# THE LOEB CLASSICAL LIBRARY

FOUNDED BY JAMES LOEB



# LIBANIUS

## II

LCL 479

# LIBANIUS

## AUTOBIOGRAPHY AND SELECTED LETTERS

### VOLUME II

EDITED AND TRANSLATED BY

A. F. NORMAN

HARVARD UNIVERSITY PRESS
CAMBRIDGE, MASSACHUSETTS
LONDON, ENGLAND
1992

First published 1992

*Library of Congress Cataloging-in-Publication Data*

Libanius.
[Selections. English & Greek. 1992]
Autobiography and selected letters / Libanius :
edited and translated by A. F. Norman.
p. cm. — (The Loeb classical library : 478–479)
Includes bibliographical references and index.
ISBN 0–674–99527–9 (v. 1)
0–674–99528–7 (v. 2)
1. Libanius—Translations into English
2. Sophists—Correspondence. 3. Orators—Antioch—
Correspondence. 4. Sophists—Biography.
5. Orators—Antioch—Biography.
I. Norman, A. F. (Albert Francis) II. Title. III. Series
PA4227.E6 1992
885′.01—dc20 [B] 91–26316 CIP

*Typeset by Chiron, Inc, Cambridge, Massachusetts.*
*Printed in Great Britain by St Edmundsbury Press Ltd,*
*Bury St Edmunds, Suffolk, on acid-free paper.*
*Bound by Hunter & Foulis Ltd, Edinburgh, Scotland.*

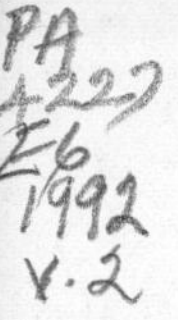

# CONTENTS

# ΛΙΒΑΝΙΟΥ ΣΟΦΙΣΤΟΥ

## 51. Θεμιστίῳ

1. Ἧκέ τις ἀγγέλλων, ὡς ἀπορρίψειάς τι ῥῆμα περὶ ἐμοῦ φαυλότερον, ἐγὼ δὲ ἠπίστησα. καὶ πάλιν ἕτερος τὸν αὐτὸν ἐκόμιζε λόγον, ἐγὼ δὲ ἦν ὁ αὐτός. τρίτος καὶ διὰ μάχης ἔφασκεν ἐλθεῖν σοι βοηθεῖν ἐμοὶ βουλόμενος. τοῦτον ἤδη καὶ μελαγχολᾶν ἡγούμην καὶ τῷ περὶ τῆς μάχης κόμπῳ τὸν περὶ τῆς βλασφημίας ἀναιρεῖν λόγον. τίς γὰρ οὕτω θρασὺς ὡς ἀντιβλέπειν τῷ Διί; 2. χωρὶς δὲ τούτων οὐδὲ ἦν εἰκός, ἐν ᾧ τοὺς πρὸ τοῦ[1] δυσμενεῖς εὖ ποιεῖς, λυπεῖν ὃν ἐν πρώτοις ἦγες τῶν φίλων καὶ ταῦτα οὐ πολὺ τῶν νεκρῶν διαφέροντα μετὰ τὰς τῶν γνωρίμων τύχας. 3. ὡς δὲ

[1] πρὸ τοῦ F (Exc. Neap. II c 32, which cites χωρὶς . . . φίλων): πρώτου Wolf (Mss.).

---

[a] Bouchery p. 162, Petit in *Ant. Class.* 26:353 f. Themistius as proconsul (a post he held until 10 Dec. 359) had nominated Priscianus for admission to the Senate; at the same time Florentius (*Ep.* 61) had summoned him to court as a candidate for higher civil service rank. This was a

## 51. To Themistius[a]

1. News reached me that you had uttered some derogatory remark about me, but I refused to believe it. Some one else came with the same story, and my attitude stayed the same. A third man claimed that he had even entered into conflict with you out of his desire to help me. Him now I thought to be quite mad;[b] by his boast about "conflict" he deprived his slander of any plausibility, for no one is so rash as to oppose Zeus.[c] 2. Moreover, it was quite inconceivable that, while treating former enemies with kindness, you would distress one whom you used to regard as among your foremost friends, particularly when I am not much better than a corpse after the misfortunes which beset my

more honorific method of entry than that proposed by Themistius. As compared with the letter to Florentius, this to Themistius is remarkable for its tartness.

[b] Aristoph. *Plut.* 12.

[c] A compliment lacking any sincerity (the battle of Zeus and the Titans, with Themistius cast as Zeus). Libanius clearly believed that Themistius had made some sour comment about him, probably upon hearing of Libanius' refusal of recent overtures made to him (see below).

οὐδενὶ ἐκείνων[2] ἐπειθόμην, αὐτό σε πειθέτω τὸ γράφειν· οὐ γὰρ ἂν τόν γε ἄλλον γεγενημένον ἐνοχλεῖν ἠξίουν. τῶν μὲν οὖν ἄλλων οὐδέν σε κεκινηκέναι νομίζω, τῆς χάριτος δὲ ἥν μοι δέδωκας ἀφαιρεῖν τὸ πλέον. 4. σὺ γὰρ δὴ κύριος μὲν ὢν ἀφελεῖν με τῆς πατρίδος μένειν ἔδωκας εὖ ποιῶν, ὃ δέ μοι τῶν οἴκοι μέγιστον ἦν, ὅπως ἔσται παρ' ὑμῖν ἔπραξας, καὶ κατῆλθεν εἰς μικρὸν ἡ χάρις. Πρισκιανὸς γὰρ ἐμοὶ τὰ πάντα καὶ τοσοῦτον ὅσον οἱ πάντες οἰκεῖοι. καὶ τοῦτο αὐτὸς ἔγνως δι' ἀγγέλων μὲν ἀπών, τῇ πείρᾳ δὲ ἥκων. 5. τοῦτον δὴ μεταστῆσαι διανοηθεὶς ἐκεῖσε ταυτί που διελέχθης πρὸς σαυτόν·[3] 'τὸν ῥήτορα ἐκεῖνον τὸν μέγαν τῇ Μεγάλῃ πόλει δοτέον. ἀλλὰ τὸ μὲν ἁπλῶς οὑτωσὶ κελεύειν τρέχειν σκαιόν τι καὶ βίαιον, δεῖ δέ τινος τέχνης. τίς οὖν αὕτη; γενέσθω τῶν ἀμφὶ βασιλέα καὶ τεθήραται. βαδιεῖται γὰρ τὴν ἐπὶ τὴν γενναίαν βουλὴν ἄγουσαν καὶ οὕτως ἕξει τὰ τοῦ δεῖνος Θεμίστιος.' 6. ἔχε

[2] οὐδενὶ ἐκείνων F. οὐδὲν ἐκείνων S Vi Vo οὐδ' ἐκεινω V.

[3] διελέχθης πρὸς σαυτόν F (αὑτόν Re, αὐτόν V S Vi) διελέχθη πρὸς αὐτόν Wolf (Vo, corrected to διειλέχθης πρὸς σαυτόν Vo[2]).

---

[d] Not only the deaths of his friends and relatives (*Or.*

friends.[d] 3. Let the very fact that I am writing this letter convince you that I was convinced by none of them, for I would not presume to trouble you if your feelings had altered. Well, I do feel that though you have changed nothing else, you are taking away from me, to a great extent, the favour you granted me. 4. You had it in your power to take my birthplace from me but generously allowed me to stay,[e] and yet you have ensured that the most precious thing I have at home should be with you, and so your favour has become minimal. Priscianus is my all in all, and means as much to me as all my relatives put together. And you yourself realized this—while absent by messengers, when present by personal observation. 5. So you conceived the idea of transferring him to you there, and you addressed yourself more or less as follows: "We have got to present that great orator to our great capital. But simply to order him to come here is peremptory and lacks finesse. Some device is needed. Well, what? Let him become a member of the emperor's entourage and we have him hooked. He will tread the path which leads to the exalted Senate, and thus Themistius will get what belongs

1.117), but also the turmoil caused by the Scythopolis trials (*Letter* 49).

[e] It is clear from *Ep.* 48 that tentative suggestions had been put to him that he should be removed to Constantinople. The aim obviously was to recruit him as one of the new senators, which to him was anathema. Libanius here implies that Themistius was at the back of this.

δὴ καὶ ἀπόλαυε καὶ σκόπει, πῶς ἂν ἐν ᾧπερ ἄξιον γένοιτο καὶ μὴ καταισχύνειε τὰ ὅπλα τὸν στρατιώτην. τῷ μὲν γὰρ οὐκ ἐπιθυμία τοῦ μείζονος, ἀρκεῖ γὰρ αὐτῷ τὸ εἶναι ἀγαθόν, ὑμῖν δὲ οὐκ ἂν ἔχοι καλῶς, εἰ δόξετε τὴν ἀξίαν ἀγνοεῖν. 7. εἰ μὲν οὖν παρ' ὑμῖν συμβάλλοι τὸ πρῶτον τῷ βασιλεῖ, τοῦ παντὸς ἐπιμελήσῃ[4] παρών· δι' ὑμῶν δὲ ὡς αὐτὸν ἐλαύνοντι γράμματα δώσεις, ταυτὶ δὲ οὐκ ἀσθενέστερα παρουσίας. 8. ἐμὲ δὲ εἴ τις μεταπέμποιτο, πρὸς θεῶν, κωλύειν. οὔτε γὰρ οὕτως ἔχει μοι τὸ σῶμα μεστή τε ἀργίας ἡ γνώμη, δι' ἣν εἰς τὴν ἀτοπίαν ἐμπέπτωκα τῆς Ἀπόλλωνος ἐρωμένης, ἣ τοῦ θεοῦ προὔθηκεν ἄνθρωπον, τοῦ Ἀπόλλωνος τὸν Ἴδαν.

[4] ἐπιμελήσῃ F (Mss.) ἐπιμελήσεται Wolf (original reading of Vo) ἐπιμελήσεσθαι Seeck.

to another." 6. Have him then; make the most of him and see that he attains the position he deserves, and do not let his arms disgrace the soldier.[f] He has no appetite for greater things: it is enough for him to be good, but it would not be right and proper for you to appear unaware of his true worth. 7. So should his first meeting with the emperor occur among you in Constantinople, you personally will arrange it all. Should he pass through on his journey to court, you will give him letters of introduction.[g] These are no less effective than your personal intervention. 8. Should anyone send for me to come, for heaven's sake stop him. Physically I am in no fit condition, mentally I am completely inactive,[h] and so I have fallen into the same silliness as the woman beloved of Apollo, who preferred a human, Idas, to the god Apollo.[i]

[f] A play on *στρατιώτης*, which Priscianus would become on entering imperial service.

[g] Constantius' precise whereabouts were then unknown in Antioch. In the autumn he had been in the capital, but had since left. In the event, Priscianus had to travel up to the Danube to find the court.

[h] He had already pleaded ill-health in *Ep.* 48. Now he hints at the breakdown he suffered after the death of his uncle.

[i] Cf. Homer *Il.* 9.557 ff. Marpessa, wooed by Apollo, preferred the mortal Idas. Libanius, wooed by the Capital, prefers Antioch.

## 52. Θεμιστίῳ

1. Ἔτι μου λέγοντος πρὸς τοὺς φίλους· 'τί τοῦτο; Θεμίστιος οὐκ ἐπιστέλλει;' φανεὶς Εὐάγριος, εἰ λάβοιμί σου γράμματα, ἤρετο. τὰ δ', ὡς ἔοικεν, ὁ μὲν ἔπεμψε τὸν δώσοντα, πρὶν δ' ἢ λαβεῖν αὐτὸς ἦν ἐπ' ἀγορᾶς. εἶτα ἀναστρέψας εἶχον τὴν φίλην ἐπιστολὴν φράζουσαν ἃ πάλαι ἠπιστάμην, ὡς αὖθις συγγένοιο τῷ βασιλεῖ. 2. σὺ μὲν ταυτὶ μόνα, παρὰ δὲ τῆς φήμης ταῦτά τε καὶ πλείω, τιμαί τε ὅτι σοι μείζους ἢ πρότερον γένοιντο τραπέζης τε κοινωνία πλείω δηλοῦσα τὴν οἰκειότητα καὶ ὡς ὅσα ἐπήγγελλες φίλων ἦν κηδομένου καὶ ὡς ὅσων μνησθείης εὐθὺς ἐν ἀμείνοσι καὶ ὡς ὁ διδοὺς παρῄει τὴν τοῦ λαμβάνοντος ἡδονήν. 3. ἔγεμον δὴ καὶ αὐτὸς ἡδονῆς αὐτὸς ἡγούμενος ἥκειν τε ἐκεῖσε καὶ ὧνπερ σὺ τετυχηκέναι καὶ ὅσαπερ σὺ κεχαρίσθαι. καὶ τῶν δικαίων γε τούτων μήτε σὺ παύσαιο διαύλων μήτε τῶν τιμῶν ὁ βασιλεύς. 4. τὸ δὲ μὴ μὲν[1] δεῖν τὴν σὴν

[1] δὲ μὴ μὲν F. μὲν μὴ Wolf (V Vo S) δὲ μὴ Vi Be.

---

[a] Bouchery p. 169 ff, F/Kr. no. 56. Themistius, as proconsul, had written to Libanius very shortly before

## 52. To Themistius[a]

1. While I was still asking my friends, "Hey! What's this? No letter from Themistius?" Eugrius[b] appeared and enquired whether I had got your letter. It turned out that he had sent somebody to deliver it, but I was in the city square before ever it arrived. So I went back home, and got your dear letter which told me what I had long been assured of, that you were once more in the emperor's company. 2. That was all the news you gave but rumour has told me this and more, and that your honours are greater than before, that your attendance at his table denotes a greater intimacy, that your professions arise from concern for your friends, that anyone you mention is immediately better off, and that his pleasure in granting such favours exceeded yours in receiving them.[c] 3. I too was filled with pleasure, for it was as though I had gone there personally, shared your success and enjoyed the favours you have received. Never may you cease from running this well-merited course,[d] nor the emperor from his honours. 4. Your statement

relinquishing office in Dec. 359. Libanius replies in the fortnight or so before news of this reached Antioch.

[b] *Agens in rebus, BLZG* 128 (i), *PLRE* 285 (3).

[c] For the honours bestowed by Constantius on Themistius cf. Them. *Or.* 31.353a ff.

[d] The course to and from the Palace, as one of the emperor's intimates.

πρὸς ἐμε γνώμην τοῖς γράμμασι κρίνεσθαι καλῶς εἰρῆσθαί μοι φαίνεται, περὶ δὲ τοῦ μὴ τοὺς λόγους ἐλθεῖν ἡμῖν οὓς ἔδειξας τίς ἂν εἴη σοι λόγος καὶ ταῦτα ἐπὶ ταῖς ἐπαγγελίαις, ἐν αἷς ἦν ὡς αὐτίκα πέμψεις; καιρὸς δὲ ἀεὶ μὲν τούτου, νῦν δὲ οὐχ ἥκιστα τὸ μὲν λέγειν ἡμῶν ἀφαιρεθέντων ὑπὸ τῆς τῶν ἑταίρων τελευτῆς, τοῦ δὲ ἀκούειν δύνασθαι μένοντος ἴσως ἔτι. 5. τήν τε οὖν ὑπόσχεσιν ἐπιτελεῖν καὶ εἴ τί σοι μετ' ἐκεῖνα πεποίηται, μὴ φθονεῖν, καὶ τό γε ᾆσμα προστιθέναι τοῦ τὸν ἀνδριάντα κεκοσμηκότος ποιητοῦ, μᾶλλον δὲ ᾧ τὸ ᾆσμα κεκόσμηκεν ὁ πρὸς τὸν σὸν τύπον ἀκολουθήσας χαλκός. τὸν μὲν γὰρ ὄνυχα εἴδομεν ἐκ τῶν πρὸς Εὐδαίμονα γραμμάτων, δεόμεθα δὲ τοῦ λέοντος. 6. Μητέριος δὲ εἷς ἦν τῶν ἀγγελλόντων τὰ σά, καὶ τοῦτο μὲν αὐτῷ κοινὸν πρὸς ἄλλους, ἀλλὰ τό γε διηγούμενον χαίρειν καὶ μικροῦ γε ὑπὸ τοῦ χαίρειν πέτεσθαι, τοῦτο δὴ αὐτὸν ἐποίει βελτίω τῶν ἄλλων ἀγγέλων.

---

[e] Aristaenetus, Hierocles, Eusebius, and his uncle Phasganius; cf. *Or.* 1.117.

[f] For the statue of Themistius cf. Them. *Or.* 4.54b. This was in acknowledgement of his *Oration* 2, and was erected c. 356. The poet is unknown.

that I should not form a judgement of your attitude towards me from your letters appears cogent to me, but what explanation could you have of the fact that the orations you have delivered have not reached me, especially after your promises that you would send them forthwith? Any time is the proper time for that, not least now, when I have been robbed of my powers of speech by the death of my friends;[e] the capacity to listen still perhaps remains unimpaired. 5. So fulfil your promise, and if you have any yet later compositions, do not begrudge me them. Send me also the epigram of the poet who did honour to your statue,[f] or rather, whose epigram was honoured by the bronze which reproduces your features. We saw a hint of it in your letter to Eudaemon;[g] we have yet to see the real thing.[h] 6. Meterius[i] was one who brought news of you: in that he is no different from others, but the pleasure he took in giving his account, when he very nearly danced for joy, is what made him better than all other messengers.

[g] Rhetor in Antioch, corresponding with both Libanius and Themistius: *BLZG* 131 (ii), *PLRE* 289 (2).

[h] "To recognise the lion simply by seeing its claw." Proverbial; cf. *Paroem. Gr.* 1.252.

[i] Meterius, father and son, were Bithynians. The father was a mutual acquaintance of Libanius and Themistius (*BLZG* 212), and may well be the one mentioned here, despite Seeck and Foerster.

## 53. Φλωρεντίῳ

1. Γλώττῃ μὲν τῇ αὐτῃ, γνώμῃ δὲ οὐ τῇ αὐτῇ τὰς ὑπὲρ τῶν φερόντων σοι πέμπομεν ἐπιστολάς, ἀλλὰ τῶν μὲν τὸν ὄχλον οὐκ ἔχοντες διαφυγεῖν ἐπιστέλλομεν, οἷς ἂν μηδὲν γίγνηται δεξιόν, οὐ φροντίς· ὑπὲρ δὲ ὧν παντὶ θυμῷ γράφομεν, καὶ προστίθεμεν εὐχὰς τοῖς γράμμασι κἂν ἐκεῖνοι τῆς σῆς ἀπολαύσωσι ῥοπῆς, ἡμέτερον τὸ κέρδος. 2. ὧν οὑτοσὶ Μίκκαλος, μᾶλλον δὲ πρῶτος τῶν ἐν τούτῳ μοι τεταγμένων. πατέρων τε γὰρ φύντες ἀλλήλοις φίλων ἐκληρονομήσαμεν τοῦδε τοῦ καλοῦ πολλά τε ὑπὲρ ἐμοῦ πεπονηκότος Ὀλυμπίου τοῦ Μίκκαλον τὸν ἀδελφὸν πλέον ἢ παῖδα φιλοῦντος αἰσχρὸν ἦν ἐμὲ μηδ᾽ ἀπὸ γραμμάτων τι συντελέσαι πρὸς τὴν ὁδόν, οὐχ ὡς οὐκ ἀρκούντων οὔτε τῶν Μικκάλου τρόπων οὔτε τῶν Ὀλυμπίου γραμμάτων ἐγεῖραί σε πρὸς συμμαχίαν. 3. πολλῶν γὰρ ὄντων ἃ ποιεῖ σοι τὸν παρὰ τῶν σπουδαίων ἔπαινον μάλιστα θαυμάζεται τὸ τοὺς πάλαι

[a] Written in early 360 for Miccalus (*PLRE* 602), elder brother of Libanius' old friend Olympius. At this time, Miccalus had two objectives: (a) to get married and continue the family line in Antioch; (b) to obtain office and so escape curial liturgies from which his brother as senator

## 53. To Florentius[a]

1. The letters I send to you on behalf of their bearers are couched in the same terms, but their intention is not the same. In some cases I write when I cannot avoid their pressing solicitations, and if they get nothing good from them, I do not care. But in the cases where my message comes from the bottom of my heart, and I add my prayers to the letter, should they enjoy your support, the gain is mine. 2. One such is the bearer Miccalus, or to be precise, the foremost of those whom I hold in this regard. Our fathers were friendly with one another, and we entered into this inheritance.[b] Olympius, who loves his brother Miccalus[c] more than a son, has laboured long on my behalf, and it would be wrong of me not to make some contribution to help him on his way even by means of a letter—not that Miccalus' own character or the letter of Olympius would not be enough to induce you to help him. 3. Though there are many grounds for causing respectable people to commend you, your habit of showing more consideration for old acquaintances

was already exempt. This second depended upon appointment by the *magister officiorum* Florentius. Miccalus did in fact marry and had a son (*Or.* 63.35), but did not obtain office until 362, when Olympius' efforts on his behalf finally prevailed (cf. *Ep.* 752).

[b] Cf. *Letters* 43.3, 49.5. Isocr. *ad Demon.* 2.

[c] Cf. *Ep.* 98; *Or.* 63.30 f.

συνήθεις πρὸ τῶν τὴν δύναμιν θεραπευόντων ἄγειν. ἀλλ᾿ ὅμως ταῦτα εἰδὼς κἀκεῖνό γε προσειδώς, ὅτι οὐδὲν ὀκνήσεις ἐν οἷς δεῖ Μίκκαλον εὖ παθεῖν, ὅπως ἔλθῃ τι τῆς τῶν πραττομένων αἰτίας εἰς τὰ ἐμὰ γράμματα, συνεφηψάμην τῆς παρακλήσεως. 4. ἔστι δὲ μέγιστον τῆς χάριτος τὸ περὶ αὐτὴν τάχος, ὑφ᾿ οὗ καὶ ἡ μικρὰ μείζων ἂν φανείη πολλάκις. μάλιστα μὲν γὰρ ἔδει καὶ οἴκοι καθημένῳ Μικκάλῳ προσελθεῖν τι τῶν τοῖς τοιούτοις πρεπόντων· ἐπεὶ δὲ ἴσως βουλόμενος τῶν τιμῶν ἡγεῖσθαι τοὺς πόνους ἐπέταξας ὁδοιπορεῖν, ὅμως ἥκει. σὺ δὲ μὴ μέλλε. οἰήσεται γάρ, εἰ ταχέως ὑποστρέψειε, μηδὲ κεκινῆσθαι. 5. ἐνθυμοῦ δὲ πάντα ὁμοῦ, τὴν ἡλικίαν, ὡς ἄγαμος ἔτι, γῆρας μητρὸς καὶ ἐπιθυμίαν, τὴν Ὀλυμπίου γνώμην, ὡς ἀνθ᾿ ἑαυτοῦ τοῦτον εὔξατο κληθῆναι πατέρα. 6. σύμπραξον οὖν, ὦ γενναῖε, πρὸς τὴν διαδοχὴν τοῦ γένους, ὡς ἐμὸν μὲν εὐτρεπίσαι τὴν νύμφην, σὸν δὲ ἀποπέμψαι λαμπρόν τε ἡμῖν καὶ ὀξέως τὸν νεανίσκον. ἐρῶ γάρ, ὡς ἂν πρέψαι νυμφίῳ, κἂν ἡ κεφαλὴ μὴ συγχωρῇ.

than for those who cultivate you for your influence elicits particular admiration. However, despite my awareness of this and of the additional fact that you will spare no effort to ensure some advantage for Miccalus, I have associated myself with him in his plea so that some of the credit for what is done will come to me and my letter. 4. The most important part of your favour is that it should be given quickly, for in this way even a small favour can often appear the greater. Preferably some honour suited to such persons should come Miccalus' way, even if he stays at home; but since, perhaps because of your wish that duty should precede honours, you have bidden him make his way to you, he is coming none the less. But you must not delay. If he comes back again quickly, he will think that he has never been removed at all. 5. Consider his case from every aspect—his youth, his unmarried state, his mother's age and her desire, and the attitude of Olympius in praying that not he but his brother be called by the name of father. 6. Noble sir, help him then in assuring the continuance of the family. My task is to adorn the bride,[d] yours to send back the young man to us with honour and quickly, for my address will be such as befits the groom, even though my migraine says me nay.

[d] With an oration celebrating this marriage.

## 54. Μοδέστῳ

1. Οἱ πρώτην αἰτοῦντες χάριν δι᾽ αὐτὸ τοῦτο λαμβάνειν ἀξιοῦσιν, ὅτι πρώτην αἰτοῦσι, παρακαλοῦντες εἰς συμμαχίαν παροιμίαν δή τινα τὴν περὶ τῆς πρώτης χάριτος. 2. ἐγὼ δὲ τῷ πολλὰς εἰληφέναι καὶ πρόσθεν[1] καὶ νῦν δὴ λαβεῖν ἰσχυρὸν εἶναί μοι νομίζω. ᾧ μὲν γὰρ οὔπω τις ἔδωκε πρότερον, ἂν αἰτοῦντι μὴ δῷ, τὸ μηδ᾽ ἄξιον εἶναι λαβεῖν ἔστιν εἰπεῖν· ὃν δὲ εὖ πεποίηκε πολλάκις, οὐκ ἔστιν ἐν τοῖς ἑξῆς ἀτιμάσαι ἢ τῶν προτέρων ἀνάγκη κατηγορεῖν ὡς οὐκ εἰς σπουδαῖον ἀνηλωμένων. 3. τί οὖν αἰτοῦμεν; ἀλλ᾽ ὅπως μή μου μέμψῃ τὸ προοίμιον ὡς μακρὸν ὑπὲρ μικρῶν· τῇ φύσει μὲν γὰρ ὃ δώσεις οὐ μέγα, τῇ δὲ τῶν λαμβανόντων ἡδονῇ μέγα. σκόπει δέ. 4. Ζηνόβιος γίνεταί μοι διδάσκαλος, παρ᾽ ἡμῖν μὲν οἰκῶν, ὢν δὲ ἐξ Ἐλούσης, ἀνεψιὸς Ἀργυρίου τοῦ πάνυ καὶ τῶν νῦν ἐν ἡμῖν λόγων, εἰ δή τινες ἐν ἡμῖν, πατὴρ ἐκεῖνος. ζῶντά τε οὖν ἐθεράπευον τὸν ἄνδρα καὶ τεθνεῶτα διὰ τῶν οἰκείων αὐτοῦ ἐκείνου πειρώμε-

[1] καὶ before πρόσθεν om. Re., F. πρόσθεν F. (V S) πρὸς Wolf (Va Vo) πρὸς τὸ Re. προσλαβεῖν Seeck.

---

[a] Modestus, as *Comes,* is asked to intervene in a local

## 54. To Modestus[a]

1. In making a first request for a favour, one expects to obtain it simply because it is the first request, since one invokes the support of that proverb about one good turn.[b] 2. However my assurance for obtaining my present request I believe lies in the fact that I have obtained many even before now, for if you do not accede to the request of someone you have never yet favoured, it might be said that he does not even deserve to get it, whereas if you have often been of service to someone, you cannot thereafter reject him, or else you must complain of your previous efforts that they were spent to no good purpose. 3. So what is my request? And see that you do not reproach my introduction to it as making a mountain out of a molehill. In itself the favour you will grant is not great, but in the pleasure it gives the recipients, great it is. But consider! 4. Zenobius, my teacher, though a native of Elusa, resided among us here. He was cousin to the excellent Argyrius[c] and the sire of whatever eloquence there may be in me. So, during his lifetime I gave him my support, and also after his death, by way of

squabble concerning the office of *eirenophylax* in Elusa, in Palestine.

[b] Cf. Soph. *Ajax* 522 χάρις χάριν τίκτει; also Eurip. *Hel.* 1224.

[c] *Principalis* of Antioch, father of Obodianus (not of Eubulus, as Seeck), and friend of Libanius and his uncle.

νος αὐτοῖς εἰς ὅσον ἔξεστι βοηθεῖν. 5. ἥκει δὲ καὶ νῦν καιρὸς βοήθειαν ἀπαιτῶν, σὺ δὲ δίδως τὸ δύνασθαι· τὸν γὰρ ὁμώνυμον ἐκείνῳ τουτονὶ καὶ συγγενῆ τεταγμένον εἰρήνης φύλακα καὶ μάλιστά γε φρουρήσαντα τὴν πόλιν ἐκβάλλει τις ἐπιθέμενος τῆς τάξεως. τὸ δὲ ὅπως, ἐγὼ μὲν οὐκ ἐρῶ, σὺ δὲ ὁρᾷς. 6. δέομαι δὴ τὸν ἐκβαλόντα ἀδίκως τοῦτο παθεῖν δικαίως, ὅπως ἐγώ τε ποιοίην τὰ δίκαια πρὸς τὸν ἀπελθόντα παιδευτὴν τήν τε τούτων πενίαν μὴ ἐλαύνωσιν οἱ δυνατώτεροι. 7. βελτίων δὲ ἢ πρόσθεν οἶδ' ὅτι φανεῖται Ζηνόβιος τῇ παρὰ σοῦ ψήφῳ τὴν ἀρχὴν κεκομισμένος.

## 55. Θεμιστίῳ

1. Πολλοῖς ἐκέλευσέ με τῶν παρ' ἡμῖν οὑτοσὶ Δωρόθεος γράφειν ἡγούμενος ἐκ πολλῶν ἀνδρῶν πολλῶν ἀπολαύσεσθαι τῶν ἀγαθῶν· φανεῖσθαι γὰρ τὸν μὲν πρᾶον ἴσως, τὸν δὲ πρόθυμον, τὸν δὲ ἀνδρεῖον, ἄλλον δυνατόν, καὶ οὕτως αὐτῷ καλὸν

[a] Introduces Dorotheus, early in 360 (Bouchery pp. 178 ff). He accompanied his patron Obodianus, who

his relatives, since I try to assist them to the best of my ability. 5. An occasion has now arisen which requires my assistance, but you are the one who can render it possible. The bearer, his relative and namesake, was appointed justice of the peace,[d] and although he has taken especial care of the city, he has been attacked and ejected from his post. As to the manner of it, I will say nothing: you may see for yourself. 6. My request is that the unjustified usurper should himself be justifiably ejected, so that I may do my duty by my dead teacher and that an influential clique may not harass this family in its poverty. 7. I know that Zenobius will be more efficient than ever if he should regain his office by your decree.

[d] The post of *eirenophylax* in a metropolis like Antioch was a minor one (cf. *Or.* 48.9); in a smaller town like Elusa the financial perquisites were enough to make it an object of competition (cf. Liebeschuetz, *Antioch* 122 f).

## 55. To Themistius[a]

1. The bearer, Dorotheus, has bidden me write to many of the people from here, for he believes that he will enjoy many benefits from many persons, with one perhaps showing his gentleness, another eagerness, another courage, and yet another his influence, and in this way the sum of his desires will

went as envoy to Constantinople in quest of assistance for his son's performance of the beast shows in Antioch (*Ep.* 113.2).

ἔσεσθαι τῆς ἐπιθυμίας τὸ κηρίον. 2. ἐγὼ δὲ ἔφην πρὸς αὐτόν ὡς οὐ πολλοῖς ἄρα δέοι γράφειν, ἀλλ' ἑνί, παρ' ᾧ τὰ πάντα. τί μὲν γὰρ ἡμερώτερον Θεμιστίου; τίς δ' οὕτω τοὺς Τυνδαρίδας ἐν τῇ περὶ τοὺς ξένους σπουδῇ τιμᾷ; παρὰ τῷ δὲ τοσαύτη προθυμία; τί δ' οὐχ ἧκεν εἰς τέλος ὧν ἥψατο; 3. ὁ δ' ὡς ἤκουσε τοὔνομα, σκιρτήσας καὶ μειδιάσας τούτου μὲν ἔφησεν ἐπιθυμεῖν, μεῖζον δὲ αὑτοῦ τὸ πρᾶγμα κρίνειν· διόπερ οὐκ αἰτῆσαι. 4. ἀλλ' εὖ ἴσθι, καὶ τούτου Δωρόθεος ἄξιος καὶ ἔτι μείζονος. ἓν δέ, οἶμαι, μεῖζον τῆς παρὰ σοῦ ῥοπῆς, ἡ παρὰ τῶν θεῶν. ὧν εἰκότως ἂν εὐμενῶν τυγχάνοι τῆς εἰς φίλους ἀρετῆς εἵνεκα. 5. οὗτος γὰρ Ἀργυρίου ἡμῖν τὸν οἶκον, ὃν ἀγαπᾷς τε καὶ ὑφ' οὗ θαυμάζῃ, σέσωκεν εἰς πάσας μὲν ἀνάγκας ἀχθείς, νικήσας δὲ καρτερίᾳ τὴν Φαλάριδος ὠμότητα, τὸ δ' ἀποθανεῖν, εἰ συμβαίη, πρὸ τοῦ τὸν ἑταῖρον ἀδικῆσαι θέμενος. 6. ζῇ μὲν γὰρ διὰ τὴν Τύχην, ὅτε δὲ ἐπ' αὐτὸν ἐφέροντο τῶν πληγῶν αἱ νιφάδες καὶ διῄκιζον[1] τοὺς ὤμους,

[1] διῄκιζον Wolf (S Vi) διώκιζον V Va Vo διηκίζοντο conj. Re. ᾔκιζον F., Bouchery

[b] κηρίον, honey(comb). Similarly *Ep.* 374.4.

be gloriously attained.[b] 2. I told him that there was no need to write to many people, only to one who possesses all these qualities: for who can be more gentle than Themistius? who so emulates the Tyndaridae in his zeal for strangers?[c] where is there such eagerness? what of the things he begins has failed to reach completion? 3. As soon as he heard your name, he jumped for joy and smiled, and said that this was what he really wanted but thought it beyond his reach and so had not asked for it. 4. Yet rest assured that Dorotheus does deserve it, and still more. There is but one thing, I believe, that counts for more than your support, that is, that of the gods. And he could expect to enjoy their favour because of his constancy towards his friends. 5. For he has preserved for us the household of Argyrius,[d] for whom you have such affection and from whom such admiration; though subjected to every compulsion, he overcame the cruelties of Phalaris[e] through his constancy and preferred to die, if need be, rather than to wrong his friend. 6. By the favour of Fortune he is still alive, when showers of blows were applied to him and scarred his shoulders, and both he and the onlookers

[c] Cf. Pind. *Ol.* 3.1. The Dioscuri protect men, especially voyagers, in times of danger.

[d] Obodianus (*BLZG* 222; cf. § 7 below and *Ep.* 113). Like other Antiochene notables he had been under suspicion in the Scythopolis trials.

[e] Tyrant of Acragas, a by-word for cruelty. His brazen bull, Diod. Sic. 9.20.

αὐτῷ τε καὶ τοῖς ὁρῶσιν ἐλπὶς ἦν, ὡς αὐτίκα δεήσει κεῖσθαι. λαβὼν δὲ ἔννοιαν, καὶ γὰρ τῶν παιδείας μετειληφότων ἀνήρ, οἵαν δόξαν ἐφ' οἵοις ὑπὲρ φίλων κινδύνοις ἐκτήσαντο τῶν παλαιοτάτων τινές, ῥήματι μὲν ψευδεῖ τὸν ἑταῖρον οὐκ ἀπώλεσε, τῇ δικαίᾳ δὲ ἀρνήσει τὸν μὲν ἐξήρπασε τῶν ξιφῶν, αὐτὸν δὲ εἰσήνεγκε τῇ φιλίᾳ τὸ σῶμα. 7. καὶ νῦν ὅταν χαίρῃς Ὀβοδιανὸν θεώμενος, τὸν Δωρόθεον παραβαλεῖν ὡς παρ' ἐκείνου τοῦτον ἔχων τοῦ τὰ τῶν φιλοσόφων δείξαντος ἐν ἑτέρῳ βίῳ. τίς ἂν οὖν ἦν οὗτος φιλοσοφῶν; καὶ γάρτοι τῆς πόλεως εὐεργέτης ᾄδεται. καὶ νῦν ὅτου ἂν οὗτος διὰ σοῦ τύχῃ, τετύχηκεν ἡ πόλις. 8. εἶχον μὲν ἕτερα μυρία λέγειν, ἐν οἷς ἐστι καὶ τὸ λόγων ἀκούειν τε ὡς ἥδιστα καὶ κριτὴν οὐ φαῦλον εἶναι, μικρὰ δὲ ἐπὶ μείζοσιν οὐκ ἂν βουλοίμην λέγειν, ἄλλως θ' ὅτε σύ μοι περὶ ἐκείνων ἐπιστελεῖς.

## 56. Σπεκτάτῳ

1. Τά τε ἄλλα με ἐτίμησεν ὁ θεῖος καὶ

[a] Early in 360 to Spectatus, his cousin and co-heir to his uncle Phasganius. Phasganius died without issue and his heirs were both immune from curial liturgies, Spectatus

anticipated that he must succumb on the spot. But bearing in mind—for he is one of those who are men of culture—the renown which some of the men of the earliest ages had won as a result of dangers incurred for their friends, he refused to cause the death of his friend by any word of falsehood, and by this forthright refusal he snatched him from the swords and offered his own person for the sake of his friendship. 7. And now, when you have the pleasure of seeing Obodianus, reflect upon Dorotheus, in the awareness that, owing to his practical demonstration of philosophic qualities in a different walk of life, you now possess Obodianus. What then would he have been like had he been a philosopher? As it is, his praises are sung as a benefactor of the city, and now, whatever he secures by your agency, our city has secured it too. 8. There are countless other things I could say,[f] including his extreme pleasure in the appreciation of eloquence and his no mean critical ability, but I would not wish to speak in tones of anticlimax, especially when you will write to tell me of those qualities.

[f] Cf. Plat. *Gorg.* 483e.

## 56. To Spectatus[a]

1. Besides the other tokens of esteem which my

because of his position in imperial service, Libanius as official sophist. The curia contested the will in order to regain control of land originally subject to curial obligations.

δὴ καὶ τελευτᾶν μέλλων ἕνα με τῶν κληρονόμων ποιεῖ τιμᾶν καὶ ταύτῃ νομίζων, ὃ δὲ ἄρα πολέμου μοι κατελίμπανεν ἀρχήν. 2. ἀλλὰ καὶ αὐτὸς εἶ τῶν τε ληψομένων τι τῶν τε ἤδη πολεμουμένων, ὥστ' εἴ τις αὐτῷ τὸ συμβησόμενον ἔσχεν εἰπεῖν, δοκεῖ μοι μήτ' ἂν ἐμὲ τῶν ἀγρῶν μήτε σὲ τῆς οἰκίας μετὰ τὴν αὑτοῦ γυναῖκα καταστῆσαι κύριον εἰδὼς ὅτι κρείττων ἡμῖν ἡσυχία χρημάτων. 3. ὁ γὰρ πολλὰ μὲν λαβὼν διὰ τὸν αὑτοῦ πατέρα, δεινὸν δὲ ἡγούμενος εἰ μὴ καὶ πάντα, χρεῶν ὄγκον ἐπιφέρει[1] τῷ θείῳ πρότερον μὲν οὐ φανέντων, νῦν δὲ ἀναφύντων. 4. πολλὴ δὲ ῥᾳστώνη δόξης ἠμεληκότι γραμμάτων εὐπορῆσαι, δι' ὧν ἔστιν ἀδίκως κερδᾶναι· παρῆλθον γὰρ ἡμῖν τοὺς ζωγράφους οἱ μιμηταὶ τῶν γραμμάτων. οἷς ἐκεῖνος χρώμενος βιάζεται δεικνύειν τὸν αὑτοῦ πατέρα δεδανεικότα τῷ θείῳ καί τινας ἀναπλάττει συνθήκας, ἃς ἔφασκεν εἰς τὸ οὖς τῆς μητρὸς αὑτοῦ καταδεδυκυίας λανθάνειν, εἶτα νῦν ἀνελκυσθῆναι. ταῦτα δέ ἐστιν ἐμὲ μὲν τῆς γῆς, σὲ δὲ

[1] ἐπιφέρει F., conj. Re. -φέροι Wolf (Mss.).

---

[b] Most of the troubles would descend upon Libanius as heir to the lands (cf. *Letter* 57). While ever Phasganius' widow survived, and probably afterwards, Spectatus' title

uncle accorded me in particular upon his deathbed he appointed me one of his heirs, thinking in this way too to accord me esteem, but it turns out that he bequeathed to me a source of hostility. 2. You yourself are also one of those who are due to inherit and are already objects of hostility. Thus I feel that, if he could have been told of what was to occur, he would have neither set me in charge of his estates nor you of his house in succession to his wife, for he knew that peace and quiet means more to us than money.[b] 3. For the claimant, who has obtained a large fortune through his own father, yet takes it amiss if he cannot lay hands on everything, and alleges a host of debts against our uncle. There has not been a sign of them before, but now they have sprung into existence. 4. It is the easiest thing for anyone who disregards his good name[c] to get a supply of documents, by which he can profit unjustly, for our copiers of documents outnumber painters. He makes use of them and tries to force his way and show that his father had advanced loans to our uncle, and he invents some contract or other, which he asserts after reaching his mother's ears was sunk in oblivion, and now has been dredged up again. This means the expulsion of you from the house and

to the family home could not be contested. Libanius is securing Spectatus' support to form a solid family front against all claimants.

[c] Cf. Plat. *Gorg.* 459c. For copyists in Antioch cf. Norman in *JHS* 80:122–126.

ἐκπεσεῖν τῆς οἰκίας. 5. ἔπειτα ἐλθὼν ὡς σὲ ταπεινὸς ἔσται καὶ πάντων ἀφεστάναι φήσει καὶ βοηθεῖν ἀξιώσει καὶ ζητεῖν οὐδὲν ἄλλο καὶ προσθήσει θεούς, οὓς καταπίνει καθ' ἡμέραν. 6. ἀλλὰ σοὶ χρηστῷ τε[2] ἔξεστιν εἶναι καὶ μὴ φενακίζεσθαι μηδὲ προδοῦναι σαυτόν τε κἀμὲ καὶ τὰ ἀρέσκοντα τῷ κειμένῳ. πρὸς δὲ τοῦτο[3] πολλαί τε ὁδοὶ καὶ παρατηρεῖν δεήσει μὴ γενέσθαι γράμματα αὐτῷ βασιλέως ἰσχυρότερα νόμων.

[2] τε F., conj. Re. γε Wolf (Mss.).
[3] τοῦτο F. τούτῳ Wolf (Mss.).

## 57. Εὐαγρίῳ

1. Τὸ Ζήζους χωρίον ἐκτήσατο μὲν ὁ θεῖος οὑμὸς οὐκ ἀδίκως, κατέσχον δὲ ἐγὼ τῇ τε τοῦ δικαίου τάξει καὶ τῇ παρὰ σοῦ βοηθείᾳ, δι' ἣν οὐκ ἔστιν ὅτε σε οὐκ ἐπαινοῦμεν, ἄλλως θ' ὅτε καὶ ἀπαράκλητος ὑπὲρ[1] ἡμῶν ἔστης. 2. νῦν τοίνυν οἱ τοῦτο γεωργοῦντες ἥκουσι περίφοβοι καί τινας

[1] ὑπὲρ F. παρ' Wolf (Mss.) παρ' ἡμῖν conj. Re.

---

[a] *BLZG* 128 (iii), *PLRE* 285 (5): *Comes Rei Privatae* 360/1 (Amm. Marc. 22.3.7). The problems of the inheritance of Phasganius continue well into 360. It appears that the outside claimants to this inheritance are attempt-

myself from the estate. 5. The next thing is that he will approach you in all humility, say that he has relinquished all, and claim that he is helping you and seeking nothing further, and he will refer also to the gods, to whose destruction he raises his glass every day.[d] 6. However, you can show your worth, and not be taken in by him, nor betray yourself or me or our uncle's last wishes. There are many ways to this end, and you must be on your guard that his documents should not have more force than the emperor's laws.

[d] The claimant is a Christian. Spectatus himself was probably Christian, but Libanius can count on family loyalty.

## 57. To Euagrius[a]

1. My uncle acquired the estate at Zezes not unjustly, and I have gained possession of it both by the forms of justice and by assistance from you, for which reason I commend you always, especially since you stood by me without any prompting. 2. Well, the tenants of this estate have come to me in alarm and report certain threats against them,

ing to scare off his tenants with threats of claims from the exchequer. This would effectively deprive him of income from the estate. Libanius attempts to forestall them by invoking the *Comes rei privatae* on his side, apparently with success since nothing more is heard of this.

ἀπαγγέλλουσιν ἀπειλάς, ἐν αἷς ἦν, ὅτι δώσουσι δίκην ὧν ἀδικοῦσι τὸν βασιλέως οἶκον ἡμᾶς τῆς ἐκείνου γῆς πεποιηκότες δεσπότας. 3. ἐμοὶ δὲ δοκοῦσιν ἀκηκοέναι μὲν τούτων οὐδέν, ἐλπίζειν δέ. καὶ θαυμαστὸν οὐδὲν ἀνθρώπους ὁμιλοῦντας ἀρότρῳ καὶ βουσὶ δείματα αὑτοῖς οὐκ ὄντα ἀναπλάττειν καὶ τὰ οὐδ'[2] ἐσόμενα γεγονέναι νομίζειν. τοιοῦτον γὰρ τὸ γεωργεῖν· ἀφελῶς ἔχειν ποιεῖ. 4. ἀλλὰ σὺ τὰ σαυτοῦ μιμούμενος καὶ φιλίαν ἣν ἐνεστήσω τηρῶν δίδαξον τοὺς δεδιότας, ὅτι κἂν ἄλλῳ μαχέσαιο τούσδε ταράττοντι.

[2] τὰ οὐδ' F., conj. Wolf, Re. τοῦ δὲ Va τοῦδ' Wolf (Vo) om. VD.

## 58. Ἀκακίῳ

1. Μεθ' ὧν ἔγραψας τὰ ἔπη θεῶν, σὺ γὰρ δὴ μόνος ἀμφότερον, ποιητής τ' ἀγαθὸς κρατερός τε ῥήτωρ, οὗτοί μοι δοκοῦσιν Ἑρμογένει προθυμίαν ἐμβαλεῖν εἰς τὸ λῦσαι τοὺς φόβους. 2. καίτοι τῆς αὐτῆς ἡμέρας εἶχέ τε τὰ παρὰ σοῦ καὶ παρελύετο τῆς ἀρχῆς, ἀλλ' ὅμως ἐν τῷ πυθμένι τοῦ

[a] To Acacius (iii) in the early months of 360. He was being canvassed either for some office or as a recruit to the

one being that they will be punished for a crime committed against the imperial house, in that they have made me master of the emperor's land. 3. It seems to me that they have not actually heard anything of this, but that they expect to do so. It is not to be wondered at that fellows familiar with the plough and oxen should invent for themselves nonexistent bogies and should take as accomplished fact things that will never happen at all. That is the way with farming: it tends to produce simplicity. 4. But please take a leaf from your own book and by maintaining the friendship you have begun, demonstrate to them in their fear that, even if anyone else disturbs them, you will take up the cudgels against him.

## 58. To Acacius[a]

1. With the help of the gods you wrote your poem—for you only are both goodly poet and doughty[b] orator—and these I feel induced in Hermogenes an eagerness to relieve you of your fears. 2. Yet on the same day as he received your message he was relieved of his office. Nevertheless,

Senate, and was reluctant to accept the position. He, with Libanius, had recourse to the praetorian prefect Hermogenes (who relinquished office before 4 Feb. 360). The certificate of exemption which he issued was the last act of his prefecture.

[b] Cf. Homer *Il.* 3.179.

πίθου τῶν γε σῶν οὐκ ἠμέλησεν, ἀλλ᾽ ἔστενεν ἅμα καὶ χάριν ἡγούμενος ἣν ἐδίδου λαμβάνειν καλῷ τε λέγων ἔργῳ κατακλείσειν τὴν ἀρχὴν ἐκέλευεν ὧν ἐχρῄζομεν. 3. ἀλλ᾽ Ἀνδρόνικος ἤγγειλεν ὡς οὐκ ἔσται σοι διάδυσις, ἀλλ᾽ ἐν βελτίονι μὲν τῷ σχήματι πάντως δὲ ἀνάγκην εἶναι διαπλεῦσαι τοῦ πόντου τὸ στόμα. τὸν γὰρ ἄνδρα ἐκεῖνον τὸν θεῖον, ᾧ σὺ τὸν υἱὸν ὁμώνυμον ἐποίησας τὸ τοῦ Κίμωνος μιμησάμενος, εἰπεῖν ἃ συνῄδει σοι πρὸς τὸν κρατοῦντα, τὸν δὲ καλεῖν. σὺ δὲ βουλεύσῃ περί τε τῶν ἐλπίδων τῶν ἐκεῖθεν καὶ τῆς ἡσυχίας. 4. ὁ δὲ ταῦτα ἀγγείλας καὶ Πρισκιανός. ὁ μὲν ἀνέγνω Τιτιανοῦ τοὺς λόγους, Πρισκιανὸς δέ, τότε γὰρ ἄσχολος ἦν, νῦν ἀπαιτεῖ, καὶ ἀποδώσομεν οὐκ ἀγνοήσαντες τὴν ἐπιστολὴν ἐν ᾗ διαλέγῃ τῷ παιδὶ περί τε φωνῆς τόνου καὶ τῶν ἐνταῦθα μεταβολῶν πνεύματός τε ἀναπαύλης καὶ τῶν ἄλλων, ὅσα βοηθεῖ τῷ λόγῳ. 5. ἅ μοι δοκεῖ μὴ μόνον τὸν νεανίσκον ἀμείνω κατα-

[c] "Niggardliness at the bottom of the jar is terrible," Hesiod *Works and Days* 368–9.

[d] Now in Antioch en route to enter his governorship of Phoenicia.

[e] To Constantinople.

though your case was the last to come out of the jar,[c] he did not neglect you: he heaved a sigh and interpreting his offer of a favour as his receipt of it, declared that he would end his term of office with a noble deed and began to order the grant of our request. 3. But Andronicus[d] informed us that there would be no way out for you: though your status would be raised, you absolutely must take boat across the Bosporus,[e] for that divinely inspired personage after whom you had named your son,[f] in exactly the same way that Cimon did,[g] had told the emperor of the qualities he knew you possessed, and it was the emperor who summoned you. You must ponder upon your expectations from that quarter as compared with the life as an ordinary citizen. 4. Priscianus[h] gave us this information too. Andronicus read Titianus' declamations; Priscianus, who was busy at the time, is asking for them now. I am going to let him have them, though I am well aware of the letter in which you address your son about voice-pitch and the changes in it, pauses for breath, and other tips for a declamation. 5. It seems to me that this will

[f] His son was Titianus, most likely named after Fabius Titianus *PLRE* 918 (6).

[g] Plut. *Cim.* 16.1, *Per.* 29.3.

[h] Cf. *Ep.* 61 and *Letter* 51 for Priscianus' summons to court some months before. He too is now in Antioch, passing through to take up his first appointment, that of *praeses Euphratensis.*

στήσειν, ἀλλὰ καὶ ἐμὲ τὸν γέροντα, καθ' οὗ τις ἤδη καὶ σκῶμμα ἀφῆκεν, ὡς εἴην ὑποκριτὴς μᾶλλον ἢ ῥήτωρ.

## 59. Δημητρίῳ

1. Ὥσπερ οἷς ἔπεμψας χρῶμαι ξενίοις, οὕτω καὶ τῇ τῆς ἐπιστολῆς ἀρχῇ χρήσομαι. κοινὰ γὰρ ἔστω μοι μὴ μόνον τὰ τῆς σῆς ἀγορᾶς τε καὶ γῆς, ἀλλὰ καὶ τὰ τῆς διανοίας. 2. λέγω τοίνυν καὶ αὐτός, ὅτι τῶν τε ἄλλων χάρις ταῖς Ὥραις καὶ ὅτι τὰς πανηγύρεις φέρουσαι φέρουσιν ἀφορμὴν τοῖς παρὰ σοῦ γράμμασιν αὐτῶν, οἶμαι, τῶν ἑορτῶν ἡδίοσι. 3. τὰ μέντοι γράμματα ἔλαβον ἀκροώμενος τῶν νέων καὶ πρὸς τὸν μηκύνοντα ἠχθόμην ἑλκόμενος ὑπὸ τῆς ἐπιστολῆς. οὐ γὰρ ᾔδειν ἀκριβῶς ὅ τι λέγοι, λύειν ἐκείνην ἐπιθυμῶν. 4. ὡς δὲ διεπαύσατο καὶ εὗρον τὰς Ὥρας ἐπαινουμένας καὶ διὰ πάντων τῶν γεγραμμένων τεταμένην τὴν ὥραν, ἀφεὶς ἃ λέξειν ἔμελλον ἐκοίνωσα τοῖς ἑταίροις τὴν ἐπιστολήν, τοῖς δὲ ἀπέχρησε. καὶ οὕτω προσετέθη τοῖς δώροις ἀπαλλαγὴ τοῦ τότε ἐπικειμένου πόνου.

improve not just your lad but an old fellow like me. Before now I have had fun poked at me as being more of an actor than an orator.

## 59. To Demetrius

1. Just as I make use of the present you sent, so I shall make use of the start of your letter too. For the produce not just of your market and your land but also of your intellect should be at my disposal. 2. Well, I too profess my gratitude to the Seasons, in particular because, in bringing on the festivals,[a] they bring the occasion for a letter from you, which is, I am sure, more pleasing than the holidays. 3. Now, I received your letter while I was listening to my students and I was annoyed by one who was longwinded, since I was attracted by your letter; for I had no precise idea of its contents and was eager to open it. 4. But when he stopped and I found the eulogy upon the Seasons and the seasonable perfection imbued in the whole composition, then I discarded the address I intended to make, and shared your letter with my companions, to their complete satisfaction. And so, in addition to your presents, I had a respite from the task that then beset me.

[a] The combined Saturnalia and New Year festivals. The letter is written early in 360.

## 60. Πρισκιανῷ

1. Πείθομαι μὴ πολλὰ εἶναί σοι τὰ πράγματα, οὐ γὰρ ἂν πολλῆς ἀπήλαυες εἰς τὸ ἐπιστέλλειν σχολῆς· ὡς τό γε κάλλος τῆς ἐπιστολῆς οὐκ ἄρχοντος ἐπιόντος πόλεις, ἀλλ᾿ ἀνδρὸς ἐργαζομένου λόγους. 2. εἰ δὲ ψεῦδος μὲν ἐκεῖνο καὶ πολλὰ τὰ πράγματα, σὺ δὲ ἀρκεῖς ἀμφοτέροις, τῶν Μουσῶν τις ἔοικέ σοι συνοικεῖν μετὰ τῆς Δίκης καὶ συλλαμβάνειν πῆ μὲν ἐκείνην, πῆ δὲ ταύτην. 3. ζητῶν δὲ ἢ τὸν Ἀβάριδος ὀϊστὸν ἢ τὴν Ὀρφέως κιθάραν μήτε τὴν κιθάραν ζήτει, τῇ γλώττῃ γὰρ τὰ ταύτης ἰσχύεις, μήτε τὸν ὀϊστόν, ἐπειδήπερ ἔχεις τὴν κιθάραν. 4. ἡ πενία κοινὸν νῦν ἀνθρώποις, ὥστε οὐ πρὸς εὐπόρους ὑπὲρ ἀπόρων ἐπιστέλλεις, ἀλλ᾿ εἰ καὶ ἡμῶν ἦρχες, ταῦτ᾿ ἂν ὠδύρου·

ἀπόλοιο δῆτ᾿, ὦ πόλεμε, πολλῶν οὕνεκα,
ὃς τοὺς Καλλίας ὀξέως Ἴρους ποιεῖς.

---

[a] To Priscianus, governor of Euphratensis, late in 360. He is evidently doing the rounds of the cities, holding the assizes.

[b] A compliment to his rhetorical ability and his success as governor.

## 60. To Priscianus[a]

1. I am sure that your troubles are not many: otherwise you would not enjoy much leisure for correspondance. Anyway, the style of your letter is not that of a governor making the rounds of cities but of a man engaged upon oratory. 2. But if I am mistaken and your troubles are many, and yet you are capable of dealing with both, it appears that one of the Muses dwells with you, and Justice also, and that first the one, then the other assists you.[b] 3. But if you seek either for the arrow of Abaris[c] or the lyre of Orpheus, do not seek for the lyre, for by your eloquence you have mastery of that, nor yet for the arrow, since you have the lyre. 4. Poverty is the common lot of mankind nowadays, and so you are not writing to the affluent on behalf of the poor. If you were governor of us also, you would complain

> "Then damn thee, War, for many a reason[d]
> Who turn the rich to beggars in a trice."[e]

[c] Herod. 4.36. The expression became proverbial, cf. Suidas *s.v.*, Iambl. *de vit. Pythag.* 19.9.

[d] Aristoph. *Clouds* 6.

[e] This line may be a composition of Libanius himself. Callias ὁ λακκόπλουτος (Plut. *Arist.* 5) becomes the proverbial millionaire (e.g., Alciphron 1.9); Irus, the beggar of the Odyssey, his opposite. Priscianus' complaints about the impoverishment of his province are acknowledged later in *Or.* 18.206, 49.2.

## 61. Πρισκιανῷ

1. Οἴκοθεν οἴκαδε Μίκκαλος παρ' Ὀλυμπίου πρὸς σὲ καὶ οὐ παρ' ἀδέλφοῦ μᾶλλον ἢ παρ' ἀδελφόν, ὅθεν μοι δοκεῖ τοῦ τε ἐν Παίοσιν ὑπεριδεῖν πλούτου καὶ τῆς ἐν ἀδικίᾳ τρυφῆς, νομίζων τὸ σοὶ συνεῖναι καὶ τῶν χρημάτων αὐτῷ καὶ τῶν[1] ἀπὸ τῆς θαλάττης ἥδιον ἔσεσθαι. 2. τοῦτον μὲν οὖν τοῦτ' ἔπεισε προκρῖναι τὴν σὴν ἀρχήν, σὺ δ' αὐτῷ καὶ χρημάτων εὕρισκες πόρους. σοὶ μὲν γὰρ κεναῖς, τούτῳ δὲ μεσταῖς ἐπανελθεῖν προσήκει χερσίν. 3. ἃ δὲ περὶ τῆς πενίας ἔγραψας μείζω τὴν ἐκεῖ τῆς τῇδε πειρώμενος δεικνύναι, ῥητορεύοντος, οὐκ ἀληθεύοντος ἦν. οἵ γέ τοι παρ' ἡμῖν προσαιτοῦντες πόλεως μέτριον, οἱ δ' ἐγγυτέρω

[1] καὶ Wolf (Mss.): om. Re., F.

---

[a] Pind. *Ol.* 7.4

[b] Miccalus, who was last seen some months before travelling to court to seek advancement, now tries to make his fortune under the protection of Priscianus, whom he knew well enough from his stay in Antioch.

[c] As Dio Cassius remarks (49.36), the Greeks, with an eye to classical literature, substituted the Homeric

## 61. To Priscianus

1. From home to home[a] goes Miccalus, from Olympius to you,[b] and does not so much leave a brother as go to one. Hence I believe that he despises the riches in Pannonia[c] and the extravagance founded in injustice, believing that association with you will be more to his taste even than the wealth that comes to him from the sea.[d] 2. This then has induced him to prefer your administration, but you can find for him sources of money too, for it is proper for you to return with hands empty, for him with hands full. 3. The comments in your letter about the state of poverty, when you try to prove that it is worse there than here, are those suited to speechifying, not to accurate truth. Admittedly the beggars among us are not too large an element in the community,[e] but if those closer to the

Paeonia for Pannonia, despite the geographical difference. For Homer Paeonia was ἐριβῶλαξ (*Il.* 17.350, 21.154)—hence the wealth. The court, which Miccalus had visited without successful outcome, had recently been operating in the Balkans.

[d] By association with the court, from which he had travelled in the sailing season.

[e] For Priscianus' comments about the poverty of his province, see preceding letter. John Chrysostom was more pessimistic in his view of poverty in Antioch. One tenth of its inhabitants are said to have needed support: *Hom. in Matth.* 66.3 (*PG* lviii, 630).

τῶν δεινῶν εἰ τούτῳ πλουτοῦσιν, Οἰδίπου τινὸς χρῄζομεν.

## 62. Ἀνδρονίκῳ

1. Μέτρον ἄριστον ἔφη τις καὶ ὁ λόγος ἀνάθημα γίγνεται τῷ Πυθίῳ. σὺ δ' ὅτι μὲν τῇ τε ἄλλῃ καὶ τῷ πλήθει τῶν βουλευτῶν μείζους τὰς πόλεις ποιεῖς, καλῶς ποιεῖς· ὅστις δὲ εἰς μείζω βουλὴν καλεῖται καὶ γέγονεν ἀντὶ Φοίνικος ἄλλο τι σεμνότερον, μήτοι τοῦτον ἀποστέρει τῆς τύχης μηδ' οὕτω φίλει τοὺς ἀρχομένους ὥστε τὴν σαυτοῦ μισεῖν. 2. ἔστω δὴ καὶ Φρατέρνῳ τῶν ἐν Φοινίκῃ λειτουργιῶν ἄφεσις, ὃν αὐτίκα δεήσει δαπανᾶν ἐν τῇ Μεγάλῃ πόλει. τὸν δὲ ἄνδρα τοῦτον εἶδον μὲν οὔπω, φίλον δὲ ἡγοῦμαι φίλῳ τε ἐμῷ καὶ μαθητῇ μέλλοντα κηδεύσειν Ἀπριγγίῳ, ὃς ἐμὲ

---

[a] Cf. Cleobulus (Diog. Laert. 1.6.6).
[b] Cf. Plat. *Prot.* 343a–b.

edge of disaster are wealthy thereby, we need another Oedipus.[f]

[f] To save us, as Thebes was delivered from the Sphinx.

## 62. To Andronicus

1. "Moderation in all things," the saying goes,[a] and the proverb has been ascribed to the Pythian.[b] In improving the cities, particularly by increasing the number of the councillors, you are doing quite right.[c] But if anyone is summoned to the Senate and has become, instead of a Phoenician, something different,[d] and more exalted, do not deprive him of his status and, in your regard for your subjects, show hostility to your home city.[e] 2. So let Fraternus too be excused the civic services in Phoenicia, for he will presently have to lay out expenditure in the capital.[f] I have not yet met the man, but I regard him as my friend since he is going to be father-in-law to my friend and pupil Apringius.[g] Apringius amazed me during the period of his

[c] Andronicus is now (360) *consularis Phoeniciae*. Part of his brief is to recruit entrants to the curiae and to prevent desertions.

[d] Membership of the Senate involves the citizenship of Constantinople and the requirement to reside there.

[e] Andronicus was a native and senator of Constantinople.

[f] For Fraternus, *PLRE* 372. On the expenditure of newly enrolled senators, see Petit in *Ant. Class.* 26:367.

[g] *BLZG* 80, *PLRE* 86.

μὲν ἐν τῷ χρόνῳ τῶν μαθήσεων ἐπιεικείᾳ τε καὶ λόγων ἐξέπληξεν ἐπιθυμίᾳ, τὴν δὲ ἡμετέραν πόλιν τῷ περὶ τὴν χορηγίαν λαμπρῷ. 3. τούτῳ τῷ νεανίσκῳ μὴ βοηθῶν μὲν ἐγὼ πάνυ ἂν ἀδικοίην, προδώσω δὲ αὐτόν, εἰ μηδενὸς ἄξιος Φρατέρνῳ φανεῖται. φανεῖται δὲ φαῦλος, εἰ σοῦ μὲν ἔχοντος τὴν ἀρχήν, ἐμοῦ δέ σε πείθειν ἔχοντος ὁ μέλλων αὐτῷ τὴν θυγατέρα δώσειν ἀδικήσεται. δόξει γὰρ Ἀπρίγγιος ὑπ' ἐμοῦ καταφρονεῖσθαι· σὲ γὰρ οὐκ ἄν ποτε μὴ δοῦναι χάριν ἐμοί. 4. ἀλλὰ δός, ἑταίρων φίλτατε, χαίρεις γὰρ ἀκούων τοῦτο μᾶλλον ἢ τὸ τῆς ἀρχῆς ὄνομα, καὶ μιᾷ πράξει τό τε δίκαιον τίμησον καὶ τῇ σαυτοῦ βοήθησον καὶ τοῦτον μὴ ἀτιμάσῃς.

## 63. Μοδέστῳ

1. Καλά γε περιμένει τοὺς ἄρχοντας τὰ ἆθλα, εἴγε ταλαιπωρήσονται μὲν καὶ τὰ αὑτῶν χείρω ποιήσουσι τῶν κοινῶν ἐπιμελούμενοι, λήψονται δὲ ἀμοιβὰς ὕβριν καὶ καταδίκην καὶ ἀτιμίαν καὶ κινδύνους. 2. ταῦτα γὰρ κεκύκλωκε νῦν τὸν ὑπὸ

studies by his impeccable conduct and his desire for eloquence, and he has amazed our city by his lavishness in the performance of the choregia. 3. It would be very wrong of me not to assist this young man, and I shall be betraying him if he appears to Fraternus to be of no esteem. And he will appear of little worth if, while you have charge of the province and I have the ability to influence you, his future father-in-law should suffer injustice, for it will be thought that Apringius is despised by me, since you would never have refused me a favour. 4. Grant it then, my dearest friend—for this is a title which you appreciate more than that of governor—and by one and the same action, honour right, assist your native city, and do not dishonour this man.

## 63. To Modestus[a]

1. It is a fine reward for our governors if, after expending their energies and reducing their private fortunes in the performance of their public duties, they get in exchange outrage, condemnation, disgrace, and danger. 2. This is the sort of thing that

[a] Written in the first part of 360, this letter illustrates the dangers that beset a provincial governor in times of financial pressure by demands made upon him by the treasury.

σοῦ μὲν οὐδὲν ἀτιμασθέντα, μεθ' ἡμῶν δὲ βεβιωκότα Τρυφωνιανόν. ἦν μὲν γὰρ ἕτοιμος χωρεῖν ἐπὶ Χαλκίδος, ὅπως ἀναγκάζοι τὰ δέοντα ποιεῖν τοὺς αὐτόθι γεωργούς, ἑστηκότα δὲ ἐπὶ τῆς βαλβῖδος περιέσχε νέφος ἀρθὲν[1] ἐκ τῶν Οὐρσουάλου χειρῶν. 3. προσπεσόντες γὰρ ἄνθρωποί τινες ἐκεῖθεν ἥκοντες καὶ θρασέως εἰσελθόντες οὗ καθεύδει χρυσόν τε ἐζήτουν καὶ καταβάλλειν ἐβόων πόσον, οἴει, χρυσόν; μὴ φαινομένου δὲ σήμαντρα πανταχοῦ, καὶ πολὺς ὁ θόρυβος, ἡ γυνὴ δὲ ἐν ἐκπλήξει καὶ τὸ βρέφος μικροῦ τῆς νηδύος οὐ κατὰ νόμον ἐξέδραμεν. 4. ἡμεῖς μὲν οὖν οὗπέρ ἐσμεν κύριοι πληροῦμεν, συναχθόμεθα τῷ φίλῳ, σὺ δὲ παρ' ᾧ τι πλέον μεθ' ἡμῶν μὲν συνάλγησον, μόνος δὲ ἐπικούρησον χρηστός τε φαινόμενος καὶ τῇ δυνάμει χρώμενος. 5. ἔστω δὲ πρῶτον μὲν τῆς χάριτος τὸ μὴ δι' ὀργῆς λαβεῖν τὴν μονήν, μᾶλλον δὲ τὸ τὴν ὀργὴν ἐπὶ τοὺς οὐκ ἀφέντας ἐξελθεῖν μετενεγκεῖν· δεύτερον δὲ τὸ λῦσαι τὴν ἐπικειμένην ζημίαν. 6. οὐκ ἔστι τῶν

[1] ἀρθὲν F., conj. Re. αἱρεθὲν (αἱ- V) Wolf (Mss.).

has now enveloped Tryphonianus[b] who has suffered no mark of your displeasure while living among us. He was all ready to set out to Chalcis to compel the peasants there to fulfil their obligations, but as he stood at the very start, he found himself in the middle of a storm raised by the agency of Ursulus.[c] 3. Some fellows from there rushed in, impudently entered his bedroom and began a search for gold and clamoured for him to produce such an amount of gold as you could not conceive. When it was not forthcoming, they planted their seals everywhere. There was a terrible hubbub; his wife was distracted, and her child was very nearly prematurely lost by miscarriage. 4. So I am doing all in my power, and show my sympathy with my friend: you, who have more influence than I, must feel the same feeling of outrage as I: show yourself a good fellow, use your influence, and be his sole source of assistance. 5. Let the first sign of your favour be that you do not take his staying here amiss,[d] rather, that you transfer your anger to those who have not permitted him to leave. Next, relieve him of the penalty imposed on him. 6. My request requires

[b] *PLRE* 924 (2). Tryphonianus' troubles stemmed from the difficulties of tax collection, for the payment of which in gold he is made personally responsible.

[c] *PLRE* 988 (1): *Comes sacrarum largitionum*, notoriously strict but efficient.

[d] He had stayed in Antioch after his demotion. He was not allowed to remain in his province while he faced a charge concerning his governorship.

ῥεόντων ἃ ζητοῦμεν, οὐδὲ γὰρ ἃ πράττεις καθημέραν τῶν ῥεόντων ἐστίν, οὐδέ γε πάσης γνώμης, ἀλλὰ τῆς σῆς μόνης. μὴ οὖν θαυμάσῃς, εἰ πάλαι διδάσκων ἡμᾶς, ὡς κἂν τοῖς ἀμηχάνοις ἰσχύεις, ἀπαιτῇ παρὰ τῶν ἐκεῖνα ὁρώντων ἕτερα ἐκείνοις ἐοικότα. 7. ἀλλ' ἐννοήσας τε ὅθεν[2] ἡ καταδίκη καὶ τὸ πρᾶγμα μεμψάμενος καὶ τὸ τῆς ζημίας μέγεθος καὶ τιμῶν ἡμᾶς καὶ βοηθῶν ἄρχοντι κατάκρας ἐλαυνομένῳ πρᾶξον, ὃ σοὶ μὲν οἴσει κόσμον, ἡμῖν δὲ εὐθυμίαν, τοῖς δὲ ἐκείνου σωτηρίαν.

[2] τε ὅθεν F. ὅθεν τε Wolf (Mss.).

## 64. Δημητρίῳ

1. Ἄμφω μὲν ἔδειξα τὼ λόγω καὶ ὅλω γε ἄμφω τὼ λόγω, τὸν μὲν νῦν τὸν μαχόμενον, τὸν δὲ πάλαι τὸν ἐπαινοῦντα· σὺ δὲ ᾤου με δείσαντα κολοιοῦ τινος θόρυβον ᾑρῆσθαι σιγᾶν καὶ γεγενῆσθαι κακὸν περὶ τὸν ἐμαυτοῦ θεῖον. 2. τὸ δὲ οὐχ οὕτως ἔχει, ἀλλ' ἃ μὲν οὐκ εἶχε κίνδυνον εἰς πολλοὺς ἐκφέρειν, ἐν πολλοῖς εἴρηται· τοῦ λόγου δὲ ἡ τρίτη μοῖρα φίλων ἐδεῖτο σαφῶν, οὓς ὀλίγοις

no irresolution—but then, your daily activities show no irresolution—nor is it a job for anyone, but for you alone. Do not be surprised, then, after long teaching us that you are capable of surmounting any impasse, if you are called upon again by those who have seen it happen to do the like once more. 7. But consider the source of origin of the verdict, and disapprove of the case and of the amount of the fine, and out of respect for me and to assist a governor who is being hounded from pillar to post, act in such a way as will bring credit to you, comfort to me, and protection to his family.

## 64. To Demetrius[a]

1. I delivered both orations, and both orations complete, the present one of criticism, the previous one of praise.[b] You thought that I was afraid of the squawking of some jay and had chosen silence and had been disloyal to my own uncle. 2. Such is not the case. Those portions, where there was no risk involved in putting them before the public, have been delivered in public, but a third of my speech

[a] Cf. Petit, "Recherches sur la publication," *Historia* 5 (1956): 487. Written in the first part of 360, about the funeral oration upon his uncle Phasganius, dead some months before.

[b] The oration was in two sections, a panegyric of his dead uncle, followed by an invective against his opponents, in particular the Caesar Gallus. He has no qualms about publishing the panegyric, but the second section received only a private hearing.

δεξάμενος τοῖς βάθροις κλείσας τὰς θύρας ἀνέγνων δεόμενος αὐτῶν, εἴ τι φαίνοιτο καλόν, σιγῇ θαυμάζειν μηδὲ τῇ βοῇ πολλοὺς ἐγείρειν. καὶ μέχρι γε τοῦ παρόντος, προσκυνῶ δὲ Ἀδράστειαν, φόβος οὐδεὶς ἐξέφυ. 3. τί τὸ φοβοῦν, ἀκοῦσαι ποθεῖς; ἐξήρπασε τοῦ τότε κρατοῦντος Φασγάνιος τὴν πόλιν οἶσθ' ὅπως ζέοντος. οὐκ ἦν οὖν τὴν τοῦδε βοήθειαν δεῖξαι μεγάλην μὴ τὴν ὠμότητα δείξαντα τὴν ἐκείνου μεγάλην. δέδεικται δή, καὶ ὁ λόγος ὧν εἰκὸς τετύχηκεν. 4. ἀλλ' ἔστι δέος μὴ τῷ μὲν λόγῳ τὸ μέρος ἔχῃ καλῶς, τὸ καλὸν δὲ τοῦτο κακὸν τέκῃ τῷ ποιητῇ. δύναται γὰρ καὶ τεθνεὼς ἐκεῖνος διὰ τοῦ ζῶντος. ὅστις οὖν οὐκ ἐπιθυμεῖ βαράθρου, κρύψαι λόγον αἱρήσεται μᾶλλον ἢ διδοὺς τρέμειν. 5. τουτὶ μὲν οὖν ἀναβολῇ δεδόσθω, τὸν δὲ ἕτερον δέξῃ δι'

---

[c] Cf. Plat. *Prot.* 325e. For the practice of the closed auditorium, common among the sophists of the day, cf. *Or.* 1.101, 2.25, Eunap. *V.S.* 483.

[d] A Platonism (e.g., *Resp.* 5.451a), now proverbial (e.g., *Or.* 1.158, 2.52; Julian *Misop.* 370b; Them. *Or.* 34.10).

required firm friends.[c] I received them on a few benches behind closed doors, and read it to them with the request that, if they felt it had any merit, they should admire it in silence and not arouse large numbers of people by their applause. And up to now—touch wood![d]—no cause for alarm has arisen. 3. Do you desire to hear what deters me? Phasganius rescued our city from the then ruler[e]—and you know what his temper was like! So it was impossible to show the extent of Phasganius' assistance without showing the extent of the other's brutality. Well, it has been delivered and the oration has met with the reception to be expected. 4. The fear is that, though this section suits the speech perfectly, this perfection may breed trouble for its composer. Even after death Gallus wields influence still through the living.[f] So anyone who does not hanker after the dungeon[g] will choose to keep the speech dark rather than to publish and be damned. 5. So let it be subject to delay. The other you will receive by the hand of a man who is

[e] The Caesar Gallus in his feud with the Antiochene notables (Amm. Marc. 14.7.2). Phasganius, connected by family ties to the praetorian prefect Thalassius who was at odds with his Caesar, and by personal opposition to Gallus' excesses, had evidently rallied the curia against him.

[f] Gallus' half-brother Julian, now Caesar. The passage indicates Libanius' insecurity at this time and his isolation from Julian.

[g] In Athens, the pit into which criminals were thrown to die, cf. Herod. 7.133.

ἀνδρὸς ἀρίστου τῶν παρ' ἡμῖν, οὗ πρότερος οὐδεὶς ἦλθεν ἐπὶ τὸ βουληθῆναι λαβεῖν. ταυτὶ δέ σοι, δι' ὧν ἡμιλλησάμην πρός τι τῶν Δημοσθένους, καὶ προάγωνε δύο, ὁ μὲν ὃν ᾔτεις, ὁ δὲ ἴσως οὐκ ἀνιάσων.

## 65. Πολυχρονίῳ

1. Τί τῆς σιγῆς ἔχεις αἰτιᾶσθαι; βραδυτῆτα νοῦ; καὶ τίς ὀξύτερος; ἀλλ' ἔνδειαν λέξεως; ὁ σαφῶς οὕτω περὶ τῶν μεγάλων διδάσκων; πόθεν οὖν ἄφωνος; οὐ λέγεις· οὐκοῦν ἀκούσῃ.[1] τῶν τροφῶν ἡμῖν περικόψας αἰσχύνῃ καὶ διαζεύξας τῶν πυρῶν τὰς κριθὰς τοὺς ἵππους ἠδικηκὼς οὐκ ἔχεις ὅ τι εἴπῃς.[2] 2. ἀλλά σοι λύω τὸν φόβον τὸ τοῦ Ἀχιλλέως εἰπών· οὐ σὺ τοῦτο λυπεῖς, ἀλλ' Ἀγαμέμνων. ὥστε θαρρῶν[3] ἴθι καὶ γράφε.

[1] ἀκούσῃ F. ἀκούσαις Mss. ἀκούσεις Wolf.
[2] εἴποις Wolf (Vo[3] A)
[3] καὶ before ἴθι Wolf (Mss.), del. Re., F.

---

[a] Seeck (*BLZG* 241) identified him as *consularis* of Phoenice; *PLRE* (711), as *domesticus* to the praetorian prefect.

[b] On the cut in Libanius' salary ordered by the new praetorian prefect Elpidius and its restoration in 362, cf. *Letter* 89.

the best of people here: no one was more beforehand than he in his desire to act as the bearer. There are enclosed my declamation against a remark of Demosthenes, and a couple of introductories, one of which you asked for;[h] the other perhaps will find favour.

[h] Cf. *Fragg.* 14, 15, 16 (Foerster, xi: 621). These were evidently written some years before (cf. *Letter* 6).

## 65. To Polychronius[a]

1. What reason have you to give for your silence? Slowness of intellect? But who is quicker than you? Weakness of diction, then? What, you who give such clear information on matters of moment! So why are you dumb? You do not reply; well, I will tell you. You are ashamed at making a cut in my allowance:[b] having sorted out the wheat from the oats and cheated your horses,[c] you have not a word to say for yourself. 2. But I relieve your fear by citing the words of Achilles, "It is not you who cause me this grief, but Agamemnon."[d] So come on now! cheer up and write.[e]

[c] A pun on πυροί, the regular term for payment in kind by the Treasury (*annona*).

[d] Homer *Il.* 1.335, 355. Agamemnon is the σκαιὸς Ἐλπίδιος of *Letter* 89.

[e] Cf. *Ep.* 32.1.

## 66. Ἀνδρονίκῳ

1. Σέβων ἐστὶ μὲν Κρής, προσήκει δέ τι κατὰ γένος τούτοις ὧν ἄρχεις. ἔστι γὰρ ἀπόγονος τῶν ἀνδρῶν ἐκείνων, οἳ ἀπὸ τῆς Εὐρώπης ἐγένοντο τῷ Διὶ κομίσαντι τὴν παρθένον ἀπὸ Φοινίκης διὰ θαλάττης εἰς Κρήτην. γέμων δὲ μαθημάτων, ἃ καὶ αὐτὸς ὁμιλῶν τε καὶ πειρώμενος εὑρήσεις, οὐ μᾶλλον τὴν γλῶτταν ἢ τοὺς τρόπους ἀγαθὸς ὑπὸ τῆς παιδεύσεως γεγένηται. 2. καὶ δὴ καὶ τόδε τῆς παιδείας· ἀνέῳξε γὰρ τοῖς ξένοις τὴν οἰκίαν καὶ πολλοὺς ἐποίησεν ἐπιλαθέσθαι τῆς οἰκείας καὶ πρὸ τῶν οἰκείων τὸ τοῦδε ποιήσασθαι. 3. δέχεται δὴ κατάραντα καὶ Φοίνικα ἄνδρα, ἀδελφὸν Εὐσεβίου τοῦ ῥήτορος ὃν πέμψαι μὲν εὔχετο σῶν, παρόντα δὲ ἐθεράπευσεν, ἀπελθόντα δὲ ἐπένθησε τά τε ἄλλα χρηστὸν ὄντα καὶ περὶ τῆς οὐσίας ἀξίως ἐπαίνου βεβουλευμένον. 4. ἀφεὶς γὰρ πονηροὺς ἀδελφοὺς πρός τε τοὺς ἄλλους καὶ πρὸς αὑτὸν ἔδωκεν ἀνδρὶ γενναίῳ πρός τε τοὺς ἄλλους καὶ πρὸς αὑτόν. οἱ δὲ ἐχρήσαντο νῦν πολλῇ κατὰ

[a] For Sebon cf. *Ep.* 306. Andronicus is governor of Phoenicia.

## 66. To Andronicus

1. Though Sebon is a Cretan, he has some lineal connection with the people you govern,[a] for he is descended from those men who were born of Europe to Zeus after he had carried the maiden from Phoenicia over the sea to Crete.[b] He is full of learning, as you will yourself discover upon association and examination, and, in consequence of his education, his virtues of character are no less than those of his eloquence. 2. Indeed it is evidence of his gentlemanliness that he opened up his home to his guests and induced many to forget their homeland and to prefer him to their own kith and kin. 3. So he welcomed a man from Phoenicia whose ship called in there, the brother of the orator Eusebius,[c] and though he prayed to send him safely on his way and cared for him while he was with him,[d] he mourned for him after his passing, as being a good fellow and, in particular, the arranger of a praiseworthy disposition of his property. 4. You see, he passed over the brothers who had behaved badly to others, and especially himself, and gave it to a man who had been good to others and himself. These brothers

[b] Cf. Plat. *Min.* 318d. Such classically inspired commendations, however tenuous their relevance, are meant to be taken seriously by educated officials.

[c] *BLZG* 142 (xiii).

[d] Cf. Homer *Od.* 15.74. Variations on this theme are common in the letters, e.g., *Epp.* 130, 179.

τῶν διαθηκῶν ἀναισχυντίᾳ. καὶ ἅμα γῦπες ἕτεροι πολλοὶ πολλαχόθεν ἐφέροντο, οὓς Σέβων ἀπεσόβησεν. 5. ἀλλ’ οὗτοί γε πάντων εἰσὶ χαλεπώτατοι νικῶντες ὥσπερ οἱ Σκύθαι, φεύγοντες γὰρ νικῶσιν. ἀλλ’ ἐκείνοις μὲν τὸ ἐπ’ ἁμαξῶν οἰκεῖν τοῦτο παρεῖχε, τούτοις δὲ ἡ τῶν ἀρχόντων τῶν μὲν νωθεία, τῶν δὲ ἑτέρα κακία. οὓς χρῆν ἀγανακτεῖν ὥσπερ αὐτοὺς ἀδικουμένους, οἱ δ’ ἐκάθευδον, Ἐλπίδιός τε ὁ Ἀριστείδης καὶ Ἀνδρόνικος ὁ Φωκίων. 6. ἀλλ’ ἄρτι δὴ μῦς πίττης. σὺ γὰρ δὴ αὐτοὺς ἐκ τοῦ σκότους πρὸς τὸ φῶς ἑλκύσεις τῶν τε δικαίων εἵνεκα καὶ νομίσας δεινὸν τοὺς μὲν οἴκοι καθημένους τρυφᾶν ἀνδραπόδων οὐδαμῇ βελτίους, Σέβωνα δὲ τὸν τῶν Ἑλλήνων ἄκρον ἐπ’ ἀλλοτρίας ἔτη τέτταρα ἀλᾶσθαι γυναικὸς οὔσης αὐτῷ καὶ παίδων. 7. εἰδότι <δ’>[1] ἂν λέγοιμι τὸν περὶ ταῦτα πόθον, δι’ ὃν ὥρμησε πολλάκις ῥίψας τὴν δίκην ἐπανελθεῖν, ὑφ’ ἡμῶν δὲ κατεκωλύθη τὸν τεθνεῶτα ἐλεούντων, εἰ τοὺς ἐχθροὺς αἰσθήσεται τὰ αὑτοῦ καρπουμένους καὶ τὸ Ὁμηρικὸν λεγόντων, ὡς αἰσχρὸν μηδὲν ἔργον φανῆναι

[1] δ’ inseruit F.

---

[e] Cf. Plat. *Lach.* 191a.

[f] Praetorian prefect from early 360.

have now behaved in very disgraceful fashion in contesting the will; and at the same time many other vultures flocked in from all sides, but Sebon scared them away. 5. But these are the worst enemies of all: they win their victories like the Scythians—in retreat.[e] The Scyths were able to do so because they lived in waggons, these people because of either the idleness or other defects of the governors. Those who should have been as angry as if they personally were the victims—Elpidius,[f] his Aristeides, and Andronicus, his Phocion[g]—had gone to sleep. 6. But they have been given enough rope.[h] You obviously will fetch them out of their hiding holes into the light, both for the sake of justice and because you think it a shame that they should sit at home in the lap of luxury, though they are in no way better than slaves, while Sebon, this first-rate Greek, should wander in exile for four years, although he has a wife and children. 7. If you knew him, I could tell you of his yearning for them: because of it he was often tempted to throw up the case and return home, but has been stopped by me out of pity for the deceased, should he see his foes reaping the fruits of what he had, and I quoted Homer, that no base deed should get the better of

[g] As Aristeides was nicknamed the Just, so was Phocion the Good; cf. Corn. Nep. *Phoc.* 1, Suidas s.v. χρηστός.

[h] Proverbial, for those who realize too late the trouble they are in; see *Paroem. Gr.* 1.206, 2.11, Dem. 50.26, Gow on Theocr. 14.51.

κρεῖττον τοῦ χρόνου. 8. δεῖξον δὴ καλῶς ἡμᾶς πεπεικότας μένειν καὶ τοῖς μὲν νόμοις χάρισαι τὸ καλέσαι τοὺς κρυπτομένους, ἡμῖν δὲ τὸ ταχέως· ὡς οὐκ ἔσται μοι λόγος, ἢν οὗτος αὖθις εἰς ἀναβολὰς ἐμπέσῃ τοῦ κατεπείγειν ὄντος ἐν σοί. τὸ γὰρ ὅτι παντὶ σθένει βοηθήσεις ἐμὴν χάριν προειπεῖν πάντα με ἀφαιρήσεται λόγον, εἰ ῥᾳθυμήσαις. ὅρα οὖν μή με ἀποφήνῃς ἀλαζόνα.

## 67. Ἀνδρονίκῳ

1. Ἦ που πολλάκις σοί τε καὶ τοῖς γνωρίμοις ὑπὲρ Φοινίκης γίγνονται λόγοι τοῦ μὲν τὴν φύσιν τῆς γῆς ὑπερεπαινοῦντος, τοῦ δὲ τὴν κρᾶσιν τῶν ὡρῶν, ἑτέρου τῆς θαλάττης τὴν φορὰν τήν τε ἄλλην καὶ ἀφ᾽ ἧς ἡ βαφή, ἣν μηνυθῆναί φασι τὸ πρῶτον τύχῃ τινὶ διὰ κυνὸς οὐδὲν εἰδότος ὧν ἔπραττεν. 2. ἀλλ᾽ ἔγωγε τὸν ἄνδρα τοῦτον ὁρίζομαι τῶν ἐν Φοινίκῃ τὸ κάλλιστον μετά γε τὰ τῶν θεῶν ἱερά. ταῦτα δὲ αὐτὸς προσκυνεῖ καὶ ἔστι τοῦτο τῶν ἐν αὐτῷ καλῶν τὸ πρῶτον, ὅτι τὸ θεῖον

[a] Introducing the philosopher Hierius, *BLZG* 175 (i), *PLRE* 430 (4); date 360. Ironically, he is the same 'foxy Hierius' responsible for Andronicus' execution after the revolt of Procopius (*Or.* 1.171).

time.[i] 8. So prove me right in having persuaded him to stay: support the law in summoning them from their hiding and me in doing it quickly, for I shall have no excuse if he is once more immersed in delays, while ever you have the power to hasten matters. My forecast that you will do all you can to help for my sake will have neither rhyme nor reason, if you are remiss. So see that you do not show me up to be a braggart.

[i] Homer *Il.* 2.298.

## 67. To Andronicus[a]

1. Often, I am sure, conversation takes place between your friends and you about Phoenicia: one lavishes praise on its fertility, another on the blending of the seasons, yet another on the produce of the sea, and particularly on the production of purple dye, which people say was first brought to light accidentally by a dog without any idea of what it was doing.[b] 2. I, however, declare that second only to the temples of the gods the finest thing in Phoenicia is the bearer.[c] He personally is devoted to them, and his understanding of religious matters is his first claim to fame. What to put second or third I

[b] A Phoenician legend, according to Pollux *Onom.* 1.45 f, suitable for narration to the governor of that province.

[c] The play on the name Hierius with ἱερά is suppressed, to be revealed in § 6.

ἐπίσταται. δεύτερον καὶ τρίτον οὐκ οἶδ' ὅ τι θείμην, πάντα γὰρ ἴσα ἀλλήλοις. 3. ἀλλ' ὅ γε καινότατον, ἐπὶ θρόνου γάρ, οἵου σύ, καθίζων ἀνέμιξε τῷ ἄρχειν τὸ φιλοσοφεῖν τῶν τι δοκούντων εἶναι καὶ ἀπειλούντων τοσοῦτον καταγελάσας ὅσον οὐκ οἶδ' εἴ τις τῶν ἄλλων ἢ τῶν ἀνδραπόδων. χρήματά τε γὰρ οὐκ εἶχον αὐτὸν ἀφελέσθαι, πῶς γὰρ τά γε οὐκ ὄντα; δεθείς τε ἡγήσαιτ' ἂν ἐν λειμῶνι διάγειν τό τε τῆς ἀρχῆς ἐκβαλεῖν οὐ στερῆσαί τινος ἦν, ἀλλ' ἀποδοῦναι σχολήν. 4. οἶμαι δέ, οὐδ' εἴ τις ἀπέσφαττεν, ἤλγησεν ἄν. οὐ γάρ, ὥσπερ οἱ πολλοί, φρίττει τὸν θάνατον, ἀλλ' οἶδεν οὔσας τοῖς γε δικαίοις ὑπὸ γῆς οὐ μικρὰς εὐφροσύνας. 5. ἥκει δή σοι θεατής τε ὧν πράττεις καὶ κριτής, προσθείην δ' ἂν καὶ ἐπαινέτης. οὗ τὴν ψῆφον ἢν λάβῃς, λήψῃ δέ, πλέον εἰς δόξαν τοῦ νῦν ὑπάρχοντος ἕξεις καὶ ταῦτα ὄντος οὐκ ὀλίγου τοῦ νῦν. 6. οὐδεὶς γὰρ τὴν ἐναντίαν Ἱερίῳ θήσεται τῷ τῶν μὲν ἄλλων διαφέροντι κατὰ τὸν τῆς φιλοσοφίας ἔρωτα, τῶν δ' αὖ φιλοσοφούντων τῷ χαίρειν ἐᾶν

πώγωνα καὶ τρίβωνα καὶ βακτηρίαν.

---

[d] Cf. Plat. *Phaed.* 82a-b, *Axioch.* 371d-e. Used by Libanius in *Letter* 71.5, *Ep.* 220.4.

hardly know, for they are all on a par with one another. 3. But the most remarkable thing is that while he occupied a governor's seat, as you do now, he mingled philosophy with government and treated the blusterers who think they are somebody with such scorn as ordinarily is reserved for the man in the street or slaves. They could not take his money away from him: that would be impossible, for he has none. If he were imprisoned, he would think that he passed his time in a meadow in paradise, and expulsion from office for him is no deprivation but the restoration of his leisure. 4. Even under the axe of the executioner, I am sure, he would utter no complaint, for unlike ordinary folk he has no fear of death: he knows that for the just at least there is in the world below no little cause for joy.[d] 5. Well, he comes to observe and to judge your actions and, I might add, to commend them too. If you gain his vote, as you will, you will have more that redounds to your credit than you possess at present, even though what you have now is no small matter. 6. No one will contradict the verdict of Hierius, for he surpasses the ordinary person in his love for philosophy, and the philosophers themselves by saying farewell to "beard and cloak and staff."[e]

[e] The three visible hallmarks of a philosopher. F. (*ad loc.*) suggested that this is not an actual quotation from comedy, but a line composed by Libanius himself reminiscent of a fragment of Phoenicides (fr. 4.17 Kassel-Austin).

## 68. Μοδέστῳ

1. Εἴη σε τὴν στοὰν ταυτηνὶ τὴν εὐρεῖάν τε καὶ μακρὰν καὶ ὑψηλὴν καὶ τῷ Διονύσῳ φίλην ἐπιτελέσαι κατὰ νοῦν καὶ σταίη γε παγίως, ἕως ἀνθρώπων γένος, σώζουσα τῷ γε ἐγείραντι τοὔνομα. 2. ἀλλ', ὦ μακάριε, μὴ τοῦθ' ἓν μόνον σκοπῶμεν, ὅπως μεγάλα ποιήσωμεν, ἀλλὰ καὶ ὅπως μηδένα ἐν οἷς ποιοῦμεν λυπήσωμεν· ὡς νῦν γε εἰσὶν οἳ στένουσιν, ὧν αὐτὸς ᾐσθόμην, καὶ οὔ σε ἀποκρύψομαι,[1] ἵν' εἴ τι φαινοίμην λέγων, παύσαις τὸ γιγνόμενον. 3. κίονας ἐκ Σελευκείας τοῖς μὲν ἐπέταξας κομίζειν, τοὺς δὲ ᾔτησας χάριν. ὁ δὲ οὕτω διειλεγμένος κύριον πεποίηκε τὸν αἰτηθέντα ἀμφοῖν. ἡ βουλὴ μὲν ὑπηρετεῖ[2] σιγῇ, τῶν δὲ ἐν ἀρχαῖς γεγενημένων οἱ μὲν ταὐτὸν ἐκείνοις ποιοῦσι καὶ κομίζουσιν, εἰσὶ δὲ οἷς δοκεῖ τὸ πρᾶγμα

[1] ἀποκρύψομαι F. ἀποκρυψαίμην Wolf (Mss.)
[2] ἡ βουλὴ μὲν ὑπηρετεῖ F. ἠβούλου μὲν ὑπηρετεῖν Wolf (Mss.)

---

[a] F/Kr. no. 30. For building in Antioch at this time cf. Petit, *Vie Municipale* 314 ff; Liebeschuetz, *Antioch* 132 ff. The initiative lies with the governor, the physical labour is imposed upon the commons, the management and the expenses entailed thereby upon the curia. Modestus exerts so much pressure to get the job done that he is squeezing even the *honorati,* who normally expected to be

## 68. To Modestus

1. My hope is that you may bring to the desired completion this great, wide, lofty portico, dear to Dionysus, and that it may stand firm while ever mankind exists, preserving the name of its builder. 2. But my dear sir, do not let us simply consider how to put up great buildings, but also how not to annoy anyone by our buildings. As things are, some people are aggrieved. I have seen them myself, and I will not conceal the fact from you, so that you may put a stop to what is happening, if I appear to be talking sense.[a] 3. Some people you have ordered to convey the columns from Seleuceia:[b] from others you have asked it as a favour. Anyone who speaks in these terms leaves the choice open to the person he asks. The city council performs its service without a murmur, but of the past holders of governmental office[c] some do the same as it does and convey them, but others, who have the dignity

and were legally immune. Libanius here puts their case. For further letters on this colonnade cf. *Epp.* 242, 617. It evidently was adjacent to the Dionysium, which still survived in the 380s (*Or.* 30.51).

[b] It is now well into the sailing season, late spring–summer 360. The transport of these columns from Seleuceia, the port of Antioch, was one of the *munera extraordinaria* imposed upon decurions; cf. *Cod. Th.* xi.16.15–18.

[c] The *honorati.*

δεινόν, οἷς ἀξία μέν ἐστι, δύναμις δὲ οὐκ ἔστι. 4. καὶ τὸ ὑπάρχου τειχίον ὀνομάζουσι τὴν στοάν, φόβος δὲ οὐ μικρὸς μὴ ἡ νῦν καλουμένη χάρις εἰς ἀνάγκην ὁμοῦ προβῇ τῶν ἔπειτα φασκόντων ἀκολουθεῖν παραδείγματι καί τις ὕστερον μέμψηται τῷ τὴν ἀρχὴν εὑρόντι. 5. ἀλλ', εἰ δοκεῖ, τῇδε ποιῶμεν· κήρυξον, εἴ τις βούλεται, τούς τε γὰρ βουλομένους εὑρήσεις διὰ τὸ δύνασθαι τούς τε οὐ δυναμένους οὐκ ἀνιάσεις. καὶ οὕτως οὐδεὶς καταράσεται τῷ ποιουμένῳ. εἴη δέ σοι μικρὰ κατασκευάζεσθαι συνηδομένων ἁπάντων ἢ βαρυνομένων τὰ τείχη Βαβυλωνίων.

## 69. Μοδέστῳ

1. Ἄκουε δὴ καὶ ἕτερον ἐπανορθώσεως χρῇζον. Ἀστερίῳ παρ' ἡμῖν οὐδεὶς ὅμοιος, οἶμαι δέ, οὐδὲ ἄλλοθι· τοσαύτην ἔσχεν ἀνὴρ ἐπιμέλειαν ἀρετῆς οὐ τοῦ γήρως αὐτῷ σβέσαντος τὰς ἀτόπους ἡδονάς, τῆς φύσεως δὲ ἐκ παιδὸς ἐπὶ τὸ σῶφρον

[a] In 360 Modestus imposed the emergency duty of the supervision of the bronze smiths of Antioch upon a curial who would normally be excused the liturgies by reason of

but not the ability, view the business with disapproval. 4. They call your portico "the Count's castle," and there is no little apprehension that the present so-called favour should finish up as compulsion, if people in future assert that they follow precedent, and that criticism thereafter be levelled at the one who first devised the practice. 5. But, if you like, let us proceed as follows: issue a proclamation, asking for volunteers, for you will find your volunteers, since they have the ability, and you will not upset those who do not have it. In this way no one will curse the construction. I would prefer you to construct something small, to everyone's delight, rather than the walls of Babylon,[d] to their annoyance.

[d] One of the wonders of the ancient world; cf. *Or.* 61.17, Herod. 1.178.

## 69. To Modestus

1. Please listen to yet another matter that requires amendment.[a] There is none among us like Asterius[b] nor, in my opinion, anywhere else. Such is the attention to virtue that he has displayed, not because old age has quenched inordinate pleasures but because right from boyhood his nature directed

age and standing. The demands necessitated by the current armament programme were causing unrest among the workers—hence the need for supervision. They were likely to strike.

[b] Decurion of Antioch, pagan, and father of the pagan Olympius (v) and Christian Eusebius (xix).

ἀγούσης, ὅθεν ἐν αἰδοῖ παρὰ τοῖς πολίταις, οὐ μᾶλλον ὢν ἔστι πρεσβύτερος ἢ ὢν ἦν τότε νεώτερος. ἐμοὶ δὲ δόξα παρίσταται ζῆν μοι τὸν θεῖον, ὅταν ἐντύχω τε τῷ πρεσβύτῃ καὶ καταστῶμεν εἰς λόγους. 2. ὅτε οὖν αὐτὸν ἐνέβαλλες εἰς καπνόν τε καὶ κτύπους χαλκέων, πράγματα[1] ὢν ἀφειστήκει πλέον ἢ καμίνων οἱ κύκνοι, λίαν ἠχθέσθην καὶ γράφειν ἕτοιμος ἦν. ἔπειτα ἐδεήθην αὐτοῦ μικρὸν ὑπομεῖναι χρόνον καὶ δοῦναι χάριν αὐτῷ τὸ σοὶ χαρίσασθαι πόνους, ὢν ἦν ἀήθης, φάσκων αὐτίκα ἥξειν τὴν λύσιν. 3. ἐπεὶ δὲ τὸ μὲν ἐκτείνεται, ταραχὴ δὲ ἐν τοῖς ἐργαζομένοις, ὁ δὲ ἡσυχίας ἐρᾷ,[2] δι' ἣν ἀρχὰς αὐτῷ πρὸς τὰς χεῖρας ἰούσας ἀπεώσατο,[3] δεῖ δὲ τοὺς χρηστοὺς ἐν τῇ σῇ δυνάμει χαίρειν, Ἀστέριος δὲ φεύγει ταῦτα ἃ διώκουσιν ἄλλοι καὶ δὴ καὶ τῆς οἰκείας[4] ἡδέως ἂν ἐκπέσοι μὴ μέλλων οἴκοι ζῆν κατὰ τὸν αὑτοῦ τρόπον, δέομαι σοῦ τὸν μὲν ἐπαινέσαι τοῦ τε τὰ αὑτοῦ πράττειν ἐθέλειν καὶ ὢν ὑπηρέτηκεν, ἐπ' ἄλλον δὲ ἀγαγεῖν

[1] πράγματα F., conj. Re. πραγμάτων Wolf (Mss.)
[2] ἐρᾷ F., conj. Re. ἤρα Wolf (Mss.)
[3] ἀπεώσατο F. ἀπώσατο Wolf (Mss.)
[4] οἰκείας F. οἰκίας Wolf (Mss.)

him towards discretion. Hence he has been held in respect by his fellow citizens, and no more by his juniors now than by his seniors then. I am impelled to believe that my uncle[c] is living yet, whenever I meet the old fellow and we fall into conversation. 2. So when you cast him into the smoke and clatter of the smithies, a business from which he is poles apart,[d] I was most upset and ready to write to you. Then I begged him to endure it for a little while, and to oblige himself by obliging you with a task to which he was unaccustomed, and asserted that presently there would come release. 3. But this is long in coming; there is unrest among the workers, and he hankers after peace and quiet, which was the reason why he rejected governmental office when it came within his grasp. Good men must rejoice in your authority, but Asterius avoids what other men pursue:[e] indeed, he would gladly be exiled from his homeland, if he cannot live at home in his own fashion. So, I beg you, commend him both for his desire to mind his own business and for the services he has rendered, and transfer your ordinance to

[c] Modestus was well acquainted with Phasganius who had died the previous year (cf. *Letter* 50). Hence the appeal to sympathy.

[d] The duty of *epimeletes* of the arms factories in Antioch was a *munus extraordinarium* which the comes could impose upon the decurions. It was not a liturgy, and there is thus no question of Asterius being excused by age.

[e] Phasganius had similarly refused office (*Or.* 1.3).

τοὐπίταγμα, πολλοὶ δὲ ὧν ἄρχεις. 4. Ἀστέριος δὲ καὶ τούτων ἀφειμένος τῶν ἔργων οὐκ ἀργὸς καθεδεῖται, τὰ γὰρ σὰ θαυμάζειν ἔργον αὐτῷ.

## 70. Μοδέστῳ

1. Συνήσθην Γεωργίῳ συναχθομένῳ τοῖς ἠτυχηκόσιν Ἀλεξανδρέων, συνήσθην δὲ καὶ σοὶ δεξαμένῳ λόγους ὑπὲρ τῶνδε παρ' ἐκείνου τοῦ πρότερον πολεμοῦντος ἐκείνοις. 2. τί δὴ λοιπόν; σαυτῷ τε κἀκείνῳ καὶ ἡμῖν καὶ τοῖς Αἰγυπτίων χαρίσασθαι δαίμοσιν. ἥξει μὲν γὰρ αὐτίκα τὸ χρυσίον, τὸ δ' αὖθις αὐτὸ γενέσθαι τῶν δεδωκότων ἀλλὰ μὴ μεῖναι τὴν ζημίαν ἐν σοί τε καὶ τῇ σῇ γνώμῃ καὶ τῇ σῇ χειρί. ἢν γὰρ μὴ βουληθῇς ἐπειχθῆναι μηδ' ἐκεῖσε πέμψῃς, ὅθεν οὐκ ἂν ἐξίοι, λείπεταί τις ἐλπὶς ἀμείνων. 3. ἄγε οὖν ὅπως ἀγωνιῇ λαμπρῶς διὰ τέλους καὶ δείξεις συνᾷδον τῷ προοιμίῳ τὸ πέρας.

---

[a] Arian bishop of Alexandria (356–61), fiercely opposed by the Alexandrian Orthodox, adherents of Athanasius. After frequent riots he engineered the expulsion of the Orthodox from their churches in 358 with the armed assis-

someone else: those whom you govern are many. 4. Asterius, even when relieved of these tasks, will not sit idle: his task will be to admire you.

## 70. To Modestus

1. I was pleased with Georgius[a] for showing sympathy towards the unfortunates of Alexandria, and I was pleased with you for entertaining the pleas made on their behalf by him who previously was at odds with them. 2. So what next? Oblige yourself, him, me, and the gods of the Egyptians. For the gold will come presently; but for it once again to belong to those who have provided it and for the fine not to be confirmed, that depends upon yourself, your resolve and your handiwork. If you refuse to be hustled and do not send it to that place from which it can never emerge,[b] there is left some hope for better things. 3. Come then, and see that yours is a brilliant performance all the way through, and produce an ending that harmonizes with the beginning.

tance of Sebastianus (for whom see *Ep.* 350); this caused further unrest, resulting in an imperial fine levied on the whole community, which Georgius, for once acting in concert with his flock, now seeks to have remitted. In this letter Libanius also joins in this unlikely alliance.

[b] Into the imperial treasury.

## 71. Ἀνδρονίκῳ

1. Ἐπ' ἐξόδῳ τῆς λειτουργίας ὁ ἀνεψιός ἐστί μου.[1] νόμος δὲ τὰ τελευταῖα καὶ μέγιστα εἶναι τῆς γε τοιαύτης λειτουργίας. ὁ δὲ καλῶς φροντίζων τῆς ὑπερβολῆς ὅπως ἐν ἑκάστῳ τῶν ποιουμένων αὐτὴ φανεῖται φροντιεῖ οὐ μόνον ἆθλα μείζω τῶν πρόσθεν τιθεὶς οὐδὲ πλείω θηρία φόνῳ διδούς, ἀλλὰ καὶ τῶν πρὸς ταῦτα ἀγωνιουμένων πολλαχόθεν ποιούμενος συλλογήν· τοῦτο γάρ ἐστιν ἀτεχνῶς τὸν κολοφῶνα ἐπιθεῖναι. 2. τῆς τοίνυν διὰ τῶν κυνηγετῶν ὑπερβολῆς ἐν σοὶ τὸ πλεῖστον. τρέφει γὰρ ἡ Φοινίκη τοὺς τὰ τοιαῦτα δεινούς. οἷς, εἰ μὲν σὺ βούλοιο, χρησόμεθα· μὴ βουλομένου δὲ κατὰ τοῦτο χωλεύσομεν. καὶ μέμψεταί τις οὐχ ἡμᾶς τοὺς ἀτυχήσαντας, ἀλλὰ τὸν ἀμνημονοῦντα τῶν φίλων. ὡς μὲν γὰρ καλοῦμεν τοὺς ἐκεῖθεν

[1] μου F. μοι Wolf (Mss.)

---

[a] F/Kr. no. 41; Liebeschuetz, "Syriarch," *Historia* 8 (1959): 113–121.

[b] Fatouros and Krischer disagree with Liebeschuetz' view that the liturgy is the Syriarchate rather than the

## 71. To Andronicus[a]

1. My cousin is approaching the end of his liturgy.[b] The custom is for the last stages also to be the most important, at least in such a liturgy as this. With a nice appreciation of the perfect, he will devise means whereby it may be achieved in every detail of his programme, not just by putting on a show bigger than any before nor yet by presenting more wild beasts for slaughter, but also by collecting from every quarter the men to fight them, for that is to cap it with the absolute peak of perfection.[c] 2. Well, perfection in the beast shows depends mainly upon you. Phoenicia produces expert huntsmen, and if you are willing, we shall employ them; if not, we will be deficient in this respect, and people will reproach not us, for our disappointment, but the one who pays no regard to his friends, for no one is unaware of the fact that we are inviting people

Olympia. However, Libanius' cousin (name unknown) had entered upon the liturgy in 356, well after his presentation of the Olympia (*Ep.* 544). He was then looking for animals for the beast shows, the most prestigious part of his duties. Now in 360 he is coming to the end of his term (Malalas p. 285 indicates a four-year tenure of the Syriarchate), and needs huntsmen for a similar showpiece. The search for huntsmen would be expected to start far in advance, and so the fact that the Olympia is only a month or two away seems to rule it out here.

[c] Cf. Zenobius 2.1, *Zenob.* 4:53.

καὶ παρ' οὗ τὴν χάριν αἰτοῦμεν οὐδεὶς ἠγνόηκε· γιγνομένου δὲ ἡμῖν οὐδενὸς εἴσονται δι' ὃν οὐ γίγνεται. τοῦτο δὲ σοὶ οὐ καλόν. 3. φιλεῖς τὴν Φοινίκην. οἶδα καὶ αὐτὸς καὶ μετ' ἐμοῦ τοῦτο οἶδε γῆ τε καὶ θάλαττα. ἀλλὰ καὶ τοῦτο ἔστι τῆς Φοινίκης ἐρῶντος ἐᾶν[2] ἡμᾶς εὖ ποιεῖν[2] τηλικαύτην πόλιν. καὶ ἅμα ἤν τι θαυμαστὸν ἐργάζωνται σοφίᾳ κρατοῦντες τὴν τῶν θηρίων φύσιν, ὁ θεατὴς ἐν τῇ τοῦ ἔργου ἡδονῇ τὴν Φοινίκην ἐπαινέσεται. 4. μὴ τοίνυν μήθ' ἡμᾶς ἀτιμάσῃς μήτ' ἐκείνην ἀδικήσῃς μηδέ γε ἁρπάσῃς πρόφασιν ἀπὸ τῶν Μοδέστου γραμμάτων εἰς τὸ μὴ δοῦναι τὴν χάριν, τὰ μὲν γὰρ ἔθει τινὶ παλαιῷ κεκόμισται, θαρροῦμεν δὲ οὐκ ἐκείνοις, ἀλλὰ τῷ σὲ βούλεσθαι τὴν ἡμετέραν οἰκίαν ἐν σχήματι φαίνεσθαι. καὶ νῦν, εἰ παρὰ σοῦ πεμφθεῖεν, οὐδεὶς πρὸ τοῦ πέμψαντος δόξει δεδωκέναι τὴν χάριν. 5. ἔδει μὲν οὖν περιεῖναί τε τὸν θεῖον ἡμῖν καὶ νῦν μεθ' ἡμῶν ἐπιστέλλειν ἢ μόνον γε ἐπιστέλλειν, ἀπέχρη γὰρ ἂν καὶ οὐδὲν ἂν ἦν ὅ τι οὐκ ἂν ἔπραττες· ἐπεὶ δὲ ἀπῆλθεν, ἐνθυμοῦ πρὸς σαυτὸν ὅτι γράφειν μὲν οὐκ ἄν τις ἀποθανὼν δύναιτο, χαίρειν δ' ἂν καὶ τελευτήσας δύναιτο. τὴν γὰρ τῶν ποιητῶν περὶ

[2] ἐᾶν . . . ποιεῖν F. ἐὰν . . . ποιῇ Wolf (Mss.)

from there or of the person to whom we direct our request. If nothing comes of it, they will know who is responsible for that. And that will be no credit to you. 3. You love Phoenicia. I know it myself, and both land and sea know it too. But it is also proper for a lover of Phoenicia to allow us to do a good turn to such a great city as ours. Moreover, if they put up a first-class show by vanquishing with their skill the beasts' brute strength, the spectators in their pleasure at the performance will praise Phoenicia. 4. Do not then disdain us or dishonour her, nor yet snatch at an excuse from Modestus'[d] letters for refusing us the favour, for they have been sent by some established protocol. I place my reliance not on them but on the fact that you wish my family to be seen to be held in honour. Now, if they are sent from you, no one will be thought to have conferred this favour before you who send them. 5. My uncle ought to be alive still and now joining with me in writing to you, or rather writing to you himself—for that would have been enough: there would be nothing you would not do. But he is dead; so reflect that, though a man cannot write to you when dead, he can still rejoice even after death. You know the views of the poets on such a subject.

[d] The *consularis* is encouraged not to be deterred by the fact that his superior, the comes, has already been approached, and has refused. In fact, the beasts were to be reserved for games to be given by the emperor (*Ep.* 218).

τῶν τοιῶνδε δόξαν ἐπίστασαι. 6. πέμπε δὴ τοὺς ἄνδρας καί τις ἔστω παρὰ σοὶ λόγος τῶν[3] Διονύσου καὶ Κορωνίδος θυγατέρων. καὶ ἃ μὲν οὐκ ἄξιον διδόναι, δοῦναι κακίας· τὸ δὲ ὅλως ἐκβαλεῖν τὰς Χάριτας οὐχ Ἑλληνικόν.

[3] τῶν F., conj. Re. τοῦ Wolf (Mss.)

## 72. Κρισπίνῳ

1. Διατριβαὶ μὲν ἡμῖν ἐπὶ λόγοις οἷαίπερ πρότερον, οὐ μέντοι γε ἡδοναὶ ταῖς ἔμπροσθεν παραπλήσιαι. τοσούτων γάρ μοι καὶ τοιούτων καὶ φίλων καὶ συγγενῶν οἰχομένων ἡ λύπη κρατεῖ καὶ τέρψις οὐδαμόθεν, ὥστ᾽ εἰ μὴ λίαν ᾐσχυνόμην, παραιτησάμενος ἂν τὰς Μούσας[1] μὴ χαλεπαίνειν λιπὼν ἂν τὴν τάξιν ἐγεώργουν. 2. ἀλλὰ ταῦτα μέν, ὅπῃ τῷ θεῷ δοκεῖ, χωρείτω· τῶν δ᾽ ἡμῖν πεποιημένων τὰ μὲν ἔχεις, τὰ δὲ οὐκ ἔχων ζητεῖς. δεῖ δή σε φράζειν, ὁπόσα ἔχεις. οὕτω γὰρ ἃ δεῖ σε λαβεῖν διδάξεις. οὐ γὰρ ἄξιον ἡμῖν κόπτεσθαι τηνάλλως τοὺς βιβλιογράφους. μήνυε δὴ καὶ τόν

[1] τὰς Μούσας F., conj. Re. ταῖς Μούσας Wolf (Mss.)

6. Send the men, then, and take some account of the daughters of Dionysus and Coronis.[e] To give what should not be given is wrong, but to expel the Graces completely is not something Greek.[f]

[e] Cf. *Ep.* 962.3; Nonnus, *Dionys.* 48.555.
[f] Cf. *Ep.* 221.4.

## 72. To Crispinus[a]

1. My classes in rhetoric are as they were before, but the pleasure derived from them is nothing like it was. Grief overwhelms me at the death of so many fine friends and relatives and I have no joy whatever,[b] so much so that, were I not utterly ashamed, after begging the Muses not to be angered,[c] I would have deserted my post and taken up farming. 2. But let this be as the god ordains. Some of my compositions you have, others you want because you do not have them. You must tell me then how many you have, for in this way you will let me know what you need to get. It is not fair for me to harass the copyists to no purpose. Tell me then,

[a] F/Kr. no. 26. For Crispinus of Heraclea, Libanius' friend at Athens, see *Or.* 1.37–30, 54; *BLZG* 112. There is no evidence to support F/Kr.'s tentative identification of Crispinus with *PLRE*'s Crispinus (4), a provincial governor of 353, or of Theophilus with the Theophilus (3), the eunuch put in charge of the library at Antioch by Julian.
[b] Cf. *Or.* 1.117 f: Aristaenetus, Eusebius, Phasganius, and his mother had all died.
[c] Cf. Plat. *Resp.* 3.387b.

τε Θεόφιλον ἐνεργὸν εὑρήσεις ἡμᾶς τέ σοι χαρίζεσθαι βουλομένους.

## 73. Μαξίμῳ

1. Τοῦ τὴν οἰκουμένην ἐκ λόγων εὖ ποιοῦντος Προαιρεσίου συγγενὴς ἐν Κουκουσῷ Φιλάστριος πολιτεύεται. τοῦτον καὶ ὡς ἄνδρα ἀγαθὸν βουλοίμην ἂν τῆς παρὰ σοῦ τυγχάνειν εὐνοίας καὶ ὅπως φαίνοιο τιμῶν τὸν χαλκοῦν μὲν ἐν Ῥώμῃ, χαλκοῦν δὲ Ἀθήνησιν ἑστηκότα. 2. τὸ δὲ αὐτὸ καὶ ἐμοί τινα τιμὴν οἴσει τῷ παρακεκληκότι καὶ δόξεις τῷ μὲν οὐδὲ γράψαντι χαρίζεσθαι, γράψαντι δὲ ἐμοὶ προσεσχηκέναι.

---

[a] *BLZG* 207 (vi), *PLRE* 583 (19). Governor of Armenia in 361.

[b] *PLRE* 731. The famous Christian sophist, teacher of Eunapius; cf. Eunap. *V.S.* 483–93. Here Libanius seeks to gain goodwill by capitalising on his reputation.

and you will find Theophilus[d] busy on the job and me ready to oblige you.

[d] Libanius' copyist; cf. Norman, "Book Trade," *JHS* 80 (1960): 122–3.

## 73. To Maximus[a]

1. Proaeresius,[b] who with his eloquence blessed the whole world, has a relative in Cucusus, Philastrius a city councillor.[c] I would be pleased for him to enjoy your goodwill as being a man of worth and for you to be seen to pay respect to the bronze statue erected in Rome and the statue at Athens.[d] 2. At one and the same time you will confer some enhancement of my own prestige, since I made the representations, and you will be thought to have obliged him without his writing while attending to me, the writer.

[c] This is the first record of the city status of Cucusus, anticipating the recorded evidence of Jones (*Cities of the Eastern Roman Empire* 183–4) by half a century. Similarly with the Armenian city of Arca (*Ep.* 245).

[d] Eunap. *V.S.* 492.

## 74. Μοδέστῳ

1. Ὁ καλόν μοι τὸ θέατρον ποιῶν Μεγέθιός ἐστιν ὁ ῥήτωρ· βοᾷ γὰρ τηλικοῦτον ὅσον ἄλλοι πεντήκοντα καὶ τούτῳ γε πολλάκις τὸν λέγοντα ἔστησε. μέγα δέ, οἶμαι, τῷ λέγοντι θερμὸς ἀκροατὴς θαύματι διακόπτων τοῦ λόγου τὸν δρόμον. 2. ἐν μὲν οὖν ταῖς ἐπιδείξεσιν ἀμείβομαι τὴν βοὴν τῷ προσγελάσαι καὶ προσδραμεῖν· νῦν δὲ εὕρηκά τι διὰ σοῦ καὶ λαμπρότερον εἰς ἀμοιβήν. χρήμασιν ἐσωφρόνισας τὸν ἀδελφὸν τὸν τοῦδε, μᾶλλον δέ, τῷ φόβῳ μὲν ἐσωφρόνισας, ὅπως δ' ἔσται λύσις τῆς ζημίας συνέπραξας. 3. καί σου γράμματα καὶ γνῶσις[1] ἀποδίδωσι τὸν ἄργυρον, ἀλλ' ὅ γε ἄργυρος, οὐκ οἶδ' ὅ τι μεμφόμενος, ἐλθεῖν αὐτοῖς εἰς χεῖρας οὐκ ἐθέλει. σὺ οὖν αὐτὸν ἢ πεῖσον ἢ ἀνάγκασον μὴ φεύγειν τοὺς δεσπότας, ὅπως τοῖς μὲν τὰ αὑτῶν ἔχειν ὑπάρχῃ, σοὶ δὲ τὸ μηδὲν ὧν κελεύσειας μάταιον εἶναι.

[1] γνῶσις F., conj. Re. γνώσεις Wolf (Mss.)

## 74. To Modestus

1. Megethius the orator[a] is the one who makes the theatre a scene of triumph for me. His cheers are as loud as fifty others put together,[b] and in this particular way he has often halted me in my declamations. Warm support from a member of the audience is, I feel, of great importance to the speaker for it intersperses the course of the speech with admiration.[c] 2. Well, in my declamations I repay his cheers smilingly by going out of my way to greet him, but now I have discovered, through you, a more notable method of repayment. You have punished his brother with a fine, or rather punished him with the threat of it and ensured means whereby he may be relieved of the penalty. 3. Your letter and its verdict was for the money to be repaid, but the money, for some reason or other, refuses to come to hand. So induce it to do so, or compel it not to evade its owners, so that they may get what is theirs and none of your commands be ineffective.

[a] *BLZG* 211. An advocate (*Epp.* 103, 1361). His grandson was Libanius' pupil in 393 (*Ep.* 1101).

[b] His applause is stentorian; cf. Homer *Il.* 5.786.

[c] Cf. Petit, *Étudiants* 100. The sophist is expected to support his adherents in return for the support they afford him.

## 75. Μοδέστῳ

1. Μηδὲν ἔστω τῶν σῶν ἀτελές. μὴ τοίνυν μηδ' Ὑπερέχιος ἥμισυ στρατιώτου μήτε ἔστω μήτε καλείσθω. τοιαῦτα γὰρ ἐπισκώπτοντες ὀνομάζουσιν αὐτὸν οἱ μέχρι τίνος προὔβη τὸ πρᾶγμα εἰδότες. 2. ἵν' οὖν ἐκείνους τε παύσωμεν τῶν σκωμμάτων καὶ τούτῳ τι γένηται τέλειον ἀγαθόν, γράφε πρὸς τὸν ἄρχοντα Γαλατῶν, τὸν χρηστὸν Ἀκάκιον, ἃ σὲ περὶ τούτου γράφειν εἰκός· ὡς τὴν προτέραν ἐπιστολὴν οὐκ ἐτολμήσαμεν Ἐκδικίῳ δεῖξαι δείσαντες μὴ περὶ τὴν ὕφαλον ῥαγῇ τὸ σκάφος. 3. πολλὰ γὰρ ἐκεῖνος τοιαῦτα ποιῶν ηὐφραίνετο καὶ δὴ καὶ τούτῳ δῆλος ἦν ποιήσων ἕλκος. ἀλλ' οὐχ ὁ νῦν ἄγων τὸ ἔθνος, ἀλλὰ καὶ τοῦ δικαίου λόγον καὶ τοῦ σοὶ χαρίζεσθαι ποιούμενος οὐδὲν διαστρέψας τῆς ἀληθείας δώσει τὰς ἀφορμὰς τῷ τέλει.

---

[a] *BLZG* 182 (i), *PLRE* 449. Petit, *Étudiants* 162–5. Libanius' favourite pupil, in his charge from 349 to 360,

## 75. To Modestus

1. Let nothing you do remain incomplete. So let Hyperechius[a] neither be nor be called a semicivil servant. That is what people who know how far matters have gone jeeringly call him. 2. So, for us to put an end to their jeers and for him to gain some unqualified advantage, write to that good fellow Acacius,[b] governor of Galatia, in terms which you may properly employ on his behalf. Your earlier letter we did not dare to show to Ecdicius[c] for fear of springing a leak! 3. You see, he took great delight in this sort of behaviour, and he clearly was going to do his best to hurt him. Not so the present governor of the province. He has a high regard for you and a desire to oblige you without doing violence to truth, and he will provide the opportunity for completing the business.

and something of a goose whom Libanius always saw as a swan. He tried to avoid curial service, aiming unsuccessfully at an official career, constantly aided by Libanius between 360 and 363. He failed to secure any confirmed official status until the reign of Julian (*Ep.* 792). He is last heard of as a supporter of Procopius in 366 (Amm. Marc. 26.8.5).

[b] *BLZG* 36 (i), *PLRE* 7 (8); governor of Galatia, 361/2.

[c] *BLZG* 125 (i), *PLRE* 276; Acacius' predecessor. As a native of Ancyra, he perhaps knew Hyperechius only too well.

## 76. Παλλαδίῳ

1. Περὶ δείλην πρωίαν ἦλθεν ὁ παῖς κομίζων τὰ βιβλία μέλλοντί μοι τῆς ὑστεραίας ἐρεῖν, καὶ οἱ δαιτυμόνες ἐκέκληντο. χρηστὸν οὖν μοί τι δηλοῦν ἐδόκει τὸ παρ᾽ ἀνδρὸς λόγους ἐργαζομένου λόγους ἀφῖχθαι δείξοντι λόγους. καί μέ τις ἀμείνων ἐλπὶς ἔχει, θεὸς δὲ οἶδε τὸ μέλλον. 2. ἢν οὖν ἀπέλθωμεν ἐκ τοῦ ἄθλου, τῶν Ἀριστείδου τε καὶ τῶν σῶν ἑξόμεθα καὶ κρινοῦμεν τὰ παλαίσματα. καίτοι τὸ Ἀριστείδην[1] φέρον σαπρὸν ὑπὸ τοῦ χρόνου καὶ τὰ πρῶτα δοκεῖν, ἐστὶν ἔχειν οὐκ ἔχειν· οὕτως ἡ μέν[2] τις συλλαβὴ φαίνεται, τὴν δὲ ζητῶν οὐκ ὄψει, ἀλλὰ δοκῶν εὑρηκέναι τὸν Θερσίτην ἐγὼ τοῦ ζητεῖν ἔτι τὸν Θερσίτην οὐκ

[1] Ἀριστείδην F., conj. Re. Ἀριστείδου Wolf (Mss.)
[2] ἡ μέν F. ἡμῖν Wolf (Mss.)

---

[a] *BLZG* 228 (vi), *PLRE* 659 (7): governor of Cilicia in 361, a scholar and bibliophile. Cf. F/Kr. no. 24.

[b] For restricted audiences at Libanius' orations, cf. *Letter* 64 and note.

## 76. To Palladius[a]

1. Early in the afternoon, your slave came and delivered the books. I was going to deliver a speech next day and the guests had been invited.[b] So I thought it a good sign that speeches had come from one engaged on speechcraft to one who was to deliver a speech. Though I am full of great expectation, heaven knows the outcome. 2. So if I come out of the ordeal,[c] I shall get hold of the works of Aristeides and yourself, and shall judge the bout between you.[d] However the book containing Aristeides is damaged by age and at first sight, it is a case of to have it and to have it not. One syllable is visible, but you will not see the next for all your searching.[e] Although I think to have found his "Thersites," I have not given up the search for the

[c] Ἆθλος and *ἀγών* are the standard sophistic terms for the delivery of an epideictic oration, which did in fact demand considerable physical effort; cf. Philostr. *V.S.* 1.25.9, Festugière, *Antioche* 166.

[d] Libanius was well known as a specialist in the works of the 2nd century sophist Aelius Aristeides (e.g. his recently composed *Or.* 64), and had been invited by Palladius to criticize his composition on a theme opposing that of the *Thersites* of Aristeides. Libanius is the author of a declamation in praise of *Thersites* (*Laud.* 4; Foerster 8:243).

[e] For the age and deterioration of the texts in Libanius' possession see Norman, "Book Trade" 124.

ἀπηλλάγην. 3. Ἀδριανὸς δέ σε οὐ διαπέφευγε μέν, ἀλλ' ἐκεῖνος ἐν τῇ σῇ κεῖται χειρί. κατέμεινε δέ, ὅπως ἀεί σου δεοίμην καὶ ἔχοις[3] ὅ τι χαρίζοιο. καίτοι τοῦτο οὐκ ὀρθῶς κεκόμψευται. πολλὰ γάρ ἐν Ἀντιμάχοιο, κἂν πέμπῃς καθημέραν, οὐδέποτε τὰ δοθέντα τῶν οὐ δοθέντων ἔσται πλείω. 4. περὶ δὲ τοῦ λόγου σου τὰ δίκαια ψηφιοῦμαι καὶ ταῦτα δικάζων ἀνώμοτος.

[3] ἔχοις ὅ τι F. ἔχῃς ὅτι Wolf (Mss.)

[f] Hadrian of Tyre, contemporary of Aristeides, also well known to Libanius (*Or.* 64.42), who challenges Palladius to produce a similar declamation on a theme of his.

## 77. Ἀνατολίῳ

1. Οἷα τετόλμηται οὐ περὶ τὸν Ἴστρον ἐγγὺς Σκυθῶν οὐδὲ ἐν τοῖς ἐσχάτοις Λιβύης, ἀλλ' ἐν Φοινίκῃ, τῷ πάντων ἡμερωτάτῳ χωρίῳ, νόμων ὄντων, ἀρχόντων ἐφεστηκότων, βασιλέως ζῶντος ἐν ὅπλοις, ὅπως ἅπαν ἀπείη βίαιον. 2. Λουκιανός τις, ἄνθρωπος ἐπὶ μικροῦ τινος σχήματος

[a] F/Kr. no. 39. Anatolius—*BLZG* 66 (ii), *PLRE* 60 (4)—was *consularis Phoenices,* 361, and father of his ex-pupils Apolinarius and Gemellus, to whom a reinforcing letter (*Ep.* 637) is sent. This letter was much admired by the Byzantines, as the frequent citations indicate (cf. Foer-

"Thersites." 3. Hadrianus[f] has not escaped your clutches: he lies in your hand, and there he stays so that I can ever request him of you, and you have the means of obliging me. Yet this quibble is not justified;[g] "there is much in the house of Antimachus,"[h] and though you send me something every day, what you give will never exceed what you have not given. 4. Concerning your oration I will give a just verdict, even though my judgement will not be on oath.

[g] Plat. *Phaedr.* 227c.

[h] Homer *Il.* 11.132. A half-quotation; the assumption that the recipient will know the rest is a compliment to his erudition.

## 77. To Anatolius[a]

1. What an outrage has been committed, not by the Danube in proximity to the Scyths nor yet on the furthest confines of Libya,[b] but in Phoenicia, the most civilized region of all, under the rule of law, of appointed governors, and of an emperor who spends his life in arms so that all violence should disappear.[c] 2. A fellow named Lucianus, holder of some minor official position, a collector of taxes from

ster *ad loc.*), and is described aptly by Liebeschuetz (*Antioch* 19) as a short *ecphrasis*.

[b] The ends of the earth, with Herodotean echoes.

[c] Constantius had for three years made Antioch his base for his Persian campaigns.

χρήματα εἰσπράττων γεωργούς τινας, ὥσπερ Διονύσιος ὤν, ὁ Σικελίας δεσπότης, ἢ Γέλων ἐκεῖνος ὁ τὴν μεγάλην δύναμιν ἔχων, ἐκώμασεν εἰς τὸν γάμον Εὐσταθίου τουτουί, πένητος μὲν καὶ πένητι συνοικοῦντος, παρεμυθεῖτο δὲ αὐτὸν ἡ σωφροσύνη τῆς γυναικός, ἣν ἀπολωλυίας αὐτῷ τῆς πόλεως, ἔστι δὲ Νικομηδεύς, ἄγεται, προῖκα δὲ εἰσέφερεν ἡ γυνὴ τὸν τρόπον. 3. ἀλλ' ὁ μὲν Ἐλπιδίου κελεύοντος ᾤχετο ἄξων ἀνθρώπους ὡς ὑφέξοντας λόγον, Λουκιανὸς δὲ τὴν ἄνθρωπον ἰδὼν ἀδίκοις ὄμμασι πλησίον οἰκοῦσαν προσπέμψαι μὲν καὶ μνησθῆναι πρὸς αὐτὴν ἔρωτος οὐκ ἐτόλμησεν, ᾔδει γὰρ οὐ πείσων, τὴν θυγατέρα δὲ ἐκέλευε χρῆσθαι τῇ γυναικί. 4. καὶ ἦσαν ἐν συνηθείᾳ καὶ πολλάκις ἦλθε παρ' ἐκείνην ἡ τούτου θυγάτηρ εἰδυῖα ὅτου χάριν ταῦτα ἐπράττετο, τοιαῦτα γὰρ ἐπαίδευε τὴν θυγατέρα. καλεῖ δή ποτε καὶ ταύτην ἐκείνη παρ' αὐτὴν ἀξιοῦσα τῶν ἴσων τυχεῖν, ἡ δέ, ὧν γὰρ ἀφειστήκει τοῖς ἔργοις, οὐδὲ ὑποπτεύειν ἠξίου, καὶ ὑπήκουσε καὶ ἦν εἴσω θυρῶν, μᾶλλον δὲ ἐν δικτύῳ. 5. κατακλείσας γὰρ αὐτὴν ὁ ὑβριστὴς ἐκεῖνος ἐν δωματίῳ καὶ φήσας δεῖν προσκυνεῖν τὴν Τύχην, εἰ τὸν βίον ἐκ

a group of peasants has behaved like Dionysius tyrant of Sicily or Gelon, the possessor of such mighty power,[d] and he has played havoc with the marriage of Eustathius, the bearer, a poor man married to a poor wife. His consolation was his wife's chastity. He married her after the destruction of his native city—he is from Nicomedeia—and as her dowry she brought him her virtue. 3. He went off, on Elpidius' orders,[e] to escort some people for examination, and Lucianus looked with lustful eyes[f] on the woman, his next-door neighbour, but he did not venture to approach her and tell her of his passion, for he knew that he would not win her over. So he ordered his daughter to handle the woman. 4. The women were well acquainted, and his daughter often visited her, knowing the reason why this occurred—for that was the way he brought up his daughter. So finally she asked her to return the visit and invited her to her home, and she, with not the slightest suspicion of behaviour from which she was poles apart in practice, consented and entered the doors—or rather, the snare. 5. That villain shut her up in a room and told her to thank her lucky stars that she, a working woman,

[d] For Dionysius the Younger's excesses against the women of Locri see Ael. *V.H.* 9.8. Gelon, however, for all his tyranny, enjoyed a good reputation.

[e] Praetorian prefect 360–1. Eustathius, *PLRE* 311 (3), was evidently in his service.

[f] Cf. *Decl.* 6.6 (Foerster 5:377). For Lucianus, *PLRE* 516 (4).

τῶν χειρῶν ποιουμένη συγκατακλίνοιτο τῷ δοῦναι δυναμένῳ, ἐπειδὴ καλῶς εὕρισκεν ὡπλισμένην τῇ σωφροσύνῃ καὶ οὔτε ὑπισχνούμενος ἔπειθεν οὔτε ἀπειλῶν κατέπληττε, χεῖρας προσῆγε καὶ ἰσχύν. ἡ δὲ ἀπεωθεῖτο καὶ ὁ τρόπος αὐτὴν ἐποίει μείζω τῆς φύσεως δεικνύειν. 6. ξίφος ἐνταῦθα ἐγύμνωσε Λουκιανός, ὦ θεοί. ἡ δὲ τοῦτο ἐπῄνεσε μόνον, εἰ ἀποθανεῖται πρὸ αἰσχροῦ τινος. ὡς δὲ ἔγνω καὶ τῆς ψυχῆς ἀφισταμένην, οἰκέτας καλεῖ καὶ σχοινία κομίζειν ἐκέλευεν, ἡ δὲ ἦν ἐπὶ κλίνης ἐν δεσμοῖς καὶ βοώσης ὑβρίζετο τὸ σῶμα. 7. εἰ μὲν οὖν ταῦτα εἰργασμένος εἰς φρέαρ ἐνέβαλε τὴν ἠδικημένην, ὥσπερ ἐν Λεύκτροις οἱ Λάκωνες ἃς ἐβιάσαντο, πονηρὸς μὲν ἂν ἦν τῇ μοιχείᾳ, πειρώμωνος δὲ ἀφανίζειν τὸ πραχθὲν ἐδόκει ἂν φοβεῖσθαι τοὺς νόμους· νῦν δ' ὥσπερ ἐνδεικνύμενος ὅτι, κἂν σύ, κἂν Μόδεστος, κἂν Ἐλπίδιος, κἂν ἅπαντες γνῶσιν ἄνθρωποι τὸ ἀδίκημα, δέος οὐδέν, ἐκπέμπει τὴν ἄνθρωπον καταγελῶν. 8. ἡ δὲ πρὸς τὸν ἄνδρα, καὶ γὰρ εὐθὺς ἀφῖκτο κατὰ τύχην, εἰποῦσα τὸ πᾶν ἐδεῖτο αὑτὴν ἀποκτεῖναι, μηδὲ γὰρ ἂν ἀτυχησάσῃ τὰ τοιαῦτα ζῆν ἔχειν καλῶς. ὁ δὲ τὴν μὲν παρέδωκεν, οἳ φυλάξουσιν,

should go to bed with a man capable of giving her things, but when he found her well defended by her chastity and was unable either to persuade her with his promises or frighten her with his threats, he laid violent hands upon her. She continued to repulse him and her virtue made her exceed the limitations of her sex. 6. Hereupon Lucianus—great heavens!—bared his sword, but she greeted this only with relief, if she should suffer death before dishonour. He saw that she was fainting and called his slaves, telling them to bring ropes; she was tied to the bed and he raped her, despite her screams. 7. Now, if after such a vile deed he had thrown the woman he had violated into a well, as the Spartans at Leuctra did with the women they raped,[g] he would be villainous in his adultery, but in his attempt to conceal his crime, he would show some semblance of fearing the laws. As it is, he almost blazons it abroad that even if you, or Modestus, or Elpidius, or all mankind condemn the crime, he has nothing to fear, and he makes fun of the wench and sends her packing. 8. But she revealed all to her husband, who, as chance would have it, had just returned, and begged him to kill her, for after such disgrace she could not live a life of honour. But he entrusted

[g] For the rape and murder of the daughters of Scedasus of Leuctra by two Spartiates see Plut. *Amat. Narr.* 3.1, p. 773d. This is the origin of the "Leuctrian curse," ultimately expiated by the Spartan defeat at Leuctra.

ὅπως μὴ αὐτὴν ἀποσφάξῃ, δεῦρο δὲ ἥκων εἰδὼς ὅτι Νικομήδειαν καὶ οὖσαν ἐφίλουν καὶ κειμένην δακρύω, ἐδεῖτό μου καὶ διδάξαι καὶ παροξῦναι διὰ γραμμάτων Μόδεστον ὡς ἐκεῖ γραψόμενος τὸν μοιχόν. 9. ἐγὼ δὲ αὐτὸν πέμπω παρὰ σὲ νομίσας τὸ μὲν ἔχειν πολὺν πόνον, τὸ δὲ ἴσην τὴν ἀκρίβειαν ἄνευ πόνων. ἀλλ', ὦ σωφρονέστατε καὶ δικαιότατε καὶ γυναικὶ συνοικῶν καὶ παῖδας γνησίους τρέφων, δεῖξον ὡς ἔστιν ὁ κωλύσων ταῦτα τολμᾶσθαι.

---

[h] Libanius naturally becomes the patron of Nicomedeians surviving near Antioch, in view of his close connections with the city and his display of loyalty and affection for it after its destruction in the earthquake of 358, for

## 78. Βασιλείῳ

1. καὶ πῶς ἂν ἐπιλαθοίμην ἡμερῶν ἐκείνων καὶ λόγων καὶ κρότων; ὡς ἔμοιγε ἀνάγραπτος ὁ βραχὺς ἐκεῖνος χρόνος καὶ πολλῶν ἐτῶν ἀντάξιος καὶ πάσης ἑορτῆς ἡδίων. ἀλλ', οἶμαι, πολλοῖς ἂν ἄνθρωπος ἐκκρουσθείη σπουδῆς ἄλλως τε καὶ ἐν πόλει τοσαύτῃ καὶ κλύδωνι μεγάλῳ τάχα που καὶ

her to the care of people to prevent her cutting her own throat, and he came here, knowing that I loved Nicomedeia while ever it existed and mourn it now that it lies in ruins.[h] He begged me to inform Modestus, and to write and enlist his support for the prosecution of the adulterer in his court. 9. But I am sending him to you, for I believe that his projected course involves much trouble, whereas he will obtain equal redress from you without trouble.[i] But my good sir, self-controlled, just, happily married, and father of sons born in wedlock as you are, show that there exists someone to stop these outrages.

which cf. *Letter* 39.

[i] Eustathius had thought to take advantage of Libanius' close relationship with Modestus, the *comes*. Libanius diverts him to the consularis, who was likely to be more amenable than the higher career official, and is, in any case, the proper official to hear the case in the first instance.

## 78. To Basileios[a]

1. And how could I forget those days, with their oratory and applause? That short period is engraved upon my mind; the equivalent of many a long year, and more pleasing than any holiday. But, I suppose, man's enthusiasms can be quenched by many things, especially in such a great city as this

[a] On the identity of this Basileios see *Letter* 19.

ἡμᾶς περικλύζοντι. 2. δεῖ δή σε τέρπεσθαι μέν, εἰ λαμβάνοις γράμματα· μὴ λαβεῖν δὲ εἰ συμβαίη, πάντα μᾶλλον εἰκάζειν ἢ ὡς οὐ σὺ παρ' ἐμοὶ τίμιος. καὶ τοὺς νεανίσκους, ὑπὲρ ὧν ὡς ἡμᾶς ἦλθες, μὴ μόνον ἐκ τῆς κηδείας, ἀλλὰ καὶ ἐμὴν χάριν φιλεῖν.

## 79. Βασσιανῷ

1. Καλῶς ἐποίησας ὀλίγοις γράμμασι πολλὴν φλυαρίαν σβέσας, ἧς ἐγὼ μὲν καὶ πρὸ τῆς ἐπιστολῆς κατεγέλων, ὡς δὲ ἧκεν ἐκείνη, πάντες. χαίρω δὲ ὅτι δῆλος εἶ χαίρων βασιλεύοντος τοῦ βασιλεύειν εἰδότος. ἐν γὰρ τῷ φάναι τὸ σκῆπτρον αὐτῷ δεδόσθαι παρὰ τοῦ παιδὸς τοῦ Κρόνου τὴν τοῦ λαβόντος ἀρετὴν μηνύεις. 2. ἐπιμελοῦ δὴ σαυτοῦ καὶ ὅπως ἔσται περὶ σοῦ λόγος βελτίων καὶ νύκτα καὶ ἡμέραν σκόπει.

---

[a] *BLZG* 95, *PLRE* 150 (2): second cousin and ex-pupil of Libanius, he belonged to the Christian and office-holding branch of the family (stemma, *PLRE* 1141). As son of Gallus' old opponent, the praetorian prefect Thalassius, he became an object of suspicion and hostile gossip

and in such turmoil as on occasion overwhelms even me. 2. You should indeed be glad to get letters. If perchance you do not, the last thing you should infer is that you do not stand high in my regard. The students, on whose behalf you visited me, you should befriend not just for your interest in their welfare but for my sake too.

## 79. To Bassianus[a]

1. You did right to put a stop to a lot of nonsense with your short letter. I said it was all ridiculous even before your letter arrived, and everybody said so afterwards. I rejoice that you so obviously rejoice at the accession to the throne[b] of one capable of occupying it, for by your comment that the sceptre was handed to him by the son of Cronos[c] you indicate the excellence of the recipient. 2. Take care of yourself, then, and ensure that you enjoy good report both night and day.

immediately upon the change of regime, Julian's enmity being reserved for his elder brother, Thalassius the younger (Amm. Marc. 22.9.16 f).

[b] Julian. The letter is therefore written about the end of November 361.

[c] The uncertainty at the change of regime is indicated by this prudently pagan reference.

## 80. Μαξίμῳ

1. Ἃ ἐποίουν ἂν περὶ Σωκράτην, εἰ κατὰ Σωκράτην ἐγεγόνειν, ὅτε αὐτῷ τὰ θηρία ἐπέκειτο, συκοφάνται τρεῖς, ταῦτ᾽ ᾤμην δεῖν καὶ νῦν ποιεῖν περὶ τὸν τὰ Σωκράτους ἐζηλωκότα. 2. ἔπραττον δ᾽ ἂν ταῦτά τε κἀκεῖνα ἂν ἐποίουν οὐχ ὑπὲρ τῶν ἐν ταῖς αἰτίαις δεδοικὼς μὴ δεινόν τι πάθωσιν — οὐδὲν γὰρ δεινὸν φιλοσόφοις ἐκλυθῆναι σώματος, μέγιστον μὲν οὖν ἀγαθόν — ἀλλ᾽ εἰδὼς ὅτι πάμμεγα κέρδος ἀνθρώποις ἀνὴρ φιλοσοφῶν καὶ οὐ πολὺ τοῦτ᾽ ἔλαττον τοῦ τοὺς θεοὺς ἀναμεμίχθαι τοῖς ἀνθρώποις καὶ συμβουλεύειν καὶ συμπράττειν, οἷα τῶν ποιητῶν λεγόντων ἀκούομεν. 3. διὰ δὴ ταῦτα μισῶ μὲν τοὺς περὶ Ἄνυτον· ὑπὲρ δὲ σοῦ τοὺς θεοὺς ἐκάλουν, τουτὶ γὰρ ἡ παρ᾽ ἐμοῦ συμμαχία, καὶ οὐκ ἦρχόν γε χάριτος ἐκείναις ταῖς φροντίσιν, ἀλλ᾽ ἠμειβόμην.

---

[a] F/Kr. no. 46, *BLZG* 208 (x), *PLRE* 583 (21). Maximus of Ephesus, extreme Neoplatonist, theurge and thaumaturge, *eminence grise* of Julian; cf. Eunap. *V.S.* 469–470; Libanius eyed him warily, as the exaggerated tone of this letter suggests, and not without reason, since Maximus was the one person at court most likely to have inspired the initial coolness between Julian and Libanius in An-

## 80. To Maximus[a]

1. I think that my present attitude towards one who is a devotee of Socrates should be such as it would be towards Socrates, had I been living in Socrates' day when those three bestial sycophants attacked him.[b] 2. In either case my attitude would not have been dictated by the fear that the accused would experience some terrible fate—for it is no terrible fate, nay rather the greatest of blessings, for philosophers to be released from the body[c]—but by the knowledge that a man engaged in philosophy is the greatest boon to mankind, not much less so than if the gods come down to associate with humans, to counsel and assist them, as we hear the poets say they do. 3. Hence I loathe Anytus and his like,[d] but on your behalf I called upon the gods—for such is my method of support—and by such considerations I was not conferring a

tioch in 362 (*Or.* 1.123).

[b] Referring to the charge of impiety brought against Socrates, Libanius remarks upon the dangers facing practising Neoplatonists in the last years of Constantius. Libanius himself was composing his *Apologia Socratis* (Foerster, 5:13) in this same year (cf. Markowski, *De Libanio Socratis Defensore* 169).

[c] Cf. Plat. *Phaed.* 67d.

[d] For the accusers of Socrates (Lycon, Meletus, and Anytus) see Plat. *Apol.* 23e, Lib. *Apol. Socr.* 175. The sophistic tradition tended to place them in reverse order of importance, often omitting Lycon, as here. Cf. Isocr. xi, *Hypothesis.*

4. οἶμαι δὲ καὶ πάντας ὀφείλειν σοι χάριν. κοινὸς γὰρ εὐεργέτης σὺ γῆς τε καὶ θαλάττης, ὁπόση μὴ βάρβαρος, θρέψας ἡμῖν καὶ δημιουργήσας βασιλέα πάντα ἄκρον, ὥσθ' οἱ πρὶν τοὺς τεθνεῶτας μακαρίζοντες νῦν βούλοιντ' ἂν εἰς τὸ Ἀργανθωνίου γῆρας ἐλθεῖν ἐκείνῳ πρότερον τοῦτο συνευχόμενοι τὸ γῆρας. 5. ᾧ δοκεῖς μοι νῦν παρεῖναι σὺ τερπόμενος, οὐ πονῶν· οὐ γὰρ ἔχεις, ὅ τι ἐπανορθώσεις τῶν πραττομένων, ἀλλ' ἐφ' ἑκάστῳ χαίρεις μετὰ πάσης ἀρετῆς γιγνομένῳ. λέγων δὲ ἥξειν παρ' ἡμᾶς καὶ ὑπισχνούμενος μετέωρον ἡμῖν πεποίηκας τὴν πόλιν ἐνθυμουμένοις, οἷον ἂν εἴη τὸ θέαμα Φοῖνιξ ἑπόμενος Ἀχιλλεῖ. 6. ἔοικα δὲ οὐκ ὀρθῶς εἰκάσαι. ποῦ γὰρ ἴσον πρὸς ταύτην τὴν συζυγίαν ἐκείνη; ἀλλ' ἐγὼ μὲν εἰκόνα πρέπουσαν ζητήσω κατὰ σχολήν, ὑμεῖς δὲ ἀφίκοισθε καὶ φανείητε ποθοῦσιν· ἐπεὶ καὶ ὁ πρόδρομος πολλοῦ γεγένηται ταῖς πόλεσιν ἄξιος, ὁ καλὸς Πυθιόδωρος. 7. τὴν γάρ τοι περὶ τοὺς θεοὺς θεραπείαν εἰς ἀκμὴν ἤγαγε πάντα βωμὸν αἵματι ῥάνας καὶ δείξας ὅτι δεῖ

---

[e] King of Tartessus in Spain, lived for 120 years and reigned for 80, Herod. 1.163. Hence, Like Nestor, proverbial for longevity.

favour, only returning one. 4. In my opinion, everyone also owes you a favour, for you are a universal benefactor of all civilized lands and seas; you have nurtured and fashioned an emperor peerless in all things, so that those who previously called the dead blessed now would want to attain the age of Arganthonius,[e] praying for this old age to come to the emperor first. 5. I think you now attend him, tasting not of toil but of pleasure, for in what he does you have nothing to amend, but you rejoice at each separate activity which is done with perfect excellence. By your statement and your promise to visit us you have set our city all agog as it reflects upon the sight it would be to see a Phoenix in the train of Achilles.[f] 6. But it is likely that my comparison is not apt, for how can such an association as that be equated with this? I shall look for a fitting comparison at leisure, but you, I trust, will come and reveal yourselves to your ardent admirers, since even your forerunner, the noble Pythiodorus,[g] is held in high esteem by the cities. 7. He has brought the worship of the gods to a high peak, bedewed every altar with the blood of sacrifice and shown that we should make our sacrifices with good

[f] Homer *Il.* 9.438 ff, especially 485 ff.

[g] *BLZG* 389, *PLRE* 756. He bore news of the changed political and religious situation in the capital, and moved on to Alexandria, where he is in October 362.

θαρρούντως θύειν. οἱ δὲ εἵποντο πηδῶντες οἱ τέως ὀκνοῦντες. 8. ἐκεῖνος μὲν οὖν χωρείτω πανταχοῦ ποιήσων ταὐτόν· ἐμοὶ δὲ ἦν μὲν διὰ πολλῶν ἀντεπιστεῖλαι, κρεῖττον δὲ ἔδοξε πέμψαι δι' ἀνδρὸς ἐοικότος τῷ κομίσαντι τἀκεῖθεν, ὅπως σε ταύτῃ γε μιμοίμην. 9. οἶμαι δὲ οὐκ ἀδικεῖν εἰς φιλοσόφων χορὸν Φουρτουνατιανὸν ἐγγράφων. κωλύσει γὰρ ἴσως οὐδέν, οὔτε ἡ χλαμὺς οὔτε ὁ κείρων.

---

[h] Libanius is certainly not replying to a personal letter from Maximus, which he would have acknowledged with expressions of even more fulsome gratitude, but to Pythiodorus' announcement of the trend of affairs at court and his open display of pagan sacrifices in Antioch, the credit for which is here given to Maximus.

## 81. Κέλσῳ

1. Εὐθὺς ἀπὸ γραμμῆς ἡμῖν ἄξιος τῶν ἐλπίδων ἐφάνης ἕνα μὲν ἄνδρα τὴν βουλὴν εὑρὼν Ἀλεξανδρείας καὶ τοῦτον, ὡς ἀκούω, χωλόν, εἰς πεντεκαίδεκα δὲ τὸν ἀριθμὸν ἐκτείνας ἐν ἡμέραις δύο βίᾳ μὲν οὐδεμιᾷ, προσδοκίαις δὲ λαμπραῖς.

---

[a] *BLZG* 104 (i), *PLRE* 193 (3): ex-pupil of both Libanius and Themistius (cf. *Letter* 44). Highly regarded by Julian (Amm. Marc. 22.9.13), he was appointed gover-

courage. Those who hitherto were laggards have followed him eagerly. 8. So may he proceed everywhere with the same intent. I could have sent my reply by a number of people, but I thought it best to do so by a man who resembles the bearer of the news from there,[h] so that in this at least I might follow in your footsteps. 9. I am not, I am sure, out of order in inscribing Fortunatianus[i] as one of the company of philosophers. There is nothing likely to prevent it—neither the robe nor the razor.[j]

[i] *BLZG* 159 (i), *PLRE* 369 (1). Pagan, at this time something of a poet and philosopher.

[j] The beard, the coarse cloak (*τρίβων*), and the staff are the standard guise for a philosopher (cf. *Letter* 67.6). Fortunatianus, though wearing the more ornate *chlamys* and shaven in the current fashion, is yet to be regarded as such.

## 81. To Celsus[a]

1. Right from scratch you showed yourself worthy of our hopes of you when you found the town council of Alexandria[b] consisting of one man—and him lame, so I am told—and inside a couple of days expanded the number to fifteen, not by any compulsion but by great expectations. 2. For by showing

nor of Cilicia in 362, where he enthusiastically promoted Julian's reform programme, in the present case, the enrolment of new decurions under the terms of *Cod. Th.* 12.1.50 of 13 March 362.

[b] Alexandria upon Issus.

2. δείξας γὰρ ὡς οὐκ ἔσονται Μυσῶν λεία τοῖς ἁρπάζουσιν οἱ βουλευταί, τοὺς μὲν ἐκ τῶν ὀρῶν κατήγαγες, τοὺς δὲ ὑπὸ κλίνας κρυπτομένους ἔπεισας ὡς ἐπὶ κέρδος τὸ λειτουργεῖν ἐκπηδᾶν. 3. καὶ ταῦτα ἠγγέλλετο μὲν ὑπὸ τῶν ἑταίρων, οἳ παρῆσαν, ὅτε ἐπράττετο, τοὺς ἀκροωμένους δὲ ἡδομένους εἶχον, καὶ οὐδεὶς ἠπίστει· τὰ γὰρ δὴ καλά τε καὶ μεγάλα συμβαίνειν ἐδόκει τῇ σῇ φύσει. 4. ἐγὼ δέ σε πολλὰ παρακεκληκὼς ἐπὶ τὴν ἀκρίβειαν καὶ τὸ δεῖν πάσας ἀνελόντα χάριτας χεῖρα ὀρέγειν ταῖς πόλεσιν ἔοικα τὸ τοῦ Περικλέους πεπονθέναι τῷ τε ἐμαυτοῦ περιπεπτωκέναι νόμῳ. τί δ' ἦν ὃ ἐκεῖνος ἔπαθε; 5. γράψας Ἀθηναίοις νόμον τὸν οὐκ ὄντα ἀμφοτέρωθεν Ἀθηναῖον τῶν τοῖς ἀστοῖς ὑπαρχόντων εἴργεσθαι τεθνεώτων αὐτῷ Ξανθίππου καὶ Παράλου τὸν ἐκ τῆς Ἀσπασίας υἱὸν ἐδεῖτο τῶν πολιτῶν πολίτην ἐγγράφειν τὰ αὑτοῦ κινῶν, οἱ δὲ ἐχαρίσαντο. 6. κἀγὼ τοίνυν τὸ ἐμαυτοῦ παραβαίνων νόμον βουλοίμην ἂν τὸν Σελεύκου τινὸς τυγχάνειν ἔξω τῶν ἐμῶν τε

---

[c] A proverb for defenceless prey, *Paroem. Gr.* 1.122, Dem. *De Cor.* 72 (and Wankel *ad loc.*).

[d] Cf. *Or.* 18.146 ff.

[e] The citizenship law of 451 BC, [Ar.] *Ath. Pol.* 26.4,

that the councillors would not be sitting ducks,[c] some you brought down from the mountains, while others who were skulking under their beds you induced to sally forth to their civic duties as to some profitable employment.[d] 3. This news was brought by your companions who were present at the event, and they kept their hearers in a state of pleasure. No one doubted the truth of it, for the great and glorious achievement seemed in keeping with your genius. 4. Yet, after my many injunctions to you to behave with scrupulous exactness and for the protection of your province to do away with all favours, it seems that like Pericles I am hoist with my own petard. Just see what happened to him. 5. He proposed a law to the Athenians stating that anyone not of Athenian descent by both parents should be barred from the rights of citizenship,[e] and then his sons Xanthippus and Paralos died; so he begged the citizens to enrol as a citizen his son by Aspasia. This was in breach of his own legislation, but they granted his request. 6. Now I too am in breach of my own rule in wishing the house of Seleucus[f] to obtain a favour above and beyond the rules we have both made for ourselves. And when you hear mention of Seleucus, you could

Plut. *Per.* 36f. The son by Aspasia was Pericles the younger.

[f] *BLZG* 272, *PLRE* 818. Seleucus was father of Olympias, supposedly the devout adherent of Chrysostom. This view is disproved by B. Schouler, "Hommages de Libanios aux femmes de son temps," *Pallas* 32 (1985): 129–133, 146n.

καὶ σῶν δογμάτων. Σέλευκον δὲ ἀκούσας οὐκ ἂν Ἀλεξάνδρας ἀμνημονεῖν δύναιο, ταύτης δὲ μνησθεὶς οὐκ ἂν ἀντιτείνειν δύναιο. δεῖ γάρ, ὥσπερ τοὺς θεοὺς πρὸ ταύτης ἄγομεν, οὕτω ταύτην πρὸ τῶν ἄλλων ἀνθρώπων. 7. οἷς οὖν αὐτὸς ἄρχων ἐχρώμην ἄν, τούτοις σὲ δεῖ φανῆναι χρώμενον ἐννοοῦντα σχῆμά τε τὸ τῆς γυναικὸς καὶ γνώμης[1] μέτρον καὶ τὴν ἄλλην ἀρετὴν καὶ ὡς ἐδοκοῦμεν ἐξ ἱεροῦ τινος ἀπιέναι παρ᾿ αὐτῆς καταβαίνοντες. 8. τῷ μὲν οὖν Περικλεῖ τὴν χάριν ἐκείνην ἀντὶ Εὐβοίας ἔδοσαν Ἀθηναῖοι καὶ Σάμου, ἐγὼ δὲ νήσους μὲν ᾐρημένας εἰπεῖν οὐκ ἔχω, τὸ δὲ μέγιστον τῶν ὑπὸ τὸν ἥλιον Ἀλεξάνδραν εἶδες Σελεύκου μὲν ἐπιτρέποντος, ἐμοῦ δὲ εἰσάγοντος.

[1] γνώμης F. φωνῆς Wolf (Mss.)

## 82. Ἰουλιανῷ

1. Εἴ τι τῶν δικαίων ἐγίγνετο, πάλαι μὲν ἐπ᾿ ἐκείνης ἂν ἦσθα τῆς ἀρχῆς, νῦν δὲ ἐπὶ μείζονος ἢ κατ᾿ ἐκείνην ἐξουσίας. ἀλλ᾿, οἶμαι, τέρπεται ἡ Τύχη τοῖς μὲν ἀμείνοσιν ἐλάττω διδοῦσα, τοῖς δὲ φαυλοτέροις μείζω καὶ διατελεῖ δὴ τοῦτο ποιοῦσα

not fail to call to mind Alexandra;[g] and upon calling her to mind, you could not make any opposition for, while we reverence the gods more than her, so we must reverence her more than the rest of mankind. 7. So your treatment of her must obviously be the same as mine would be, were I governor: you should reflect upon the lady's rank, her depth of intellect and her other virtues, and how, upon leaving her presence, we felt that we were departing from a holy shrine. 8. Well, the Athenians granted Pericles that favour in return for his recovery of Euboea and Samos. I cannot speak of the capture of any island, but you have, in Alexandra, beheld the finest thing under the sun, referred to you by Seleucus and introduced by me.

[g] *BLZG* 56. The tone of this description, as well as indicating Libanius' appreciation of her intellectual qualities, shows that she was pagan.

## 82. To Julianus[a]

1. If everybody had his due, you would have been in that office long ago and now would be in a position of still higher authority. However, Fortune, I suppose, enjoys giving too little to the good and too much to the bad, and continues to behave so,

[a] *BLZG* 189 (ii), *PLRE* 470 (12): Julian's maternal uncle, appointed *Comes Orientis* in 362. An apostate, he was instrumental in putting Julian's restoration of paganism into effect. He died suddenly in office early in 363. This letter is one of congratulation upon his appointment.

καθάπερ φοβουμένη μὴ τῆς ἰσχύος αὐτῆς ἐπιλαθώμεθα. 2. ἐγὼ δὲ ὅτι μὲν ὁμοίως ἡδέως καὶ λέγω καὶ τῆς σῆς ἀκοῆς τυγχάνω—καὶ γὰρ οἶσθα πηδᾶν λέγοντος—οὐκ ἀγνοεῖς· πλῆθος δὲ ἐπιστολῶν τὸ τῶν πραγμάτων πλῆθος οὐκ ἀφῆκε γενέσθαι. πολλοὶ μὲν γὰρ οἷς δεῖ βοηθεῖν, οἱ δ' ὑπερπηδῶντες πολλῶν δυνάμεις ἐπὶ τὴν ἐμὴν καταφεύγουσιν ἀσθένειαν ἀτόπῳ κεχρημένοι πάθει, συκίνην ἀνθ' Ἑρμιόνος ζητοῦντες ἐπικουρίαν. 3. ἐμοὶ δὲ ἀνάγκη παρέχειν ἐμαυτόν, τί γὰρ ἄν τις καὶ ποιοῖ; ἔπειτα μικρὰ δεομένων μὲν ὠφελῶ, χρόνος δὲ ἀναλίσκεται, γράμματα δὲ ὑμῖν οὐχ ὅσα βούλεσθε γίγνεται.

---

[b] Libanius refers to his ill health in the summer of 362. He uses a combination of two proverbs (1) *Paroem. Gr.* 2.210 συκίνη ἐπικουρία, fig wood being notoriously brittle and

## 83. Βακχίῳ

1. Οἱ μὲν ἰδόντες εὐδαιμονέστεροι τὰ περὶ τὴν Ἄρτεμιν σοὶ πεφιλοτιμημένα, γεγόναμεν δὲ καὶ αὐτοὶ τοῖς ἠγγελμένοις ἡδίους καὶ οὐκ ἴσον μὲν

---

[a] *BLZG* 93. The letter is written in late spring, probably May 362. Bacchius of Tarsus, an old friend and correspondent of Libanius and friend of Demetrius, had

as though afraid that we should forget her power. 2. You are not unaware that I have equal pleasure in speaking and in having you as an auditor—indeed you know how to leap with enthusiasm at my speeches, but the volume of business has not allowed a volume of correspondence to be forthcoming. For there are many whom I must assist; they bypass the influence of a large number of persons and have recourse to my weakness, an irrational piece of behaviour, since they crave the assistance of a broken reed instead of something stronger.[b] 3. But I needs must offer my services, for what else could one do? In consequence, though I am of little assistance to them in their needs, time is spent, and letters are not forthcoming in the quantity that you wish.

unreliable, and (2) ἀνθ' Ἑρμιόνος, a safe refuge for suppliants, from the temple of Kore and Demeter at Hermione; *Paroem. Gr.* 1.38.

## 83. To Bacchius[a]

1. Those who saw the celebrations you made in honour of Artemis are more than fortunate.[b] I too am the happier on receiving news of it, not so much

last visited Libanius in Antioch in 360 (*Ep.* 186).

[b] He had taken advantage of Julian's religious reforms to recover a statue of Artemis from Christian hands, as implied in *Ep.* 712, and to reinstitute the cult with due ceremony, including an inaugural oration from Demetrius. He was installed as priest of the cult (§ 4).

ἐκείνοις, οὐ πολὺ δὲ ἔλαττον εἴχομεν. 2. ὁ γάρ σοι τὰ γράμματα φέρων οὗτος ἐκόμιζέ μοι τῶν πεποιημένων τὸν λόγον, ὅθεν μὲν σὺ τὴν θεὸν ἦγες καὶ ἐν ὅτῳ σχήματι, ὅπως δὲ ὡπλισμένην, σὸν δὲ εἶναι τὴν σκευὴν ἀνάλωμα. 3. καὶ τῶν ἱερείων ἐμνήσθη τοῦ τε ἀργυροῦ συὸς καὶ τῆς ἐλάφου πομπῆς τε διηγήσατο κόσμον πλῆθός τε δαιτυμόνων καὶ πλῆθος ἡμερῶν ἐν πότῳ καὶ τὸ κάλλιστον· προσθεῖναι γὰρ ἔφησε τὴν ἀπὸ τῶν λόγων τὸν καλὸν Δημήτριον ἑστίασιν, ὥστε με σκιρτήμασιν ἔχεσθαι καὶ συνήδεσθαί σοι τῆς περὶ τὴν Ἄρτεμιν θεραπείας. 4. ἀλλὰ σύ γε παισί τε παραδοίης τὴν ἱερωσύνην τῆς τε τῶν θυσιῶν ἐπανόδου γῇ τε καὶ θάλαττα πάντα ἀπολαύοι τὸν χρόνον.

## 84. Κέλσῳ

1. Ἔδωκεν ἡ ἀρχή σοι πλεονεκτῆσαι ἡμῶν καὶ προεντυχεῖν τῷ καλῷ Φουρτουνατιανῷ. ἡμῶν γὰρ ἔτ᾽ ἐν μαντείαις ὄντων καὶ ἄλλην ἄλλου λέγοντος ἡμέραν, εἰς ἣν αὐτὸν εἰκὸς φανεῖσθαι, σὺ τὸν ἄνδρα εἶχές τε καὶ εἱστίας, ἀνθειστία δὲ σὲ κἀκεῖνος, ὡς εἰκός, οἷς εἶχε, καλλίονι θοίνῃ, τοῖς περὶ τοῦ βασιλέως λόγοις, ἐν οἷς ἦν ὅτι καὶ σὲ

as they, but not very much less. 2. The bearer of your letter personally gave me the account of what took place, of the place from which you conducted the goddess and with what pomp and equipment, and that the ceremonial was all at your expense. 3. He told me of sacrificial offerings, the silver boar, the deer, and related the order of the procession, the number of diners and the number of days of feasting and drinking, and, best of all, he told me that the noble Demetrius had capped it with a feast of eloquence. In consequence I leapt in excitement and shared your joy in the cult of Artemis. 4. May you hand down your priestly office to your sons, and may land and sea enjoy the return of the sacrifices for all time.

## 84. To Celsus

1. Your office has allowed you to gain the advantage over me and to meet the noble Fortunatianus before I do.[a] We are still peering into the future: different people give different forecasts of the probable date of his arrival here, while you have him and feast him and he in turn feasts you, I am sure, with the finer fare at his disposal, his conversations about the emperor, of which both his friendship

[a] Fortunatianus, commended to Maximus at court (*Letter* 80) has had his audience with Julian.

φιλεῖ καὶ ἡμῶν οὐκ ἀμνημονεῖ. 2. κατηγορούμενος δὲ ἐπὶ τῷ μὴ γράψαι καὶ παρὰ τούτῳ καὶ ἔτι πρότερον παρὰ τοῖς πρέσβεσιν, οἶσθα γὰρ ἃ πρὸς ἑκατέρους εἶπεν, οὔπω δύναμαι καταγνῶναι τῆς ἐμαυτοῦ σιωπῆς οὐδ' ὡς ἦν μοι κάλλιον ἐπεσταλκότα εἶναι πεισθῆναι. τῆς γὰρ νῦν οὔσης αἰτίας ἡ τότ' ἂν γενομένη χαλεπωτέρα τ' ἂν ἦν καὶ οὐκ ἐῶσα τὸν φεύγοντα ἀντιβλέπειν τῷ διώκοντι. 3. πρότερον μὲν οὖν τὸ τῆς βασιλείας μέγεθος ὀκνεῖν ἐποίει γράφειν· νῦν δὲ δὴ καὶ τὸ κάλλος τῶν βασιλέως ἐπιστολῶν διπλοῦν ποιεῖ τὸν φόβον. καὶ γὰρ εἰ τὰ ἄλλα παρ' ἡμῖν, ἀλλ' οὐ τό γε φῶς ὅσον ἐν τοῖς ἐκείνου. μάλιστα γὰρ ὧν ἴσμεν ἰσχὺν ἁνὴρ[1] συνεκέρασε σαφηνείᾳ.

[1] ἁνὴρ F. ἀνὴρ Wolf (Mss.)

---

[b] Of the embassies of congratulation arriving in Constantinople to greet the new emperor that from Antioch was the last to appear (Jul. Misop. 367c), a fact that Julian did not allow them to forget. Libanius, pleading ill-health (*Ep.* 697), had refused to be a member of the embassy and

for you and mindfulness of me form part. 2. Although arraigned both before him and still earlier before our envoys for not writing[b]—and you know the comments he made on each occasion—I still cannot condemn my silence or convince myself that it would have been more proper for me to have written. The accusation[c] which would then have been levelled at me would have been more serious than the present one, and would not permit the defendant to look the accuser in the eye. 3. No, the might of majesty made me hesitate to write then, but now too the beauty of the emperor's letters redoubles my fear. Whatever other qualities mine possess, they certainly do not have the radiance that is presented in his. He, more than any man I know, has united force with clarity.[d]

had even felt unable to send any personal message to Julian or to friends at court—hence his uneasiness in early 362 and the complaints of Julian here mentioned. For this embassy see *Epp.* 698, 702; Petit, *Vie Municipale* 416 f.

[c] Of sycophancy.

[d] Libanius (*Or.* 13.52) claims to have influenced Julian's epistolary style; cf. also *Or.* 15.6 f, 18.14 ff.

## 85. Κέλσῳ

1. Οὐκ ἀγνοεῖς τουτονὶ Διογένη ὄντα πολίτην ἡμέτερον, τῷ δ' οὐ τοῦτο μόνον πρὸς ἡμᾶς ἐστιν, ἀλλὰ καὶ ἆθλον ὑπέστη ποτὲ προσόμοιον τῷ Ζωπύρου. 2. μὴ καταφρόνει δὲ μήτε τῶν πολέμων, οὓς πολεμοῦσιν οἱ σοφισταί, μήτε τῶν ἐν αὐτοῖς ἀριστευόντων νέων, ὧν ὁ Διογένης οὗτος. ἔδοξε γὰρ ἡμῖν δάκνειν ποτὲ μετὰ παιδιᾶς Ἀκάκιον. 3. ἡ δὲ ἦν ἀπόστασις μαθητοῦ πεπλασμένη ζητοῦσα δὴ τὸν ὡς ἄριστα ὑποκρινόμενον τὸ δρᾶμα, βελτίων δὲ οὐδεὶς ἐδόκει τοῦ Διογένους. 4. ὁ δὲ ἐφάνη καλλίων ἢ προσεδοκήθη. καὶ γὰρ ἐπιστεύθη ταχέως καὶ ῥημάτων ἤκουσε τῶν ἐκ κολακείας καὶ παρέπεμπε μὲν ὡς ἂν μαθητὴς ὀχούμενον, ἀπεπήδα δὲ περὶ τὰς θύρας ὡς τοὺς ἡμετέρους, οἳ ἐκάθηντο θέατρον αὐτῷ. καὶ οὕτως ἀντὶ τῆς Βαβυλῶνος εἴχομεν ἀφορμὴν εἰς γέλωτα

[a] Diogenes, protagonist of Libanius' students in a display of sophistic feuding, is commended to Celsus, governor of Cilicia, in repayment of this personal obligation. See F/Kr. no. 17, Festugière, *Antioche* 431 f, Petit, *Étudiants* 106.

Bitter professional rivalries were an accepted part of a sophist's career. The accepted technique was to try to

## 85. To Celsus

1. You are not unaware that the bearer, Diogenes,[a] is a fellow citizen of mine, but this is not his only recommendation in my eyes: he also undertook a task similar to that of Zopyrus.[b] 2. And do not despise either the wars waged by the sophists or the prowess displayed therein by the students,[c] of whom Diogenes was one. We once decided to play a trick on Acacius and annoy him. 3. The trick was to fake the desertion of a pupil, and it required the best possible actor for the farce. No one appeared better than Diogenes. 4. He turned out even better than expected, for he soon carried conviction and listened to words of flattery. In his role of pupil, he began to escort him as he rode along, but, as he got to his door, he dashed off to my boys who had taken up their positions as spectators of the scene. We might not have taken Babylon, but we had a

outdo a rival by getting his students away from him by whatever means, deceit, flattery, bribery, even, at Athens, by force. According to Libanius, Acacius had tried most of these methods (cf. *Ep.* 555); the loyal Diogenes retaliates by making a laughing-stock of Acacius.

[b] Cf. Herod. 3.150 ff for the deception practised by Zopyrus against the Babylonians which brought about the recapture of the place by Darius.

[c] E.g. *Or.* 1.14–25, Eunap. *V.S.* 482 ff.

καὶ οὐδὲ ὁ θεῖος ἡμῖν ἐνταῦθα ἠδύνατο μὴ γελᾶν. 5. σκόπει οὖν ὅπως αὐτῷ τὸν μισθὸν ἀποδώσεις τῆς τόλμης ἐπὶ τὸν ἀποστεροῦντα χρέους τινὸς βοηθήσας.

## 86. Ἰουλιανῷ

1. Ἀλλ' εἰ καὶ μὴ πρὸς ἡμᾶς ἐπιστέλλεις, ἡμεῖς γε τοῖς σοῖς ἑστιώμεθα γράμμασιν. ὅταν γὰρ ὅτι τις ἔλαβε μάθωμεν, εὐθὺς ἡμεῖς πλησίον καὶ ἢ πείσαντες ἢ κρατήσαντες ἀκόντων ἀνέγνωμεν. 2. τὸ μὲν οὖν κέρδος οὐχ ἧττον ἡμῶν ἢ 'κείνων, τὸ τετιμῆσθαι δὲ παρ' ἐκείνοις μόνοις. ἐρῶμεν δὲ καὶ αὐτοὶ τιμῆς, ἐπειδὴ καὶ φίλτρου τοῦ παρὰ σοί. δῆλον γὰρ ὡς, εἴ τι τιμήσεις, οὐκ ἄνευ γε τοῦ φιλεῖν τοῦτο ποιήσεις.

## 87. Ὑπερεχίῳ

1. Συνησθεὶς σοί τε καὶ τῷ σῷ πατρί, τῷ μὲν τῆς εἰς σὲ μεγαλοψυχίας, σοὶ δὲ τοῦ τὸν πατέρα

[a] F/Kr. no. 75. For Hyperechius see *Letter* 75. This letter, dated to May–June 362, is supported by others to Hyperechius' brother-in-law Albanius and to the governor of Galatia, Acacius (*Epp.* 730, 732). His father Maximus had just given him control of the family property, and the

huge store of laughter; not even my uncle could forebear to chuckle at it. 5. So ensure that you reward him for his hardihood[d] by helping him against one who seeks to deprive him of some debt.

[d] An oration against the practice of accepting deserting students is composed some twenty years after this (*Or.* 43 of 383).

## 86. To Julianus[a]

1. Well, even if you do not write to me, I feast on your letters, for whenever I find out that anyone has received one, I present myself forthwith, and either by persuasion or by overpowering his reluctance I get to read it. 2. So my gain is no less than theirs, though the honour is theirs alone. But I too am desirous of honour, as I am of some token of affection from you. For clearly, if you honour me at all, you will do so not without some feeling of regard.

[a] Julianus has evidently not replied to the congratulations of *Letter* 82, and Libanius is becoming restive in his isolation from the new regime.

## 87. To Hyperechius[a]

1. I congratulate both your father and you, him upon his generosity[b] towards you, and you upon so

question of his future career is once more a matter of debate.

[b] On *megalopsychia*, cf. G. Downey, "The Pagan Virtue of Megalopsychia in Byzantine Syria," *TAPA* 76 (1945): 283 ff.

ἀρέσκειν, ὥστ᾿ ἐκείνου ζῶντος πάντων καταστῆναι κύριον, ἐν τοῖς δευτέροις σὲ μὲν ὁμοίως ἐπαινεῖν ἔχω, τὸν δὲ οὐκέτι. 2. σὺ μὲν γὰρ τῶν τε ἡμετέρων μεμνημένος λόγων καὶ τὸ πρᾶγμα ἐξετάζων ὀρθῶς οἷος εἶ τῇ πατρίδι λειτουργεῖν, ἐξ οὗ δόξα τε καὶ δύναμις γένοιτ᾿ ἂν καὶ πρὸ τούτων γε τὸ τὰ δίκαια πρὸς τὴν οἰκείαν[1] ποιεῖν· ὁ δὲ σὲ πέμπει ῥίψοντα τὰ ὄντα εἰς τὴν θάλατταν. εἰ γὰρ μήτε ἐκεῖ μέγα τι παρὰ τὴν δαπάνην ἕξεις οἴκοι τε οὐκ ἰσχύσεις ἑτέρωθι δαπανώμενος, πῶς οὐκ ἀπολεῖταί σοι τὰ χρήματα τῇ ψήφῳ τοῦ δεδωκότος; 3. πεῖθε οὖν αὐτὸν μὴ τὴν ἐν τῇ παροιμίᾳ μιμεῖσθαι βοῦν μηδ᾿ ὃ ἠμέλχθη γάλα λακτίσαντα ἐκχέαι. πρὸς γὰρ τῇ περὶ τὰ χρήματα βλάβῃ καὶ εἰς τὴν πόλιν ζημιώσῃ. 4. εἰ μέντοι πολιτεύοιο τοῖς καθ᾿ ἡμέραν παρὰ τοῖς ἄρχουσιν ἀγῶσιν, ἀμείνων ἔσῃ καὶ τὸ νῦν ἐπαινούμενον ῥεῦμα πλέον ἐργάσῃ· πράξας δὲ ἃ ᾿κείνῳ δοκεῖ, τῆς μὲν οὐσίας οὐ μικρὸν ἀφαιρήσεις, ἐν ἀργίᾳ δὲ καὶ ὕπνῳ τὸν λοιπὸν βιώσῃ χρόνον τὰ μὲν τῶν πέλας ὁρῶν αὐξόμενα, σοὶ δὲ πλὴν ὀνόματος κενοῦ γεγενημέ-

[1] οἰκείαν F (Ath.) οἰκίαν Wolf (other Mss.).

---

[c] Maximus was pressing him to apply to join the Sen-

pleasing your father that in his own lifetime he has put you in complete control of his property. However on the next move, though I can commend you in similar terms, I cannot do so with him. 2. If you remember my words and weigh the matter correctly, you can be of service to your city, in consequence of which you may obtain fame and influence and, more important still, do justice by your own community, but he is sending you to throw your possessions into the sea. If you will get no great reward comparable with your expenditure, and if owing to your expenditure elsewhere you have no influence at home, your fortune is bound to be wasted by the decision of its donor.[c] 3. So persuade him not to behave like the proverbial[d] cow that kicks over the bucket and spills the milk, for besides the financial loss you will harm yourself with regard to your home town. 4. If, however, as a councillor you participate in its daily disputations before the governors, you will be all the better and you will enhance that flow of eloquence for which you are now commended. If you do what he wants, you will lose no small part of your property and will live the rest of your life in idleness and sloth, seeing the fortunes of your neighbours increase while you get nothing

ate, advice of which Libanius disapproves. Instead, he advises him to answer the call for curial service.

[d] There is no known proverb in these terms, but compare English, "crying over spilt milk."

νον οὐδέν. 5. πρόσαγε δὴ πᾶσαν μὲν πεῖραν, πάσας δὲ δεήσεις τῷ πατρὶ καὶ μὴ Καδμείαν νίκην ἐπίτρεπε νικᾶν ἐκείνῳ. γιγνέσθω δὲ μετὰ σοῦ καὶ ἡ μήτηρ, ἀκούω δὲ αὐτὴν νοῦν ἔχειν, καὶ τὸ μηδὲ ἐμοὶ τὴν βουλὴν ἀρέσκειν τὴν ἐκείνου λεγέσθω. ἴσως γὰρ νουθετούμενος λύσει δόγμα πονηρόν, ὅπερ μοι δοκεῖ πρὸς τὴν ἀπραγμοσύνην τὴν αὑτοῦ κεκυρωκέναι νῦν. ἅτε γὰρ ἐν ὄρεσι καὶ θήρᾳ τὰ πολλὰ διάγων μισεῖ τοὺς ἐκ τῶν ἐπ' ἀγορᾶς ἄθλων ἱδρῶτας. 6. ἀλλ' ἐκεῖνος μὲν ταῦτα φευγέτω, σοὶ δὲ ἐπιτρεπέτω παλαίειν. νῦν γὰρ οὐ Μάξιμον οἶμαι πολιτεύεσθαι δεῖν τὸν τῶν ἀγρῶν φίλον, ἀλλ' Ὑπερέχιον τὸν Μαξίμου τὸν θορύβους ἐπιστάμενον φέρειν. 7. ἐγὼ μὲν ταῦτα παραινῶ καί φημι λυσιτελήσειν ὑμῖν· ληρεῖν δὲ εἰ δόξαιμι νῦν, ἀλλ' ὕστερόν γε ἐπαινέσεσθε τὴν γνώμην, ὃ τὸν μὲν σύμβουλον κοσμήσει, τὸν οὐκ[2] ἐπαινοῦντα δὲ οὐκ ὀνήσει.

[2] οὐκ F (V): om. Wolf (other Mss.).

but an empty title. 5. Then apply every means, and use every entreaty upon your father, and do not allow him to gain a Cadmeian victory.[e] Let your mother too be with you in this—she is a sensible woman, I hear—and let it be noted that his plan does not meet with my approval either. On receipt of such advice he will perhaps rescind an ill-advised decision which in my opinion he has adopted now with an eye to his own retirement, for since he spends most of his time in the mountains hunting he dislikes the sweat that comes from the exertions of the city square. 6. Well, let him retire from them but allow you to compete in them, for now, I believe, it is not the country-loving Maximus who must participate in civic life, but Maximus' son Hyperechius, who has the ability to endure its hurly-burly. 7. This is my advice: I assert that it will be to your advantage. If I now be thought to be talking nonsense, you will certainly approve my opinion later, and though it may be a feather in my cap to have given the advice, it will be of no use to you if you do not approve it.

[e] A victory disastrous to victors and vanquished alike; cf. *Paroem. Gr.* 1.97 and references.

## 88. Κέλσῳ

1. Οὐκ ἔφθη σε[1] ἀφεὶς ὁ βασιλεὺς καὶ συνέμιξεν ἐμοὶ καὶ μικροῦ μὲν σιγῇ παρέδραμεν ἠλλοιωμένου μοι τοῦ προσώπου καὶ χρόνῳ καὶ νόσῳ, φράσαντος δὲ τοῦ θείου τε καὶ ὁμωνύμου πρὸς αὐτόν, ὃς εἴην, κίνησίν τε ἐκινήθη θαυμαστὴν ἐπὶ τοῦ ἵππου καὶ τῆς δεξιᾶς λαβόμενος οὐ μεθίει σκώμμασί τε χαριεστάτοις καὶ ῥόδων ἡδίοσιν ἔπαττέ με καὶ αὐτὸν οὐκ ἀπεχόμενον τοῦ σκώπτειν. ὁ δὲ ἀμφοτέροις ἦν θαυμαστός, οἷς τε ἔλεγεν οἷς τε ἠνείχετο. 2. μικρὰ δὲ αὐτὸν ἀναπαύσας καὶ τὴν πόλιν ἁμίλλαις ἵππων εὐφράνας ἐκέλευέ με λέγειν. καὶ εἶπον παρακληθείς, οὐκ ἐνοχλήσας, ὁ δὲ ἐτέρπετο βεβαιῶν μοι τὸ προοίμιον· ἔφην γὰρ αὐτὸν ἐν προοιμίῳ πάντα τἀμὰ καλὰ νομιεῖν ὑπὸ

[1] ἔφθη σε F., conj. Re. (S) ἔφθησε most Mss. ἔφθησεν Wolf (Mo D)

[a] F/Kr. no. 47. Celsus, as governor of Cilicia, escorted Julian to the frontier of his province, where the emperor was welcomed by a reception committee from the province of Syria, including Libanius. The date of the meeting was 18 July 362, during the festival of the Adonia which marked the end of the religious year and was a day of mourning, a bad omen according to Ammianus (22.9.15; cf.

## 88. To Celsus

1. Almost as soon as the emperor left you he met me.[a] He almost passed me by in silence since my face is so ravaged by time and illness,[b] but his uncle and namesake[c] told him who I was, and he was remarkably excited as he sat his horse. He grasped my hand and would not let go, and he showered me with jests most delightful and sweeter than roses,[d] and I did not refrain from jesting myself. He was admirable both for the remarks he passed and those he suffered. 2. After he had rested himself for a while and entertained the city with horse races, he bade me deliver an oration. I did so at his command and not through any solicitation of mine, and his pleasure confirmed what I said in the introduction, for in the introduction I said that he would regard all my utterances as excellent because of his

Bidez, *Vie de Julien* 400). There is a significant difference of tone between this letter and his later account in *Or.* 1.120.

[b] Julian had not seen Libanius since their days in Nicomedeia, some 15 years before. In any case, at this time Libanius had been plagued by ill-health for some years; cf. *Epp.* 695, 727, 738.

[c] Julianus, *Comes Orientis*.

[d] Aristoph. *Clouds* 1331. Julian's behaviour here is not in keeping with the imperial station, any more than his greeting to Maximus in the Senate (cf. *Or.* 18.155 f; Amm. Marc. 22.7.3). For Libanius it is justified by their common literary interests—hence the σκώμματα.

τοῦ ἐρᾶν. καὶ οὕτως ἐξέβη. 3. σὺ δὲ καὶ αὐτὸς μὲν εἶ τῶν εἰπόντων καὶ ψήφου τετυχηκότων ἐγγύθεν σοι τῶν θεῶν ἀπὸ τοῦ βωμοῦ βοηθούντων καὶ παρεχόντων πρὸς τὸ θάλπος ἀνδρείαν· τοσοῦτον δὲ ἀπέσχες πέμψαι μοι τὸν λόγον, ὥστ' οὐδ' ὅτι εἴρηκας ἔγραψας, ἀλλὰ πρὸς μὲν Ὀλύμπιον εἰρωνευόμενος ἔφης ἐμέσαι, πρὸς δὲ ἡμᾶς οὐδὲ τοῦτο.

---

[e] *Or.* 13: for ἐρᾶν cf. *Or.* 13.3. Both now and later Libanius insists that he did not push himself into Julian's notice or favour, nor did he seek any personal advantage; cf. *Letter* 97, *Or.* 15.7, *Or.* 1.121 ff.

## 89. Ἰουλιανῷ

1. Κατήγαγεν ἡμᾶς εἰς τὴν τιμὴν ὁ χρηστὸς Σαλούτιος,[1] ἧς ἐτύγχανεν ἐξεληλακὼς ὁ σκαιὸς Ἐλπίδιος· ἃ γὰρ ἐκεῖνος ὑβρίζων ἀφείλετο, ταῦθ' οὗτος παύων τὴν ὕβριν ἀπέδωκε. 2. τὸ μὲν οὖν ἥμισυ τῆς τροφῆς ἐνταῦθα φέρομεν, θάτερον δὲ ἐκ

[1] Σαλούτιος F. Σαλούστιος Wolf (Mss.).

---

[a] *BLZG* 191 (vii), *PLRE* 472 (15); a close friend of Libanius, he was in office as *consularis Phoenices* by 3 Sept. 362.

[b] *BLZG* 265, *PLRE* 814 (Secundus 3), Julian's *praetorian prefect*, in office by Dec. 361, in succession to

affection.[e] And so it turned out. 3. You too are among those who have delivered orations and had judgement passed upon them, when the gods were at hand to assist you from the altar and to encourage you to warm to the task, but so far from sending me your oration, you did not even write to tell me that you had delivered it; in mock modesty you told Olympius that you spewed it out, but me you have not told even that much.[f]

[f] As Libanius' old friend Olympius had reported, Celsus had delivered an extempore address of welcome to Julian. The notion is Aristeidean, as is the description in *Or.* 1.120 of the meeting of the emperor and the sophist: cf. Philostr. *V.S.* 2.9.2.

## 89. To Julianus[a]

1. The excellent Salutius[b] has restored me to that privilege from which that dunce Elpidius had ejected me, for that of which he outrageously deprived me, Salutius has returned to me, so putting an end to the outrage.[c] 2. Now, half of my salary I get from here: the other half he bade me

Elpidius (Amm. Marc. 22.3.1).

[c] In 359/60 Elpidius—Helpidius i (*BLZG* 168), 4 (*PLRE* 414)—had cancelled part of Libanius' subvention paid in kind (*Letter* 65). This was now restored by authority of Salutius, half to be remitted from Phoenicia and half from Syria (ἐνταῦθα)—not Constantinople, as Petit (*Vie Municipale* 409). On Libanius' wealth and its sources, cf. Petit, App. 3.

Φοινίκης ἐκέλευσεν ἔχειν ἐνθυμηθείς, οἶμαι, τοῦθ' ὅτι σοῦ τῆς Φοινίκης ἄρχοντος καλῶς μοι τὸ πρᾶγμα κείσεται. 3. βεβαίωσον τοίνυν τῷ φίλῳ τὰς ἐλπίδας.

## 90. Ἀκακίῳ

1. Τῶν πολλῶν ἐκείνων καὶ γενναίων λόγων, οὓς τὸ μὲν πρῶτον ἐν Φοινίκῃ, μετὰ ταῦτα δὲ τῇδε, νῦν δὲ πράττεις ἐν Παλαιστίνῃ τῇ καλῇ—πῶς γὰρ οὐ καλὴ τοῦ γε παρὰ σοὶ κάλλους ἐρῶσα;—τούτων δὴ τῶν γενναίων ἐκγόνων οὐχ ἧττω σοι δόξαν ἤνεγκαν οὓς Εὐτρόπιος ἐποίησε. 2. καὶ γὰρ οὗτοι σοὶ τοῦ γε σπείραντος, ὥστ' ἔδοξεν οὐ μᾶλλον τῇ μορφῇ τὴν συγγένειαν μηνύειν ἢ τῷ τύπῳ τῶν λόγων, ἐν οἷς δεικνύει μετὰ ῥώμης δρόμον, τοῦτο δὴ τὸ ὑμέτερον. 3. οὕτω δὲ ὢν ῥήτωρ ἀγαθὸς οὕτως ἐστὶ χρηστός, ὥστ' αἰσθόμενος ὅτι με βούλοιο τιμᾶσθαι, πᾶσιν οἷς εἰς σέ καὶ πρὸς ἐμὲ κέχρηται καθάπερ ἐμὸς ὢν ἀδελ-

[a] Libanius' rival during his first years in Antioch, he had removed to Caesarea in 361 (cf. Petit: Libanios, *Autobiographie,* Discours 1, p. 236). The present letter with its fulsome admiration contrasts sharply with the spiteful

have from Phoenicia. His idea was, I believe, that my business would be properly settled since you are governor of Phoenicia. 3. Please confirm the expectations of your friend.

## 90. To Acacius[a]

1. Of that mass of noble eloquence which you produced first in Phoenicia, then here, and now in Palestine the beautiful—for beautiful she must be in her passion for the beauty that is in you—of those noble productions of yours none has brought you more renown than the compositions of Eutropius.[b] 2. Indeed they bear the mark of their origin: he seemed to indicate this relationship not so much by his physical characteristics as by the stamp of his oratory in which he displays fluency combined with force—your attributes, in fact. 3. He is so good an orator and so decent a fellow that, since he saw that you wished me to receive respect, he has treated me just as he treats you, just as though he

comment of *Or.* 1.120. Acacius, even in absence, retained some rhetorical standing in Antioch, and so despatches an oration to Julian—here praised but later damned by Libanius.

[b] Cf. *Ep.* 1304. According to Seeck, *BLZG* 151 (iv), this Eutropius was to become the historian. However, in *PLRE* 317, the historian is to be identified with Seeck's Eutropius (iii), and Acacius' nephew rightly sinks into anonymity.

φιδοῦς τε καὶ μαθητής. 4. τοιγαροῦν καὶ αὐτὸς εἰς τοὺς πάλαι συνήθεις τὸν ἄνδρα ἐνέγραψα καὶ πρὸ πολλῶν γε τῶν πάλαι, παρῄει γὰρ δὴ πολλοὺς ἐν τῷ φιλεῖν. ὅθεν αὐτῷ καὶ τὰ μικρὰ τῶν ἐμῶν—πάντα δὲ οἶμαι μικρὰ τἀμά, τί γὰρ ἄν τις αὑτὸν ἀγνοοίη καὶ ταῦτα βοῶντος ἀνδρὸς σοφοῦ δεῖν γιγνώσκειν αὑτόν;—ἀλλ' αὐτῶν γε τούτων καὶ τὰ σμικρότατα ἠγάπα καὶ οὐκ ἔστιν ὃ ἐγὼ μὲν εἶπον, ὁ δὲ οὐκ ἀκήκοεν, οὐδ' αὖ ἤκουσε μέν, οὐ σὺν ἐπαίνῳ δέ. 5. οὗτος τοίνυν ὁ καλὸς κἀγαθὸς καὶ δίκαιος εἶναι βουλόμενος ἔστιν ὅ τι με ἠδίκησε. καὶ σκόπει γε τὴν γραφήν· ἠδίκηκέ με Εὐτρόπιος τὸν λόγον, ὃν εὖ μὲν ποιῶν Ἀκάκιος ἔγραψεν, εὖ δὲ ποιῶν ἔπεμψε, τῷ βασιλεῖ δεδωκὼς πρὶν ἐμοί. 6. καὶ τὴν μὲν αἰτίαν ἐπὶ τὸν πρεσβύτην οἴσει, καὶ γὰρ πρὸς ἐμὲ τοιαῦτα ἐσοφίζετο· σὺ δὲ μὴ πίστευε, οὐδὲ γὰρ ἐγώ. καὶ γὰρ εἰ σφόδρα ἐστὶ δεινός, ἀλλὰ πρότεροι γεγόναμεν ἐγώ τε καὶ σύ. πάντως δὲ οἶδεν ἃ τοῖς πρεσβυτέροις δέδωκεν Ὅμηρος. 7. λεγέτω μὲν οὖν μηδέν, ἔργῳ δὲ ἀπολογείσθω, καὶ μιμείσθω τὸν Ἀχιλλέα

were my own nephew and pupil. 4. In consequence I too have enlisted him among my acquaintances of long standing—more so than many of them, for he surpasses them in his affection. Hence even my trifles—and all my stuff in my opinion consists of trifles: how could anyone be ignorant of himself, especially when a philosopher proclaims the need of self-knowlege?[c]—even the smallest of these trifles he welcomed. Every single utterance of mine he listened to, and did not just listen, but listened with approval. 5. Yet this fine gentleman, despite his desire to play fair, has done me wrong in one particular. Just look at my indictment: Eutropius has done me wrong by presenting the oration which Acacius was good enough to write and to send, to the emperor before he did so to me. 6. And he will cast the blame upon the old fellow[d]—indeed such was the excuse he devised for me. But do not believe him: I certainly do not. However clever he may be, you and I were born before he was. In any case, he knows the respect Homer accords to men who are getting on in years.[e] 7. So do not let him say a word, but let him defend himself in deed, and take a leaf out of Achilles' book,

[c] Foerster cites Thales (Diels/Kranz, *Fr. Vorsokr.* 1.72). The aphorism is attributed to Delphi.

[d] Acacius.

[e] Homer *Il.* 15.204.

κύριος ὤν, ὥσπερ ἐκεῖνος, ἰᾶσθαι τὸ τραῦμα.

## 91. Βακχίῳ

1. Ἐπιμελοῦ τῶν ἱερῶν, ὦ καλὲ Βάκχιε, καὶ πλήθει θυσιῶν καὶ τελετῶν ἀκριβείᾳ καὶ τῷ τὰ κείμενα ἀνιστάναι. δεῖ γάρ σε καὶ περὶ τοὺς θεοὺς εὐσεβεῖν καὶ τῷ βασιλεῖ χαρίζεσθαι καὶ τὴν πατρίδα καλλίω ποιεῖν. δίδου μέντοι καὶ χάριτας ἐν τῷ φυλάττειν τὴν σπουδήν. θεάς τε γὰρ οὔσας οὕτω τιμήσεις τὰς Χάριτας καὶ ἅμα ἔξεστι μήτ' ἐκείνων ἀμελεῖν καὶ πρᾷον εἶναι. 2. γενοῦ δή μοι τοιοῦτος ἐν οἷς εἰσπράττεις Βασιλικὸν[1] μερίσας αὐτῷ τὴν καταβολήν, ὥστε τὸ μὲν θεῖναι, τὸ δὲ εὐτρεπίσαι. τῶν γὰρ Αἰμιλιανοῦ τρόπων ἐπελάβετο μὲν οὐδείς, ἐγὼ δὲ καὶ ἐπαινέτης. οὐ γὰρ

[1] Βασιλικὸν F. (Ath., -οῖς V) Βασιλίσκον Wolf (other Mss.).

[a] Proceeding in accordance with Julian's edict, Bacchius is pressing for the restitution of property taken from the temple of Artemis, whose cult he is now restoring (*Ep.* 712; for the edict, Julian *ELF* no. 42). Libanius here, as elsewhere, protests against excess in enforcing repayment from owners of temple property who were not guilty of having acquired it by reprehensible means: Basilicus and

for, like him, he has it in his power to heal the wound.[f]

[f] Cf. *Ep.* 1105. Telephus of Mysia was wounded by the spear of Achilles, and could be cured by it alone: see *Paroem. Gr.* 2.763.

## 91. To Bacchius

1. Protect your shrines, noble Bacchius, by the number of victims, the exactness of ritual and the restoration of those in ruins, for you must reverence the gods, oblige the emperor and beautify your city.[a] Yet in maintaining your zeal, leave some room for grace and favour too, for in this way you will honour the Graces,[b] who are divine, and it is also possible for you not to neglect them and to show kindness. 2. Please show kindness, then, in the demands you are making on Basilicus, and divide up his contribution so that he may pay part and retain the rest. No one has complained of Aemilianus' conduct, and I have gone so far as to commend him, for he was not

Aemilianus, evidently Christians, were such possessors. This policy of reconciliation he always claims is that enjoined by Julian himself (e.g. *Or.* 18.121 ff).

[b] A favourite pun in such pleas for consideration. χάρις, however, like the contemporary use of *gratia,* can approach graft, and Libanius is at pains, not always successfully, to dissociate himself from such imputations (as in *Letter* 97). Hence the insistence here upon the divinity of the Graces.

ἦν τῶν ὑβριζόντων καὶ ταῦτα ἐνόν, εἴπερ ἐβούλετο. 3. δῶμεν δὴ μισθοὺς αὐτῷ τῆς καλοκἀγαθίας ἀφελόντες τῆς εἰσπράξεως οὐ τὸ ἐπείγειν, ἀλλὰ τὸ λίαν.

## 92. Σελεύκῳ

1. Μόλις ἥψω τῶν σαυτοῦ καὶ γέγονας ἐπιστάτης τῶν τῇ σῇ πρεπόντων φύσει. πρότερον δὲ ἄρα Ἡρακλῆς ταλασίας ἠναγκάζου φροντίζειν καὶ λύειν στάσεις ἀνθρώπων, οἷς ἡδέως ἂν προσέθηκας πολέμους. 2. ἀλλ' ἐκεῖνα μὲν εὖ ποιοῦντα οἴχεται, τὰ δὲ νῦν βωμοὶ καὶ νεῴ καὶ τεμένη καὶ ἀγάλματα κοσμούμενα μὲν ὑπὸ σοῦ, κοσμοῦντα δὲ σὲ καὶ γένος. 3. ἔχων δὴ τηλικούτους συμμάχους κωφὰ μὲν ἡγοῦ τὰ τῶν ἀνοσίων βέλη, κάθιζε δὲ κλάοντας τοὺς καταγελάσαντας πολὺν δὴ χρόνον τῶν βελτιόνων. ὀφείλεις δὲ χάριν τοῖς θεοῖς πατὴρ γεγονώς. ἣν ἀποδοῦναί σε χρὴ βοηθοῦντα τῶν ἱερῶν τοῖς κειμένοις. 4. ταυτὶ μὲν οὖν οἶδ' ὅτι ποιήσεις, ὥστ' εἶναι πολὺ τὰ διὰ σοῦ τῶν ἑτέ-

---

[a] On the chronology of *Letters* 92–95 see Appendix.

[b] Cf. *PLRE* 818. The reference is to Seleucus' brief career of office; but the suggestion there that this included

one of the aggressors, though he could have been, had he wished. 3. Let us reward him for his sense of responsibility by taking from the demand not the necessity for payment but the excess of it.

## 92. To Seleucus[a]

1. At long last you have gained possession of what is yours and have become supervisor of what naturally becomes you. Before this, to be sure, you were forced to be a Heracles busy at the loom, and to resolve the quarrels of men against whom you would cheerfully have gone to war.[b] 2. But that is past, and good riddance. Now you deal with altars, temples, precincts, and statues which you glorify and which glorify you and your family.[c] 3. Since you have such powerful allies to support you, think of the weapons of the unholy as vain, and those who for long enough laughed their betters to scorn, set them down to weeping and wailing. You owe a debt to the gods for becoming a father, and you must repay it by helping the temples that are in ruins. 4. I know that you will do so, and that in consequence those you restore will be far more glori-

the duty of requisition officer for woollens is hypothetical. The contrast seems no more than that of the congenial as opposed to the distasteful, symbolized by Heracles as a woman in Omphale's court.

[c] Seleucus now became chief priest of a province, perhaps Cilicia, under Julian's religious reforms.

ρωθι καλλίω· τὰ δ' ἡμέτερα, μικροῦ με τοῦ θέρους ἡ κεφαλὴ κατηνάγκασεν αὐξηθέντος τοῦ κακοῦ χρησμῷ κιβδήλῳ. 5. νοσῶν δὴ τὸ σῶμα πῶς ἂν δυναίμην οἷος πρὶν εἶναι περὶ τοὺς λόγους, ὃς οὐδὲν οὔτε λέγειν οὔτ' ἀκούειν βούλομαι πλὴν περὶ τῆς κεφαλῆς; 6. ὕμνηται μὲν οὖν ὁ γενναῖός μοι βασιλεύς, βραχεῖ δέ τινι μάλα λόγῳ· φασὶ δὲ αὐτὸν εἶναι καλόν, ἀλλ' ἐγὼ οὐ πείθομαι, καὶ διὰ τοῦτο κρύψας ἔχω. ἢν οὖν παρέλθῃ τὸ νέφος καὶ τῆς Αἴτνης ἀπαλλαγῶ καὶ κομίσωμαί τινας δυνάμεις, καὶ γράψω τι τοῦ πέμπειν ἄξιον, ὃ πρὸ ὑμῶν ληψόμενος οὐκ ἔσται.

---

[d] For the consultation of the oracle for his migraine in summer 362 see *Epp.* 706–7.

[e] Libanius' health had been one of his greatest worries. A near breakdown in 359 had been followed by this lowness of spirit (cf. *Or.* 1.117 f).

## 93. Βασιλεῖ Ἰουλιανῷ

1. Ἔπεμψά σοι τὸν λόγον μικρὸν ὑπὲρ μεγάλων πραγμάτων. τοῦ δὲ καὶ μείζω γενέσθαι λόγον σὺ δήπου κύριος, εἰ δοίης ἀφ' ὧν ἂν γένοιτο

---

[a] The cover note accompanying the text of *Or.* 13 (cf. Bidez, ed., Julien, *Oeuvres Complètes, Lettres* 1.2.110); it

ous than those elsewhere. As for myself, my migraine nearly had its way with me during the summer: the trouble was heightened by a false oracle.[d] 5. In my physical affliction, my attitude towards oratory could not possibly be the same as before, for I do not want to speak or hear of anything except my head.[e] 6. Our noble emperor has had his praises sung, but in a quite short speech. People say it is a good one, but I do not agree, and so I keep it hidden.[f] If the cloud passes, and I rid myself of this incubus[g] and regain some of my powers, then I will write something worth sending, and no one will get it before you do.

[f] *Or.* 13. For his reluctance to publish see Petit, "Recherches sur la publication."

[g] For Etna, *Ep.* 1312. Zeus punished Typhon (Pind. *Pyth.* 1.34 ff, Aesch. *P.V.* 354 f), or Enceladus (Virgil *Georg.* 1.471, Oppian *Cyn.* 1.273) by burying them under it.

## 93. To the Emperor Julian

1. I have sent you a small oration on great matters.[a] You certainly have it in your power to make the oration even greater, if you give me the

dates to late August 362. Both Seeck and Silomon dated it to 357, ignoring the importance of βασιλεῖ in the superscription. Foerster's tentative dating to 360 is no better, for the same reason. There is no evidence for any such oration to Julian at either time.

μείζων. 2. δοὺς μὲν οὖν δηλώσεις ὅτι με τεχνίτην ἐγκωμίων ἡγῇ· μὴ δοὺς δὲ δώσεις ἕτερα ὑποπτεύειν.

## 94. Ἰουλιανῷ αὐτοκράτορι

1. Εἰ ταυτὶ γλώττης ἀργοτέρας, τίς ἂν εἴης αὐτὴν ἀκονῶν; ἀλλὰ σοὶ[1] μὲν ἐν τῷ στόματι λόγων οἰκοῦσι πηγαὶ κρείττους ἢ δεῖσθαι ἐπιρροῆς· ἡμεῖς δὲ ἢν μὴ καθημέραν ἀρδώμεθα, λείπεται σιγᾶν. 2. τὸν λόγον δὲ ζητεῖς μὲν ἔρημον βοηθοῦ λαβεῖν καὶ διὰ τοῦτό σοι Πρίσκος ὁ καλὸς μέλλει,[2] δέχου δὲ ὅμως. πάντως ὅ τι ἂν γνῷς, στέρξομεν.

[1] σοὶ F. (V): σοῦ Wolf (other Mss.), Bidez-Cumont.
[2] μέλλει F. (V): μέλει Bidez-Cumont (*ELF* p. 152)

---

[a] This is Libanius' reply to Julian *ELF* no. 96 (374 b–d), the opening words referring specifically to Julian's postscript where he excuses his use of dictation and adds καίτοι μοι καὶ τὴν γλῶτταν εἶναι συμβέβηκεν ὑπὸ τῆς ἀνασκησίας ἀργοτέραν καὶ ἀδιάρθρωτον. The delay in receiving *Or.* 13 had evidently disconcerted Julian who, informed by Priscus that Libanius was engaged upon the composition of another oration, required it to be forwarded without delay (ζητεῖς μὲν ἔρημον βοηθοῦ λαβεῖν). The oration is that for Aristophanes (*Or.* 14). Both Julian and Libanius are deliberate in their reference to Soph. *Phil.* 97 ff.

material for it to grow. 2. If you do, you will show that you regard me as a craftsman of panegyric; if not, you will give reason to suspect the contrary.[b]

[b] The further material solicited from the emperor results in *Or.* 12.

## 94. To the Emperor Julian

1. If this is the product of an unpractised tongue,[a] what would you be like if you sharpened it? No! on your lips dwell springs of eloquence so strong as to require no stimulus.[b] As for me, unless I nurture mine each day, my only alternative is silence.[c] 2. You seek to have my oration bereft of its protection, and hence your noble Priscus is waiting.[d] Still, receive it. In any case I shall acquiesce in whatever you decide.

[b] Plat. *Tim.* 75e.

[c] The first section of this letter appears as *Letter* 9 in the correspondence between Basil and Libanius (*Ep.* 1588; Foerster 11:583). Despite the argument of Seeck (*BLZG* 33 f), Libanius would never have repeated himself in such a context. The deliberate transference of the receipt of this literary compliment from the leader of the pagan reaction to the foremost Christian protagonist of his day can only be taken as proof of the falsity of the collection.

[d] Priscus, the Neoplatonist philosopher and Julian's intimate, acted as intermediary to resolve the initial coolness between Libanius and the emperor (*Or.* 1.123 f). He had been waiting a couple of days for Libanius to finish the speech (Julian 374b), and then delivered it without delay.

## 95. Ἰουλιανῷ αὐτοκράτορι[1]

1. Ἐγὼ μὲν Ἀριστοφάνει τὰς ἀμοιβάς, σὺ δὲ ἀπέδωκας ἐμοὶ τοῦ περὶ σὲ φίλτρου λαμπροῦ τε καὶ σφοδροῦ καὶ οὔτε θεοὺς οὔτε ἀνθρώπους λανθάνοντος· ὡς νῦν γε μικροῦ πέτομαι πρὸς ὕψος ἀρθεὶς ὑπὸ τῆς ἐπιστολῆς, ἐλπίδας τε ἐνεγκούσης καὶ τὸν λόγον μοι κοσμούσης. καὶ μικρά μοι πάντα ἤδη φαίνεται, Μίδου πλοῦτος, κάλλος Νιρέως, Κρίσωνος τάχος, Πολυδάμαντος ῥώμη, μάχαιρα Πηλέως. 2. δοκῶ δ' ἄν μοι μηδ' ἂν τοῦ νέκταρος μετασχὼν ἡσθῆναι μᾶλλον ἢ νῦν, ὅτε μοι βασιλεύς, ὃν πάλαι Πλάτων ζητῶν ὀψέ ποθ' εὗρε, τήν τε γνώμην ἐπῄνεσε τόν τε λόγον ἐθαύμασε καὶ τιμῶν τῇ τοῦ δώσειν ὑποσχέσει τῷ μετ' ἐμοῦ σκοπεῖν ἐθέλειν ὃ δοῦναι δεῖ τιμᾷ μειζόνως. 3. οὐκ ἄρα ὁ τὴν Αἶγα τὴν οὐρανίαν ἐπι-

[1] Cf. Bidez-Cumont, *Recherches sur la tradition manuscrite des lettres de l'empéreur Julien,* p. 128; and *ELF* p. 154.

---

[a] After reading the oration for Aristophanes, Julian sent Libanius a letter of ecstatic approval (*ELF* no. 97); Libanius acknowledges this reply. Once again he cites almost verbatim Julian's opening words as the introduction to his own letter.

## 95. To the Emperor Julian

1. I have paid my debt to Aristophanes,[a] but you have repaid me for my strong and sincere affection for you which is not unnoticed by either gods or men. So now I almost take wing, uplifted by your letter which has given me hope and glorified my oration. And now everything else seems but paltry to me—the wealth of Midas, the beauty of Nireus, the speed of Crison, the strength of Polydamas, the sword of Peleus.[b] 2. I feel that, even if I sipped nectar, my joy would be no greater than now, when an emperor, whom Plato sought long ago and found at last,[c] has commended my resolution and admired my oration, and, while honouring me with the promise to make a grant, honours me more greatly by his wish to investigate with me what grant he should make.[d] 3. So, after all, it is not the watcher of the

[b] The wealth of Midas is legendary, as is the beauty of Nireus (Homer *Il.* 2.671 ff), while the sword of Peleus was given him as the reward for *σωφροσύνη* (cf. *Paroem. Gr.* 1.123, 446). The prowess of the athletes Crison of Himera, a sprinter of the middle 5th century, and of Polydamas of Scotussa later (cf. Pausan. 5.23.4 and 6.5, 7.27.1) had become legendary by Plato's time (cf. *Prot.* 335e, *Legg.* 8.840a, *Resp.* 1.338c).

[c] Plat. *Resp.* 5.473c ff.

[d] Cf. Jul. *ELF* no. 97 (382a): *δίκαιος δὲ εἶ μὴ συμβουλεύειν μόνον ὅ τι χρὴ βοηθεῖν ἀνδρὶ τοὺς θεοὺς ἀδόλως τετιμηκότι, ἀλλὰ καὶ ὃν χρὴ τρόπον.*

τέλλουσαν παρατηρῶν παντὸς ἂν τύχοι, ὅπου γε ἐμοὶ τοῦτο οὐ σπουδάσαντι τὰ μέγιστα γίγνεται, κἂν δεηθῶ τοῦ καλοῦ, βασιλεὺς ἕτοιμος εἰς τὴν χάριν θεὸν τὴν ἐν οὐρανῷ μιμούμενος; 4. ἡ μὲν οὖν ἐπιστολή σου προσκείσεται τῷ λόγῳ, μηνύουσα παισὶν Ἑλλήνων ὡς οὐ μάτην ἐξεπέμφθη τὸ βέλος, καὶ φιλοτιμήσεται τοῖς μὲν ὑπ' ἐμοῦ γεγραμμένοις Ἀριστοφάνης, τοῖς ὑπὸ σοῦ δὲ ἐπεσταλμένοις ἐγώ, μᾶλλον δέ, ἀμφότεροι τοῖς τε ἐπεσταλμένοις τοῖς τε δοθησομένοις· σεμνότεροι γὰρ ἀμφοτέροις ἀμφότεροι. 5. δεῖ δέ σε τὸν φόβον Ἀριστοφάνους μαθεῖν, ὅπως ἂν καὶ γελάσαις. τῶν τις εἰσιέναι παρὰ σὲ δείλης εἰωθότων ἥκων ἐπὶ θύρας, εἶτα κωλυθεὶς ὡς σοῦ τινα ποιοῦντος λόγον ἤγγειλεν ἡμῖν, καὶ φόβος εὐθὺς μὴ παλαῖσαι προελόμενος πρὸς τὸν λόγον καταβάλῃς μὲν τὸν διδάσκαλον, Ἀριστοφάνει δὲ τὸ Νείλου περιστήσῃς κακόν. 6. δρόμος οὖν παρὰ τὸν καλὸν Ἐλπίδιον· ὁ δὲ μαθὼν ἐφ' ᾧ δεδοίκαμεν ἀνεκάγχασεν. εἶθ' οὕτως ἀνεπνεύσαμεν καὶ μικρὸν ὕστερον δεχόμεθα τὴν καλὴν ἐπιστολήν.

---

[e] Amalthea, the goat who suckled Zeus, translated to form the constellation. Various explanations were current

rising of the Goat in heaven who achieves everything, when I achieve supreme success without pressing for it, and if I am in need of any good thing, the emperor is ready for the favour, behaving like the goddess in the sky.[e] 4. Your letter, then, will be attached to the oration informing the sons of Greece that my bolt was not discharged in vain, and Aristophanes will take pride in my writings and I in the letter you have sent, or rather both of us will take pride in what you sent and what you will grant, for both of us will enjoy more prestige for both reasons. 5. But you must understand what Aristophanes was afraid of; it may amuse you. One of those who normally attend you in the afternoon came to your doors and was refused entry, since it was said that you were composing a speech. He reported this to us, and immediately the alarm was raised that you had chosen to enter the lists against my oration, and would lay your teacher low and visit Aristophanes with the punishment you dealt Neilus.[f] 6. So we hurried to the noble Elpidius[g] who, on learning the reason for our trepidation, burst out laughing. So then we breathed again and shortly afterwards I received your wonderful letter.

in antiquity. The first observers of its rising were sure to obtain their wish, so Suid. *s.v.* αἴξ. Cf. *Paroem. Gr.* 1.8, 44.

[f] Cf. *Or.* 18.198; Julian *ELF* no. 82 (443c ff).

[g] Cf. *Or.* 14.35. *BLZG* (Helpidius) 170 (ii), *PLRE* 415 (6), *comes rerum privatarum.*

## 96. Δημητρίῳ

1. Δευτέρων φασὶν ἀμεινόνων ἤ, εἰ βούλει γε, εὐτυχεστέρων· ταύτῃ γὰρ κατῆρεν, οἶπερ ἐπέμπετο, καὶ οὐκ ἔλαφος ἀντὶ παρθένου. διάγομεν δὲ τὰ μὲν χαίροντες, τὰ δὲ οὐχ οὕτω διὰ τὴν τῆς ἀγορᾶς πενίαν. 2. λόγος δὲ ὁ μὲν εἰς τὴν πανήγυριν ἔτι μέλλει κρύπτεσθαι μὲν ἐθέλων, ἑλκόμενος δὲ εἰς μέσον παρὰ τοῦ βασιλέως καὶ ἴσως φανεῖται· δεῖ γὰρ ἐκεῖνον κρατεῖν· ἃ δ᾽ ἐπὶ τῷ πυρὶ καὶ οἷς ἔδρασεν ἅμα δάκρυσιν ἐφθεγξάμην, ἀπέσταλκά σοι. 3. τέχνης δὲ γέμων καὶ τῶν τοῖς πρεσβυτέροις πεποιημένων οὐ δήπου καταγνώσῃ τοῦ τὰ τοιαῦτα θρηνοῦντος.

---

[a] *Paroem. Gr.* 1.62.

[b] The miraculous rescue of Iphigeneia by Artemis, and her substitution of a deer for sacrifice by the Greeks at Aulis; cf. Eurip. *I.T.* 28. Libanius congratulates himself on his good relations with Julian.

[c] For the famine of winter 362/3 in Antioch, see Petit, *Vie Municipale* 109–118.

## 96. To Demetrius

1. Second thoughts are better, so the proverb[a] goes—or luckier, if you prefer it so, for here things have proceeded on their intended course, and no two ways about it.[b] But on some counts our life is happy, on others not so because of the shortages in the market.[c] 2. My panegyric still dallies on; it wants to stay under cover but it is being forced out into the open by the emperor.[d] It will probably make its appearance, for the emperor's will must prevail. I have sent you the lament I delivered upon the fire and its ravages.[e] 3. You have the craft and the compositions of earlier writers at your finger tips, but you will certainly not condemn a monody on such a subject.

[d] *Or.* 12. This letter is therefore written some little time after 1 Jan.

[e] The Monody on the Temple at Daphne, which survives only in fragments (*Or.* 60). Libanius is to serve as a member of the commission of enquiry into its cause, cf. *Letter* 107.

## 97. Ἀντιπάτρῳ

1. Ἔοικας ἀνδρὸς πονηροῦ γραμμάτων ἐπιθυμεῖν, εἴτε διὰ χρόνου μῆκος ἐπιλέλησμαι φίλου εἴθ' ὑπό τινος εὐπραξίας αὐτὸ τοῦτο ἔπαθον, καὶ θαυμάζω γε, ὅπως οὐ κέρδος ἡγήσω τοῦ τὰ τοιαῦτα νοσοῦντος ἀπηλλάχθαι. 2. ἐγὼ δὲ τῆς μὲν κοινῆς εὐτυχίας ἔχω τὸ μέρος ἀρχόμενος ὑπὸ βασιλέως ἀρίστου, τοῖς δὲ ἰδίοις οὐδένα παρελήλυθα τῶν γειτόνων. οὔτε γὰρ οἰκοδομῶ λαμπρῶς οὔτε γῆν ἐώνημαι πολλὴν οὔθ' ὑπὸ ῥαβδούχων παραπέμπομαι παιόντων καὶ φοβούντων οὐδ' ὑπισχνοῦμαι μεγάλα οὐδ' ἐχθρὸν ἠμυνάμην. 3. τίνα τοίνυν ὄγκον ἑωρακὼς ὑβρίζεις; τίς μηνυτὴς ἢ τίς μάντεων τοῦτον ἔφρασέ σοι τὸν ὄγκον; εἴσειμι παρὰ τὸν βασιλέα καλούμενος, ἄλλως δὲ οὐδαμῶς, τοῦτο δὲ οὐ συνεχῶς. εἰσελθὼν ἀκούω

---

[a] F/Kr. no. 49, *BLZG* 77, *PLRE* 73 (1). A pagan, otherwise unknown, who had by early 363 resumed a long-interrupted acquaintance with a letter criticizing Libanius for his arrogant conduct under Julian and accusing him of feathering his own nest. Such criticisms he had to rebut for the rest of his life, e.g. *Letter* 124 (of 364), *Or.* 1.125 (of

## 97. To Antipater[a]

1. It seems that you are desirous of a letter from a rascal if either through lapse of time I have forgotten a friend or am affected in exactly the same way by success, and I am surprised that you do not think it to your advantage to be rid of a man with such an ailment. 2. I participate in the universal well-being, as a subject of an excellent emperor, but I have never in my private affairs outdone any of my neighbours. I go in for no ostentatious building;[b] I have not purchased much landed estate; I am not escorted by lictors who lash out with their staves and create alarm, nor yet do I make huge promises or revenge myself upon an enemy. 3. Where then is the arrogance that you insultingly see in me? What informer, what clairvoyant has told you of this arrogance? I attend the emperor upon invitation, and not otherwise, and then not all the time. On entering his presence, I listen to his words, for he is

374), *Or.* 2.8 (of 381), *Or.* 51.30 (of 388). This letter reveals that they were voiced even before Julian's death, and reflect the jockeying for position at court which is suggested by Libanius himself in *Or.* 1.123. Antipater (*pace PLRE*), disappointed of preferment to a priesthood by Julian, blamed Libanius for lack of support.

[b] That is, he does not behave like the average *honoratus* or *principalis,* whose passion for building, commended in *Or.* 11.227, is repeatedly criticized later, e.g. *Or.* 2.55, *Or.* 50.

λέγοντος, καὶ γάρ ἐστι Σειρήν, καὶ ὅ τι φθέγξαιτο, συγγράμματος τοῦτο οὐ χεῖρον. ἀμείνων γενόμενος τὴν γνώμην ἄπειμι παρακληθεὶς εἰς λόγους τοῖς τοῦ βασιλέως λόγοις. 4. οὗτοι τῶν εἰσόδων οἱ καρποί. τὸ δὲ 'τὸν δεῖνα μέν, ὦ βασιλεῦ, παῦσον ἄρχοντα, ὁ δεῖνα δὲ ἀρξάτω, καὶ τῷ μὲν γενέσθω τιμή, τὸν δὲ ἔκβαλε τῶν ὄντων,' ταῦτα δὴ τὰ ἐπὶ τοῦ Πραξίλλης Ἀδώνιδος οἴχεται. καὶ νῦν ὡς ἀληθῶς εἰς ἔργον ἥκει τὸ τοῦ κρατοῦντος ὄνομα. 5. οὐ μὴν ἀλλ', εἰ καὶ σφόδρα τις ἦν τῶν γε τοιούτων ἐξουσία, τῶν φευγόντων ἂν ἐγενόμην τὸν ὄγκον ὥσπερ τι φορτίον οὐ φορητόν. πιστεύοις δ' ἄν μοι δικαίως, εἰ μὴ ὅπερ αἰτιᾷ πέπονθας καὶ ἐπιλέλησαί μου τοῦ τρόπου. 6. καὶ μὴν κἀκεῖνό γε ἄτοπον εὔχεσθαι μὲν ζῆν ἐν τοῖς αὐτοῖς πράγμασι, καινὰ δὲ ποιεῖν καὶ οἷα οὔπω πρότερον. ἀνάμνησον γάρ με, τί σου γράμμα πρὸ τοῦδε πρὸς ἡμᾶς ἧκεν εἰς Συρίαν, ἀλλ' οὐκ ἂν ἔχοις. οὐκοῦν ἕτερος γέγονας καὶ αἰτῶν παρὰ τῶν θεῶν ὁ αὐτὸς εἶναι τέμνεις ἄλλην ὁδὸν ἑκὼν ἡδίω μὲν ἐμοί, ταῖς δὲ σαῖς εὐχαῖς μαχομένην. 7. ἀλλὰ ταύτην μὲν ἰὼν καὶ

[c] The Sirens of the Odyssey gave rise to this proverb applied to oratory, cf. Suid. *s.v.*

a Siren indeed;[c] any utterance of his is not inferior to a composition. Invited to his discourse, I depart with intellect improved by the emperor's discourse. 4. This is the fruit of my attendance. But anything like, "Sire, demote this man from office; promote that one," or "Let him enjoy honour, but expel the other from his property"—all that is just nonsense.[d] Now the term "ruler" really has become reality. 5. For all that, even if I enjoyed full authority in matters such as this, I would have been one to reject such arrogance as an intolerable burden, and you would fully believe me, were it not that your attitude is the same as the one you impute to me and that you have forgotten the way I behave. 6. Besides, it is stupid to pray to live in an unchanged environment and yet to go in for innovations previously unheard of. Remind me what letter of yours has ever up to now come to me in Syria—but you cannot. So you are the one who has altered: you pray the gods to remain the same, but yet of your own free will you strike out on another way: it may be more pleasant to me, but it conflicts with what you pray for. 7. But do not stop travel-

[d] Cf. Praxilla fr. 1 (=*Paroem. Gr.* 1.89). Praxilla of Sicyon, a 5th century poet, wrote of Adonis in the underworld. When he was asked what he missed from the world above, he replied the sun, the moon, cucumbers, apples, and pears—which became proverbial for its silliness. See also Suid. s.v. ἠλιθιάζω.

γράφων μὴ παύσαιο, βουλοίμην δ' ἂν σε καὶ περὶ ἡμῶν ἐπιεικεστέραν ζητεῖν αἰτίαν καὶ ὅταν γράμματα μὴ λάβῃς, μᾶλλον τοῖς διακόνοις ὡς ἠμεληκόσιν ἐγκαλεῖν ἢ τὸν φίλον νομίζειν εὐθὺς γεγονέναι κακόν, ὃς ἐβουλήθη μὲν σοὶ τὴν ἱερωσύνην γενέσθαι, τοῦ φθάσαντος δὲ ἡττήθη τοῦτ' αὐτὸ δίκαιον ἔχοντος τὸ προειληφέναι.

## 98. Ἰουλιανῷ αὐτοκράτορι

1. Ὅσα κατηγόρησα τῆς ὁδοῦ, καὶ γὰρ ἦν χαλεπή, τοσαῦτα ἐμαυτοῦ καὶ ἔτι πλείω ταχέως ἀναστρέψας, ἀλλ' οὐκ ἐπ' αὐτὸν ἐλθὼν τὸν σταθμὸν καὶ δοὺς ἐμαυτῷ τὸ καὶ τῆς ὑστεραίας ἅμα τῷ ἡλίῳ τὴν θείαν ἰδεῖν κεφαλήν. 2. καὶ γὰρ οὐδ' ἡ πόλις με εἶχε παραμυθεῖσθαι πράττουσα κακῶς. λέγω δὲ κακοπραγίαν οὐ τὴν τῶν ὠνίων σπάνιν, ἀλλ' ὅτι πονηρὰ καὶ κακὴ καὶ ἀχάριστος κέκριται καὶ δοκεῖ τῷ τηλικαύτην μὲν ἀρχήν, πλείω δὲ φρόνησιν κεκτημένῳ. 3. ἕως

[a] Julian left Antioch for his Persian campaign on 5 March 363, with threats and resentment against the Antiochenes (already pilloried in the *Misopogon*); Ammianus (23.2.3–5) sets the scene. The Antiochenes sought to make their peace, but Julian would have none of it.

ling it and writing to me; though I could wish you to look for some better grounded complaint against me, and when you do not receive a letter, to accuse our servants of negligence rather than jump to the conclusion that a friend of yours has played you false, when he wanted you to get the priesthood but was worsted by one who got there first and whose sole claim was that he had got there first.

## 98. To the Emperor Julian[a]

1. The complaints I made about my journey—and a toilsome one it was—I made, and more besides, against myself for returning so quickly and for not going as far as the actual post station and allowing myself, at the next day's dawn also, the sight of your revered person.[b] 2. And the city, in her misery, could give me no consolation either. And when I speak of misery, I do not mean the shortage of goods on sale, but that she has been judged base, wicked and ungrateful, and is believed so by him who possesses so mighty an empire and an intellect mightier yet. 3. Thus, while ever I

Despite this rebuff to the city's envoys, Libanius was to persist in his efforts to reconcile his city and his emperor with the composition and despatch of *Orations* 15 and 16, which however failed to reach him (*Or.* 17.37).

[b] The post station was Litarba (Jul. *Ep.* 98). Libanius, in frail health, escorted the emperor and his fellow citizens part of the way, but had turned back before the envoys received their final rebuff there.

μὲν οὖν Ἄλκιμός μοι παρῆν, εἶχον τὸν δεχόμενον τοὺς λόγους, ἐν οἷς ἐμαυτόν τε ᾐτιώμην καὶ περὶ τῆς εἰς ἐμαυτὸν παρὰ σοῦ διεξῄειν τιμῆς· ὡς δὲ ἐκεῖνος ἀπῆρε, τὴν ὀροφὴν ἐποιούμην ἀντὶ τοῦ φίλου. 4. πρὸς ἣν ἀναβλέπων κείμενος ἐπὶ τῆς κλίνης 'νῦν,' ἔλεγον, 'ὁ βασιλεὺς ἐκάλει· νῦν εἰσιὼν ἐκαθήμην, καὶ γὰρ τοῦτο ἐδίδου, νῦν ὑπὲρ τῆς πόλεως ἠγωνιζόμην, καὶ γὰρ τοῦτο ἐξῆν ὑπὲρ τῶν βασιλέα λελυπηκότων πρὸς βασιλέα λέγειν· ὁ δὲ ἐκράτει μὲν δίκαιά τε ἐγκαλῶν καὶ δυνάμενος εἰπεῖν, ἐγὼ δὲ φιλονεικῶν οὔτε ἐμισούμην οὔτε ἐξεβαλλόμην.' 5. τοιούτοις ἐμαυτὸν εὐωχῶ καὶ αἰτῶ παρὰ τῶν θεῶν πρῶτον μὲν σὲ ποιῆσαι κρείττω τῶν πολεμίων· ἔπειθ' ἡμῖν ἐνταῦθα δεῖξαι καθάπερ ἔμπροσθεν. 6. ἔστι τι καὶ τρίτον ἐν ταῖς εὐχαῖς, ὃ ἐκεῖνοι μὲν ἀκηκόασι, πρὸς σὲ δὲ οὐκ ἐρῶ· δεινὸς γὰρ σύ γε τὸ τρίτον τοῦθ' εὑρεῖν ἀπὸ τοῦ τὸν εὐχόμενον ἐμὲ κρύπτειν ὅπερ ηὐξάμην, καὶ δέδοικα δὴ μὴ τοὐναντίον αἰτήσῃς. 7. ἀλλὰ νῦν μὲν διάβαινε τοὺς ποταμοὺς καὶ ποταμοῦ φοβερώτερος ἔμπιπτε τοῖς

[c] The teacher from Nicomedeia, long friendly with Libanius and with Julian, had visited the court in Antioch in winter 362/3.

had Alcimus[c] with me, I had someone to listen to my utterances of self-criticism and narration of the honour conferred on me by you. Upon his departure, however, I addressed myself not to my friend, but to the ceiling. 4. I lay on my bed, looking up at it, and said to myself, "Now the emperor issued his invitation to me. Now I entered his presence and sat down, for even that he allowed me to do. Now I entered the lists on my city's behalf, for I was even allowed so to address the emperor on behalf of those who had upset the emperor. But he emerged the victor: his complaints were just and he had the ability to express them, but though I sought to oppose him, I was neither hated by him nor expelled from his presence." 5. Such are the thoughts on which I feast myself; and I pray the gods first to give you victory over your foes, and then to show you to us here, as before.[d] 6. There is also a third object in my prayers.[e] The gods have heard it, but I shall not disclose it to you, for you anyway are clever enough to discover this third thing from the fact that I, who pray for it, seek to conceal the object of my prayers, and so I am afraid that you will request its opposite. 7. But now cross your rivers,[f] and more dread than any river fall upon those archers,

[d] And so, give up the threat to transfer the imperial residence from Antioch to Tarsus when he returned from campaign.

[e] That he would remarry and have sons to complete his task; cf. *Or.* 17.32, 18.294.

[f] The Tigris and Euphrates, to attack the Persians (here archers).

τοξόταις, μετὰ ταῦτα δὲ βουλεύσῃ περὶ ὧν βεβουλεύσεσθαι φῄς. ἐμὲ δὲ εὐφραίνων μὴ κάμῃς οἷς ἔξεστι τὸν ἀπόντα· ὡς ἔγωγε ἐπιστελῶ προκαλούμενος γράμματα τὰ σὰ ἀπὸ μέσης μάχης πιστεύων ὅτι καὶ ταῦτ᾽ ἂν εἴη τῆς σῆς φύσεως τάττειν τε ὁμοῦ στρατὸν καὶ τιτρώσκειν καὶ ἐπιστέλλειν. 8. οὕτως ὑπὸ τοῦ σώματος ἀδικοῦμαι μέλλων ἀκούειν ἃ χρῆν ὁρᾶν· Σέλευκος δὲ ὁ μακάριος ὄψεται καλῶς προθεὶς καὶ γυναικὸς ἀγαθῆς καὶ παιδὸς ἀγαπητῆς τὴν ἀπὸ τοῦ τοιούτῳ βασιλεῖ διακονεῖν εὔκλειαν.

## 99. Νικοκλεῖ

1. Οὐκ ἄδηλον ὅτι δι᾽ ὅσων ἦλθες πόλεων, πάσας ἐνέπλησας τῶν ὑπὲρ ἡμῶν λόγων. καὶ γὰρ ἐνταῦθα, ὡς ἤρξω τοῦτο ποιεῖν, πάντα ὦτα ἐνέπλησας τῶν τε βουλομένων τῶν τε οὐκ ἐθελόντων, τοῖς μὲν χαριζόμενος, τοὺς δὲ ἀνιῶν· ὥστε θαυμάσαιμ᾽ ἂν εἰ μὴ παραπλήσια καὶ πρὸς τοὺς γεωργοὺς ἐβόας, ὅσοι μέχρι τῆς λεωφόρου τὰς αὔλακας ἔτεμνον. 2. ἐμοὶ δὲ μείζω μὲν ταῦτα τῆς Συρακουσίων δεκάτης, μικρῷ δὲ ἐλάττω τῶν

---

[a] For Nicocles, see *Letter* 23.

and thereafter take counsel upon the matters you say you intend to do. Never weary of giving me joy by whatever means possible while I am apart from you. I will write to you, inviting letters from you written in the midst of battle, for I am confident that your genius has the capacity simultaneously to deploy your array, to inflict casualties and to write a letter. 8. My physical health lets me down so badly that I shall listen to what I ought to see. But our blessed Seleucus will see it, for he has nobly preferred the glory of serving such a monarch to his good wife and beloved daughter.[g]

[g] Cf. *Letter* 142. He was to compose a history of the expedition.

## 99. To Nicocles[a]

1. Quite clearly you filled all the cities through which you journeyed with eloquence on my behalf, for here, when you began to do so, you filled every ear both of those who wished it and of those who did not, delighting some and annoying others.[b] So I would be surprised that you did not broadcast similar stories even to the peasants who drove their furrows to the edge of the highway. 2. This means more to me than the tithes of Syracuse,[c] and falls

[b] He had recently visited Julian in Antioch as envoy of Constantinople after riots there in winter 362/3 (cf. *Ep.* 1368).

[c] For the proverbial wealth of Syracuse see Strabo vi.2.4, and of its tithes, *Paroem. Gr.* 1.418 and 455.

εἰς τὸν ὑμέτερον νομοθέτην ὑπὸ τοῦ θεοῦ λεχθέντων. ὃς γὰρ οὔτ᾽ ἂν κολακεύσαις, οὐδὲ γὰρ βασιλέως σύ γε τύχην, μὴ ὅτι γε σοφιστήν, οὔτ᾽ ἂν ἀγνοήσαις λόγου κάλλος ἢ αἶσχος, πῶς οὐκ ἐπαινῶν τόν γε ἐπαινούμενον μέγαν ποιεῖς καὶ λαμπρὸν ἐν Ἑλλήνων χοροῖς; 3. ἡμεῖς δὲ σὲ ἐπαινοῦντες μὲν οὐ παυόμεθα, ποιοῦμεν δὲ παραπλήσιον ὥσπερ ἂν εἴ τις πυροὺς χρησάμενος ἀποδοίη κριθὰς αὐτῷ τῷ μέτρῳ. τὸ μὲν γὰρ μέτρον οὗτος ἐτήρησεν, ἀπέδωκε δὲ οὐκ εἰς ἅπαν. 4. οὐδὲ γὰρ ἐκεῖνος, οὗ νῦν ἐμνήσθην, ὁ Λακωνικὸς τιμηθεὶς ὑπὸ τοῦ χρησμοῦ εἰ τὸν Πύθιον αὐτὸς ἀντεκόσμησεν ἔπεσιν, ἴσον ἂν ἦν, οὐδ᾽ εἰ πάνυ πολλὰ ἦν τὰ ἔπη. 5. ἐνταῦθα μὲν οὖν λειπόμεθα, φιλοῦντες δὲ ἢ νικῶμεν ἢ πάντως γε οὐ νικώμεθα. πρὸς τοσοῦτον δὲ ἥκω τοῦ θαρρεῖν σοι καὶ οἴεσθαι παντὸς ἂν τυχεῖν, ὥστε καὶ τῶν ἡμετέρων φίλων τοὺς ἐκεῖσε ἰόντας καὶ δεομένους φίλων ἐπὶ τὰς σὰς πέμπω θύρας ὡς σοῦ γνώμην μὲν τὴν ἐμὴν εἰς αὐτοὺς μιμησομένου, ῥώμῃ δὲ μείζονι χρησομένου. 6. δι᾽ οὗ δὲ ταύτην λαμβάνεις τὴν ἐπιστολήν, μὴ ἕνα νόμιζε τῶν πολλῶν, ἀλλ᾽ υἱέος μοι διαφέρειν οὐδέν. αἴτιον δὲ

only little short of that greeting given to your lawgiver by the god.[d] You would not go in for flattery—not even of an emperor's station, let alone of a sophist—nor would you fail to recognise beauty or deficiency of style, so obviously by your commendations you make the object of them great and glorious among the companies of the Hellenes. 3. I never cease commending you, but my behaviour is very like that of one who borrows wheat and pays back barley to the same measure, for he, while keeping to the measure, does not make repayment in full.[e] 4. Not even that Laconian whom I have just mentioned would have been equal to the task if, after being honoured by the oracle, he had himself repaid Pythian Apollo in verse, however many the verses. 5. In this, then, I am an also-ran, but as regards affection I am a clear winner, or in any case, no loser. Such is my confidence in you and my belief in complete success that I also send to your door those of my friends who travel your way and need friends to help them, since I am sure that you will adopt my attitude towards them, but will employ a greater effectiveness. 6. The bearer of this letter do not regard as one of the common run, but as no different from a son to me. The reason lies in his modesty, his

[d] Nicocles was a Spartan (*Or.* 1.31). Hence the flattering reference to the greeting given by Apollo to Lycurgus the lawgiver (Herod. 1.65.2).

[e] Thus κριθοφαγία was noted as a military punishment as early as Polybius (6.38.4).

<ἡ>[1] ἐπιείκεια καὶ τὸ αἰδεῖσθαί τε καὶ δόξης ἐπιθυμεῖν καὶ λαβεῖν ἐπαινέτας τοὺς γέροντας, ὧν καὶ πρῶτον καὶ μάλιστα τὸν θεῖον τὸν ἐμόν, ὃν εἰδὼς εἰδείης ἂν καὶ τοῦτον· οὐ γὰρ ἂν ἐκεῖνος τὸν οὐκ ἀγαθὸν ἐθαύμασε. 7. μέλει δὲ καὶ Μοδέστῳ τοῦ νεανίσκου τὸ μὲν πρῶτον ὑπ᾽ ἐμοῦ παρακληθέντι, μετὰ δὲ τὴν πεῖραν ὑφ᾽ ἑαυτοῦ. ὄψει δὲ αὐτὸν τὰ πατρὸς εἰς Ὑπερέχιον τουτονὶ σπουδάζοντα, ἀλλ᾽ οὐδὲν οἷον εἰς προστασίαν ὁ δαιμόνιος Νικοκλῆς· οὕτω γὰρ κἀκεῖνος αὐτὸν ἐπαινέσεται σπουδάζων, εἰ ὅτι καὶ σοὶ χαριεῖται γνοίη. 8. μαθέτω τοίνυν οὗτος ἀκούσας διαρρήδην ἐκ τοῦ σοῦ στόματος ὡς προσιὼν οὐκ ἐνοχλήσει, μᾶλλον δὲ ὡς, εἰ δι᾽ ἄλλου τῶν αὑτοῦ τι θήσεται, σύ γε ἠδίκησαι καὶ λήψῃ τοῦδε δίκην.

[1] <ἡ> ins. F.

[f] Promoted by Julian in 362 from *Comes Orientis* to prefect of Constantinople, where he, like Nicocles here, was once more solicited to forward the career of Hyperechius (*Ep.* 804). Hyperechius himself acts as messenger to Nico-

respect, his desire for renown, and his success in winning the commendations of his elders, and first and foremost of them, of my uncle. If you had known him, you would know the bearer too, for he would never have admired anyone but the good. 7. Modestus[f] too is interested in the lad, at first at my prompting, but later, upon closer acquaintance, at his own. You will see him showing a father's zeal for Hyperechius here, but that is as nothing compared with the support provided by the gifted Nicocles; for even Modestus will be more zealous in his commendation of him, if he realizes that he is obliging you also. 8. So let the bearer understand when he hears it explicitly stated from your own mouth that he will cause you no annoyance by presenting himself to you, and better still, that if he transacts his business through any other person, you will feel yourself aggrieved and punish him for it.

cles, Modestus, and Clearchus, as well as to other notables and officials en route (*BLZG* 396). He had arrived in Antioch too late and had missed the chance of gaining favour there, and had, on Libanius' advice, posted to Constantinople to bring influence to bear in the meantime until Julian returned from campaign (*Ep.* 805).

## 100. Ἰουλιανῷ αὐτοκράτορι

1. Ἐγὼ τὴν ἀρχὴν τὴν Ἀλεξάνδρου τὸ πρῶτον ἐδυσχέραινον, ὁμολογῶ, καὶ τὸ τοὺς ἀτιμοτάτους[1] τῶν παρ' ἡμῖν ἐπιμελεῖσθαι τούτων δὴ τὸ πρὶν οὐ τῶν ἐνδόξων ὕβριν ἡγούμην καὶ οὐκ ἄρχοντος ἔργον, ἀλλὰ καὶ τὴν εἰς χρήματα ζημίαν πυκνήν τινα οὖσαν ἀσθενεστέραν ᾤμην ποιήσειν τὴν πόλιν, πλέον δὲ οὐδέν. 2. νῦν δὲ ὁ καρπός τε ἀνεδόθη τῆς τραχύτητος καὶ ᾄδω παλινωδίαν. οἱ γὰρ δὴ πρὸ[2] μεσημβρίας ἐκεῖνοι λελουμένοι καὶ κοιμώμενοι Λακωνικοί τινες γεγένηνται τοὺς τρόπους καὶ καρτερικοί, καὶ πρὸς τῇ ἡμέρᾳ τῆς νυκτὸς οὐκ ὀλίγον πονοῦσιν ὥσπερ προσηλωμένοι ταῖς Ἀλεξάνδρου θύραις. 3. ὁ δ' εἰ βοήσειεν ἔνδοθεν, σείεται πάντα, ὥστ' οὐδὲ σιδήρου μοι δεήσεσθαι δοκεῖν τοῦ ἀπειλεῖν ἀποχρῶντος ἐνεργούς τε ὁμοῦ καὶ σώφρονας ποιεῖν τοὺς ἀργούς τε καὶ θρασεῖς. 4. τεθεράπευται δὲ καὶ ἡ Καλλιόπη τῆς σῆς γνώμης ἀξίως οὐ μόνον ἱπποδρο-

[1] ἀτιμοτάτους F., conj. Re. ἐντιμοτάτους Wolf (Mss.)
[2] πρὸ F., conj. Re. πρὸς Wolf (Mss.)

---

[a] This is the last extant letter of Libanius to Julian,

## 100. To the Emperor Julian[a]

1. At first, I confess, I disapproved of Alexander's[b] appointment to office. When the least regarded among us were put in charge of matters which in times past were discredited, I believed that to be a scandal and no part of a governor's job. Besides, I thought that the repeated financial losses would weaken the city and have no other result. 2. But now the fruits of his severity have appeared, and I make my recantation. Those fellows who used to be bathed and abed before noon have become really Spartan in their habits[c] and tough, and they spend not only their days but no small part of their nights at their job, as though nailed to Alexander's doors. 3. If he calls out from inside, everything is set all a flutter, so that it seems to me that he will have no need of the sword at all: his threats are enough to make the lazy and the insolent industrious and well-behaved. 4. Calliope too has had her share of honour in a manner according to your wish, not just in horse races but also in the pleasures of

written after the festival of Calliope, tutelary goddess and Fortune of Antioch, held early in May, when Julian was deep inside Persian territory.

[b] Appointed *consularis Syriae* as a means of punishing Antioch, to bring the unruly city under control (Amm. Marc. 23.2.3). He was to apply an aggressively pagan policy.

[c] Proverbial, then as now.

μίαις, ἀλλὰ καὶ ταῖς ἐπὶ σκηνῆς χάρισι καὶ τέθυται ἐν θεάτρῳ τῇ θεῷ καὶ μετετάξατο παρ' ἡμᾶς οὐ μικρὸν μέρος, ὥσθ' ἥ τε βοὴ λαμπρὰ θεοί τε ἐν τῇ βοῇ καλοῦνται. δηλῶν δὲ ὁ ἄρχων ὡς χαίρει τῇ τοιαύτῃ βοῇ μείζω ταύτην ἀπὸ πλειόνων προκαλεῖται. 5. τοσοῦτόν ἐστιν, ὦ βασιλεῦ, μαντικὴ τοῖς ἀνθρώποις διδάσκουσα, τί ποιῶν ἄν τις ἄριστα διοικοίη καὶ οἶκον καὶ πόλιν καὶ ἔθνος καὶ βασιλείαν.

---

[d] Julian's policy was to ensure, by the reinstitution of these sacrifices and acclamations, that the normal round of

## 101. Ἀκακίῳ

1. Ἡ πόλις ἐκείνη ἡ λαμπρὰ καὶ μεγάλη, ᾗ καὶ σαυτὸν ἔδειξας[1] καὶ παρ' ᾗ τετίμησαι, πολλοῖς κακοῖς διασέσεισται λιμῷ τε μεμαχημένη καὶ βασιλεῖ δόξασα εἶναι κακοῦργος, καὶ διετελέσαμεν ἱκετεύοντες μέν, ἐκφυγεῖν δὲ τὴν δόξαν οὐ δυνηθέντες. 2. σὺ δὲ ἄρα εὐδαίμων εὖ πραττούσης μὲν ἀπολαύσας, τῶν ἑτέρων δὲ οὐ κοινωνήσας, πλὴν εἰ ταύτῃ σέ τις κεκοινωνηκέναι φαίη, ὅτι ἃ φερομένης καλῶς ἐπέπρακτο ἄν σοι, ταῦτα τῇ τοῦ

[1] ᾗ καὶ σαυτὸν ἔδειξας F. καὶ ᾗ σαυτὸν ἐδίδαξας Wolf (Mss.).

the stage. Sacrifices were performed to the goddess in the theatre, and many people have come over to our side, so that the applause rings loud and the gods are invoked in that applause; and the governor, by showing his pleasure at cries of this kind, invites more of them from more people.[d] 5. Such, Sire, is the power of divination which teaches mankind the means by which family, city, province, and empire may best be administered.

entertainment was desecularized. Alexander's energetic application of this as a means of proselytizing was immediately successful.

## 101. To Acacius[a]

1. That great and glorious city, to which you displayed yourself also, and by which you have been honoured, has been buffeted by many blows. She has been beset by famine and is regarded as criminal by our emperor,[b] and we have continued, despite our supplications, unable to escape this ill repute. 2. Lucky you! You enjoyed its prosperity and had no part of the opposite, save insofar as it may be said that you partake to this extent, that what you would have accomplished here if things went well with her has been prevented by the distemper of the

[a] Libanius' one-time rival in Antioch had been settled in Caesarea since 361.

[b] Cf. *Letter* 98.2 and *Ep.* 813.2. The famine is first recorded as ended in *Ep.* 824.

καιροῦ χαλεπότητι διεκωλύθη. 3. ὅπῃ γὰρ ἔλθοιμεν, ἀθυμία πανταχοῦ, καὶ οἱ λόγοι μάτην ἀνηλοῦντο· προσιόντων δὲ οἱ δοῦναι κύριοι τὰς θύρας ἀπέκλειον, ὅπως ἡμῶν μὴ ἀκούοιεν τῆς φωνῆς· εἰς τοσοῦτον δυνάμεως ἥκομεν. ἀλλ' ἢν θεῶν τις λύσῃ τὸν ζόφον, ἔργου τε αὖθις ἑξόμεθα καὶ ἴσως οὐκ ἀτυχήσομεν.

## 102. Θεμιστίῳ

1. Ὤιμην ἀφεῖσθαι πάσης αἰτίας μετ' ἐκείνην τὴν ἐπιστολὴν καὶ γνώμην εἶναι σοὶ πρὸς ἐμὲ τὴν πρὸ τῶν ἐγκλημάτων. σὺ δ' ἄρα ἐχθρόν τέ με ἡγοῦ καὶ δίκην ἐπιθήσειν ἔμελλες. 2. καίτοι ὅ γε θαυμαστὸς Ἁρποκρατίων μένειν ἔφασκε τὴν παλαιὰν φιλίαν θαρρεῖν τε ἐκέλευεν ὡς σοῦ γε οὐ μεταβεβλημένου. ἐξηπατώμεθα δέ, ὡς ἔοικεν, ἐγώ τε κἀκεῖνος οὐ μικρόν τινα χρόνον, καὶ ἴσως ἐκέρδαινον ἀπατώμενος, εἰ τὸ μὴ λυπεῖσθαι κέρδος ἦν. 3. ὡς δὲ ἦλθεν ὁ λόγος καὶ διεδόθη

[a] Cf. Bouchery pp. 217–220. In 362 a rift occurred in the friendship of Libanius and Themistius. Themistius had taken amiss comments made by Libanius and reported back concerning his conduct and had written a letter of complaint, to which *Ep.* 793 (here referred to)

times. 3. For wherever I go, there is despondency everywhere, and my eloquence is spent in vain. At my approach, people capable of granting my request shut their doors so as not to hear my voice, so far has my influence shrunk. But if some god disperses the cloud, I shall apply myself again to the task, and perhaps I shall not fail.[c]

[c] He has been engaged upon the composition of *Or.* 15, addressed to the absent Julian, and of *Or.* 16, reproving his fellow citizens. His vulnerability in Julian's absence is here marked, his lack of influence with the *consularis* Alexander being dramatically exaggerated.

## 102. To Themistius

1. I thought that after that letter I was freed of every charge and that your attitude towards me was as it was before the complaints were made.[a] Yet it seems that you thought me your enemy and were going to punish me. 2. However the admirable Harpocration[b] assured me that our long-standing friendship still remained and bade me be of good cheer, for your feelings at least had not changed. But, so it seems, we were deluded, he and I, for no little time, and perhaps I gained from my delusion, if it be a gain not to suffer pain. 3. But when your

sought to make amends, unsuccessfully it appears.

[b] An Egyptian poet and rhetor who was teaching in Antioch up to 358, and then moved to Constantinople, cf. *Letter* 29.

μετὰ τῶν γραμμάτων καὶ ἤκουον τοῦ δεῖνος 'ἐμοὶ πέπομφε βιβλίον Θεμίστιος' λέγοντος καὶ τοῦ δεῖνος ταὐτὸ καὶ τρίτου καὶ τετάρτου καὶ μόνος ἦν Ἀργείων ἀγέραστος, τότ' ἔφην πρὸς ἐμαυτὸν ὡς οὔπω διαλλαγαί, κρατεῖ δὲ ὁ θυμὸς ἔτι καὶ παρόν μοι λαβεῖν τὸν λόγον οὐκ ἔλαβον, ὅπως μὴ γνοίην ἃ μὴ ἐθέλεις, καὶ ὠδυνώμην μὲν ἀπεχόμενος θοίνης οὕτω καλῆς, ἠνειχόμην δέ, ὅπως μὴ γένηταί τι ὧν οὐκ ἐβούλου. 4. εἰ μὲν οὖν ἔτι χαλεπαίνειν οἴει δεῖν, μὴ ἐπίστελλε μηδ' εἰρωνεύου· τῆς ὀργῆς δὲ εἰ πέπαυσαι, πρόσθες ἐπιστολῇ τὸν λόγον. ἥδιον γὰρ ἀναγνώσομαι πέμποντος αὐτοῦ τοῦ δημιουργοῦ τὸ τέχνημα.

---

[c] An oration now lost. O. Seeck and H. Schenkl—"Eine verlorene Rede des Themistios," *Rh. Mus.* 61 (1906): 554–544—identified it with the Φιλόπολις, the protheoria of which they published, interpreting it as the introduction of an oration addressed to Julian. However, Dagron (*L'empire romain d'orient* 218–229) shows conclusively that it introduces *Oration* 4, which was addressed to Constantius in 357. The oration to Julian to which Libanius here refers was, in fact, a panegyric composed by Themistius and sent to Julian in celebration of his 4th consulship (1 Jan. 363). Since it remained unknown in Antioch until

oration[c] arrived and was distributed along with your letters, I heard first one, then another, yet a third and a fourth saying "Themistius has sent me a copy of his work," and I "alone of the Argives was without a prize."[d] Then I told myself that there was no reconciliation yet, that your resentment still held sway, and that, though I could have received your oration, I had not done so, so that I should not get to know things you do not want me to know. For all my pain at being excluded from such a glorious feast,[e] I endured it so that nothing should seem contrary to your wishes. 4. Now, if you think that you must still be angry, do not write but have done with pretence. If however your anger has ceased, append a copy of your speech to a letter,[f] for I shall read the composition with all the more pleasure if it is sent by its creator.

the arrival of these copies, it must have been sent to Julian to reach him after he had left Antioch in March.

[d] Homer *Il.* 1.119.

[e] Plat. *Phaedr.* 236e.

[f] Themistius sent a copy; cf. *Letter* 116.

## 103. Βηλαίῳ

1. Ἐγένετό μοι φίλος Ὠρίων, ὅτε εὐτύχει· νῦν δὲ πράττει μὲν ἐκεῖνος κακῶς, τηρῶ δὲ ἐγὼ τὴν γνώμην· αἰσχύνομαι γὰρ εἰ καὶ αὐτὸς ὑπὸ τῇ παροιμίᾳ γενήσομαι καὶ δόξω φεύγειν ἠτυχηκότα φίλον.[1] 2. ταῦτα δὲ τρὶς ἤδη πρὸς σὲ βοῶ· τὸ μὲν πρῶτον ἐν γράμμασιν, ἔπειτα πρὸς παρόντα, νῦν δὲ ὥσπερ τὸ πρῶτον. καὶ γὰρ εἰ διέστηκεν ἡμῶν τῇ περὶ τὸ θεῖον δόξῃ, βλάπτοι μὲν ἂν αὐτόν, εἴπερ ἐξηπάτηται, παρὰ δὲ τῶν συνήθων οὐκ ἂν εἰκότως πολεμοῖτο. 3. ἠξίουν δὲ ἔγωγε καὶ τοὺς νῦν ἐγκειμένους αὐτῷ μεμνῆσθαι ὧν αὐτοῖς ἐβοήθησε πολλάκις καὶ μᾶλλον ἀποδοῦναι χάριν ἢ ζητεῖν κατορύξαι ζῶντα τὸν εὐεργέτην· οὗ τὴν συγγένειαν ἐλαύνοντες πάλαι καὶ Μυσῶν

[1] Schol. Ath. in marg.: οὕτω γὰρ ἡ παροιμία λέγει· φίλου κακῶς πράττοντος ἐκποδὼν φίλοι ( = Menander *Mon.* 32)

---

[a] F/Kr. no. 51. *BLZG* 97, *PLRE* 160. Belaeus, a rhetor and devout pagan, was governor of Arabia in 362/3. The metropolis of the province, Bostra, was riddled with religious faction. Julian issued an edict strictly ordering both sides to refrain from looting and physical violence (1 Aug. 362; *ELF* 114, 435d ff; cf. Sozomen *H.E.* 5.15.11 f). The paying-off of old scores continued nonetheless, and

## 103. To Belaeus[a]

1. Orion was my friend in the days of his prosperity. Now that things go badly with him, I maintain the same attitude, for I am ashamed to lay myself open to the proverbial stricture and be thought to desert a friend in need.[b] 2. Three times now I have made this point to you: first by letter, then to you personally, and now as on the first occasion. Even if he differs from me on matters of religious belief, it is his own look-out if he has been misled,[c] but he could not reasonably be an object of hostility to his acquaintances. 3. I beg his present persecutors to remember the number of times he has assisted them and to repay his kindness rather than to bury their benefactor alive;[d] but for a long time now they have been harrying his kinsfolk and descending on their property like a

Orion, a Christian ex-governor, and his family were driven from their property, under the pretext of reclaiming temple possessions. Libanius certainly showed consistency in support of his friend Orion.

[b] The scholia quote Menander (*Monostich*: 32): "when a friend is in trouble, his friends disappear."

[c] As in his previous letter to Belaeus (*Ep.* 763), Libanius uses the wording of Julian's letter to the Bostraeans (*ELF* 114, 436d: τὰ γοῦν πλήθη τὰ παρὰ τῶν λεγομένων κληρικῶν ἐξηπατημένα), while also asserting that Orion's one-time friends had now become his enemies.

[d] Cf. Herod. 3.35, 7.114. Xen. *Anab.* 5.8.11; *Mem.* 1.2.55.

λείαν πεποιημένοι τἀκείνων τελευτῶντες ἥκουσιν ἐπὶ τὸ τοῦδε σῶμα ὡς ταύτῃ γε χαριούμενοι τοῖς θεοῖς, πλεῖστον ἀπέχοντες τοῦ περὶ τὰς τῶν θεῶν τιμὰς νόμου. 4. ἀλλὰ τοὺς μὲν πολλοὺς οὐδὲν θαυμαστὸν ἄνευ λογισμοῦ φέρεσθαι καὶ ποιεῖν ἀντὶ τῶν καλῶν τὰ ἡδέα· σὲ δὲ τὸν ἀπὸ τοῦ παιδεύοντος θρόνου πρὸς τὸν ψήφου κύριον ἥκοντα κατέχειν τοὺς τοιούτους εἰκὸς καὶ πείθειν ἢ ἔργῳ κωλύειν. 5. εἰ μὲν οὖν ἔχει χρήματα τῶν ἱερῶν Ὡρίων καὶ δύναιτ' ἂν ἐκτῖσαι, παιέσθω, κεντείσθω, τὰ τοῦ Μαρσύου πασχέτω, δίκαιος γάρ, εἰ παρὸν ἀποδόντα ἀπηλλάχθαι χρημάτων ἐστὶν ἥττων καὶ πάντ' ἂν ὑπομείνειεν, ὅπως ἔχοι χρυσίον· εἰ δ' ἐστὶν Ἶρος καὶ πεινῶν ἐκοιμήθη πολλάκις, οὐκ οἶδα, τί ἂν κερδαίνοιμεν ἀπὸ τῆς αἰκίας, δι' ἣν εὐδοκιμήσει παρὰ τοῖς ἡμῖν ἐναντίοις. 6. εἰ δὲ δὴ καὶ ἀποθανεῖν αὐτῷ δεδεμένῳ συμβαίη, σκόπει ποῖ τὸ πρᾶγμα ἥξει, καὶ ὅρα μὴ πολλοὺς Μάρκους ἀποφήνῃς. Μάρκος ἐκεῖνος

---

[e] An argument repeated from *Ep.* 763.6. For the proverb see *Letter* 81 note c.

[f] The provincial governor is for Libanius δικαστής, for the Codes *iudex*.

[g] τῶν ἱερῶν Ὡρίων, an evocative word-play.

[h] Marsyas, flayed alive by Apollo for daring to compete with him in music.

sitting duck,[e] and finally they attack him in person, as though in this way they will please the gods, though they are miles away from the usual manner of honouring the gods. 4. It is no surprise that the common folk should behave irrationally and should not do what is right but what is pleasant: but you, who have stepped from the teacher's chair to the judgement seat,[f] can be expected to restrain such as them, and to apply persuasion or actual coercion to them. 5. Now, if Orion is in possession of any temple property[g] and could repay it, beat him by all means, lash him, flay him like Marsyas,[h] for he would deserve it, if he is so influenced by money and is ready to put up with anything so as to keep his gold, when he could pay up and have done. But if he is beggared[i] and has often gone to bed hungry, I do not know what advantage we would gain from flogging him. That will merely raise his prestige among our opponents. 6. In fact, if it should happen that he should even die while in prison, just consider where matters will end. See that you do not produce any number of people like Marcus. That fellow Marcus[j] was racked and flogged, his beard

[i] Irus (Homer *Od.* 18.6) became the stock personification of beggary.

[j] Marcus, bishop of Arethusa in Syria, had been responsible for the destruction of the temple there, and had suffered severe physical punishment for it; cf. Sozomen *H.E.* 5.10, Greg. Naz. *Or.* 4.91, Theodoret *H.E.* 3.7.6 ff.

κρεμάμενος καὶ μαστιγούμενος καὶ τοῦ πώγωνος αὐτῷ τιλλομένου πάντα ἐνεγκὼν ἀνδρείως νῦν ἰσόθεός ἐστι ταῖς τιμαῖς, κἂν φανῇ που, περιμάχητος εὐθύς. καὶ ταῦτα εἰδὼς βασιλεὺς ἀλγεῖ μὲν ὑπὲρ τοῦ νεώ, τὸν δὲ ἄνδρα οὐκ ἀπέκτεινε. 7. νόμισον δὴ νόμον τὴν Μάρκου σωτηρίαν καὶ τὸν Ὠρίωνα σώσας ἔκπεμπε μὴ θαυμαζόμενον. φησὶ μὲν γὰρ οὐδὲν ἡρπακέναι, κείσθω δὲ εἰληφώς. τί οὖν; εἰ πάντα ἀνήλωται, μέταλλα χρυσίου προσδοκᾷς εὑρήσειν ἐν τῷ δέρματι; 8. μή, πρὸς Διός, ἑταῖρε καὶ δικαστά, μὴ σύ τι πάθῃς ἀβέλτερον, ἀλλ', εἰ δεῖ δίκην αὐτὸν ὑποσχεῖν, ἄτρωτος περινοστείτω μηδεμίαν ἔχων εἰς φιλοτιμίαν ἀφορμήν.

## 104. Ἀλεξάνδρῳ

1. Ἠισθόμην σε συμβουλὰς ἡδέως δεχόμενον καὶ ταῦτα εὖ ἥκοντα φρενῶν, ὡς μηδὲν δεῖσθαι τῶν ἃ δεῖ ποιεῖν ἐρούντων. καί μοι δοκεῖς ζηλῶσαι τὸν Εὐαγόραν τοῦ ἐπαίνου καὶ βουληθῆναι δοῦναι τοῖς γράφουσιν ἴσα καὶ περὶ σοῦ διελθεῖν. 2. τοῦτό με πείθει λέγειν ὅ τι ἂν ἡγῶμαι συμφέρειν. πρὸς παρόντα μὲν οὖν λέγω, πρὸς ἀπόντα δὲ γράφω. σὺ δ' οὕτω μου χαίρεις τοῖς γράμμα-

was plucked out, and yet he endured it all bravely, and now is almost divine in prestige. Whenever he makes an appearance, people jostle to see him. And that is what our emperor knew: though he grieved for the temple, he did not execute the fellow. 7. So take Marcus' survival as your rule: leave Orion unharmed and do not release him to be an object of admiration. He says that he has taken nothing illegally—but suppose he had! What then? If it is all spent, do you expect to find a gold mine in his hide? 8. No, by Zeus, entertain no feelings of inhumanity, my friend and governor:[k] if he must be punished, let him go home unmarked with no cause for giving himself airs.

[k] Cf. Dem. *Fals. Leg.* 338—a reference most cogently directed to a teacher of rhetoric, as Belaeus had been.

## 104. To Alexander

1. I realize that you gladly accept advice even though so well endowed with intelligence as to have no need of people to tell you what you should do. It seems to me that you envy Euagoras his praise and want to allow writers to give a similar account of yourself too.[a] 2. This encourages me to tell you of whatever is, in my opinion, to your advantage; and you are so pleased with my letters that even at

[a] Isocr. *Euag.* 3.

σιν, ὥστ᾽ αὐτὰ καὶ δειπνῶν τοῖς δαιτυμόσιν εἰσάγειν, ὃ ποιήσειν οἶμαί σε καὶ περὶ ταῦτα. 3. ἐπέβης Ἀπαμείας εὖ ποιῶν τῆς τοῦ Διὸς φίλης, ἣ τὸν Δία τιμῶσα διέμεινεν, ὅτ᾽ ἦσαν τιμωρίαι τοῦ τιμᾶν τοὺς θεούς. φύσις δὲ τῶν ἀνδρῶν τοιάδε· παρακαλούμενοι μὲν σὺν ἐπαίνοις κἂν λύκου πτερὰ δοῖεν κἂν ὀρνίθων γάλα· προσούσης δὲ ὕβρεως ταραχθέντες ὑπ᾽ ἀθυμίας οὐδ᾽ ἂν πρὸς τὰ ῥᾷστα τῶν ἔργων ἀρκοῖεν, ῥᾳδίως δ᾽ ἂν οἰκίας ἀφέντες καὶ θύρας ἀνοίξαντες καὶ γῆς ἀποστάντες φέροιντο οἷ συμβαίνοι. ἐνθυμοῦ δή, πότερον βέλτιον ἥμερον φανέντα τὰ ἔργα ἐπιτελεῖν ἢ χαλεπὸν ὄντα χαλεπὰς τὰς πράξεις ποιεῖν. 4. ἀλλ᾽ ὅπως μὴ βοήσῃς πρὸς τὸ ῥηθὲν μηδὲ ὀργισθῇς· κρατήσεις μὲν γὰρ καὶ ἀκόντων, μακρῷ δὲ ἄμεινον ἑκόντων. τί γὰρ ἥδιον τοῦ τὰ μὲν ἔργα πράττεσθαι, τοὺς δὲ ἄνδρας ἑορτάζειν; ἑορτὴ δέ ἐστιν οὐχ ὅταν θύῃ τις στένων καὶ δεσμὸν ἐλπίζων, ἀλλ᾽ ὅταν ἀκριβῶς ἀπηλλαγμένος δέους σπένδῃ καὶ θύῃ. 5. ἄφελε δὴ καὶ τοῦ τῆς φωνῆς μεγέ-

[b] Apamea contained a strong pagan nucleus. Libanius records a celebration of the Olympia there in 361 (*Epp.* 663, 668). And a generation later, during the officially inspired attacks on the temples, the pagans maintained a guard; see Sozomen *H.E.* vii.15.

dinner you introduce them to your guests, as I think you will do with this one also. 3. You visited Apamea, and very properly, for she is dear to Zeus and continued to reverence Zeus when punishment were reserved for reverencing the gods.[b] But the character of the people is of this sort; if they are encouraged and praised, they will do anything—even the impossible:[c] but if force is applied, they become frantic with despair and are incapable of even the easiest of tasks: without compunction they would depart from their homes, leave their doors wide open, and desert the land, rushing away no matter where.[d] Consider then whether it is better to show oneself to be gentle and to get one's job done or to be a hard man and make hard work of doing one's duty. 4. And please do not protest in irritation at my remarks. You will prevail over them, however unwilling they may be, but better by far, with their good will. What is more pleasant then to get one's job done and for them to treat it as a holiday? And a holiday it is, not when sacrifices are made with grumblings and in expectation of arrest, but when libations and sacrifices are offered in an atmosphere quite free from fear. 5. And have

[c] λύκου πτερά, the proverbially impossible; cf. *Paroem. Gr.* 1.270. Similarly ὀρνίθων γάλα (*Paroem. Gr.* 1.231). Comic in origin, Aristoph. *Wasps* 508, *Birds* 733.

[d] On the flight from the councils, *Or.* 2.33 ff, *Or.* 48 and 49. See also Jones, *Later Roman Empire* 740 ff, Liebeschuetz, *Antioch* 174 ff, Petit, *Vie Municipale 321 ff.*

θους καὶ τοῦ τῶν ἀπειλῶν πλήθους, καὶ τὰς ἁλύσεις ταύτας μόνοι δεξάσθων φονεῖς καὶ τοιχωρύχοι καὶ οὓς δεῖ τεθνάναι. ἡ βουλὴ δέ σοι πάντα ἄπληκτος ποιήσει τὸ ὡς οὐ πεπλήξεται πεισθεῖσα. 6. αἰσχύνθητι δὲ αὐτῶν, ὦ 'γαθέ, τὸν φόβον, δι' ὃν οὐ καθεύδουσιν, ὥς ἐμοί τις ἤγγειλεν εἰπὼν ἄν, εἰ καὶ μὴ ὧδε εἶχον. ἔστω δέ σοι τοῦ φόβου σημεῖον τὸ πρὶν ἥκειν θέρος ἐκπεπληρῶσθαι ταῦτα ὧν ἤρχοντο φθινοπώρου μεσοῦντος, οὐχ ὅτι χρηστῶν ἀπέλαυσαν τῶν ὡρῶν ἢ τῶν τῆς γῆς ὠδίνων καλῶν, καὶ γὰρ ἐκείνη ἡ πέρυσι διψῶσα οὐκ ἔπιεν, ἀλλ' ὁ 'Αλέξανδρος καὶ τὰ ἀδύνατα δυνατὰ κατέστησεν. ὁπότ' οὖν γέμουσι δέους, τί ἂν τις αὐτοὺς προσέτι πλήττοι; 7. χωρὶς οὖν ἔστω τὰ Μυσῶν καὶ Φρυγῶν· ἡμεῖς μὲν γὰρ οἱ Φρύγες ἠδικήκαμεν τὸν Μενέλαον, καὶ ὅ τι ἂν πάθωμεν, δίκη τοῦτο καλεῖται· οἱ Μυσοὶ δὲ οὐχ ἡρπάκασι τὴν Ἑλένην. ὥστ' οὐχ ἕξομεν εἰς ὅ τι ἀνοίσομεν, ἤν τι λυπῶμεν.

done with heightened tones and hosts of threats: let murderers, burglars, and those who deserve to be put to death be the only ones to be confined in these fetters. The council will obey you implicitly without being flogged once it is convinced that it is not going to be flogged. 6. My good sir, respect their fear, for that is what gives them no sleep of nights, as I was told by one who would have told me the truth also if they had been otherwise affected. Take it as a sign of their fear that before the coming of summer they have completed what they began in mid-autumn not because they had enjoyed good seasons or great productivity of their land—indeed last year it was athirst and drought-stricken[e]—but because Alexander made a possibility even of the impossible.[f] So how could they be further frightened when they are already filled with fear? 7. Make some distinction between Mysians and Phrygians.[g] We are the Phrygians who have done wrong to Menelaus: any suffering we undergo has the name of punishment. But the Mysians were not responsible for the rape of Helen. Thus we shall have nothing to refer to by way of excuse, if we do them harm.

[e] Compare the famine in Antioch in 362/3.

[f] Cf. Isocr. *Demon.* 7.

[g] χωρὶς τὰ Φρυγῶν καὶ Μυσῶν ὁρίσματα, cf. *Paroem. Gr.* 2.130, and note. In the Trojan War, the Greeks also raided the territory of the Mysians, whose king, Telephus, protested that they were innocent of any crime against the Greeks.

## 105. Γαϊανῷ

1. Οὐκ οἶδ' ὁπότε τοῖς Θαλασσίου παισὶν ὑπάρξει τῶν δικαίων ἐν Φοινίκῃ τυχεῖν, εἰ μὴ νῦν τῶν ἀδικούντων ἔσονται κρείττους, ὅτε Γαϊανὸς ὁ καλὸς κἀγαθὸς καὶ ῥητορικὸς καὶ ἀρχικὸς ἐργηγορυίᾳ τῇ ψυχῇ τὰ τῆς Φοινίκης ἐφορᾷ. 2. καὶ τὴν μὲν ἐκ τοῦ γένους οὖσάν μοι πρὸς τὴν περὶ αὐτοὺς εὔνοιαν ἀνάγκην οὐκ ἀγνοεῖς οὐδ' ὅτι Βασσιανῷ καὶ δεύτερον ὑπάρχει δίκαιον, τὸ παρ' ἐμοί τε καὶ ἐν ταῖς ἐμαῖς διατριβαῖς καὶ τραφῆναι καὶ ἀνδρωθῆναι· οὔσης δέ μοι καὶ πρὸς σὲ φιλίας καὶ τοῦτο πάντων ἐπισταμένων ἀμφοτέρωθεν ἂν ἠλεγχόμην κακὸς ὧν τε φροντίζειν ἔδει, τούτους προδιδοὺς καὶ μὴ τολμῶν ἐπιστεῖλαι φίλῳ πάλαι δὴ βεβαιοῦντι τοὔνομα τοῖς ἔργοις. 3. ἐν κεφαλαίῳ μὲν οὖν, μελέτω σοι τῶν ἐμῶν συγγενῶν· τοῦτο δὲ οὐ λύει τὴν τῶν νόμων φυλακήν, ἀλλ' ἔστι κἀκείνους μὴ κινεῖν καὶ τούτοις ἐπικουρεῖν·

---

[a] *BLZG* 160, *PLRE* 378 (6): governor of Phoenicia, 362/3.

[b] Libanius' kinsman by marriage and praetorian prefect, 351–3. The enmity with Gallus made his sons, also Christian, highly suspect to Julian. Ammianus (22.9.16 f) records attacks on the younger Thalassius in 362, and

## 105. To Gaianus[a]

1. I do not know when ever the sons of Thalassius[b] will get justice in Phoenicia unless they prevail over those who do them wrong while that true gentleman, Gaianus, a born orator and governor, watches over Phoenicia, wakeful and alert. 2. You are not unaware of the ties of goodwill that bind me to them through our family connections, or yet of the fact that Bassianus has a second claim upon me, in that he was brought up and grew to manhood as my pupil and at my lectures.[c] Since I am also friendly with you, as everyone well knows, I would be proved a rogue on both counts if I betrayed those who should be my concern and if I did not venture to write to a friend who has long justified the term by his actions. 3. To sum up, then, please show concern for my relatives. This does not imply any relaxation of the maintenance of law: it is possible both to leave them undisturbed and

Julian's reconciliation with him. The family was wealthy, with property not only in Syria and Phoenicia but also in Euphratensis, where they faced the same problems as here (*Ep.* 1404).

[c] *PLRE* 150 (2). Although the family had admittedly appropriated temple property, the personal tie between teacher and pupil gave Libanius reason for intervention. As an advocate, rhetor trained, Gaianus could accept this argument with sympathy.

ὧν τὸ μέν ἐστιν ἐν τῇ τῶν ὀφειλομένων εἰσπράξει, τὸ δὲ ἐν τῷ μὴ πάντα ἐξεῖναι τοῖς τῷ καιρῷ χρωμένοις. 4. ἔχεις δὲ τῶν πραγμάτων καὶ τῆς ἀληθείας διδάσκαλον Ἑρμείαν, ἄνθρωπον καὶ φύσει καὶ παιδεύσει βέλτιστον, ἀλλὰ καὶ τὸν εὐνοῦχον μέντοι Μαρτύριον, ὃν οὐ φήσεις εἶναι τούτων δὴ τῶν πολλῶν εὐνούχων, ἀλλ' ἔστιν οἷος πιστεύεσθαί τε ἂν εἰκότως καὶ ἐπαινεῖσθαι δικαίως. 5. ὅταν οὖν ὦσιν οἱ καταβοῶντες ὡς πάντα ἡρπάκαμεν, μετέστω καὶ τούτοις παρρησίας καὶ τάχα εὑρήσεις μείζω τῶν πράξεων τὰ ἐγκλήματα. 6. ἡμᾶς δὲ δεῖ χαίρειν μὲν τῶν ἱερῶν ἀνισταμένων, μὴ μέντοι προστιθέναι τῇ ἐπανορθώσει πικρίας, ἵν' ἐξῇ τοῖς τότε πραττομένοις ἐπιτιμῶντας μηδὲν ἀντακούειν ἴσον. οἷον γὰρ[1] καὶ τὸ νῦν γινόμενον. 7. μετέπλασαν νεὼς εἰς οἰκίαν οἱ Θαλασσίου πρᾶγμα ποιοῦντες ἀρέσκον τῷ κρατοῦντι τότε, καὶ οὐκ ἐπαινῶ μέν, ἦν δ' οὖν τῶν τότε τὰ τοιαῦτα νόμων. ταύτην δὴ τὴν οἰκίαν ἔχοντες οἱ Φοίνικες καὶ καρπούμενοι

[1] γὰρ Wolf (V) γε F.

---

[d] Hermeias has appeared in Libanius' pleas to Andronicus, a previous governor of Phoenicia (*Epp.* 151, 225, 271).

to assist these people, for one aspect of the matter involves the collection of a debt, the other the prevention of those who misuse the present situation from doing exactly as they like. 4. As your informant upon the true facts of the case you have Hermeias,[d] who is an excellent person both by character and upbringing, and also the eunuch Martyrius, whom you will admit not to be one of the ordinary run of eunuchs but a person whom you can reasonably trust and justifiably commend. 5. So whenever people appear and accuse us of wholesale pillage, let these too be allowed to speak freely, and you will perhaps find that the complaints are out of all proportion to the facts. 6. Though we are bound to rejoice at the restoration of the temples, we must not surround the reform with an atmosphere of bitterness, in case we in our turn may hear similar accusations made against us—for this is the sort of thing that is happening in the present instance. 7. The sons of Thalassius converted temples into a house: they acted in conformity with the policy adopted by the emperor of the day.[e] I do not approve of it, but anyway this was legal at the time. Now the Phoenicians are in possession of the house and enjoy the revenue

Bassiana, the widow of the elder Thalassius, was very interested in his activities (*Ep.* 225). Thus he is hardly likely to be an impartial witness now. Martyrius is otherwise unknown.

[e] Constantius.

κελεύουσι καὶ τοὺς νεὼς αὐτοῖς ἀνοικοδομεῖν. 8. πῶς, ὦ βέλτιστοι; δεῖ γὰρ ἡμᾶς ἢ τῆς οἰκίας κρατοῦντας ἀνοικοδομεῖν ἐκείνους ἢ τούτων ἐκβεβλημένους ἀπηλλάχθαι πραγμάτων. ἀλλ', οἶμαι, διπλᾶ εἰσπράττειν ἐθέλουσιν. οἱ θεοὶ δὲ οὐ μιμοῦνται τοὺς ὠμοὺς τῶν δανειζόντων, ἀλλ' ἤν τις ἀποδιδῷ τἀκείνων, οὐκ ἂν αὐτὸν ἡδέως ἀγχόμενον ἴδοιεν. 9. τὴν αὐτὴν δὴ ψῆφον καὶ ὁ τοῖς θεοῖς φίλος οἴσει Γαϊανός, ἄλλως θ' ὅτε τὸ τοὺς Θαλασσίου κακῶς ποιεῖν ἀναγκάζον οἴχεται.

## 106. Ῥουφίνῳ

1. Ὁ φίλον συκοφαντούμενον ἐξαιρούμενος τῶν αἰτιῶν οὐ τοσοῦτον πράττει μόνον, ὅσον ἐκείνῳ λύει τὸν κίνδυνον, ἀλλὰ καὶ ὃν ἐξαπατηθῆναι κωλύει, μετὰ τοῦ τυχόντος τῆς συνηγορίας ὠφελεῖ· ὁ μὲν γὰρ οὐκ ἔδοξεν ἀδίκως κακός, ὁ δὲ οὐχ ἡγήσατο πονηρὸν τὸν χρηστόν. 2. δέξαι δή μου τὸν ὑπὲρ Λητοΐου λόγον ὡς καὶ τῆς σῆς δόξης κηδομένου. Λητόϊος ἐπὶ τὸν νυνὶ πόνον ὑπὸ τοῦ

[a] *Comes Orientis,* 363, in succession to Julianus. *BLZG* 254 (v), *PLRE* 775 (11).

[b] *Principalis* of Antioch, for whom cf. *BLZG* 197 (i). A

from it, and yet they bid them rebuild the temples for them as well.[f] 8. How, my dear people, can this be? We must either be in possession of the house to rebuild them, or if expelled from them, we should be rid of such complications. In my opinion they want to exact a double indemnity. But the gods do not take the line of harsh creditors: if anyone restores some of their property to them, they would not be glad to see him with a noose around his neck. 9. This same verdict will be given also by Gaianus, the friend of the gods, especially when the reason that compels the family of Thalassius to be subjected to such ill-treatment is over and done with.

[f] This seems to be a case of the same kind as that in Ammianus (22.9.16).

## 106. To Rufinus[a]

1. Anyone rescuing a friend falsely accused from charges made against him is not only effective in relieving him of his danger, but also a benefactor of the person who receives his advocacy, together with the man whom he stops from being duped. The one avoids being wrongly regarded as a bad man; the other avoids believing the good man to be bad. 2. So receive my plea for Letoius[b] as evidence of concern for your good name, too. Letoius, directed

very different picture of Letoius is given by Theodoret (*H.R.* 14).

παρ' ἡμῖν ἄρχοντος ἀγόμενος τὰ μὲν ἄρχοντι πειθόμενος, τὰ δ' οἴκτῳ τῆς πατρίδος δέχεται τὴν διακονίαν εἰδὼς μέν, ἐν οἵῳ χειμῶνι τολμᾷ πλεῖν, οὐκ ἀξιῶν δὲ τὴν ἀσφάλειαν τὴν αὑτοῦ πρὸ τῆς πόλεως θέσθαι. 3. ὢν δὲ καὶ ἄλλως μισοπόνηρος καὶ ἅττα πιστευθείη, πανταχοῦ φυλάττων ἀκριβῶς ὑπὸ τοῦ καιροῦ τὸν τρόπον ἐπέτεινε καὶ περιῄει κεκραγώς, κύνα μιμούμενος πολεμοῦντα λύκοις. πολλοὶ δὲ ἦσαν οἱ λύκοι καὶ ἔδει κυνὸς οὐ νωθροῦ τινος καὶ ἄρτῳ μικρῷ πραϋνομένου, ἀλλ' εἰδότος τά τε ἄλλα καὶ δακεῖν. 4. διὰ πολλῶν μὲν οὖν ἦλθεν ἰχνεύων τε τἀδικήματα καὶ ἀγανακτῶν καὶ τὰ μὲν εἰς δικαστήριον ἄγων, ἔστι δὲ οὗ καὶ αὐτὸς κολάζων, ὁπόσα δίδου τὸ σχῆμα. ἤδη δέ τις καὶ τῶν εἰς τὴν σὴν τελούντων στρατιὰν ἔδρασέ τι μέμψεως ἄξιον καὶ οὐκ ἔλαθε καὶ ἤλγησεν, ὅτι μὴ ἐπῃνεῖτο ἁμαρτάνων. 5. ἔσχε δὴ καὶ τοὺς συναλγοῦντας, πολὺ δέ γε πλείους τοὺς ἐπιτιμῶντας ἀπὸ τῆς αὐτῆς στρατιᾶς, ἄνδρας ἐπιεικεῖς καὶ εἰδότας αἰδεῖσθαι. ἀλλ' οἵ γε οὐ τοιοῦτοι παρακολουθοῦσι τῷ Λητοΐῳ πολεμοῦντες ἀπὸ παντὸς πειρώμενοι πλέκειν αἰτίας. 6. εἰ

[c] Alexander, implementing Julian's law concerning curial recruitment (*ELF* 47 of 13 March 362) had ordered

to his present task by our governor,[c] in deference to the governor and from commiseration for his native city, accepted the service, and though knowing full well the tempest through which he ventured to sail, he yet refused to prefer his own safety to that of his country. 3. He dislikes evil on principle, and everywhere carefully protected what had been entrusted to him, and as the present occasion demanded he developed this line of conduct and set up a hue and cry, like a hound fighting wolves. And the wolves were many; there was need of a hound with some spirit, not the sort of one to be cajoled with a bit of bread, but one which most of all knows how to bite. 4. So his activities were widespread: he tracked down acts of wrongdoing, showed his resentment of them, bringing some cases to court, while on occasion he personally inflicted the punishments his position allowed. One individual attached to your own staff whose actions were reprehensible was found out and took offence that his misconduct was not commended. 5. He had some sympathisers too, but many more critics from this same staff, decent people and with some sense of shame. But those who are not like that join him in opposition to Letoius and try to concoct charges against him on any ground. 6. Well, if you were

Letoius to undertake the difficult and invidious duty of reclaiming fugitive decurions for the curia of Antioch. Elsewhere (*Or.* 48.32; 49.19) he is noted as having reclaimed three serving officers from the army.

μὲν οὖν παρὼν ἐτύγχανες, ἐκεῖνοί τ᾿ ἂν ἧττω ἐψεύδοντο καὶ ὁ ἐλέγξων ἐγγὺς ἂν ἦν· νῦν δὲ φοβούμεθα τὰς ἐν ταῖς ἐπιστολαῖς συκοφαντίας. καὶ ὡς μὲν οὐκ εἶ τῶν ταχὺ πειθομένων, ἴσμεν, ὃ καὶ τὸν Λητόϊον ὤνησεν· ὡς τῷ γε πλήθει τῶν βλασφημιῶν ἀπόλωλε, νῦν δ᾿ ἔστιν ὅ τι καὶ ὑπώπτευσε τῶν εἰρημένων· ἀλλ᾿ ἂν ὁ ψευδόμενος συνεχῶς ἐγκείμενος τοῦτο ποιῇ, δέος ἐστὶ μὴ φενακίσῃ τῷ χρόνῳ. 7. δέομαι δὴ σοῦ μήτ᾿ ἀπιστῆσαι μήτε πιστεῦσαι τοῖς κατηγόροις, πρὶν ἂν καὶ τῆς ἀπολογίας ἀκούσῃς. ἀπολογήσομαι δὲ ἐγώ, κἂν ἐκεῖνος ἀδικεῖν δόξῃ, κατ᾿ ἀμφοῖν ἡ ψῆφος ἐξενεχθήτω.[1]

[1] ἐξενεχθήτω F. ἐνεχθήτω Wolf (V).

## 107. Ἡλιοδώρῳ

1. Ὤιμην ἀπαλλαγὴν γεγονέναι Βιταλίῳ πραγμάτων τὴν ἡμέραν ἐκείνην, ἐν ᾗ μηδὲν αὐτὸν ἀδικεῖν ἔγνωμεν Ἀστέριός τε καὶ σὺ καὶ ἐγώ· οἱ δ᾿ οὔτ ἀγροίκων οὔθ᾿ ἱερέων πρᾶγμα ποιοῦσιν

---

[a] *BLZG* 166 (i). Probably identical with the Heliodorus charged with dabbling in astrology (Amm. Marc. 29.1.5), preliminary to the uncovering of the so-called conspiracy of Theodorus in 371.

[b] *PLRE* 971. He was almost certainly Christian,

here in person, they would not resort to so many lies, and there would be one at hand to refute them. As it is, I am afraid of the calumnies they make against him in their letters. I know that you are not one to be easily persuaded; this has worked to Letoius' advantage even, else he would be overwhelmed by the weight of their charges. As things stand, he has some suspicion of these stories, and it is to be feared that, if the liar proceeds with his continual attacks, he will in course of time hoodwink you. 7. This I beg you, not to lose faith or to rely on his accusers until you have heard his explanation too. I shall present it, and if he be judged guilty, then let your verdict be given against us both.

## 107. To Heliodorus[a]

1. I thought that Vitalius[b] had got rid of his troubles on that day when Asterius,[c] you, and I decided that he had done no wrong.[d] But when the same

because he was here accused of arson, even though acquitted, and he was appointed proconsul of Asia in the Christian reaction under Jovian later in this year (*Ep.* 1231).

[c] Cf. *Letter* 69.

[d] Ammianus (22.13), while reporting the charge of arson, gives another report of the cause of the blaze. The constitution of this investigating commission of three is most unusual: none was an official, and only one was of curial status. So it was not a duty passed on by the authorities to the curia. It would appear that the course of action which Libanius requires of Heliodorus in § 3 is that of moral suasion only. For the burning of the temple, cf. *Or.* 60 and references in Julian *ELF* 105.

αὖθις ἐπὶ τὸν αὐτὸν ἰόντες καὶ οὐκ ἴσασιν ὡς τὸν μὲν εἰς χρήματα βλάψαι ἐπιχειροῦσιν, ἡμᾶς δὲ ὑβρίζουσιν οἱ τότε τούτων ἀφέμενοι. 2. εἰ γὰρ ἐκεῖνοι νῦν δικαίως ἐγκαλοῦσιν ἡμῖν, ἀδίκως οὗτος ἐφαίνετο καθαρὸς τῆς αἰτίας. ἀλλ' ἴσως οὐχ οἱ δικάζοντες ἠδίκουν, ἀλλ' οἱ μὴ θέλοντες διακρίνειν ἀπὸ τῶν ἐμβαλόντων τὸ πῦρ τοὺς μόνον τεθεαμένους. 3. κάτεχε τοίνυν αὐτοὺς καὶ νουθέτει καὶ μὴ ἐπίτρεπε τοιαῦτα ἐπιστέλλειν, ἵν' αὐτοῖς οἱ θεοὶ χαίρωσι τῶν ψυχῶν πρὸ τῶν ναῶν ἐπιμελουμένοις.[1] ἀπαιτούμενος δὲ τὰ τοιαῦτα παρ' ἡμῶν μὴ θαύμαζε· καλὸς γὰρ ὢν κἀγαθὸς εἰκότως ἐπὶ τὰ καλὰ τῶν ἔργων ὑπ' ἡμῶν παρακαλῇ.

[1] ἐπιμελουμένοις F. ἐπιμελομένοις Wolf (V).

## 108. Δουλκιτίῳ

1. Ὅτι μὲν καὶ ἡμᾶς, ὥσπερ Φοίνικάς τε καὶ Θρᾷκας καὶ νῦν Ἴωνας, ἐπὶ σωτηρίᾳ μετὰ μείζονος παραλήψῃ τοῦ σχήματος, ἴσμεν καλῶς· πάντως δὲ μαντικῆς[1] ἅπασα ὁδὸς ἀνέῳκται καὶ δεινὸν οὐδὲν τὸ μέλλον εἰδέναι. 2. ἀλλὰ τότε

[1] μαντικῆς Wolf (V) μαντικῇ F.

man is subjected to their attacks, then people are not behaving like either peasants or priests, and they do not realize that, even though they once relieved him of such burdens, they are trying to inflict financial harm on him and insulting us. 2. If they now are justified in accusing us, he obviously was unjustifiably cleared of the charge. But it may be that it was not the commission of investigation that was at fault, but those people who refuse to distinguish mere onlookers from the arsonists. 3. So bring them to heel, admonish them and do not let them send such letters, so that the gods may be pleased with them for showing more concern for souls than for shrines. Do not be surprised at the receipt of such a request from me: you are a fine gentleman, and it is only natural that you should receive encouragement from me to actions that are fine.

## 108. To Dulcitius[a]

1. I am well aware that you will receive the task of protecting us with status enhanced, as was the case with Phoenicia and Thrace, and now with Ionia. Certainly the way is clear for divination and there is no harm in knowing what is to come.

[a] A letter requesting aid in the collection of beasts for the shows of the Syriarch, Celsus. A similar letter is sent to Caesarius, vicar of Asia at this time. Dulcitius' career is repeated more unflatteringly in *Or.* 42.24.

μὲν ἡμῖν προσθήκαις τε καὶ κόσμοις μείζω τε ποιήσεις καὶ καλλίω τὴν πόλιν· νῦν δ' ἔξεστί σοι τοσοῦτον ἀπέχοντι λαμπρῦναι μὲν τῶν πολιτευομένων ἕνα, χαρίσασθαι δὲ τοῖς ὀφθαλμοῖς τοῦ δήμου, μᾶλλον δέ, πολλοῖς δήμοις, ὁπόσους καλεῖν ἐπὶ τὴν θέαν εἰώθαμεν, ἣν γενέσθαι χαριεστάτην σὺ κύριος. 3. καὶ ὅπως γε, ἄκουσον. ἐν τοῖς παρ' ἡμῖν λειτουργοῦσίν ἐστι συριάρχης ὀνόματι καλῷ τιμώμενος διὰ τὸ μέγεθος τῆς δαπάνης· καὶ γὰρ ὁ Πακτωλὸς αὐτῷ μικρὸν καὶ τὰ Κινύρου καὶ τὰ Γύγου. 4. οὗτος ἄρχει μὲν οὐδενός, δεῖ δὲ αὐτὸν τὰ αὑτοῦ νῦν μὲν ἡνιόχων ποιεῖν, νῦν δὲ τῶν εἰς τὸ θέατρον εἰσιόντων κυνηγέτας τε ἀγείρειν κούφους καὶ θηρία κρείττω τέχνης ἁπάσης. ἐπαινεῖται γὰρ ὁ δαπανώμενος, ὅταν οἱ μὲν ἥκωσι πεπαιδευμένοι, τὰ δὲ ὅταν καὶ οὕτω κρατῇ· ἄρκτος δὲ ἡττωμένη καὶ πάρδαλις νικωμένη τοῦ χορηγοῦντος ἐγκλήματα. 5. ταύτην δὴ νίκην ἀπὸ τῶν ὑμετέρων ἡμῖν ἐλπὶς ὁρῶν ἔσεσθαι. καὶ

[b] The title is mentioned only here and in *Letter* 119. Note that invitations are sent out to the cities for this show.

[c] The reference to Pactolus and Gyges is very appropri-

2. In that case, you will make our city bigger and better with additions and adornments. As it is, you have it in your power, though so far away, to glorify one of our city councillors, and to delight the eyes of our citizens, or rather of the citizens of many places whom we have normally invited to the spectacle; and this you are able to make most popular. 3. Just listen how this is to be done. Among those who perform civic duties among us the Syriarch[b] enjoys a prestigious title for the huge amount he expends. Pactolus and the wealth of Cinyras and of Gyges are a mere nothing to him.[c] 4. He is not a governor, but he must at times turn his possessions over to the chariot drivers, or to people who walk the stage, and collect nimble huntsman and animals that can overcome all their skill, for the person who puts up the money earns praise when the hunters come in well-trained and the animals get the better of them despite that. For a bear to be beaten or a panther conquered is a criticism of the sponsor of the show.[d] 5. Well, we can expect a victory of this kind to come from your mountains,[e] for the den-

ate, however proverbial it may be, in a letter to a governor of Asia.

[d] After Constantine's ban on gladiatorial shows, beast chases became the most popular form of mass entertainment. The cost to the sponsors was no less, since both beasts and hunters were imported.

[e] Ida, in particular; cf. *Ep.* 1399.

γὰρ μεγάλα καὶ θυμοῦ γέμοντα καὶ οὐκ ἂν παρακρουσθέντα τὰ τῆς ὕλης ἐκείνης θρέμματα. 6. Πολύκαρπος μὲν οὖν ὠνήσεται, τὸ δὲ δεινά τε αὐτὸν πρίασθαι καὶ μὴ ἔλαττον σχεῖν τῶν κωλυόντων καὶ δυνηθῆναι ὁπόσα βουλόμεθα σὸν ἂν εἴη καὶ τῆς σῆς φιλανθρωπίας τε καὶ τῆς πρὸς ἡμᾶς φιλίας, εἰ μή τι αὐτὴν λέλυκεν. οἶμαι δὲ οὐδὲν ἐκείνων ἰσχυρότερον γεγονέναι τῶν δεσμῶν. 7. καὶ ταῦτα πρῶτον μὲν παρ' ὅλης οἴου τῆς πόλεως ἀκούειν, ἔπειτα παρὰ τοῦ καλοῦ Σαλουτίου[2] καὶ τρίτου γε τοῦ χρηστοῦ Ῥουφίνου. καὶ γὰρ οὗτοι τὰ αὐτὰ ἂν ἔγραφον, εἰ μὴ ὁ μὲν ἤλαυνε Πέρσας, Ῥουφῖνος δὲ πλησίον ἦν τῶν ἐκεῖνα δρώντων. ὅμως δὲ εἴσονταί σοι χάριν ὥσπερ αὐτοὶ ταῦτα ἐπεσταλκότες. 8. καλὸν δὲ μηδὲ ἡμᾶς ἀτιμάζειν τοὺς περὶ τὸν Ἑρμῆν διατρίβοντας, ὅπως ἐμμένωμεν ταῖς διατριβαῖς καὶ μὴ τοῦ ἄρχειν ἐπιθυμῶμεν ὡς οὐκ ὂν ἄλλως ἔργου τυχεῖν.

[2] Σαλουτίου F. Σαλουστίου Wolf (V).

---

[f] Celsus' agent, as in *Ep.* 1399.5. Otherwise unknown.

[g] Praetorian prefect. The letter is written during Julian's Persian campaign and before the news of his death.

izens of your forests are huge, full of fight and not easily overcome. 6. So Polycarpus[f] will purchase them, but for him to buy the fiercest and not to be worsted by those who would stop him, and for him to be able to do all we wish, would depend on you, your kindness and your friendship for me, if it has not been broken. Nothing, I think, can be stronger than such ties. 7. On this matter, imagine that you are listening, first to our whole city, then to the noble Salutius,[g] and thirdly to the good Rufinus.[h] They too would be writing in the same vein, were it not that Salutius is engaged in the invasion of Persia and Rufinus is nearby in support of those so engaged. Still, they will be as grateful to you as though they had written this themselves. 8. It is right for you not to dishonour us either, whose lives are spent in the pursuit of eloquence, so that we may stay in our studies and not hanker after office with the notion that we could never get results otherwise.[i]

[h] *Comes Orientis,* then on the frontier in support of the campaign.

[i] It may be noted that Celsus is not mentioned by name in this letter; the prestigious title of Syriarch is enough to impress Dulcitius. Nor does the letter contain any of the classical allusions expected in correspondence between men of culture. Dulcitius is a self-made man.

109. Ἀριστοφάνει

1. Οἶμαι μὲν τὴν Φήμην καὶ νῦν ὃ πάλαι πεποιηκέναι καὶ διδάξαι τοὺς Ἕλληνας τὰ πάθη τῶν βαρβάρων, οἶσθα γὰρ ὡς πρότερον αὐτῇ τι τοιοῦτον ἐπέπρακτο, ὅτε τοῦ νενικηκότος στρατοπέδου τὴν νίκην ἤγγειλε τῷ μέλλοντι μαχεῖσθαι στρατοπέδῳ καὶ ἐπέρρωσεν—εἰ δ' οὖν οὔπω ἥκει εἰς ὑμᾶς λόγος, ἀλλ' ἴστωσαν οἱ Ἕλληνες ὅτι αὐτοῖς δίκην διδόασιν οἱ ἀπόγονοι Δαρείου καὶ Ξέρξου πυρὶ τὰς αὑτῶν πόλεις ἀπολλυμένας ὁρῶντες οἱ προπέρυσι τὰς ἡμετέρας κατασκάπτοντες. 2. ὡς γὰρ ἐνέβαλε βασιλεὺς ἅμα ἦρι ᾗ οὐκ ᾤοντο, εἴχοντο εὐθὺς Ἀσσύριοι, κῶμαι πολλαὶ καὶ ὀλίγαι πόλεις· οὐ γὰρ ἦσαν πολλαί. εἶτ' ἀφυπνισθεὶς ὁ Πέρσης ἐξεπλάγη τε καὶ ἔφυγεν, ὁ δ' ἐδίωκε πάντα ἀμαχεὶ λαμβάνων, μᾶλλον δέ, τὰ πλείω μὲν ἄνευ μάχης, ἀπέκτεινε δὲ καὶ ἑξακισχι-

[a] After his pardon, Aristophanes had returned to Greece to take up the post which Julian had finally chosen for him (*ELF* 97). According to Seeck, this was the proconsulate of Achaea, but as Bidez pointed out (*Lettres* pp. 26, 178), this post was held by Vettius Agorius Praetextatus. *PLRE* suggested the vicariate of Macedonia. Petit (*Autobiographie* 242n.) canvasses the possibility that Aristophanes was simply appointed *agens in rebus* with wide-ranging powers of supervision over the restoration of

## 109. To Aristophanes[a]

1. Rumour, I think, has done what she did long ago and told the Greeks of the plight of the barbarians—for of course you know how in the past she performed something of the sort when she reported the victory of the conquering army to the army which was just going to engage, and so strengthened its morale.[b] Anyhow, even if the story has not yet come your way, Greeks should certainly know that the descendants of Darius and Xerxes are being punished by seeing their own cities being put to the flames when a year or two ago they were responsible for the utter destruction of ours.[c] 2. As soon as the emperor invaded early in the spring by a route which surprised them, the Assyrians were taken straightaway[d]—villages in large numbers and a few cities, for they have not got many cities. The Persians rudely awakened, then fled in alarm, while the emperor in hot pursuit captured everything without a blow, or rather he captured the greater part without fighting, but he killed 6,000 of them who had come out on reconnais-

pagan religion in the Balkan provinces.

[b] Herod. 9.100; the Greeks at Mycale heard the rumour of the victory of Plataea. The conjunction of Xerxes' invasion of Greece with Julian's Persian campaign forms a typically sophistic introduction to his formal requests of §§ 4–5.

[c] Amida, Singara, and Bezabde captured by the Persians (Amm. Marc. 19.8; 20.6 f).

[d] Cf. Amm. Marc. 23.3.

λίους ἥκοντας ὡς ἐς κατασκοπὴν καὶ ἅμα ἐπ' ἔργον, εἰ συμβαίη. 3. καὶ ταῦτα ἀγγέλλουσιν οἱ ἐπὶ τῶν πτηνῶν διαιτώμενοι καμήλων—τετιμήσθω γὰρ αὐτοῖς τὸ τάχος τῷ ὀνόματι τῶν πτερῶν—ἐλπίς τε ἥξειν τὸν βασιλέα τὸν μὲν νῦν ἄρχοντα ἄγοντα, παραδόντα δὲ τῷ φεύγοντι τὴν ἀρχήν. 4. τόθ' ἡμῖν ἥξει καὶ παρὰ σοῦ γράμματα πάντων πανταχόθεν δεῦρο θεόντων. εἰ δ' ἐγγένοιτο καὶ νῦν ἐλθεῖν, μὴ ὄκνει· βουλοίμην γὰρ ἂν εἰδέναι, ὅσην τε χώραν ἐπῆλθες καὶ ὅ τι δρῶν καὶ εἴ τι τῶν λανθανόντων γεγύμνωται καὶ ὅπως ὡμιλήκαμεν τοῖς ἀνθρώποις καὶ τὸ μέγιστον, εἰ ἡ Τύχη συλλαμβάνει. 5. ταυτὶ μὲν ἐπιστελεῖς, τῷ φέροντι δέ σοι τὴν ἐπιστολὴν πάντα ποίησον λεῖα καὶ σύμπραξον ἐφ' ἃ ἥκει. ἥκει δὲ ἐπανάξων πολῖτιν ἡμετέραν, ᾗ γάμος ἐν Μακεδονίᾳ. 6. καὶ ὁ παρὰ σοὶ δὲ νεανίσκος χρώμενος περὶ τὰς δίκας τοῖς λόγοις ἔστω ἐν λόγῳ καὶ μὴ βλαπτέσθω τῷ μὴ μετ' ἐμῶν πεπλευκέναι γραμμάτων· ὁ μὲν γὰρ ᾔτει, ἐγὼ δὲ ἠρρώστουν. ὁ δὲ κυβερνήτης ἐπὶ τὴν ναῦν ἐκάλει, καὶ ἔδει νικᾶν τὸν ἄνεμον.

sance and also for any action that might take place. 3. And this is the news that is brought by those messengers on their winged camels—their speed ought to receive due recognition with the word "wings"—and we expect our emperor to come with the present king a captive in his train, after handing over the kingdom to the one whom he had exiled.[e] 4. Then letters will come to us even from you, for everyone will hurry here from everywhere. But if they could possibly come now, do not hold back, for I would like to know of the lands to which you have gone and what you are doing. Has all that is not obvious been laid bare? How have we got on with the people? In particular, is Fortune on our side? 5. You will write and tell me all this. As for the bearer of my letter to you, make all plain sailing for him and assist him in the object for which he has come—which is to escort home a lady, a citizen of ours, who is married in Macedonia. 6. And the young fellow whom you have with you employing his eloquence on the law, let him be held in esteem and let it be no detriment to him that he set sail without a letter from me. He asked me for one, but I was ill, the captain was calling him aboard, and the wind brooked no waiting.

[e] King Sapor and Hormisdas (*PLRE* 443 (2)), the exile.

## 110. Ἀλεξάνδρῳ

1. Ἥψαντο τῶν εὐθυνῶν ὅ τε χρηστὸς Καλλιόπιος καὶ ὅτῳ ἡ ἐπωνυμία ἀπὸ τοῦ σανδάλου, ὑπὲρ οὗ δημοσίᾳ χρὴ εὔχεσθαι καὶ θεοῖς καὶ θεαῖς παρελθεῖν αὐτὸν μήκει βίου τὸν Ἀργανθώνιον δικαιότερον ὄντα τοῦ Ῥαδαμάνθυος· ταυτὶ γὰρ καὶ αὐτὸς ἐπείσθης. 2. στρέφοντες δὲ τὸ πρᾶγμα μαθεῖν δύνανται οὐδέν· οὔτε γὰρ τοῖς καπήλοις ἐν γράμμασιν ἐσώζετο τὰ τότε πραττόμενα, οὐδὲ γὰρ ἥξειν εὐθυνῶν ἀνάγκην ἤλπισαν, τῶν τε διδασκόντων οὐκ ὄντων πῶς ἂν γένοιντο λογισταί; 3. ὁ μὲν οὖν πόνος πολὺς καὶ αἱ ἀπειλαί, καί πού τις καὶ ἐδάκρυσε καὶ μικροῦ πληγὰς ἔλαβε, προϊόντος δέ, οἶμαι, τοῦ πράγματος ἔσονται καὶ πολλαί. θαυμάσαιμι δ' ἂν εἴ τις σαφέστερος ἐξετασμὸς ἔσται ταῖς πληγαῖς. 4. ἃ οὖν νῦν τε ἔστι καὶ ἀπὸ τούτων ἔσται, μὴ ἀγνόει. νῦν μὲν ἀποσπώμενοι τῶν ἐργαστηρίων στένουσιν ἐν τῷ

---

[a] *BLZG* 101 (ii), *PLRE* 174 (1).

[b] Unknown. The use of nicknames at this time is com-

## 110. To Alexander

1. Both the good Calliopius[a] and the man with the nickname from the sandal[b]—and for him we should offer public prayer to gods and goddesses that he should in length of life surpass Arganthonius,[c] since he is more just than Rhadamanthys,[d] which was your own opinion, too—these have tackled the investigation. 2. Despite examining the matter from every angle[e] they cannot find out anything about it. The shopkeepers had not kept any written record of what took place at that time, for they had not the slightest notion that there would be need for an enquiry—and how can auditors be effective without anyone to give the information? 3. Well, their labours were long, the threats many: one or two set up a lament and were very nearly flogged, and as the business drags on, flogging there will be aplenty, I think. But I would be surprised if the examination becomes any the clearer with floggings. 4. So do not ignore what is happening now and what will happen in consequence of it. Now they are dragged away from their

mon, especially among the upper classes. Thus Strategius was called Musonianus (*PLRE* 611), Anatolius (60) Azutrio, Proclus (747) Coccus.

[c] Cf. *Letter* 80.4.

[d] Cf. *Or.* 16.19.

[e] Demosth. *Meid.* 116.

τῆς Τύχης ἱερῷ τρίβοντες χρόνους καὶ τὸ αὑτῶν οὐκ ἐώμενοι ποιεῖν· ἢν δὲ πάνυ μακρὸν τοῦτο ᾖ, ζητήσουσιν οὗ ἐργάζεσθαι ἐξέσται. 5. ἡ δὲ τούτων ἀθυμία καὶ οἱ φόβοι λόγους ἔτεκον καὶ ὑποψίας, ὑφ' ὧν ἡ ἀγορὰ γίνεται χείρων, καὶ δέος μὴ τὸ νῦν ἄνθος ἀποβάλῃ δόξῃς[1] τε ὃ ἔδωκας ἀφῃρῆσθαι. 6. ταῦτ' ἐγὼ καὶ σὲ καὶ τὴν ἐμαυτοῦ φιλῶν ἐπέσταλκα. εἰ δ' ἔξω φέρομαι λογισμῶν ὀρθῶν, ἐμοὶ μὲν ἔστω συγγνώμη, νικάτω δὲ ὃ μέλλει συνοίσειν.

[1] δόξῃς F. δόξεις Wolf (V)

---

[f] It is uncertain what malpractices of the market traders were under investigation by this high-powered commission of enquiry (Calliopius himself was *honoratus*). A census was being conducted at this time (*Ep.* 1412), but it was perhaps more likely to be concerned with problems arising from the famine of the previous year.

workshops[f] and pass their time moaning and groaning in the temple of Fortune,[g] forbidden to ply their own trade. If this goes on for any length of time, they will look for somewhere where they will be allowed to ply it. 5. Their disappointment and their fears have engendered comments and suspicions that impair our market, and people are afraid that its present prosperity will be lost and you will be thought to have taken away what you gave. 6. I have written you this letter out of affection both for you and for my own city. If I exceed the bounds of true reasoning, then pardon me and let what will be to the general good prevail.

[g] In 359 (*Letter* 45), the temple of Tyche had lost the classes of students it had once had, temples and teaching being closely connected (*Or.* 1.102). By 363, as Petit (*Vie Municipale* 107) remarks, it had became little more than a public meeting place. Thus when Julian was greeted with acclamations in the Tychaeum he protested strongly at this confusion of a temple with a theatre (Julian, *Lettres* no. 176, ed. Bidez-Cumont). The secularization had taken place as a result of Constantius' policies of the middle 350s (*Cod. Th.* 16.10.4).

## 111. Ἐντρεχίῳ

1. Ἀπὸ χαιρούσης τῆς ψυχῆς ἐπέσταλκας οὔπω τῇ φήμῃ βεβλημένος. οὐ μὴν ἔθ' ὁμοίως ἔχων δέξῃ τὴν ἐπιστολήν. οἶμαι γὰρ ἤδη καὶ παρ' ὑμᾶς ἀφῖχθαι τοῦ κακοῦ τὸν λόγον τοσοῦτον κερδάναντας, ὅσον ὑστέρους πεπύσθαι. 2. καὶ ἔγωγε θαυμάσαιμ' ἂν εἰ ἔτι δυνήσῃ μακρὰς οὕτω καὶ καλὰς πέμπειν ἐπιστολάς, οὐ πείσῃ δὲ ὅπερ ἐγώ. τὸ δὲ ἐμὸν πάθος, ἀπ' ἐκείνης τῆς ἡμέρας ἄφωνος ὡς εἰπεῖν γέγονα καὶ κατέλυσα τὸ γράφειν. 'τὸν πάντα δ' ὄλβον ἦμαρ ἕν μ' ἀφείλετο.' 3. ἀλλ' ἐκ τραγῳδίας μὲν πολλὰ μὲν ἐγώ, πολλὰ δὲ σύ, πολλὰ δὲ τῶν εὖ φρονούντων ἕκαστος φθεγξόμεθα τοιαύτης οἰχομένης κεφαλῆς· ἐφ' ᾧ δὲ σὲ μάλιστα ἠγάσθην, ἐκεῖνό ἐστιν, ὅτι τῶν ἄλλων ὑπὸ τῶν ἐν ταῖς ἀρχαῖς πραγμάτων ἀμβλυνομένων τὴν γλῶτταν, ὥστ' ἤδη καὶ τῶν σοφιστῶν τινες ἐνταῦθ' ἥκοντες ἀπέβαλον τὴν ἰσχύν, σὺ μόνος μετὰ τῶν πόλεων τὴν γλῶτταν ἀμείνω πεποίηκας καὶ θεραπεύεις μὲν ἐκείνας ὡς

---

[a] *BLZG* 126, *PLRE* 278 (1).

[b] The news of Julian's death had reached Antioch by

## 111. To Entrechius[a]

1. You wrote your letter with joyful heart, for you had not yet been smitten by the news.[b] You will certainly not feel the same way when you receive the reply, for I am sure that by now the tale of woe has reached you too, though you are this much better off that you heard it after we did.[c] 2. I would be surprised if you can still send such fine, long letters without being affected as I am. As for my reactions, from the day I heard the news I have been practically dumb and I have given up writing. "A single day robbed me of all my joy."[d] 3. You and I and every man of good will will cite many a quotation from tragedy now that such a person has departed. In fact, what pleased me most in you is this: when other people had their eloquence blunted by the business of office, so much so that even certain sophists who attained that position threw away their abilities, you alone have improved the condition both of your eloquence and of the cities and, while administering them as well as if you had

early July, and this letter marks Libanius' immediate reaction to it. He records his emotions in retrospect in *Or.* 1.135. His grief did not allow him to speak or write for some considerable time (*Ep.* 1422.2; cf. *Or.* 17.38), and he resumed his declamations only after New Year 364 (*Letter* 123, *Epp.* 1194, 1430).

[c] Entrechius was at this time governor of Pisidia, appointed by Julian.

[d] Eurip. *Hec.* 285.

ἀφεστηκὼς λόγων, λέγεις δὲ ὡς ἓν τοῦτο ἐργαζόμενος μόνον. 4. καὶ τούτου γε αἴτιον ἡγοῦμαι τὸν οὐκ ἔτ' ὄντα βασιλέα· ἐλογίζου γὰρ ὡς ἄτοπον, εἰ ὁ μὲν ἐν ταῖς ὑπὲρ ὅλης τῆς γῆς φροντίσιν εἴχετο τῶν βιβλίων, σὺ δ' ἐκεῖνον θαυμάζων οὐκ εἰς ἔργον ἄξεις τὸν ἔπαινον. 5. ἀλλ', ὦ 'γαθέ, βιβλία μὲν ἐν χερσὶν ἀεὶ κείσθω, γενναῖα μέντοι καὶ σοφὰ καὶ πατέρων ἀγαθῶν· σὺ δ' ἐπὶ φαῦλα καὶ ἄμορφα τὰ ἡμέτερα φέρῃ καὶ οὐ δέδοικας μή σε λαβόντα διαφθείρῃ. 6. ἀλλ' ὑπὲρ μὲν τούτων ἄμεινον βουλεύσῃ· τῆς δ' εἰς τὸν ἑταῖρον προθυμίας τε καὶ σπουδῆς τίνα σοι μισθὸν ἑτοιμάσωμεν;[1] χρήματα; ἀλλ' οὐ θαυμάζεις χρυσίον θαυμάζων τὸν Περικλέα. ἀλλ' ἐπαίνους; ἀλλ' ἀπὸ παντὸς ὁμοίως σοι τοῦτό γε στόματος. 7. ὅσων[2] γὰρ ἂν νέος ὢν ἄρχοις, ἐπιμελὲς ἅπασιν ἀνερωτᾶν, ἐν ᾧ νῦν τὰ Πισιδῶν. εἶτ' ἀκούοντες νόμους ἄρχοντος γνώμῃ βεβαιουμένους καὶ τὰ κείμενα ἀνιστάμενα κοινοὺς ἐπαίνους εἰς σέ τε καὶ τὸν δόντα τὴν ἀρχὴν ᾄδουσι. 8. λείπεται δὴ θεοὺς αἰτεῖν δι' ἀρχῶν εἰς γῆράς σε ἀφικέσθαι τηροῦντα τὴν ἐκ τῆς νεότητος ἀρξαμένην ἀρετήν.

[1] ἑτοιμάσωμεν F. (S Vind.) -άσομεν Wolf (V Par.)
[2] ὅσων F., conj. Re. ὅσῳ Wolf (Mss.)

given up rhetoric, you yet speak as though engaged solely on this profession. 4. The reason for this, in my opinion, is our departed emperor. You regarded it as absurd if he, despite his preoccupation for the whole world, held fast to his books, yet you, despite your admiration for him, should not put this admiration into effect. 5. My good friend, let books always be in your hands—noble, wise books produced of good stock, and you come to my shapeless trifles with no fear that their receipt will corrupt you. 6. On this matter your decision will be a better one. But for your eager support for our comrade what reward am I to make ready for you? Money? Yet, as an admirer of Pericles, you do not admire gold.[e] Praises, then? But these you have from every tongue alike. 7. For all the people whom you may govern while still a young man make it their business to enquire how Pisidia is faring now. Then, on learning that law is supported by its governor's decree and that what was cast down is now being restored, they sing the praises alike of yourself and of him who gave you that office. 8. What remains, then, is to pray heaven that you may reach old age by a career of office, maintaining that excellence which displayed itself in your youth.[f]

[e] Thuc. 2.65.5.
[f] Cf. *Ep.* 13 of 353/4 and *Letter* 153 of 388.

## 112. Σαλουτίῳ[1]

1. Ἀνεκτήσω με τοῖς γράμμασι κείμενον ἀπ' ἐκείνης τῆς ἡμέρας, ἣν οὐκ ἂν σε δέοι διδάσκειν, ἀλλ' αὐτὸς εἰκάζεις. ἔγνω δὲ τοῦτο καλῶς καὶ Πρίσκος ὁ καλός, ὃς εὑρὼν ἐοικότα με τοῖς ἰχθύσι τοῖς ἐπὶ τῆς ἠιόνος λειποψυχοῦσιν ἐπεχείρει μὲν ἀνιστάναι φάρμακα ἔχων ἐπὶ τὰ πάθη τῆς ψυχῆς οὐκ ἀσθενῆ, μικρὸν δὲ ἴσχυσεν ἐν πολλαῖς ἡμέραις. 2. ἐλθούσης δέ σου τῆς ἐπιστολῆς 'οἴου σοι,' φησί, 'ζῆν ἐκεῖνον εἰς τοῦτον βλέπων σωτῆρα μὲν ἐθνῶν, κηδεμόνα δὲ φίλων.' καὶ ἐγὼ κατὰ μικρὸν ἐμαυτὸν ἐπειρώμην συναγείρειν διεσκεδασμένον τε καὶ ὄντα οὐδέν. 3. εἰ δ' ἀπὸ γραμμάτων μόνων τοσοῦτον ὑπῆρξεν ἡμῖν, πόσον τι οἴει γενήσεσθαι φανείσης τῆς ἱερᾶς κεφαλῆς; ἡ κεφαλὴ δέ με καὶ τοῦτο ἠδίκηκεν ἡ ἐμὴ μήτε ἥλιον ἀνεχομένη μήθ' ὅσα ταλαιπωρεῖν ὁδοιποροῦντα ἀνάγκη, ὅτι ἃ ἐξῆν ἔχειν ἤδη δραμόντα, περιμένειν πεποίηκεν οἴκοι καθήμενον. 4. εὖ γὰρ ἴσθι ὅτι, εἰ κύριος ἦν ἐλθεῖν, οὐδεὶς ἂν με τῶν πολλὰ

[1] Σαλουστίῳ Wolf (V)

---

[a] Julian's praetorian prefect, retained in office after he declined imperial rank, is with the retiring army. The

## 112. To Salutius[a]

1. In your letter you found me prostrate from that day, of which there is no need to tell you but which you guess for yourself. The noble Priscus[b] knew this well enough, when he found me like a fish stranded on the seashore and tried to revive me with cures for my distress of spirit, and these though not weak, had little effect over many days. 2. But when your letter came, he said to me, "Think that your dead emperor still lives while ever you look upon this saviour of his provinces and protector of his friends," and I tried little by little to pull myself together, though I was distracted and a mere nothing. 3. If such was the effect upon me merely of your letter, how much do you think it will be at the sight of your revered self? As for my own self, my head has played me false, since it cannot endure the sun or the enforced fatigue of travel, because it has made me sit at home and put up with everything I could possibly experience on a journey. 4. Rest assured that, if I were able to come, nobody who possessed many a carriage and pair would

letter is written before 22 Oct. 363, when Jovian was in Antioch (*Cod. Th.* 10.19.2).

[b] Priscus, along with Maximus, had accompanied Julian on his campaign and had been at his deathbed. Clearly he had left the new court very soon after that, staying some time in Antioch on his return home.

ζεύγη κεκτημένων ἔφθη· τοσοῦτος ἔρως ἐγκατέσπαρται ταῖς ἁπάντων ψυχαῖς περὶ σὲ καὶ τὸ σὸν κάλλος, οὗ πᾶσα μὲν ἀπολέλαυκε πόλις, πᾶς δὲ οἶκος καὶ ἀνὴρ καὶ πρό γε πολλῶν ἐγώ. ὁ γὰρ Εὐάγριος ἄρχων Ὀλυμπίου μὲν βουληθέντος, ἐμοῦ δὲ φράσαντος, σοῦ δὲ δράσαντος, τιμὴ τοῦτο ἐμή. 5. πῶς οὖν τοιαῦτα λαβὼν οὐκ ἐπέστελλον; οὐδὲν ποικίλον ἐρῶ, ἀλλ᾽ ᾐδούμην, ὦ ᾿γαθέ, καὶ ὤκνουν, μὴ αὐτῷ τῷ τιμᾶσθαι δόξω θρασὺς γεγονέναι καὶ γραμμάτων ἄρχειν, ἐν οἷς ἀκολουθεῖν ἔδει. 6. νῦν οὖν ἐπειδὴ γράφεις καὶ προτρέπεις, εἴσῃ Λυδὸν εἰς πεδίον προκαλούμενος. μᾶλλον δέ, τὴν ταχίστην ἡμῖν ἥκων ἄνελε τὴν τῶν γραμμάτων χρείαν τῇ συνουσίᾳ.

have outpaced me, for such is the passion that has been sown in the souls of all for you and for your noble qualities. These every city has enjoyed, every home, every man, and, before them all, myself. For Euagrius became a governor at the wish of Olympius,[c] at the instance of myself and by your doing, but this was an honour to me. 5. How then was it that after such generosity I did not write? I will not prevaricate:[d] I felt shame and reluctance, my good sir, lest it appear that I had become too conceited at this honour and be thought to be taking the lead in a correspondence where I ought to be following it. 6. So now, when you write and invite me to reply, you will realize that you are inviting me on to ground of my own choosing.[e] But better still, come and visit us as soon as you can, and by your presence do away with the need of writing.

[c] Euagrius—*BLZG* 128 (iv), *PLRE* 285 (6)—was a younger brother of Libanius' old friend Olympius (ii). After various vicissitudes in political life, beginning with this appointment, he became leader of the Christian church in Antioch.

[d] Plat. *Meno* 75e, *Gorg.* 491d.

[e] Cf. *Ep.* 617.2, *Paroem. Gr.* 2.509 ἐπὶ τῶν θᾶττον βουλομένων τι δρᾶσαι καὶ προθύμως.

## 113. Ἐλπιδίῳ[1]

1. Χαίρω ὅτι τῆς τοῦ βασιλέως εὐνοίας ἀπολαύεις. τεκμαίρομαι δὲ τοῦτο τῷ μένειν σε ἐπὶ τῆς ἀρχῆς· εἰ γὰρ μὴ 'κεῖνο ἦν, οὐδὲ τοῦτο ἂν ἦν. 2. ὁ δὲ πρὸς Σέλευκον πόλεμος εἰ μὲν καταλέλυται — εἰ δὲ μή, ἀλλὰ λυθήτω γε, πρὸς Διός. εἴτε γὰρ πρότερος ἐλύπεις, εἰκός τοι σὲ καὶ ἄρξαι τῆς εἰρήνης, εἴτε παρ' ἐκείνῳ τὸ ἔγκλημα, μεῖζον σοὶ ταύτῃ τὸ θαῦμα· οὐ γὰρ οὕτω τὸ ἀμύνασθαι ὡς τὸ παρὸν ἀμύνασθαι μὴ βουληθῆναι θαυμάζεται· τὸ μὲν γὰρ καὶ τῶν βαρβάρων καὶ τῶν θηρίων, τὸ δὲ Ἑλληνικὸν καὶ Ἀθηναίων καὶ θεοῖς ἐοικότων. 3. ἀναμιμνήσκου δὲ ἐκείνου τοῦ παρέχοντός σοι δακρύων ἀφορμὴν ἑαυτὸν ἀποθανόντα καὶ τάχα γε εὑρήσεις αὐτὸν ἀφέντα πολλοῖς αἰτίας οὐ μικρὰς οὐδ' οἷαι ὑμᾶς συνέκρουσαν. ἀλλ' οἶσθα δὴ τοὺς ὀκτὼ καὶ τὰ ἐκείνων ξίφη· ὃ μεθ' ἡμῶν ἐπαινῶν τότε πῶς ἂν δύναιο μὴ μιμεῖσθαι νῦν; 4. εἰ δέ τοι Ἀτρείδης μὲν ἀπήχθετο καὶ δέδοκται τηρεῖν τὴν ὀργήν, σὺ δ' ἀλλὰ τὴν γυναῖκα τῶν ἔμπροσ-

[1] Ἐλπιδίῳ F., Seeck (V) Οὐλπιανῷ Wolf (S Vind.)

[a] *BLZG* 170 (ii), *PLRE* 415 (6). Appointed *Comes Rei Privatae* in 362 by Julian, he was initially retained in office

## 113. To Elpidius[a]

1. I am glad that you enjoy the emperor's favour—a fact which I deduce from your continuance in office, for the one follows on the other. 2. If your feud with Seleucus is finally over—well and good: if it is not, then for heaven's sake get it over. If you were the first to give offence, it is reasonable for you to make the first overtures for peace too: if the blame lies with him, you will get more admiration by so doing, for retaliation is not so much admired as the refusal to indulge in it when one can.[b] That is savage and brutal: this self-denial is in the Hellenic and Athenian tradition, a mark of men who are the image of gods. 3. Remember him who by his death gave you cause for tears: you will probably find that he excused many people for faults that were not trivial nor yet such as caused you to be at loggerheads. Indeed, you know those eight and their swords.[c] You commended him for his action then, as I did; so how can you fail to follow his lead now? 4. And if the son of Atreus was angered and determined to maintain his wrath,[d] at any rate regard his wife[e] as deserving of her former

by Jovian, but soon succeeded by Caesarius. The quarrel between him and Seleucus, two of the devoted followers of Julian, was most distressing to Libanius.

[b] Cf. *Letter* 126.3, Plat. *Crito* 49d.

[c] Cf. *Or.* 18.199, where the conspirators number ten.

[d] Homer *Il.* 9.115 f.

[e] Alexandra, *BLZG* 56, *PLRE* 44.

θεν ἀξίου καὶ τὸ αἰδεῖσθαι φύλαττε, ἣ οὔτε Ἀσσυρίους εἶδεν οὔτε Εὐφράτην οὔτε ἐκοινώνησε τῆς ἐκεῖ παιδιᾶς· οὕτω γάρ μοι καλεῖν ἥδιον.

## 114. Σκυλακίῳ

1. Οἶμαι καὶ σὲ πεπλῆχθαι τὴν ψυχήν, ὥσπερ ἡμεῖς· τῶν τε γὰρ αὐτῶν ἐτυγχάνομεν ἐρῶντες καὶ τῶν αὐτῶν ἐστερήμεθα, ἀνδρὸς ἑταίρου τε καὶ φίλου.[1] εἰ δὲ βασιλέα προσεῖπον ἑταῖρον, δεινὸν[2] οὐδέν· αὐτὸς γὰρ ἡμᾶς οὕτω κέκληκε φθάσας καὶ τὸν ἐκείνου βεβαιοῦμεν ἐν τῷ ὀνόματι νόμον. 2. πάντων δὲ ὄντων μοι τῶν τότε ἡδονῆς ἀξίων μέγιστον ἦν ἡ σὴ φιλία γενομένη τε ὁμοῦ καὶ εἰς ἀκμὴν ἐλθοῦσα, πρότερον οὐκ οἶδ' ὅπως οὐκ ἐθελήσασα γενέσθαι, πλὴν εἰ τοῦτο εἴποις, ὅτι μοι τὸν χρόνον ἐκεῖνον ὑπερβολὰς ἀγαθῶν ἐνεγκεῖν ἔδει. 3. ἀναμιμνήσκου γάρ, ὅσα τε ἐσπουδάσαμεν ὅσα τε ἐπαίσαμεν[3] ἐμμελῶς τούς τι οἰομένους

[1] φίλου F. (V) βασιλέως Wolf (other Mss.).
[2] δεινὸν F. (V) θαυμαστὸν Wolf (other Mss.).
[3] ἐπαίσαμεν F. (V) ἐπαίξαμεν Wolf (other Mss.).

[a] *BLZG* 271 (ii), *PLRE* 811 (2). F/Kr. no. 55. Teacher of law in Berytus, a confirmed pagan corresponding with

due and maintain your courtesy, for she did not see Assyria or the Euphrates or share in your fun there—for that is the term I prefer to apply to it.

## 114. To Scylacius[a]

1. You too are as aghast as I am, I believe, for we both loved the same thing and were robbed of it—of a dear friend and comrade. For me to call an emperor comrade is nothing out of the way, for he himself called us that first and we confirm the precedent he set by using the term.[b] 2. Of all the things that then gave me joy the greatest was your friendship which, no sooner had it come into being, than it reached perfection. Somehow or other it had refused to come about before, unless you were to argue that that period inevitably must produce a superabundance of blessings for me. 3. Just remember what we did both in jest and in earnest[c] simply to prove wrong those people who thought

Libanius in 363/4. The inference from § 6 is that the letter was composed about the beginning of the academic session in early October.

[b] For Julian's breaches of imperial etiquette and the criticisms aroused cf. *Or.* 1.129; Amm. Marc. 22.7.3; Socr. *H.E.* 3.1 (fin). In his letters to Libanius Julian twice addresses him as ἀδελφὲ ποθεινότατε καὶ προσφιλέστατε (*ELF* 96–7), an attitude which does violence to the majesty of the emperor.

[c] Cf. Plat. *Gorg.* 481b.

εἶναι καταλύοντες ἐλέγχοις καὶ ποθοῦντες ἑσπέραν καὶ θέοντες ἐπὶ τὴν συνουσίαν, ἐν ᾗ βραχέα μὲν ἔλεγον, πλείω δὲ ἤκουον. ἔρρεον δὲ ἐκ τοῦ σοῦ στόματος οἱ λόγοι τῶν τοῦ Νέστορος οὐ χείρους, οὓς ὁ δεξάμενος εἰς φρόνησιν ἐπιδοὺς ἀπῄει. 4. διὰ δὴ ταῦτα πάντα, ὥσπερ αὐτὸς ἐκεῖνος ὁ Πύλιος, τὴν ἀκμὴν ποθῶ τῶν χρόνων ἐκείνων. ἀλλ' οὔπως ἅμα πάντα. εἰ τότε εὐτύχουν, νῦν αὖτέ με γῆρας ἱκάνει, λύπης ἔργον μᾶλλον ἢ πλήθους ἐτῶν. 5. παραμυθήσομαι δ' οὖν ἐμαυτὸν οἷς τε ἐπιστέλλω πρὸς σὲ τοῖς τε ἥξουσι παρὰ σοῦ. πρώτην δὲ Ἕλληνι δι' ἀνδρὸς Ἕλληνος πέμπων ἐπιστολὴν ἴσως οὐκ ἀδικῶ, τῷ δὲ οὐχ Ἕλληνι μόνον, ἀλλὰ καὶ χρηστῷ συμβέβηκεν εἶναι. προσερεῖ δέ τις αὐτὸν καὶ εὐδαίμονα, τῆς σῆς εἰ τύχοι προνοίας. 6. τεύξεται δὲ καὶ διὰ τὸν τρόπον καὶ τοῦ γένους ἕνεκα καὶ τῶν γραμμάτων καὶ τῆς γε αἰτίας καθ' ἣν ἥκει. νόμους γὰρ ἐκ Φοινίκης κτησάμενος εἰς τὴν Ἑλλάδα κομίσαι βούλεται τοῖς ἀδικουμένοις λιμένα.

themselves to be somebody, and how we longed for evening to come and hurried to that gathering where I said little and heard much. Eloquence flowed from your lips no worse than that of Nestor,[d] and any who received it went away with intellect improved. 4. For all these reasons then, like that old man of Pylos himself, I long for the perfection of those days;[e] but we cannot have everything at once. If I was happy then, but "now old age comes upon me,"[f] it is the result of grief rather than length of years. 5. So I will console myself with the letters I write to you and those which will reach me from you. Perhaps I am not at fault in sending this first letter to a Hellene by means of a Hellene, for he happens to be not just a Hellene but a genuine one, too.[g] He will also be accounted happy and fortunate if he enjoys your consideration. 6. And enjoy it he will both because of his character and for the sake of his family, his literary abilities and the reason for his coming, for, after acquiring a knowledge of law in Phoenicia, he wants to take it to Greece as a protection for the victims of injustice.

[d] Cf. Homer *Il.* 1.247 ff.

[e] *Ibid.* 11.670.

[f] *Ibid.* 4.320.

[g] The bearer is unknown. His introduction has a triple nuance; he is a Hellene by birth, by his education in the classics, and by religion.

## 115. Φιλαγρίῳ

1. Ὅτι μὲν ἀπεσώθης,[1] καλῶς ποιεῖς· ἔδει μέντοι σε τὸ τῶν χαιρόντων δρῶντα τοῖς φίλοις ἐπιστέλλειν διδάσκοντα ἡλίκον διέφυγες κλύδωνα. 2. ἀλλ', οἶμαι, καταφρονεῖς ἡμῶν ἅτε τὸν πόλεμον ἐν γράμμασιν ἔχων εἰδὼς ὅτι σου δεῖσθαι δεήσει τοὺς σοφιστάς, οἷς ἔρως εἰπεῖν τι περὶ τῶν πεπραγμένων. ἀκούω γάρ σε τὸ ἀεὶ γινόμενον γραφόμενον σκέπτεσθαι[2] χωρίων τε φύσεις καὶ μέτρα πόλεων καὶ ὕψος φρουρίων καὶ ποταμῶν πλάτος καὶ ὅσα δρᾶσαί τε καὶ παθεῖν συνέβη. 3. ἀλλ' εἰ μὲν ἡμῖν χαριζόμενος τοῦτο ἐποίεις, τῆς αὐτῆς ἦν δήπου γνώμης καὶ τὸ ἐπιστεῖλαι· εἰ δὲ σαυτῷ καὶ τοῖς συστρατευσαμένοις, ἡμᾶς γ' ἐχρῆν ἐξ ἐπιστολῆς εὐφρᾶναι. 4. ἃ μέντοι φρονῶ περὶ τῶν γεγραμμένων, σοὶ φράσω. οὐ μᾶλλον ἐγὼ σοῦ δεήσομαι ἀναγινώσκειν ἢ ἐμοῦ σὺ τὰ ὦτά με παρασχεῖν. σὺ μὲν γὰρ ἐμὲ διδάξεις ἔργα γυμνά, ἐγὼ δὲ αὐτὰ τοῖς ἐκ τῶν λόγων ἐσθήμασιν ἀμφιέσω. βούλοιο δ' ἂν κοσμηθῆναι τὰς πράξεις, ὥσπερ ἐγὼ μὴ ἀγνοῆσαι τὰ ἔργα. 5. ἀλλ' ἐν μὲν ἐκείνοις τὸ μὲν δώσεις, τὸ δὲ κερδανεῖς· ἕως

[1] <χαίρων> καλῶς suggested F.

[2] σκέπτεσθαι F. ἕπεσθαι Wolf (V)

## 115. To Philagrius[a]

1. I am glad that you are safe. Still you should act as though you are glad and write to tell your friends of the tempest from which you have escaped. 2. I suppose it is that you look down on me, since you have the story of the campaign written down and know that sophists will have to approach you when they have the urge to speak of its happenings, for I am told that you examine and put into writing every particular, the nature of the localities, the dimensions of cities, height of fortresses, width of rivers, and all the successes and reverses. 3. If you did so as a favour to me, surely you would be consistent in your attitude if you wrote to me: if it was for yourself and your fellow combatants, then at least you ought to bless my heart with a letter. 4. As for my feelings about what you have written, they are as follows: I will no more ask you to read them than you ask me to lend you my ears. You will inform me of the bare facts; I will dress them in the robes of rhetoric. You would want your actions displayed to best advantage, as I would wish not to be ignorant of what happened. 5. But herein you will be both the giver and the gainer. While you are

[a] *BLZG* 237 (iv), *PLRE* 693 (2), a loyal officer of Julian (Amm. Marc. 21.4.2 ff), who reappears as *Comes Orientis* in 382 (*Or.* 1.206 ff). Libanius has had time to recover from the first shock of Julian's death and is now casting around for information about the expedition for his orations on Julian. Philagrius is still with the retreating army. The time is October.

δ' ἂν ἀπῇς, χαρίζου δι' ὧν ἔξεστι τοῖς ἀποῦσιν, ἄλλως θ' ὅτε σοι καὶ βέλτιον[3] μηνύειν ἔνι βασιλέως περὶ πάντα τε ἀρετὴν καὶ πρός σέ τινα χρηστότητα. θαυμαστὸν δὲ οὐδὲν διακόνῳ βελτίστῳ τὸν οὐκ ἂν πονηροῖς χρησάμενον χαίρειν. 6. τοῦ τε οὖν γράφειν ἔχου καὶ Σάλβιον ὄντα μου φίλον καὶ σαυτοῦ νόμιζε· ὃς ἐνοχλήσει μέν σε οὐδέν, ἐπίσταται δὲ μεμνῆσθαι χάριτος.

[3] βέλτιον F. βελτίω V om. Wolf.

## 116. Θεμιστίῳ

1. Ἔλαβόν σου τὸν λόγον, καλὸν ὑπὲρ ἀνδρὸς καλοῦ, συγχωρήσεις δὲ καλὸν εἶναι τὸν κοσμηθέντα τῷ λόγῳ. καὶ γὰρ εἰ τέθνηκεν, ἀλλ' ἥ γε Ἀλήθεια ζῇ πολλῶν ψευδομένων στομάτων ἰσχυροτέρα. 2. λαβὼν δὲ καὶ προσελόμενος Κέλσον εἰς τὴν τοῦ λόγου κρίσιν ἀνέγνων ἔτι ζῶντος τοῦ ἐπαινουμένου πηδῶν ἐφ' ἑκάστῳ, ταὐτὰ δὲ ἡμῖν καὶ τὸν Κέλσον κατεῖχε, θεώμενος δὲ τὴν ἐφ' ἑκάστῳ τέχνην καὶ τὸ καινὸν τῆς εὑρέσεως καὶ τὸ τρίπωλον ἅρμα δαιμόνων τὸ καλλιζυγὲς καὶ τὰς

[a] Bouchery p. 223, F/Kr. no. 60. This letter, written in Oct.–Nov. 363, acknowledges receipt of the copy of the oration he had requested in *Letter* 102.

not with me, oblige me as absent friends can, especially when you can give me a better account of our emperor's excellence in general and any kindness of his towards you. For it is no surprise if he who would never have employed a bad subordinate was pleased with a very good one. 6. So get down to writing. Regard my friend Salvius[b] as your own friend too; he will not be a nuisance and he knows how to remember a kindness.

[b] Salvius, father of an ex-pupil, appears in various requests between 363 and 365; cf. *Epp.* 1433, 1276, 1464.

## 116. To Themistius

1. I have received your speech, a noble speech upon a noble man, for you will concede that the person honoured by it was noble.[a] Even if he is dead, Truth at least lives on, more potent than many lying mouths. 2. On receiving it, I got Celsus to assist me in the assessment of the speech and I read it while the person you praised was still alive. My excitement mounted at each new detail, and Celsus was affected just as I was, and as I observed the artistry of each particular, the originality of conception,[b] the "glorious threefold team of gods"[c]

[b] εὕρεσις = *inventio*. Cf. Hermogenes Περὶ Εὑρέσεως (*Rhet. Gr.* 2.177 ff).

[c] Cf. Eurip. *Andr.* 277 f and schol. The goddesses were Hera, Athena, and Aphrodite: the personification of dignity, clarity, and grace (a citation from Themistius' speech. So Dagron, p. 225).

ἀνάγκας αἷς ἐδέθησαν καὶ τὰς τῶν ἐγκωμίων εἰσόδους καὶ τῆς λέξεως τὴν χάριν ἕτοιμος ἦν βιβλίον ὑπὲρ τοῦ βιβλίου ποιεῖν· τοσαῦτα ἐπέρρει τῆς τε ἀναγνώσεως χωρούσης καὶ ἀπιόντων ἤδη καὶ μάλιστά γε δὴ τῆς νυκτός· οὐ γὰρ εἴα καθεύδειν ὁ λόγος ἐνδιαιτώμενος τῇ ψυχῇ. 3. μέλλοντος δέ μου τῆς γραφῆς ἅπτεσθαι φερόμενος ὁ τῆς σφαγῆς λόγος ἐνέπεσεν εἰς τὴν πόλιν, καὶ πάντα διεσκέδαστο καὶ ἓν ἠπιστάμην μόνον, δακρύειν. ὃ καὶ νῦν εὑρὼν ποιοῦντά με Κλέαρχος ἐπετίμησε μέν, οὐ μὴν ἔπαυσεν· οὐδὲ οὐδ' ἐγὼ τοὺς χαίροντας. 4. μὴ τοίνυν θαύμαζε σιγῶντος· οὐ γὰρ τῶν πενθούντων τὸ λέγειν οὐδὲ τὸ γράφειν. τῆς λύπης δὲ εἰ μὲν ὁ χρόνος ἀπαλλαγὴν οἴσει, θεὸς οἶδε. σὺ δ' εἰ πρεσβεύων ἀφῖξο, τάχ' ἂν ἤρκεσας τῇ σαυτοῦ σοφίᾳ τὴν ἐμὴν ψυχὴν ἰώμενος, ἀλλ', οἶμαι, ἔφυγες ἄνδρα ἀτυχοῦντα. 5. καὶ περὶ Κλεάρχου μὲν ὡς ἐρῶντος γράφεις καὶ φῄς αὐτῷ πρὸ τῆς πρεσβείας εἶναι τοὐμόν· σὺ δ' οὔθ' ὡς ἐρῶν οὔθ' ὡς ἐρασθείς ποτε ἦλθες. καίτοι τὴν βουλὴν ἀμήχανον τὴν σὴν ὑπερβῆναι πειθώ, δι'

---

[d] Cf. *Or.* 11.186.

[e] Cf. Philostr. *V.S.* 22.4 (of Polemo): καὶ καθεύδειν γε οὐκ ἐᾷ.

[f] *BLZG* 108, *PLRE* 211. He had been a member of the

and the ties with which they were bound together,[d] the introductions to your commendations and the graceful diction, I was quite prepared to write a book upon your own book. So many were the thoughts that flowed over me, both as the reading progressed and afterwards when we had parted, and particularly during the night, for your speech which had impressed itself in my mind allowed me no sleep.[e] 3. Just as I was about to begin writing, the news of his murder descended on the city: everything fell to pieces and the only thing I was capable of doing was to weep. Clearchus[f] found me doing that just now and reproved me for it, but he did not stop me. Nor did I stop people from rejoicing, either.[g] 4. Do not then be surprised at my silence; speeches do not belong with mourning, nor yet does letter-writing. Heaven knows whether time will bring relief from my grief. If you had come here on the embassy, you would perhaps have succeeded in curing my soul by your philosophy,[h] but, I suppose, you avoided a man distressed. 5. In your letter you speak of Clearchus as an admirer of mine, and say that he thinks more of me than of the embassy. But you have never come either as admiring or as admired. Yet the senate could not possibly

embassy from the Senate of Constantinople to congratulate Jovian upon his accession.

[g] On the rejoicing in Antioch at the death of Julian cf. *Letter* 120.2.

[h] Plat. *Hipp. Min.* 372e.

ἢν πλείω γεωργεῖ καὶ γεγένηται μείζων, ἀλλ', οἶμαι, ἐξωμόσω· χρῆν γάρ με καὶ ταύτῃ κακῶς παθεῖν.

---

i As proconsul of Constantinople in 359 Themistius had increased the numbers of the Senate from 300 to 2000 (Them. *Or.* 34.13). By this increase in numbers, the amount of landed property vested in its members had also increased.

## 117. Ὑπερεχίῳ

1. Οὐδέν σε δεῖ νῦν ἀθυμεῖν, ὅτι μή σοι τὸν Μίδου, τοῦ ὑμετέρου προγόνου, δέδωκεν ἡ Τύχη χρυσόν, ὥστ' ἐξεῖναι, ὅ τι ἂν ἐθέλῃς, ὠνεῖσθαι πολλὴν τῶν μικρῶν ἐξ ἀφθόνων διδόντα τιμήν. οὐ γὰρ τῶν πρίασθαι δυναμένων τὸ ἄρχειν, ἀλλὰ τῶν δυναμένων ἄρχειν τὸ τῶν πόλεων[1] ἐπιστατεῖν. 2. εἰ μὲν οὖν μηδέν σοι συνῄδειν χρηστόν, ἤλγουν ἂν ὡς οὐκ ὂν τῷ τοιούτῳ πρὸς τὰ τοιαῦτα παρελθεῖν· νῦν δέ — νοῦς γὰρ ἔστι σοι καὶ γλῶττα ἀγαθὴ καὶ οὐκ ἂν εἰς πλῆθος πραγμάτων ἐμπεσὼν θορυβοῖο[2] — πολλὰς ἐλπίδας ἔχω τάξεως σέ τινος καὶ σχήματος ἐπιβήσεσθαι. 3. δεῖ δὲ μὴ

[1] δυναμένων ἄρχειν τὸ τῶν πόλεων F. (V) πόλεσιν εἰδότων Wolf (other Mss.).

[2] θορυβοῖς Wolf (Par.).

have ignored your powers of persuasion, for because of them its lands cover a wider area and its numbers have increased.[i] You refused,[j] I am sure, for here too I am bound to suffer.[k]

[j] Cf. Demosth. *Fals. Leg.* 121 f. Themistius had excused himself from being a member of this embassy, as Demosthenes had done before him.

[k] Cf. Herod. 1.8. Libanius has to bear the disappointment of not meeting Themistius again, as well as his grief at Julian's death.

## 117. To Hyperechius

1. There is no need for you to feel disappointed now because Fortune has not given you the gold of your ancestor Midas[a] for you to be able to purchase anything you like, paying from your wealth a big price for trifles. The government of cities does not belong to those who can buy office but to those who can wield it. 2. So if I were unaware of your capabilities, I would be sorry for you because of the impossibility of such a person attaining such a position. As it is—you have intelligence, a fine tongue, and you would not be put out by involvement in a mass of business—I have good hopes that you will enter upon some post with official rank. 3. But

[a] Midas was king of ancient Phrygia, son of Gordias, and founder of the temple of Cybele at Pessinus—the area later covered by the province of Galatia with its capital Ancyra, the home town of Hyperechius.

τὰ μέγιστα εὐθὺς ζητεῖν μηδ' ἐν πίθῳ τὴν κεραμείαν, φασίν, ἀλλὰ κἂν μικρὰ διδῷ τις, δέχεσθαι μεθ' ἡδονῆς νομίζοντα ἀφορμὴν ἔσεσθαι τοῖς μεγάλοις τὰ μικρά. ἡ γὰρ ἐν ταῖς ἐλάττοσι τῶν τεχνῶν ἐπίδειξις ταχέως ἀνέῳξε τὰς τῶν λαμπροτέρων θύρας. 4. ὑπὲρ δὲ τούτων λόγοι τέ μοι γεγένηνται πρὸς τὸν ἄριστον Καισάριον καὶ γράμματα πρὸς τὸν αὐτὸν φέρεται. ἃ σὺ δὴ λαβὼν αἰδοῦ καὶ πειρῶ φαίνεσθαι φρόνησιν ἔχων, ἡνίκα ἂν σε δοκιμάζῃ.[3] δεινὸς δὲ ἀνὴρ ἐξ ὄνυχος τὸν λέοντα. 5. 'ἐγὼ μὲν οὖν ὁ αὐτός εἰμι,' φησὶ Περικλῆς· σὺ δ' οὐ παύσῃ μεταβολὴν ὑφορώμενος;

[3] ἄν σε δοκιμάζῃ F. (V) ἂν δοκιμάζῃ Wolf (other Mss.).

---

[b] Proverbial by Plato's time; cf. *Lach.* 187b.

[c] Lately *vicarius Asiae,* he had been summoned to Jovian's court at Antioch, where Libanius had had this conversation. Promoted to *Comes rei privatae,* he is now

## 118. Δατιανῷ

1. Οὐκ Ἐνδυμίωνες ἐγενόμεθα τὴν νύκτα ἐκεί-

---

[a] Datianus, out of favour with Julian, had immediately been restored to court by Jovian. The relation of this comedy of errors is to excuse Libanius of the apparent

you must not aim at the top straightaway nor yet try to run before you can walk, as they say.[b] You should be glad to accept whatever is offered, however small, and you should think that small beginnings lead on to great things. A demonstration of proficiency in minor matters quickly opens the door to something higher. 4. I have been in conversation with the excellent Caesarius[c] on the subject, and my letter to him is on its way. Take it and make your respects to him and try to show yourself a man of sense, when he tries you out. He is very good at summing up at a glance.[d] 5. "I am the man I always was," says Pericles.[e] Will you not stop suspecting me of a change of heart?

en route with Jovian to Ancyra, where Hyperechius is instructed to present his letter of introduction (*Ep.* 1443).

[d] The proverb "telling a lion from its claw" goes back as far as Alcaeus; Plut. *de Defec. Orac.* 410c and *Paroem. Gr.* 1.252.

[e] Thuc. 1.140.1; cf. *Ep.* 752.

## 118. To Datianus[a]

1. We were not at all like Endymion[b] that night

discourtesy of failing to see him off when he left Antioch to rejoin Jovian on his way to Constantinople.

[b] Endymion, beloved of Selene; Zeus granted him his choice, which was an everlasting sleep, in which he remained forever youthful (Apollod. 1.56, *Paroem. Gr.* 1.75).

νην, ἐν ᾗ τὸν καλὸν βασιλέα ἡμῖν διώκων ἀπῇρας· εἰ γὰρ δὴ καὶ πρότερον Ἐνδυμίωνες ἦμεν, τότ᾽ ἂν πάντως ἀπεωσάμεθα τὸν ὕπνον. ἀλλ᾽ ἄκουσον παιδιὰν Τύχης ἤ, εἰ βούλει, ἐπήρειαν. 2. ἑσπέρας ἀλλήλοις παραγγείλαντες πράττειν, ὅπως σε προπέμψομεν,[1] διελύθημεν λελουμένοι. ἄρτι δὲ τῶν ἡμιόνων ὑπηγμένων τῷ ζυγῷ[2] δραμὼν ὁ παῖς ὃς ταῦτα τηρεῖν ἐτέτακτο κινεῖ με καὶ ἀφυπνίζει. ἐγὼ δὲ τὸν μὲν ὡς Ὀλύμπιον πέμπω ταὐτὸ ποιήσοντα, ἕτερον δὲ καθίζω πρὸ τῶν θυρῶν κελεύσας, ὁπότε παρίοις, βοῆσαι· διὰ γὰρ τῆς στοᾶς ᾤμην σαυτόν τε βαδιεῖσθαι καὶ τὸ ζεῦγος. 3. ἕως ἦν καὶ ἐθαύμαζον οὐδενὸς καλοῦντος καὶ καταβὰς ἔπαιον τὸν οἰκέτην ὡς προδότην μοι τῆς σπουδῆς. ὁ δ᾽ ἔφασκε μὲν οὐδὲν ἀδικεῖν, πείθειν δὲ οὐκ εἶχεν. ἀλλ᾽ ἐγὼ μὲν ἐθυμούμην, σὺ δ᾽ ἄρα ἑτέραν ἦλθες ἐπὶ τὴν γέφυραν τὴν ἐπώνυμον Ταυρέου. ταῦτα γὰρ ὕστερον ἐπυθόμην, ἃ πρὶν μαθεῖν χαλεπὸς ἦν ἅπαντι τῷ φανέντι. καὶ δεινὸν ἐποιούμην Ὀλύμπιον μὲν

[1] προπέμψομεν F. παραπέμψομεν Wolf (Ms.)
[2] τῷ ζυγῷ F., conj. Re. τῶν ζυγῶν Wolf (Ms.)

when you set out to follow in the train of our noble emperor.[c] Even if we had been before, at that moment we would have totally rejected sleep. But now listen to fortune's sport—or, if you would have it so, spite. 2. In the evening, after encouraging one another to act and set you on your way, we had a bath and went home. As soon as your mules were put to the carriage, the slave who had been detailed to look out for this, ran and shook me awake. I sent him to Olympius[d] to do the same, and I stationed another in my doorway to shout and tell me when you were passing, for I thought that you and your carriage would go by way of the colonnade. 3. Dawn came and I was surprised to receive no call; so I went down and began to beat my servant for failing me in my desire. He tried to tell me that he had done no wrong but he could not convince me; I was in a rage, but you, after all, went the other way to the bridge of Taureus.[e] That is what I learned later, but before finding it out I was out of temper with everyone I saw. I was annoyed that Olympius had succeeded in his part because of

[c] Jovian had arrived in Antioch by 22 Oct. and had left by mid-winter.

[d] Olympius (ii), Libanius' old friend.

[e] The bridge of the Taurean Gate, lying at the southwest corner of the city walls, was the main crossing point of the Orontes for roads north and west. For a convenient plan of Antioch, showing colonnades, bridges, and municipal buildings see Petit, *Vie Municipale* 127.

δι᾽ ἐμὲ τετυχηκέναι ἔργου, πεδηθῆναι δὲ ἐμέ. 4. μετὰ τοιαύτης ὀργῆς ἐπὶ τῆς κλίνης ἐκείμην, ἀναβὰς δὲ Ὀλύμπιος ὁ μὲν εὐδαιμόνιζεν ἐμὲ εἰδὼς τῶν ἐμῶν οὐδέν, ἐγὼ δὲ ἐκεῖνον οὐδ᾽ αὐτὸς εἰδὼς τἀκείνου, ἀλλ᾽ ὁ μὲν ᾤετο ἐμὲ προπεπομφέναι καὶ τὸ μέχρι τίνος; ἠρώτα, ἐγὼ δὲ ἐκεῖνον, καὶ προσῆν ταὐτὸν ἐρώτημα. 5. <καὶ>[3] εἶπον ὡς μηνύσαιμι καὶ τὸν οἰκέτην ἐμεμφόμην· ὁ δ᾽ ἐκεῖνον μὲν ἀπέλυεν αἰτίας διὰ τῆς γεφύρας ἣν ἔφην, τὸν αὑτοῦ δὲ ἀποπνίξειν ἠπείλει σαφῶς αὑτὸν ἠδικηκότα· τὸν γὰρ δὴ ἵππον ῥᾳθύμως ἑλκόμενον ἐλευθερῶσαι μὲν ἑαυτὸν τῆς τοῦ ἱπποκόμου χειρός, φέρεσθαι δὲ διὰ τῶν στενωπῶν ἀπολαύοντα τῆς σελήνης, καὶ οὕτω δὴ τὸν μὲν ἐπὶ τὴν θήραν τοῦ ἵππου τραπέσθαι, τὸν ἱπποκόμον, αὑτὸν δὲ ἄπρακτον ἀναστρέψαι λυπούμενον. 6. ‘τοιόνδ᾽ ἀπέβη τὸ πρᾶγμα,’ φησὶν ἡ τραγῳδία. σὺ δὲ σύγγνωθί τε γελάσας καὶ τῇ γνώμῃ τὰ ἡμέτερα κρῖνον, καὶ τάχα οὐ κακοὺς εὑρήσεις.

[3] <καὶ> F., conj. Re.

me, while I had been bound hand and foot. 4. In such a temper I was lying on my bed when up the stairs came Olympius. He began to congratulate me in ignorance of what had happened to me, and I him, myself ignorant of what had happened to him. He thought that I had gone to see you off, and "How far did you go?" he enquired. I thought he had done the same, and put the same question. 5. I told him that I had sent him the news, and I started to blame my servant; he cleared him of blame by telling me of the bridge I mentioned, but swore that he would throttle his own man who had obviously let him down. He told me that his horse was carelessly handled, got free from the hands of the groom and galloped away through the side streets to enjoy a moonlight jaunt, and that in consequence the groom went off to chase the animal while he returned home frustrated and annoyed. 6. "Such is the end of our story"[f]—so it is said in tragedy. Pardon us with a chuckle: judge us by our intention, and perhaps you will find us not at all bad.

[f] A stock Euripidean conclusion. Five of his extant plays end with this line.

## 119. Καισαρίῳ

1. Κατὰ νόμον ἀρχαῖον ὅ τε συριάρχης εὖ παθεῖν ἠξίωσεν ὅ τε μέγας βασιλεὺς ἐπένευσε, καὶ γράμματα μέν, ὥς φασι, γεγένηται, μένει δὲ ἐν τοῖς πρὸ τῶν γραμμάτων ὁ συριάρχης καὶ τῶν δωρεῶν οὔτε μικρὸν οὔτε μεῖζον ἀπολαύσας φαίνεται. 2. τὸ δὲ αἴτιον, οὐδεὶς ἡμῖν τῶν ἀρχαίων ἑταίρων ἐν βασιλείοις δυνατός. εἰ δ' ἦν Καισάριος ὁ χρηστός, πᾶς ἂν ἐκινεῖτο λίθος καὶ τὰ ἔργα ταῖς ἐπιστολαῖς εὐθὺς ἂν ἠκολούθει. 3. ἆρ' οὐ δοκοῦμέν σοι ἀδικεῖσθαι, ὅτι πρῶτον τοιαῦτα ἠναγκάσμεθα γράφειν; πῶς γὰρ ἀνεκτόν, ὦ πρὸς Διός, ἡνίκα δοκοῦμεν εὐτυχεῖν, τῶν εἰωθότων ἀτυχεῖν, καὶ λόγον μὲν εἶναι πολύν, ὡς ἄρα ἐξ οὐρίων θέομεν παρὰ τὴν σὴν δύναμιν, ἑστάναι δὲ ἡμῖν τὴν ναῦν ὥσπερ δεδεμένην; 4. πότερον, ὦ 'γαθέ, μεταβέβλησαι καὶ μισεῖς ἢ φιλεῖς μέν, ἀπερρᾳθύμηκας δέ; καὶ δεῖ τι προσδοκᾶν ἢ μηδὲ ἐλπίζειν ἔτι; καὶ ταύτην οἶδ' ὅτι τὴν ἐπιστολὴν

---

[a] Cf. Liebeschuetz, "The Syriarch" 115 ff; *Antioch* 141.

To Caesarius as *Comes rei privatae,* repeating the request, ignored in *Ep.* 1399, for official assistance for Celsus, the Syriarch of 364. The Syriarch was responsible for the annual presidency of the κοινόν of Syrian cities in

## 119. To Caesarius[a]

1. In accordance with long established custom the Syriarch has asked to receive assistance and our great emperor[b] has consented. A letter of assent is said to have been composed, but the Syriarch remains in the same condition as before the letter, and obviously enjoys no part of what he has been awarded, whether small or great. 2. The reason is that none of our old friends has any influence at court. If the good Caesarius had, no stone would be left unturned[c] and results would immediately follow upon our letters. 3. Does it not seem to you that we are the injured party in that for the first time we have been forced to write in this strain? Good heavens! it is surely intolerable to be unsuccessful in getting what we usually do when thought to be successful, and for it to be common gossip that our course is set fair because of your influence,[d] and yet for us to be in the doldrums, as though fast at anchor! 4. Has your attitude changed, good sir? Have you taken a dislike for us? Or are you still our friend, and yet utterly neglectful of us? Should we still look forward to something or have we no hope

honour of the emperor; he received an imperial subvention to help cover the enormous expense, but it had to be applied for and, as here, it could be slow in coming.

[b] Jovian.

[c] Cf. Eurip. *Heracl.* 1002; Zenobius 2.24 (*Zenob.* 4:196).

[d] *Paroem. Gr.* 2.408.

ἀρχὴν ποιήσῃ θυμοῦ, θυμὸς δὲ οὐκ ὀλιγάκις ἐποίησεν ἔχθραν. ἔστι δέ, οἶμαι, μετριώτερον ἀμελεῖσθαι μισούμενον ἢ καλούμενον φίλον μηδὲν ἔχειν τοῦ μισουμένου πλέον. 5. φήσεις ὑπέραντλος εἶναι τῷ πλήθει τῶν πραττομένων. τοῦτο δ' ἂν εἴη καὶ τὸ δεινόν, ὅτι μὴ τῶν πολλῶν ἓν καὶ τοῦτο ἦν τῶν ἀξίων πεπρᾶχθαι. εἰ γὰρ αὖ τὰ μὲν ἔδει τιμᾶν, τὰ δὲ ἀπορρίπτειν, οὐ δήπου γε Κέλσον καὶ τὴν Κέλσου λειτουργίαν τῶν οὐ σπουδῆς ἀξίων ἔδει κεκρίσθαι.

## 120. Σκυλακίῳ[1]

1. Οὐδέπω με πεπαυμένον δακρύων εἰς μείζω θρῆνον ἐνέβαλες διὰ τῆς ἐπιστολῆς· οὕτως ἀκριβῶς διελέχθης περί τε τῶν ἀγαθῶν ὧν ποτε ἀπελαύομεν καὶ περὶ τῶν γενομένων ἄν, εἴ τις ἡμῖν θεῶν ἀποδεδώκει τὸν τὰς νίκας ἀνῃρημένον. 2. ἐκεῖνον μὲν οὖν μᾶλλον ἐπαινοῦσιν οἱ πληγέν-

[1] Σκυλακίῳ F. (V) Ἀριστοφάνει τῷ Κορινθίῳ Wolf (other Mss.).

---

[a] F/Kr. no. 53. Written about the end of November 363 since Jovian is still in Antioch, in acknowledgement of

at all now? I know that you will regard this letter as a cause for anger, and anger not seldom has caused enmity. But it is, I feel, more respectable for an object of your dislike to be ignored than for a so-called friend to have no advantage over one you dislike. 5. You will tell me that you are overwhelmed by pressure of business.[e] It would be the worst part of it for this job too not to be one of the many that need doing. However, if you must defer to this and reject that, then certainly Celsus and his duties ought not to be judged unworthy of your concern.

[e] Cf. Eurip. *Hippol.* 767.

## 120. To Scylacius[a]

1. When I had not yet ceased from tears you cast me into deeper mourning by means of your letter, for you expressed so precisely those blessings we once enjoyed and those which would have come to pass had any of the gods restored him to us after he had won his victories. 2. Those whom he smote

Scylacius' reply to his first letter (*Letter* 114 above). F/Kr. 398 f and 405 f deny that the addressee here is identical with the Scylacius of *Letter* 114, wrongly. There is, however, confusion in the Mss. concerning the superscription, all save V reading Ἀριστοφάνει τῷ Κορινθίῳ—a reading disproved by *Letter* 133.3 and *Ep.* 1214.1.

τες ἢ ὑπὲρ ὧν παρετάξατο· τούτων δέ γε καὶ ὠρχήσαντό τινες δύο πόλεις, ὧν ὑπὲρ τῆς ἑτέρας αἰσχύνομαι. 3. καὶ συγγνώμη γε αὐτοῖς. ὁ γὰρ κακὸς εἶναι βουλόμενος τὸν οὐκ ἐῶντα εἶναι κακὸν ἐχθρὸν εἶναι ἡγεῖται, κἂν ἀποθανεῖν συμβῇ τὸν σωφρονιστήν, ὁ μὴ δυνάμενος σωφρονῆσαι χαίρει διὰ τὸ ἐξεῖναι ἤδη εἶναι κακόν. τοιούτῳ συζῶμεν ὄχλῳ θεοῖς τε ἐχθρῷ κἀκείνῳ, περὶ οὗ σὺ καλῶς δοξάζεις τοῦ τῶν θεῶν αὐτὸν γραφόμενος χοροῦ. 4. ἐγὼ δὲ καὶ αὐτὸς ταῦτά τε ὑπείληφα καὶ ἅμα στένω λογιζόμενος, τίνα μὲν ἠλπίσθη, τίνα δὲ ἐξέβη. καὶ γὰρ εἰ 'κεῖνος μετὰ τῶν κρειττόνων, ἀλλὰ τά γε ἐμὰ χείρω· λεγέσθω γὰρ οὕτως, ὅτι ἐμά. 5. οἷον γὰρ ἂν ἦν τὸν μὲν ἐκ Μήδων, σὲ δὲ ἐκ Φοινίκης ἀφῖχθαι, τὸν μὲν αἰχμαλώτους ἄγοντα, σὲ δὲ ὀψόμενον τὰ ἆθλα τῶν πόνων, ἐμὲ δὲ λέγειν τι περὶ τῶν πεπραγμένων, μικρὸν ὑπὲρ μεγάλων, ἐκεῖνον δὲ εἶναι τὸν τὰ αὑτοῦ διηγούμε-

---

[b] For the awe in which the Persians held Julian cf. *Or.* 18.305, 24.18 ff.

[c] The rejoicing in Antioch is graphically narrated by Theodoret *H.E.* 3.28 not merely in the churches but in theatres, and with feastings and holidays. Despite the protests of Libanius and his fellow pagans, this was not

praise him more than do those for whom he fought.[b] Why, of these a couple of cities even danced for joy at the event, and for one of them I am ashamed.[c] 3. Yet they can be forgiven, for when a man wants to be a rogue he regards as his enemy anyone who prevents him being one, and if it happens that this disciplinarian should be killed, then he, incapable of self-discipline, is glad of the opportunity to be a rogue now. That is the sort of crew among whom my life is spent—enemies of gods and of him whom you rightly describe by enrolling him in the company of the gods.[d] 4. I too have reached this conclusion, and at the same time I grieve in reflecting upon what we hoped and what came to pass.[e] If he indeed is in heaven with those higher powers, my condition at least has taken a turn for the worse—and let us simply say my condition. 5. For what would it have been like for him to have arrived from Persia with his train of prisoners, and you from Phoenicia to see the rewards of his labours,[f] and for me to deliver some slight oration upon his great achieve-

unexpected considering the influential part the city had played in the history and development of Christianity over the past three centuries. The other city is presumably Constantinople.

[d] Cf. *Or.* 18.304.

[e] Cf. the tragic conclusions of Euripides, *Letter* 118.6 note.

[f] That is, to see Libanius deliver a panegyric to Julian upon his achievements.

νον. ἦλθεν ἂν καὶ νέφος κολοιῶν,[2] γέλως ἐμοί τε καὶ σοί, λέγειν μὲν οὐκ ἐπισταμένων, παίειν δὲ ἄλλους ἐπιχειρούντων ἀντὶ τῆς αὑτῶν ἀμαθίας. 6. τοιαύτην ἡμᾶς πανήγυριν ὁ δαίμων ἀφείλετο. καί μοι πολλοὶ μεθ' ὅπλων ἐπέθεντο καὶ ἐκείμην ἂν ὡς μήποτε ἰσχῦσαι,[3] εἰ μή με ἐξήρπασεν ὅστις καὶ τὸν Ἄρη δεδεμένον ἐξέκλεψε. καὶ νῦν δέ τις ἀφῆκε βέλος κρυπτόμενος, καὶ ἐνεγεγράμμην ὡς δὴ δεινὰ ποιῶν, ἀλλὰ πάλιν θεῶν τις κωφὸν τὸ βέλος ἐποίησε καὶ μένω κατὰ χώραν ἐλπίσας ἀνάσπαστος ἔσεσθαι. 7. τοῖς μὲν οὖν τοιούτοις τοξόταις ἀρέσειέ ποτε λῦσαι τὰς νευράς· γῆ δὲ ἡ Περσῶν ἐφθάρη μὲν ἱκανῶς· τὸν δ' ὑπὲρ τῶν ἔργων λόγον ἀπῄτουν μὲν τῶν ἀπανελθόντων τοὺς φίλους καὶ οὓς εἰκὸς ἦν μὴ τῆς περὶ τῶν τοιούτων ἀμελῆσαι γραφῆς, φάσκων δὲ ἕκαστος καὶ

[2] Schol. Mo: τοὺς μοναχούς φησι κολοιοὺς ὁ δυσσεβής.

[3] μήποτε ἰσχῦσαι F. δήποτε ἰσχῦσαι Lacap. δὴ τότε ἰσχύσας Mss. μὴ τότε ἰσχύσας Wolf.

---

[g] Cf. Homer *Il.* 17.755. The scholiast here equates the daws with monks, the black-robed disturbers of the peace of *Or.* 30.8.

[h] The plot is mentioned in *Or.* 1.136 f, where the complicity of Jovian is hinted.

ments, and him to be the one to relate his own actions. A crowd of daws[g] would have flocked around too, and made of themselves a laughing stock for you and me, for though they have no ability in speaking, they try to attack others in return for their own stupidity. 6. Such is the celebration of which fate has robbed us. As for myself, many people have made armed attack upon me, and I would have been laid low, unable ever to prevail,[h] had not I been rescued by him who stole away Ares too when he was enchained.[i] And as it is, a bolt has been aimed at me from cover, and I have been accused of disloyalty, but once again one of the gods has rendered the bolt harmless[j] and I stay where I am, in expectation of not being uprooted. 7. So I trust that sometime the strings of archers such as these may be loosed. The land of Persia has been properly ravaged. I have been requesting an account of the actions from my friends out of those who have returned, and from people who are likely not to have been neglectful of a written account of such matters,

[i] Homer *Il.* 5.389 f. The divine rescuer is Hermes, appropriate in Libanius' case as the patron deity of oratory.

[j] Homer *Il.* 11.390. This appears to be the same charge as that in *Ep.* 1453, where certain δυνατοί, who had returned to favour under Jovian, concoct allegations against him. In *Or.* 1.138 one of the moving spirits is a "barbarian," who may conceivably be Arintheus (so Petit, *Autobiographie* 247).

ἔχειν καὶ δώσειν ἔδωκεν οὐδείς, ἀλλ᾿ οὐδ᾿ ἀπὸ στόματος ἐδίδαξεν. ὁ μὲν γὰρ οἰχόμενος ὠλιγωρεῖτο, πᾶσα δὲ ἡ σπουδὴ τὰ περὶ αὑτὸν ἑκάστῳ. 8. στρατιῶται δέ τινες οὐ πρότερόν με εἰδότες ἔδοσαν ἡμερῶν τέ τινων ἀριθμὸν καὶ ὁδοῦ μέτρα καὶ προσηγορίας τόπων· ἔργων δὲ οὐδαμοῦ διήγησις τὸ πᾶν δυναμένη μηνῦσαι, ἀλλ᾿ ἀμυδρὰ καὶ σκιὰ καὶ συγγραφέως οὐχ ὑπηρετοῦντα στόματι. 9. εἰ δή σοι καὶ τούτων ἐπιθυμία, ποίει μοι δῆλον, καί σοι ἥξει τὰ τῶν στρατιωτῶν· οὗτοι γὰρ καὶ ἔγραψαν, ἡμεῖς δὲ ἄλλους ἠλπίζομεν.

[k] Libanius draws a distinction between the one-time members of Julian's court who have remained silent, and the serving soldiers who have been more forthcoming.

## 121. Ἀνδρονίκῳ

1. Τοῖς τῆς Φοινίκης ἀγαθοῖς κοσμεῖται τὸ κάλλιστον τῆς γῆς τοῦ μὲν ἀρίστου πάντων ἄρχοντος, τοῦ δὲ μετ᾿ ἐκεῖνον ἀρίστου παρεδρεύοντος. ὃν ὅπως τὸ πρῶτον εἴδομεν, ἄκουσον. 2. ἥκομεν ἐγώ τε καὶ Ὀλύμπιος εἰς τὸ Ἐλευσίνιον καὶ

[a] F/Kr. no. 78. Andronicus is now in retirement in Phoenicia.

but though every one says he can and will provide the material, no one has done so—in fact, has not even informed by word of mouth. Our dead hero is slighted: every one's concern is for himself. 8. Some soldiers, previously unacquainted with me, have given me a list of some dates, marching distances, and names of places, but at no time have I received a fully detailed narrative of events, but a shapeless, shadowy tale, unsuited to the lips of a historian.[k] 9. If you have a desire for this information too, let me know and the soldiers' story will be sent to you. They have even put it into writing, and I hope for others to do the same.

Philagrius (*Letter* 115) would be one of these. At this time he is engaged upon the composition of *Oration* 17, and his research for *Oration* 18, which is to appear within the next two years, continues.

## 121. To Andronicus[a]

1. The fairest spot in all the world is ennobled by the glories of Phoenicia, since its governor[b] is the best of men, and the next best is his assessor. And just listen to how I first set eyes on him. 2. Olympius and I had gone to the Eleusinium[c]

[b] Marius, *BLZG* 204, *PLRE* 561 (1). The name of his assessor, the bearer of the letter, is not known.

[c] Olympius (ii) and Libanius were in Daphne, strolling in the gardens near the temple of Artemis Eleusinia (for the foundation legend of which cf. *Or.* 11.109).

ἦμεν ἐν μέσῳ κήπων· τοιοῦτος γὰρ ἐκεῖνος ὁ στενωπός, κῆπος ὁ μὲν ἔνθεν, ὁ δὲ ἔνθεν. ὁρῶμεν οὖν ἄνδρα ἐφ' ἵππου ξένον καὶ πλῆθος ἀκολούθων, καὶ πρὶν πρὸς ἀλλήλους εἰπεῖν· 'τίς οὗτος;' ὁρῶμεν ἀποβάντα καὶ προσείπομεν ἀλλήλους. 3. ὁ δὲ παρά του τῶν[1] παίδων λαβὼν ἐπιστολὰς ἡμῖν ἔδωκεν, εἰπὼν παρ' ὧν. ἐγὼ δὲ οἷς μὲν ἔλαβον ἡδόμην, τῷ δὲ μὴ καὶ Γαϊανοῦ γράμματα ἔχειν ἠχθόμην. ὁ δὲ λύπην τινὰ ἀπήγγελλεν ἐκείνου νομίζοντος ἀπημελῆσθαι. μικρὸν δὴ πρὸς ταῦτα ἀπολογησάμενος ἐπορευόμην ἔτ' ἔχων δεδεμένας τὰς ἐπιστολὰς καὶ τοσοῦτον εἰδὼς μόνον, ὡς ἐκ Φοινίκης ὁ δούς. 4. διενοούμην μὲν οὖν ὡς ἀναγνωσόμενος οἴκοι, διελεγόμην δὲ πρὸς Ὀλύμπιον ὡς περὶ χρηστοῦ τοῦ δόντος ἑωρακὼς τὴν ψυχὴν διὰ τῆς μορφῆς. ἔλαμπε γὰρ τὸ 'κείνης ὡς ἀληθῶς κάλλος διὰ τῶν ὀμμάτων. ἐντυχὼν δέ τις ἡμῖν τῶν ἐκεῖνον βουλομένων ἰδεῖν ἤρετο, εἰ τὸν ἄνδρα εἴδομεν, εἰπὼν τοὔνομα καὶ ἐφ' ὅτῳ ἥκει. καὶ οὕτως ἤδη τὸ πᾶν εἴχομεν. 5. καὶ σοὶ χάρις τῶν γραμμάτων, μᾶλλον δέ, τῆς φιλίας·

[1] παρά του τῶν F., conj. Re. παρὰ τούτων Wolf (Ms.)

and were in the middle of the gardens, for the pathway is such that it has a garden on either side. Well, we saw a stranger on horseback and a mass of attendants, and before we could ask each other "Who's this?" we saw him dismount and we exchanged greetings. 3. He took letters from one of his slaves and gave them to us, telling us from whom they came. I was delighted with those I got, but I was disappointed at not getting a letter from Gaianus[d] too. The bearer told me that Gaianus was rather put out and thought that he had been slighted. I made a few remarks of excuse and went on, still holding the letters unopened, knowing only that the bearer came from Phoenicia. 4. Well, my intention was to read them at home, and I chatted with Olympius and said how fine a fellow the bearer was, for I had seen his character in his face; its quality really shone in his eyes.[e] I was met by someone who wanted to see him and inquired if we had seen him, and he told us his name and why he had come, and so we now knew the whole story. 5. I am grateful to you for your letter or—should I say—for his friendship; for you ensured this in your letter,[f]

[d] Former governor of Phoenicia, replaced by Marius.

[e] So also *Epp.* 839.2, 860.1.

[f] The compliment to the addressee is enhanced by the compliment to the bearer and by taking him as a friend thereafter. For the importance of the bearer in such letters cf. F/Kr. p. 225 ff.

τοῦτο γὰρ ἐν αὐτοῖς ἔπραττες καὶ νῦν ἀλλήλοις χρώμεθα. λόγους δέ σοι πέμψομεν πολλούς· εἰ δὲ φαύλους, ὁ μὴ καλῶν ἐπιθυμῶν αὑτῷ μεμφέσθω. τιμὴν δέ σε οὐκ ἀπαιτήσομεν, ἣν ἔχομεν. ἔχομεν δὲ οὐκ ἀργύριον οὐδὲ χρυσίον, ἀλλ᾽ ὃ πολλῷ πάντων μεῖζον χρημάτων καὶ τῶν Κροίσου καὶ τῶν Γύγου καὶ τῶν Κινύρου, φιλίαν ἀνδρὸς τά τε ἄλλα γενναίου καὶ ῥητορικοῦ. 6. τί οὖν ἄν τις ἐγγυητὴν καταστήσειε δῶρον οὕτω μέγα τούτῳ δούς, παρ᾽ οὗ μικρὰ λαβεῖν ἀξιοῖ; ταυτὶ μὲν οὖν ὕστερόν σοι ποιήσομεν ὥστε σε λαμβάνοντα καμεῖν· περὶ δὲ τῆς τοῦ βασιλέως ἐπιστολῆς δοκεῖς μοι μείζω τῶν ὄντων εἰρηκὼς κεναῖς ἐλπίσιν ἀπατᾶν τοὺς ἀτυχοῦντας. ἡ δέ ἐστιν ὑπόσχεσις μὲν πρὸς ἐμὲ βοηθείας, βοήθεια δὲ οὔπω, παρ᾽ ἧς ὠφελοῖτ᾽ ἂν ὁ νόθος. νῦν δέ ἐσμεν ἐν τῷ πρίν. 7. ὅμως δὲ αὐτὴν ἀπέσταλκα τοῦ παῦσαι τὰς μετρίους ἐλπίδας τοῖς εἰς ταὐτὸν μὲν ἥκουσί μοι κατὰ τὴν τύχην, οὐκ οἶδα δὲ εἰ τὴν τύχην ὥσπερ ἐγὼ φέρειν ἐπισταμένοις.

---

[g] The stock millionaires appear, as usual, in such commonplaces.

and now we are on close terms with each other. I will send you plenty of speeches. If they are not worth much, then anyone who hankers after what is no good has only himself to blame. I shall not demand any payment from you, for I have it already—not in silver or gold, but something that far surpasses all the treasures of Croesus, Gyges, and Cinyras,[g] the friendship of a noble man, and particularly, of one endowed with eloquence. 6. What can anyone require as guarantee when he has presented such a splendid gift to one from whom he can expect slight return? Anyway, I shall make it up to you in the future so that you will be weary of taking. On the matter of the emperor's letter, I feel that you have exaggerated, and that you flatter the unfortunate with vain hopes. It is a promise to assist me, but there is no assistance as yet which might benefit my illegitimate son.[h] We are as we were. 7. Still, I have sent it, so as to stop those who are in the same position as myself, and who perhaps learn to bear their lot as I do, from indulging their slight hopes.

[h] Cimon (Arabius) was Libanius' only son by a slave woman (*Letter* 188.5), and so barred from legitimate inheritance by *Cod. Th.* iv.6.2. Julian had promised to allow an exemption but had not lived to do it (*Or.* 17.37). Jovian here offers only vague promises. Valentinian's edict of 371 (*Cod. Th.* iv.6.4) resulted in some improvement but not for long (*Or.* 1.145; 195).

## 122. Νικοκλεῖ

1. Καὶ τὰ λοιπὰ τοῦ πολέμου ὡς ἐπολεμήθη καὶ ὡς ὁ μὲν ἐπὶ πᾶν μανίας ἀφίκετο, κρείττω δὲ ἦν τὰ ἡμέτερα διὰ τοὺς ὑπὸ σοῦ κληθέντας θεούς, καὶ ὅτι κρύψας αὑτὸν οἴκοι μένει περιῃρημένος τὸ θράσος ὁ τὰ τῶν γιγάντων μιμούμενος, πάντα ἀναγγελεῖ σοι δι᾽ ἀκριβείας ὁ γενναῖος Ἑρκουκιανός. 2. καλῶ δὲ αὐτὸν γενναῖον, ὅτι πόσον τέ ἐστιν ὁ διδάσκαλος οἶδε καὶ τὰς τιμὰς οἳ τούτοις ὀφείλονται καὶ οὐκ ὀφείλειν αἱρεῖται μᾶλλον ἢ ἐκτίνειν·[1] ἀνθ᾽ ὧν αὐτὸν ἐλπίζω σὺν εὐδαιμονίᾳ περάσειν τὸν βίον τά τε ἄλλα καὶ παῖδας ὁρῶντα ἀγαθοὺς ἐν ταῖς σαῖς χερσί. 3. ταῦτα μὲν οὖν τελοίη θεός· σὺ δέ μοι μὴ πάσης τῆς ἡμετέρας κατηγορεῖν μηδὲ τὴν ἑνὸς μοχθηρίαν πόλεως ὅλης ἔγκλημα ποιεῖσθαι, ἀλλ᾽ εἰδέναι διαιρεῖν ἀπὸ τῶν δυσσεβῶν τοὺς οὐ τοιούτους· ὡς οἵ πολλοί γε καὶ κατεβόησαν καὶ ἐστέναξαν καὶ κατηράσαντο τῷ τὴν σὴν ἀγνοήσαντι φιλοσοφίαν. 4. πεντεκαίδεκα δὲ μυριάδας ἀνθρώπων πάντας εἶναι χρη-

[1] καὶ . . . ἐκτίνειν F. (V) om. Wolf (other Mss.).

---

[a] Seeck (p. 414) suggested that this was part of the Christian reaction after Julian, when the Bishop of An-

## 122. To Nicocles

1. Concerning the rest of the hostilities and their conduct, and the ranting and raving of our antagonist,[a] despite which we prevailed by reason of the gods whom you invoked, and the manner in which he, who sought to imitate the actions of the giants,[b] stays at home in hiding with his arrogance abashed—all this the noble Herculianus[c] will report to you accurately. 2. I call him noble because he knows how much his teacher[d] means, and he chooses not to be under obligation to these people rather than to repay it. Hence I trust that he will spend his life in happiness especially when he sees his fine children in your hands. 3. May heaven bring this to fruition! But please do not accuse my city as a whole nor yet make one man's shortcomings a ground for complaint against the complete community, but know how to differentiate the pious from the impious. At any rate, the majority decried and bewailed and called down curses upon the fellow who knew not your philosophy. 4. I do not know whether it is possible for 150,000 people

tioch pressed Jovian during his stay in the city for firm action against the leading pagans. Though sympathetic, Jovian contented himself with an edict of tolerance.

[b] Cf. Eurip. *Ion* 987 f.

[c] Son of Hermogenes (ii) of Amm. Marc. 14.10.2; cf. *Ep.* 828. See *PLRE* (Herculanus) 420 (1).

[d] Libanius himself.

στοὺς οὐκ οἶδα εἰ τῶν δυνατῶν· οὐδὲ γὰρ ἐν τῇ σῇ Σπάρτῃ, καίτοι τῇ Σπάρτῃ Λυκοῦργος διδάσκαλος, πάντες ἄμεμπτοι καὶ κατὰ τοὺς νόμους ζῶντες, ἀλλ' ἤδη τις καὶ δειλὸς ἔδοξεν, οὗ τοὐναντίον ἐκ παιδὸς ἐδιδάσκετο.

---

[e] This rough figure for the population of Antioch may be compared with Chrysostom's 200,000 (*Hom. in S. Ignat.* 4,

## 123. Δημητρίῳ

1. Οἶδα οὐ πρὸς πολλὰς ἀποκρινάμενος ἐπιστολάς. αἴτιον δὲ ἡ λύπη, ἣν ἐπ' ἐκείνῳ τῷ πεπτωκότι λυπούμενος οὐκ αἰσχύνομαι, ἐπεὶ καὶ τὰς ἐπιδείξεις τῶν λόγων πολὺν δὴ παύσας χρόνον νῦν μόλις ἀνενεωσάμην. 2. δοκεῖς δέ μοι καὶ αὐτὸς ἐπαινεῖν μου τὴν ἀθυμίαν. οὐδαμοῦ γὰρ ἐνεκάλεσας τὴν πολλαχοῦ σιωπὴν ὡς ἂν ἔχουσαν τὸ εὔλογον. 3. ἡ βραδυτὴς δέ σοι τῶν ξενίων μακρὰν ἡμῖν πεποίηκε τὴν ἑορτήν. ἄρτι γὰρ εἰσιόντας εἰς τὸ πονεῖν ἥκοντα πάλιν ἡμᾶς εἰς τὸ ποιεῖν ἃ τῶν ἑορταζόντων ἐστὶ κατέστησε καὶ συνηγωνίσατο τοῖς πολλοῖς, οἳ πάντα φασὶ τὸν μῆνα δεῖν ποιεῖν ἑορτήν· ὥστ' οὐκ αἰτιάσομαι τὸν

all to be good:[e] even in your Sparta, though Sparta has Lycurgus for a teacher, not everyone has been beyond reproach and lived in accordance with the laws. At times some of them have been regarded even as cowards, though from boyhood they had been schooled to be the opposite.

*PG* 50.591), with 100,000 Christians (*Hom. in Matth.* 85.2, *PG* 58.762). The literary evidence is collected by Downey, *History of Antioch in Syria* pp. 580 f.

## 123. To Demetrius

1. I know that I reply to few letters. The reason is the grief that I am not ashamed to feel for our fallen hero, for it is only now and with difficulty that I have recommenced my declamations, after stopping them for a long time.[a] 2. I believe that you too commend me for my dejection, for you have not reproached me for my blanket of silence, obviously since there is good reason for it. 3. The delay in the arrival of your presents has made my holiday a long one.[b] They came just after I had resumed work and once more set me in holiday mood and provided support for those many people who contend that we should be on holiday for the whole month. Hence, I shall not complain against

[a] Cf. *Or.* 17.38; *Letter* 116 for his inability to compose or declaim after the news of Julian's death.

[b] The conventional New Year's gifts (cf. *Or.* 9.8), received a month late, dating this letter to mid-February at the earliest.

χειμῶνα μᾶλλον κλείσαντα τότε τὴν ὁδὸν ἢ φίλον ἡγήσομαι τὴν εὐφροσύνην ἐκτείναντα.

## 124. Ἰουλιανῷ[1]

1. Καλὰ παρὰ καλοῦ γράμματα βραδέως ἥκει. τύχην δ' ἥντινα λέγεις μεταπεσεῖν μοι, δι' ἣν οὐκέτ' ἔχω τοὺς θεραπεύοντας, μόλις ἠδυνήθην μαθεῖν ὅτιπερ τὴν τελευτὴν τοῦ βασιλέως λέγεις. 2. ἐγὼ δὲ ἐφίλουν μὲν ἐκεῖνον οὐχ ἧττον ἢ τὴν ἐμαυτοῦ μητέρα καὶ ἐφιλούμην γε μᾶλλον ἢ οἱ πάνυ δοκοῦντες· οὐ μὴν ταῖς γε ὡς αὐτὸν εἰσόδοις εἰς τὸ τοὺς μὲν μείζους ἢ προσῆκε ποιεῖν, τοὺς δὲ ταπεινοῦν[2] κατεχρησάμην. 3. ἀλλ' οὐδ' ἐμπορίαν τὸ πρᾶγμα ἐποιησάμην. οὐδ' ἔστιν εἰπεῖν ὡς δραχμῇ πλουσιώτερος ἐκ τῶν βασιλείων ἐγενόμην, ὅς γε οὐδ' ὅσα ἦν ἐκεῖ τῶν παππῴων μοι οὔτ' αὐτὸς ἠξίουν ἀπολαβεῖν οὔτε ἀναγκάζοντος ἐδεξάμην. Ἀριστοφάνει δὲ καὶ τὸ δοθὲν ἐκεῖνο

[1] Ἰουλιανῷ ] τῷ αὐτῷ (sc. Δομνίωνι) Wolf (Par.)
[2] ταπεινοῦν ] ταπεινοὺς Wolf (S Par.)

---

[a] F/Kr. no. 54, pp. 402 ff. *BLZG* 191 (viii), *PLRE* 471 (14). A Christian, corresponding with Libanius for the past five years and enjoying his support as recently as 363 (*Ep.* 1367), had addressed a disparaging comment to him after Julian's death, eliciting this balanced and dignified

the winter weather for closing the roads then, but rather consider its friendliness in extending my season of good cheer.

## 124. To Julianus[a]

1. A fine letter from a fine fellow has been slow in arriving. As for the change of fortune that you say has befallen me,[b] whereby I no longer have people to defer to me, I found it hard to realize that you were referring to the death of the emperor. 2. I loved him no less than my own mother, and I was loved far more than those who really seemed to be. Anyway, I never employed my audiences with him to raise up some to undeserved heights, or to depress others.[c] 3. Nor yet did I turn this into a traffic for gain, nor can it be alleged that I became a penny the richer from the imperial coffers, for I never asked for the return of all my grandfather's fortune which lay there,[d] nor did I accept it when he pressed it on me. Even that paltry grant to Aristophanes was the

reply. No further correspondence between them is known.

[b] Cf. Isocr. *Philipp.* 44.

[c] This criticism was made against him all his life, and was always rebutted in these terms; cf. *Letter* 97, *Or.* 1.125; 51.30. He remained consistently loyal to Julian's memory, even to the extent of formally renouncing friendship with Polycles for slighting it (*Or.* 37.2 ff).

[d] Following the revolt of Eugenius in 303 (for which see *Or.* 11.158 ff, 19.45 f, 20.18 ff), Libanius' grandfather and a Brasidas (great-uncle?) were executed and their property confiscated. This still remained imperial property.

τὸ μικρὸν ἔργον ἦν λόγου τινός, οὐκ ἐμὴ δέησις. 4. ἀτυχὴς μὲν οὖν εἶναι φίλου τοιούτου στερηθεὶς ὁμολογῶ, κόλακας δὲ οὐκ ἀπολώλεκα, ὅς γε οὐδὲ ἐκτησάμην. φίλοι δὲ οἱ πρὸ τοῦ καὶ νῦν, καὶ ἡδίους γε νῦν ἐπαινοῦντές μου τὸν τρόπον, ὃν οὐκ ἐπῆρε καιρὸς ὑβρίσαι. 5. σὺ δὲ καὶ νῦν ἐπιστέλλων χαρίζῃ καὶ τότε. εἰ <δὲ>[3] τοῖς αὐτοῖς ἐβούλου τιμᾶν, τιμᾶν ἔδοξας ἂν ἄνδρα ἑταῖρον, ἀλλ᾽ οὐ κολακεύειν τύχην.

[3] <δὲ> F.

## 125. Ἐλπιδίῳ

1. Ἕτερα μὲν ἠλπίσαμεν περὶ τῶν Ὀλυμπίων, ὅτι δὴ λαμπρότατα τῶν πώποτε ἔσται τῶν τε σῶν ὀφθαλμῶν τυγχάνοντα κἀκείνων τῶν μεγάλων τε καὶ καλῶν καὶ φοβερῶν, οὓς ζημίαν ἡλίῳ φήσαιμ᾽ ἂν οὐκ ὄντας ἔτι· πληροῦμεν δὲ ὅμως τὰ πρὸς τὸν θεὸν οὕτως ὅπως ἂν ἐξῇ. 2. σοὶ δὲ ἄρα εἵμαρτο πάντως τι τὴν πανήγυριν ὠφελῆσαι. φέρων γάρ

---

[a] F/Kr. no. 43, *BLZG* (Helpidius) 170 (ii), *PLRE* 415 (6); appointed *Comes rei privatae* by Jovian, he is now proconsul of Asia, a promotion made presumably after Jovian's death.

[b] Julian, cf. Amm. Marc. 15.8.16. His death is a disaster (a) to those who live in this world, under the sun, (b) to

consequence of an oration, not a request from me.[e] 4. So I concede that I am unfortunate in the loss of such a friend, but I have not lost any flatterers for I never had any. My earlier friends are my friends now, and more pleasing to me now in their commendations of my conduct, which was not inspired to insolence by the accident of Fortune. 5. By writing to me now you give me pleasure, as you did then. But had you wished to honour me in the same manner, you would have got a name for honouring a friend, not of truckling to fortune.

[e] *Or.* 14; cf. *Or.* 1.125. The term τὸ μικρόν, though deliberately used as suitable to the present context, can hardly describe a provincial governorship and reinforces Petit's suggestion of some minor post devised for Aristophanes by Julian.

## 125. To Elpidius[a]

1. Our expectations for the Olympia were very different from this, for we thought to make it the most glorious celebration ever, under your gaze and that of that great, noble, and awe-inspiring person whose death, I venture to assert, is a disaster to the world of light.[b] However we fulfil our duty towards the god in the best way we can. 2. But destiny meant you to help the festival in any case. Fate has

Helios, whose devotee he was. Despite Libanius' aversion to games and spectacles, he supports them here from motives of religious conformity and devotion to Julian's memory, as well as of local patriotism.

σε κατέστησεν εἰς τοῦτο ὁ δαίμων ὥστε ἐν σοὶ κεῖσθαι τὸ πλέον τῆς ἑορτῆς. ἡ γὰρ δὴ Ἰωνία τά τε ἄλλα καλὴ καὶ ἀθλητῶν γενναίων εὔφορος, οὓς ὁ μὲν τὸν ἀγῶνα τιθεὶς μεταπέμπεται τῇ παρὰ τοῦ στεφάνου δόξῃ καὶ χρήματα προστιθείς· μέγιστον δ', εἰ γνοῖεν ὅτι καὶ σοί τις σπουδὴ τούτους ἑτέρων προκεκρίσθαι. δῆλον γὰρ ὅτι καὶ γονεῦσι τοῖς αὑτῶν καὶ τοῖς ἄλλοις οἰκείοις οἰήσονται συμφέρειν τὸ ποιεῖν ἀφ' ὧν ἡδίων ἔσῃ. 3. δέχου δὴ τὸν παρ' ἡμῶν, ὥσπερ εἴωθας, ἡμέρως καὶ μὴ μόνον ὅτου ἂν δέηται πράττειν, ἀλλὰ καὶ ὅ τι ἂν ἀγνοῇ, καὶ τοῦτο φράζειν τε καὶ πράττειν.

## 126. Δατιανῷ

1. Μόλις ἐκινήθησαν οἱ πρεσβευταὶ παρ' ἡμῶν ὑπὸ φόβου θαυμαστοῦ, τὸν φόβον δὲ ἐνεποίει τὸ σὲ πρὸς τὴν πόλιν ἐσχηκέναι χαλεπῶς. 2. οἱ μὲν

---

[a] F/Kr. no. 29. *BLZG* 113 ff, the offence given by the Antiochenes being treated in detail on p. 115.

[b] The official embassy of the city to congratulate Valentinian on his accession (26 Feb. 364) also had the duty of appeasing Datianus for violence committed against his

taken you and placed you in your present position so that the greater part of the celebrations depends upon you: for Ionia, besides its other claims to fame, is productive of first-rate athletes, and the president of the games is inviting them to attend, offering prizes in money over and above the prestige of the victor's crown.[c] Their greatest inducement would be for them to know that you also are eager for them to be judged victors over the rest; for obviously they will regard it as advantageous to their parents and other relations to behave in a manner pleasing to you. 3. Then extend your usual kind welcome to our emissary, and do not be content with acting as he asks but, if there is anything of which he is unaware, remind him of it and act upon it.

[c] The Olympia of 364, in honour of Zeus Olympius, to be held in Daphne, presented by Sabinus (*Epp.* 1179, 1181).

## 126. To Datianus[a]

1. The envoys left us reluctantly urged on by a remarkable fear, a fear induced by your displeasure towards the city.[b] 2. Now those against whom

property in and near Antioch. It seems that on the arrival of news of the death of Jovian, under whom Datianus had regained all the influence lost under Julian, a mob looted the property he had amassed in the city, and the council could not or would not do anything to prevent it. In any case, they were as usual held responsible.

οὖν ἐν ταῖς αἰτίαις ὀμνύουσιν ἦ μὴν ἠναγκασμένοι ποιῆσαι ἃ πεποιήκασι καὶ ταῖς μὲν χερσὶν αὑτῶν, τῇ γνώμῃ δὲ ἑτέρου πεπορθῆσθαι τοὺς ἀγρούς· ἐγὼ δὲ πεισθεὶς τούτους ἠδικηκέναι καὶ κοινὴν εἶναι τῆς βουλῆς τὴν ἁμαρτίαν, οἵ γε οὐκ ἐκώλυον, ἀναμνησθῆναί σε βούλομαι τῶν σεαυτοῦ λόγων, ἐν οἷς ἡμῖν διηγοῦ πολλάκις ὡς οἷς ἐγκαλεῖν εἶχες, τούτους ὄντας ἐν χρείᾳ συμμάχων ὤρθωσας. 3. τὸν γὰρ ὡς καλῶν ἐκείνων μεμνημένον οὐ πάνυ καλὸν τὸν αὑτοῦ παραβαίνειν νόμον. ἀδικεῖ μὲν γὰρ οὐδὲν ὁ ἀμυνόμενος, ἔστι δὲ βελτίων ὁ παρὸν τιμωρίαν λαβεῖν οὐκ ἐθελήσας. τοῦ μὲν γὰρ πολλὰ τὰ παραδείγματα καὶ πανταχοῦ, καὶ καθ' ἡμέραν τοὺς ἀμυνομένους ὁρῶμεν, τὸ δὲ δοῦναι συγγνώμην θεοῦ τε καὶ θεῷ παραπλησίου. εἰ δὲ προσέσται τῷ μὴ λαβεῖν τὴν δίκην καὶ τὸ βοηθῆσαι τοῖς ὀφείλουσι τὴν δίκην, Ἡράκλεις, ὡς στεφάνων ἄξιον. 4. ἔτι δὲ τὸ μὲν ἀσθενῶς διακείμενον παρὰ τοῦ μέγα δυναμένου δυνηθῆναι δίκην λαβεῖν τάχ' ἄν τις θαυμάσειεν ὡς οὐκ ὂν τῶν ῥᾳδίων· ὅταν δέ τις ἰσχὺν ἡλίκην σὺ κεκτημένος — καὶ μένοις γε ἐπὶ τῆς ἰσχύος — ἐλαύνῃ τοὺς ἀσθενεῖς, μάλα οὐχ ἡδὺ τὸ θέαμα. οὐδὲ γὰρ ὁ Ἡρακλῆς εἰ νοσοῦντας καὶ κειμένους ἀνθρώπους

your complaints are made take their solemn oath that they did what they have done under compulsion, and though it was by their hands, it was by the will of another that your estates were ravaged. However, I am convinced that they have done wrong and the fault is that of the council as a whole, for they did not try to stop it, but I would like you to recall your own words, in which you often told us that you have raised up people who needed allies though you had complaints against them. 3. It is not very nice for one, after recalling those kindnesses, to transgress his own rule. Self-defence is not wrong, but refusal to exact legitimate punishment is better. We see plenty of examples of this, of people employing self defence, everywhere and every day, but to forgive is a divine act and approximates to divinity. If, in addition to refusing to inflict punishment, aid is proffered to those deserving of punishment, upon my word, this indeed deserves crowns.[c] 4. Moreover, for the weak to be capable of punishing the strong may well occasion surprise, for it is not an easy matter; but whenever anyone possesses such strength as yours—and may you remain in possession of it—and harasses the weak, it is a most unpleasant spectacle. Even Heracles, if he harried and cast aside the ailing and the fallen,

[c] The argument resembles that of *Letter* 113, where Libanius tries to act as mediator to two friends.

ἕλκων ἐρρίπτει, θαυμαστὸν ἂν ἦν. 5. καὶ μήν, εἰ μὲν οἰόμενοι πείσεσθαί τι κακὸν ἥκουσι, κρείττων φάνηθι τῆς τῶν ἁμαρτανόντων ἐλπίδος· εἰ δὲ θαρροῦσιν ὡς σοῦ γε οὐκ ἂν λυπήσαντος, μὴ χείρων γένῃ τῆς ἐλπίδος. 6. οἶδα γὰρ ἐγὼ πολλοὺς ἐκ μὲν τοῦ μετ' ὀργῆς τι πρᾶξαι βραχὺν ἡσθέντας χρόνον, ὕστερον δὲ ἀνιωμένους ἐφ' οἷς ἥσθησαν, ἑτέρους δὲ πάντα τὸν χρόνον ἡδομένους διὰ τὸ μὴ τὴν ἡδονὴν ἐκείνην ἡσθῆναι τὴν ἀπὸ τοῦ χαρίσασθαι τῷ θυμῷ συμβαίνουσαν. 7. εἰ μὲν οὖν μὴ πολλὰ περὶ τὴν πόλιν ἡμῶν ἐπεπονήκεις, ἥττων ἂν ἦν ἡ μέμψις, εἰ τὰ νῦν ἔβλαπτες· ἐπεὶ δὲ σώζων καὶ κοινῇ πάντας καὶ καθ' ἕκαστον ἐν μέρει καὶ ῥυόμενος καὶ χεῖρα ὀρέγων καὶ κοσμῶν οἰκοδομίαις τὴν πόλιν διατελεῖς, μὴ διαφθείρῃς πολλὰς καὶ λαμπρὰς εὐεργεσίας ἐν τῷ τελευταίῳ, μηδ', ἂν ἐγὼ τὰ βελτίω διηγῶμαι, λόγος ἕτερος ἐπεισίτω τὸ δυσχερὲς περιφέρων, ἀλλ' ἔστω πᾶσα περὶ σοῦ διήγησις καθαρὰ τοῦ χείρονος. 8. <εἰ>[1] ἥξεις ὡς ἡμᾶς θεοῦ διδόντος, ἐμπλήσομέν σοι τὴν οἰκίαν οἱ τὸ προσειπεῖν σε κέρδος ἡγούμενοι. πότερον οὖν κάλλιον λέγειν σε τὰς αἰτίας, ὑπὲρ ὧν ἔτρωσας διὰ τῶν πρέσβεων τὴν πόλιν, ἢ

[1] <εἰ> F.

would be no cause for admiration.[d] 5. Indeed, if they have come expecting to experience some evil, reveal yourself as rising superior to expectations of the culprits, and if they confidently expect you not to harm them, do not fall short of their expectations. 6. I know that many people take a momentary pleasure from acting in anger, and later are sorry that they have been so pleased, but others have pleasure all the time since they do not experience that pleasure which comes from gratifying their temper. 7. So had it not been for your many past exertions for the city, there would be less reason to reproach you if you harm her now. But since you continually protect us, both collectively and individually, and rescue us, stretch your protecting hand over us, and adorn our city with buildings, do not ruin your many glorious benefactions at this last moment, nor yet, if my account concentrates on the brighter side, let any contradictory account make its appearance and introduce an element of hostility. Let every account of you be free from ill. 8. If, by grace of god, you come to us, we who think it a boon to address you will fill your house. So which is the nobler course—for you to dwell on the accusation for which you afflict our city through our envoys, or to pride yourself on sending away those who deserve

[d] Heracles, by his labours, was regarded as benefactor of frail mortals.

φιλοτιμεῖσθαι τῷ τοὺς τραυμάτων ἀξίους εὖ πεπονθότας ἀποπέμψαι; 9. ἔστι δὲ οὐ περὶ τοῦ παρόντος σοι μόνον ὁ λόγος χρόνου· τῶν μὲν γὰρ ἄλλων ἡμῶν ὁ τελευτήσας εὐθὺς ἐν λήθῃ, τὸ δὲ σὸν λαμπρόν τε καὶ κρεῖττον ἢ σβεσθῆναι, ὅ τε γὰρ ὕπατος αἵ τε ἐκ βασιλέων τιμαὶ καὶ τὸ βασιλέων τοῦ μὲν μαθητήν, τοῦ δὲ γενέσθαι διδάσκαλον, ἔτι δὲ οἰκιῶν κάλλη καὶ λουτρῶν πλῆθός τε καὶ μέγεθος καὶ χάρις, πάντα ταῦτα τοὔνομα καθέξει, κἂν τὸ σῶμα ἀπέλθῃ. 10. δὸς δὴ τοῖς ἐσομένοις λέγειν ὡς οὗτος μέντοι τὴν Ἀντιόχου πόλιν οὐ πάντα ἄμεμπτον εἰς αὐτὸν λαβὼν ἔχων ἀνατρέψαι τε καὶ καταδῦσαι διεφύλαξεν οὐχ ἧττον ἐν τῷ καιρῷ τῶν ἐγκλημάτων ἢ ὅτε βελτίστην ἡγεῖτο. 11. ταῦθ᾽ ὅτε ἐπέστελλον, ἦσαν οἳ ληρεῖν με ἐνόμιζον καὶ λύκου, φασί, πτερὰ ζητεῖν· οὐ γὰρ ἂν πεῖσαι. ἐγὼ δὲ ἐκείνους οἷς ἐδόξαζον ληρεῖν ἡγούμην· πεῖσαι γὰρ ἂν καὶ ταῦτ᾽ ἐμαντευόμην, οὐ τῇ τέχνῃ Κάλχαντος, ἀλλ᾽ εἰς τὴν σὴν ἀποβλέπων γνώμην τε καὶ φύσιν. σὺ δ᾽, οἶμαι, κύριος ἢ δεῖξαί με μάντιν

[e] Of 358. Cf. *Letter* 47.5; Amm. Marc. 17.5.1.

[f] He began his career under Constantine (τοῦ μὲν) and was adviser to Constantius (τοῦ δὲ), to whom he acted as

such affliction as recipients of your kindness? 9. Nor do I address myself to the present moment only. Any of us ordinary folk who dies is immediately forgotten, but your achievements are glorious and too great to be suppressed—your consulship,[e] the honours received from emperors, your position as pupil of one and teacher of another,[f] and the beauty of your buildings[g] and the number, size, and charm of your baths—all this will immortalize your name, even though the body passes away. 10. Allow future ages to say that here was a man who found the city of Antioch not entirely beyond reproach as regards himself, yet though it was in his power to ruin and destroy it, he gave it no less protection at the very time of his reproaches against it than when he held it in the highest regard. 11. When I was writing this, some people thought me a fool, wishful to see pigs fly—as the proverb has it:[h] they said I would never convince you. But I thought them the fools for thinking so. I forecast that I would persuade you even in this, not because I used the art of Calchas, but by reference to your intellect and character. You have it in your power, I believe, either to

Nestor (*Ep.* 114.7; cf. *Ep.* 490).

[g] For Datianus' buildings in Antioch, constructed in the 350s when he was in attendance upon Constantius, see *Ep.* 114.5, 435.6 (baths), *Letter* 13.7 (portico). The current fashion by notables of building in the city is praised in *Or.* 11.194, though later decried.

[h] Cf. *Letter* 21.2 note.

φαῦλον ἢ Τειρεσίου βελτίω.

## 127. Σαλουτίῳ

1. Ἔδει μέν σοι τὸν οἶκον ἅπαντα εἶναι σῶν καὶ μήτε μικρὸν μήτε μεῖζον ἀπὸ τοῦ Φθόνου βέλος ἐφ' ὑμᾶς ἐλθεῖν, ἀλλ' ᾗ σὺ κέχρησαι περὶ τοὺς ἀρχομένους φιλανθρωπίᾳ, ταύτῃ πρὸς σὲ τοὺς θεούς. 2. ἴσθι μέντοι θαῦμά σοι γενόμενον ἀπὸ τῆς συμφορᾶς. ἁπάντων γὰρ ἡμῶν οὕτως ἀφόρητον τὸ πρᾶγμα ἡγουμένων ὥστε μηδὲ τὴν ἐκ λόγου τολμᾶν προσάγειν παραμυθίαν σὺ γενναίως ἤνεγκας τὴν τῆς Τύχης προσβολὴν νομίσας πολὺ ταύτην μείζω εἶναι τὴν ἀριστείαν ἢ ὅσας αἱ πρὸς ἀνθρώπους δέχονται μάχαι. τὰ γὰρ παρὰ τῶν ποιητῶν περὶ τῆς ἀνθρωπείας εἰρημένα φύσεως εἰδὼς μετὰ τῶν ἐκεῖθεν ἐπῳδῶν παρετάξω καί σε οὐκ ἔκλινε τοσοῦτον κακόν. 3. ἀλλ' ὁ μὲν ἐπηρεάσας ἡμῖν δαίμων — καὶ γὰρ ἐμὲ νόμιζε τῶν πενθησάντων εἶναι — τρέποιτο ἐφ' ἑτέρους, ἐπειδὴ

---

[a] Salutius, Julian's praetorian prefect, retained by Jovian, is kept in this same post by Valentinian. Libanius speaks of one emperor; thus he is writing before news came

show me up as a poor forecaster or as one better than Teiresias.[i]

[i] Calchas, the seer of the Greeks at Troy, and Teiresias, the two most famous prophets of classical myth.

## 127. To Salutius[a]

1. By rights, your whole household should be safe, with no shaft of Envy, either small or great, to attack you: the humanity you employed towards your subjects, the gods should employ towards you. 2. Yet be assured that you have won admiration in consequence of your misfortune. We all regarded the occurrence as so intolerable that we could not even bring ourselves to extend an address of consolation, but you have courageously borne the buffetings of Fortune, thinking heroism here to be superior to any that is revealed in battle against humans.[b] You know all that the poets have said about human nature,[c] and supported by their protecting charms you took up your position and were not put to rout by such misfortune. 3. I trust that the destiny which loomed over us—for you must regard me too as one of those afflicted—may be diverted against others, since it is desirous of

of the elevation of Valens to be Valentinian's partner on 28 March 364.

[b] A close relative of his had died at about the same time as Valentinian's accession.

[c] Cf. Eurip. *Alc.* 780 f.

τοῦ κακῶς ποιεῖν ὥσπερ τινὸς γέρως ἐπιθυμεῖ· τὴν δὲ πρεσβείαν ἡμῖν τυχοῦσαν ἁπάντων ἀπόπεμψον· ὡς οὐκ ἔστιν ὅτε οὐκ εὖ ἐποίησας ἁπλῶς ὅ τι ἐπαγγείλαιμεν δίκαιον τοῦτο καλῶν καὶ βασιλέα πείθων ὡς καλὰ μὲν αἰτοῦμεν, καλὸν δὲ τὰ τοιαῦτα χαρίζεσθαι.

## 128. Θεμιστίῳ

1. Βοήθησον τοῖς πρέσβεσι τὰ εἰκότα διά τε τὴν πόλιν ἥ σε πολλάκις ἐθαύμασε καὶ τὸν βασιλέα, ᾧ τὸν στέφανον[1] φέρουσιν. εἰ δ' ἐστί τι καὶ τοὐμὸν ἔτι παρὰ σοί — πείθομαι δὲ ὡς ἔστι — τρίτον τοῦτο ἡμῖν ὠφελείτω τὴν πρεσβείαν. 2. ἔστι μὲν γὰρ οὐ μικρὸν οὐδ' ὅσα τῆς τοῦ κρατίστου δὴ Σαλουτίου γνώμης[2] πρὸς ταῦτα σὲ συλλαβεῖν εἰκάζω, ὅτι ἀεί σοι καὶ τὸ βασίλειον εὖ

[1] καὶ τὸ with a lacuna of 12 letters Ms. τὸν βασιλέα, ᾧ τὸν Seeck (p. 424) τὸν στέφανον ὃν F., conj. Re.

[2] δὴ Σαλουτίου (Σαλουστίου Ms.) γνώμης Wolf, Bouchery (Ms.) δεῖ Σαλουτίου γνώμης, <μεῖζον δὲ> F., conj. Re.

---

[a] Bouchery p. 243. A companion letter to the two preceding, delivered by the embassy which was taking the

inflicting harm, as though this were the prize. But return our embassy to us successful on all points. You have always been our benefactor; every single thing we have requested you describe as justified, and persuade the emperor that our plea is honourable and that it is honourable to accede to such pleas.[d]

[d] The embassy has acted as messengers to Alcimus in Nicomedeia, and to Datianus, Salutius, and Themistius at court in Constantinople.

## 128. To Themistius

1. Provide our envoys with all reasonable assistance, both for the city that has often admired you and for the emperor to whom they bring the crown.[a] And if you still have any regard for me too, and I am sure that you have, let this be a third reason for helping our embassy. 2. It is no minor matter, nor yet, I think, such as for you to enlist the full support of the excellent Salutius upon it,[b] because the palace has always opened its doors to you—and

crown (*aurum coronarium*) for Valentinian; late March–April 364.

[b] He flatters Themistius with the assertion that, since he has direct access to court, it will be unnecessary for him to engage the attention of the praetorian prefect on the matter in question—which remains unknown. More immediate are his good offices to appease the affronted Datianus (cf. *Letter* 126).

ποιοῦν ἀνέῳκται. τεκμαίρομαι δὲ τῇ τε σῇ καὶ τῇ τοῦ βασιλέως ἀρετῇ· ὁ μὲν γὰρ ἀνδρῶν ἁπάντων, σὺ δὲ φιλοσόφων ἄριστος. 3. δὸς δὴ σαυτὸν τοῖς ἡμετέροις πολίταις καὶ τοῦ πολλαῖς θύραις ἐνοχλεῖν ἀπάλλαξον. κἂν τὸν φίλτατον ἡμῖν Δατιανὸν αἴσθῃ δυσκόλως ἔχοντα καὶ μεμνημένον τινῶν ἀγροικότερον πεπραγμένων ἢ πάντα παῦε τὸν θυμὸν ἢ ὅσον ἔξεστιν ἀφαίρει.

## 129. Ἀλκίμῳ

1. Μὴ θαυμάσῃς εἰ τὰ πολλὰ σιγῶν ἄνθρωπος οὐκ ἐπέστειλά σοι. σιγῶ δὲ ὑπ᾽ ἀθυμίας, ἣν τὸ μὲν πρῶτον ἐνέθηκέ μοι τὸ τῆς ὑμετέρας πτῶμα· φίλη γὰρ ἐπὶ φίλοις ἀνδράσιν ἔκειτο πόλις. 2. ἐπηύξησε δὲ τὴν λύπην θεῖός τε ἀπελθὼν καὶ μήτηρ. καὶ μέμνησαι δὴ τῶν ὀδυρμῶν, οὓς περὶ αὐτῶν ἐποιούμην. ὁ δὲ δὴ κολοφὼν δόρυ καὶ αἷμα καὶ θάνατος. τὸ δὲ ὅθεν ἴσασιν οἱ πάντα

[a] The despairing tone of this letter written to an intimate friend is in stark contrast with the accompanying letters directed to officials and courtiers. It may also be compared with his narration of the same sequence of

rightly so.[c] This I infer from the emperor's virtue and your own, he being preeminent among all men, you among philosophers. 3. Provide your services then to my fellow citizens and rid them of the need to trouble many doors. And if you see our dearest Datianus ill disposed to us, and reminding himself of some boorish behaviour on our part, either stop his anger completely or reduce it as much as you can.

[c] Flattery here becomes ironical: Themistius always finds the doors of the palace open to him, no matter who is on the throne.

## 129. To Alcimus

1. Do not be surprised that I, a fellow who languishes in silence for the most part, have not written to you. My silence is due to the despondency which I first experienced at the disastrous fall of your city, for a dear city was laid low and dear friends with it.[a] 2. The deaths of my uncle and my mother heightened my grief. Just remember the lamentations I uttered over them.[b] But what capped it all was that spear, the bloodshed and death. The omniscient gods know where that came

events in 374 in *Or.* 1.117, where distress is disguised by sophistic technique.

[b] On the death of Phasganius, *Letter* 50, 64; for the monody on his mother, *Or.* 2.69, 55.3.

εἰδότες. οἶσθα δὲ καὶ αὐτὸς ὡς διεκείμεθα δεδιότες μὴ τὰ γενόμενα γένηται. 3. ὃν οὖν ἔπληττε φόβος οὐ σαφής, τίν' οἴει ψυχὴν ἔχειν ἔργου φανέντος; ἆρ' ἂν πιστεύσαις ὡς ἀπειρήκασιν ὑπὸ τῶν ἐμῶν θρήνων οἱ συνοικοῦντες ἐμοὶ θεῶν τε καὶ γῆς καὶ ἀέρος καὶ οὐρανοῦ καὶ πάντων[1] ἐγκαλουμένων[2] ληγούσης τε ἡμέρας καὶ νυκτὸς ἀρχομένης, καὶ πάλιν ληγούσης μὲν νυκτός, ἀρχομένης δὲ ἡμέρας; οὐ γάρ ἐστιν ἐλπὶς δυναμένη τοῦ τραύματος ἀφελεῖν, ἀλλὰ τὸ μὲν ἀπολωλὸς μέγιστον, ὁ δὲ ὄλεθρος ὅλος.[3] τὸ δὲ ἢ σὲ δεῦρο ἄξον ἢ ἐμὲ παρ' ὑμᾶς οὐκ ἔστιν. ἀλλ' ἀτεχνῶς ἔτι ζῶντες τεθνήκαμεν. 4. ὅπερ οὖν ἔφην, μὴ σιγῶντός μου θαύμαζε, σιγῆς γὰρ[4] ὁ καιρός, ἀλλ' εἴ τι καὶ μικρὸν ἐπιστέλλειν δυναίμην.

1 πάντων F., conj. Re. πάντα Wolf (Mss.)
2 ἐγκαλουμένων F. (Ath.) ἐγκαλοῦμεν Wolf (V)
3 ὅλος F. οἷος Ath. om. Wolf (V)
4 γὰρ F., conj. Re. καὶ Wolf (Mss.)

## 130. Εὐελπιστίῳ

1. Καλῶς ἐποίησαν οἱ θεοὶ σοί τε δείξαντες τὴν

from,[c] but you personally know how fearful we were that the event that actually occurred should come to pass. 3. If some uncertain foreboding alarmed me, what do you think my feelings were when it became a reality? You may well believe that the members of my household have grown weary of my laments in reproach against gods, earth, air, heaven, and all creation, at the end of the day and the coming of night, and again at the ending of night and the coming of the day. I have no hope which can cure me of my wound: the loss is irreparable, the ruin complete. There is nothing to attract either you here or me there, but I am simply dead alive.[d] 4. So, as I have said, do not be surprised at my silence, for it is a time for silence. Rather be surprised that I can write to you, however briefly.

[c] Responsibility for Julian's death, already described as murder (σφαγή, *Letters* 116, 133), is here canvassed with suspicious suspension of judgement. In *Or.* 18.275 it is imputed to the Christians. By *Or.* 24.6 ff this imputation has become certainty, notwithstanding the evidence of others, like Ammianus.

[d] Cf. Eurip. fr. 833, quoted by Plat. *Gorg.* 492e.

## 130. To Euelpistius[a]

1. The gods did right in revealing your own city

[a] *BLZG* 132. Seeck's note on him follows Wolf's reading. In fact, he had not been in Antioch to take part in Julian's campaign, and so Libanius had been deprived of his company.

οἰκείαν[1] καὶ τῇ Λακεδαίμονι τὸ μέγιστον ἀποδόντες φυλακτήριον. ἐπαινοῖντο δ᾽ ἂν δικαίως, καὶ ὅτι τῆς εἰσβολῆς ἐκείνης τῆς οὐ πάντα εὐτυχοῦς οὐ[2] μετέσχες. καίτοι ἡμεῖς γε ἠγανακτοῦμεν ὡς ἂν ἠδικημένοι. σοφώτεροι δὲ ἄρα οἱ κρείττους, δι᾽ οὓς οὐκ εἶδες τετρωμένον, οὗ τὸ τραῦμα ἀκούων οὐ φέρεις. 2. ἐκείνῳ μὲν οὖν ἴσον νέμοιεν[3] τῇ περὶ αὐτοὺς θεραπείᾳ· Περγάμιος δὲ ὁ σοί τε καὶ ἐκείνοις φίλος τὰς μεγάλας καὶ πολυανθρώπους πόλεις καὶ παρ᾽ αἷς κῶμος καὶ μέθη καὶ τὸ τὰ χείρω τιμᾶν ἀφεὶς εἰς Σπάρτην ἥκει τὴν σώφρονα, μᾶλλον δέ, εἰς σέ, δι᾽ ὃν ἡ Σπάρτη τοιαύτη, καὶ οἴεται πολλῶν τε καὶ ἀγαθῶν πλήρης ἔσεσθαι μαθημάτων. καὶ ὀρθῶς οἴεται. ἐγὼ γὰρ τὸ σοὶ συνεῖναι τοῦ θεοῖς μὲν ἔλαττον ἡγοῦμαι, κρεῖττον δὲ ἧς ἂν εἴπῃς ἑτέρας ὁμιλίας. 3. δέχου δὴ τὸν ἑταῖρον ἡδέως καὶ ποιοῦ πολίτην· ὡς οὐ μέμψεταί γε ταύτην ὁ Λυκοῦργος τὴν ποίησιν. ἐγὼ δὲ αὐτόν, εἰ μὲν ἔλθοι ποτὲ παρὰ σοῦ, μεμνημένον ἰδὼν ἡσθήσομαι· μένοντος δὲ παρὰ

[1] οἰκείαν F., conj. Re. οἰκίαν Wolf (Mss.)

[2] οὐ F. (V) om. Wolf

[3] ἐκείνῳ μὲν οὖν ἴσον νέμοιεν F. (V) ἐκεῖνον μὲν οὖν ἴσως νέμοιεν Re. (Ath.) νέμοι ἐν Wolf.

to you and in granting to Lacedaemon her greatest protection. They could be rightly praised also because you took no part in that great but not entirely successful invasion. Yet we took it amiss, as though we had suffered harm—but the higher powers were wiser than we after all; you find the tale of his wounding intolerable, but because of them you did not see him mortally wounded. 2. May they then, grant him equal recompense for his devotion to them! But Pergamius[b] is a friend of yours and of them, and he has passed by the large and populous cities[c] where there is revelry and drunkenness and no respect for decency and has come to Sparta the prudent—or, I should say, to you because of whom Sparta is as she is, and he thinks to have his fill of many fine studies. And he thinks aright, for I regard association with you as inferior to that with gods but superior to any other companionship one could mention. 3. Then welcome my friend gladly and create him a citizen, for Lycurgus will not voice disapproval of such a creation. If ever he returns from his visit to you, I shall be pleased to see him recall it, and if he remains with you, even so

[b] Pergamius is the bearer of letters to Nicocles (*Ep.* 1211), and to Aristophanes in Corinth (*Ep.* 1214), as well as to Euelpistius in Sparta. He reappears in *Or.* 1.176 as implicated in the conspiracy of Theodorus. Libanius' comment there is more in keeping with Ammianus' disparaging remarks about him (29.1.25).

[c] In particular, and as usual, Constantinople.

σοὶ καὶ οὕτως ἄξιον εἰπεῖν ὡς ἡσθήσομαι. τὸ γὰρ τοῦτον οὗ προσήκει ποιεῖσθαι τὰς διατριβὰς ἐμαυτοῦ κέρδος ἡγήσομαι.

## 131. Πρισκιανῷ[1]

1. Θόρυβός τις ἐν τοῖς παρ᾽ ἡμῖν ἐγένετο Ἰουδαίοις[2] ὡς ἥξοντος ἐπὶ τὴν ἀρχὴν πονηροῦ τινος γέροντος, ὃν ἔχοντα αὐτὴν πρότερον ἐξέβαλον τυραννίδα ποιήσαντα τὴν ἀρχήν. καὶ οἴονται τοῦτο ἐπιτάξειν τὸν τῶν ἀρχόντων τῶν παρ᾽ αὐτοῖς ἄρχοντα σοῦ τοῦτο ἐθέλοντος. δέξασθαι γάρ σε τοῦ γέροντος ἱκετείας ἀγνοοῦντα αὐτοῦ τὸν τρόπον, ὃν οὐδὲ τὸ γῆρας ἐδυνήθη διορθώσασθαι. 2. ταῦτα οἴονται μὲν οὕτως ἔχειν οἱ τεταραγμένοι, πεῖσαι δὲ οὐ δυνηθέντες τοῦτο ἐδυνήθησαν ἀναγκάσαι με γράψαι. σὺ δὲ καὶ ἐμοὶ καὶ ἐκείνοις σύγγνωθι, ἐμοὶ μὲν ἡττηθέντι τοσούτων, τοῖς δὲ

[1] The superscription of the Ms. is τῷ αὐτῷ (i.e. Priscianus). Seeck (*BLZG* 103, 245), however, argued that the recipient was the Callistio of *Ep.* 1233.

[2] Ἰουδαίοις F., conj. Re. ἰου with illegible compendium in Ms. ἰοῦσι Wolf.

---

[a] *BLZG* 244 (i), *PLRE* 727 (i). Libanius' letters provide all the information about Priscianus that we possess.

[b] Cf. M. Stern, *Greek and Latin Authors on Jews and*

it is right to mention how happy I will be, for I shall count it my personal gain for him to pass his time where it is right for him to do so.

## 131. To Priscianus[a]

1. Some disturbance has arisen among the Jews here at the prospect of the entry into authority over them of a wicked elder whom they had previously expelled from this position for making a tyranny of it. And they believe that the supreme leader who has authority over their own leaders will ordain this at your behest, since you have, so they say, accepted the pleas of this elder in ignorance of his behaviour, which even his age could not correct.[b] 2. In their alarm that is how they think matters stand, and though they have not been able to convince me of this, they have been able to force me to write to you. Pardon both them and me, me for yielding to force of

*Judaism* (Jerusalem, 1980), 2:598–599. The Jewish community in Antioch is disturbed by rumours of the reinstatement of an unpopular elder, who had already been ejected from this office for misconduct. He had appealed to Libanius' friend Priscianus, governor of Palestine, for his support in persuading the highest Jewish authority, the patriarch in Tiberias, to secure this return. The Antiochene Jews now approach Libanius, asking him to induce Priscianus to refrain from such support. The ἀρχή to which this rogue elder aspires is the gerousiarchy in Antioch. For a different interpretation see R. L. Wilken, *John Chrysostom and the Jews* (California, 1983) 60–61.

παθοῦσιν, ὃ τῶν ὄχλων ἐστί, τὸ ῥᾳδίως ἐξαπατᾶσθαι.

## 132. Πρισκιανῷ

1. Οἱ τὸν ἥλιον οὗτοι θεραπεύοντες ἄνευ αἵματος καὶ τιμῶντες θεὸν προσηγορίᾳ δευτέρᾳ καὶ τὴν γαστέρα κολάζοντες καὶ ἐν κέρδει ποιούμενοι τὴν τῆς τελευτῆς ἡμέραν πολλαχοῦ μέν εἰσι τῆς γῆς, πανταχοῦ δὲ ὀλίγοι. καὶ ἀδικοῦσι μὲν οὐδένα, λυποῦνται δὲ ὑπ' ἐνίων. 2. βούλομαι δὲ τοὺς ἐν Παλαιστίνῃ τούτων διατρίβοντας τὴν σὴν ἀρετὴν ἔχειν καταφυγὴν καὶ εἶναί σφισιν ἄδειαν καὶ μὴ ἐξεῖναι τοῖς βουλομένοις εἰς αὐτοὺς ὑβρίζειν.

---

[a] Manichaeism.

[b] προσηγορίᾳ δευτέρᾳ refers to the second grade of Manichaean worshippers, the *auditores,* as distinct from the *electi.* The terminology of Libanius betrays no more detailed knowledge of the sect than was to be expected of any shrewd observer.

numbers, them for behaving as the mass of people do, and becoming easily the victims of deception.

## 132. To Priscianus

1. The bearers are of that sect[a] which worships the sun without blood offerings and, as members of the second category, honour it as a god: they restrain their bellies and regard the day of their death as a blessing.[b] They exist in many quarters of the world, but everywhere their numbers are small. They do no harm to anyone, but they are persecuted by some people.[c] 2. I would like those of them who live in Palestine to have your excellence as their refuge and to enjoy security, and would-be aggressors not to be permitted to do them violence.[d]

[c] After Diocletian there was no official persecution of Manichaeism until the legislation of Theodosius (*Cod. Th.* xv.5.7–9). Meantime, however, sectarian struggles inside the Christian church made it a target for religious zealotry. Titus, bishop of Bostra, was prominent in presenting it as heresy.

[d] Libanius' plea for toleration is on a par with his pleas for persecuted individuals and groups, whether they be Christian, pagan, or Jew; it is indicative of the nature of the man, not of his religious beliefs.

## 133. Ἀριστοφάνει

1. Ἐπὶ τὴν τῶν γραϊδίων ἥκεις ἐπιστολήν· μακρά τε γὰρ ἡ ἐπιστολή σου καὶ τὸ μῆκος αὐτῆς ἐξ ἑνὸς ἐγκλήματος, τοῦ οὐκ ἐπεσταλκέναι με πολὺν ἤδη χρόνον, τοῦτο δὲ πολὺ πολλαχοῦ παρὰ πολλῶν. 2. ἐγὼ δέ σε ἠξίουν ἐκ μέσης ἥκοντα τῆς Ἑλλάδος γράφειν τι διαφεῦγον τὸν ὄχλον. σὺ δ' ἔοικας ἀμελεῖν λόγων καὶ ταῦτα λόγους μεταπεμπόμενος, οὐ γὰρ δὴ πέμπων, οὐ γὰρ ἐβουλήθης. 3. ἐθαύμασα δὲ ὅτι σιγὴν αἰτιᾷ τινος μετὰ τὴν τοῦ βασιλέως ἐκείνου σφαγήν. οὐ γὰρ τοῦτο δεινόν, εἴ τις ἐκείνου φίλος ἐσίγησεν, ἀλλ' ἐκεῖνο μᾶλλον, εἰ λέγων καὶ γράφων καὶ ἐπιστέλλων ἐφαίνετο. 4. τί δ' ἂν σοι καὶ ἐπέστελλον; ὅτι τέθνηκεν; ἀλλὰ τοῦτό γε καὶ ὠκεανὸς ᾔδει. ἀλλ' ὅτι φέρω; ἀλλὰ μεῖζον τὸ κακὸν ἢ φέρειν. ἀλλ' ὅτι οὐ φέρω; τοῦτο δὲ οὐκ ἦν σοι δῆλον; ἀλλ' ὑπὲρ τῆς ἐν χερσὶν ἀρχῆς ἔδει τι παραινεῖν

[a] Aristophanes has replied to Libanius' letter of spring 364 (*Ep.* 1214), which, *pace* Seeck, was the first written to him after Julian's death. He had now retired from the post to which Julian had appointed him. He had begun a spirited defence of Julian's memory, and was now engaged

## 133. To Aristophanes[a]

1. You have set about writing your letter like an old maid. Your letter is long and its whole length consists of one complaint, that I have not written to you for a long time now. But this is something that often happens, everywhere and with a lot of people. 2. I expected you, coming from the heart of Greece,[b] to write something different from the common herd, but it appears that you are not interested in eloquence, even though you send and ask me for some, for you send me none. You refused to do so. 3. I am surprised that you accuse anyone of staying silent after the murder[c] of our noble emperor. The scandal is not for any friend of his to stay silent, but rather for him to be seen speaking, writing, and sending letters. 4. And what would I have to write to you about? His death? But Ocean itself knows that much. That I endure it? But the evil is too great to be endured with equanimity. My lack of equanimity, then? But did you not know about that already? The need to proffer advice, then, upon the post you held, and hope and expectation of one to fol-

upon a collection of oratory relevant to the subject (§2). Bidez (Julien, *Oeuvres Complètes* I.ii.114) canvasses the possibility that Aristophanes is responsible for the first collection of Julian's letters.

[b] Aristophanes had now retired home to Corinth.

[c] See *Letter* 129 note c.

καὶ περὶ δευτέρας ἐλπίδας ὑποτείνειν; ἀλλ' ᾔδειν ὅτι τῆς μὲν ἐκβεβλῆσθαι δεῖ, τὸ δ' ὑπὲρ ἄλλης τι λέγειν εἰς ἑτέρους ἥκει. 5. ταχύ μοι δοκεῖς, ὦ φίλε Ἀριστόφανες, ἐπιλελῆσθαι τῆς θείας ἐκείνης κεφαλῆς. οὐ γὰρ ἂν τοιαῦτα οὔτε ἐπεζήτεις οὔτε ἐπετίμας. ἐπιστολὰς δὲ τὰς ἐκείνου πρὸς ἐμὲ καὶ πρὸς ἐκεῖνον ἐμὰς τὰς μὲν πέμψω, τὰς δὲ οὔ. κρίσει δὲ ἑκάτερον ἔσται· τὰς μὲν γὰρ οὐδὲν δεινὸν φανῆναι, τὰς δὲ ἴσως. 6. ὁ δ' οἰόμενος λόγῳ με τετιμωρῆσθαι τοὺς περὶ αὐτοῦ βλασφημοῦντας καὶ τοιαύτης ἀκοῆς ἐπιθυμῶν, ὅτι μὲν μισεῖ τοὺς ἐκεῖνον μισοῦντας, καλῶς ποιεῖ· μὴ μέντοι με οὕτως οἰέσθω Μελιτίδην ὡς ἀγνοεῖν οὐκ ἀκίνδυνον τὸ τοιαύτας δίκας λαμβάνειν· οἱ γὰρ αὐτοὶ καὶ βλασφημοῦσι καὶ δύνανται. 7. ἐκείνῳ μὲν οὖν ἀρκεῖ τὸ πλὴν ὀλίγων ἅπαντας αὐτὸν ποθεῖν· σοῦ δὲ ἐπαινῶ τὸ ἔργων ἐπιθυμεῖν καὶ τὸ μὴ ἑλέσθαι καθεύδειν, ἐπειδήπερ ἔξεστιν. ἄξιον δὲ ἐπαίνου καὶ τὸ πρὸς τὸν ἄριστον Ὀλύμπιον βλέψαι γνώμην ἄδολόν τε καὶ φιλότιμον καὶ δύναμιν ἱκανὴν <ἔχοντα>.[1]

[1] <ἔχοντα> F., conj. Re.

[d] Libanius' prudence is not without reason. Antioch

low? But I knew that you were bound to be ejected from the one, and talk of another would depend on other people. 5. It seems to me, my dear Aristophanes, that you have soon forgotten his sacred majesty: otherwise you would not make such requests or complaints. Of the letters which passed between him and me, I will send you some but not all. It will be a matter of judgement, for though there is no harm in publishing some of them, there may perhaps be, in the case of others.[d] 6. If anyone thinks that I by an oration[e] have exacted vengeance from those who slander him and is desirous of hearing it because he hates those who hate him, he is quite right. But do not let him think me such a simpleton[f] as to be unaware that the exaction of such punishment is not without danger, for the same people who slander him hold the reins of power. 7. So it is enough for him that all save a few long for him. I commend you for your desire for action and your refusal to be a sluggard, though you could be. It is also commendable to have regard to the excellent Olympius,[g] for his disposition is guileless and generous and he is influential enough.

remained a hotbed of Christian extremism; and the attitude of the new emperors towards religious matters and towards Julian's memory was as yet uncertain.

[e] The Monody on Julian, itself unpublished; cf. Petit, "Recherches sur la publication . . ." p. 486.

[f] Cf. *Or.* 17.8; Suidas s.v. γελοῖος.

[g] *BLZG* 224 (v), *PLRE* 645 (9). Now governor of Achaea, cf. *Ep.* 1258.

## 134. Νικοκλεῖ

1. Τί δαί; ᾤου, πρὸς Διός, ἐν λειμῶσιν ἡμῖν καὶ ἄνθεσι καὶ ἡσυχίᾳ τὸν ὑπόλοιπον ἔσεσθαι βίον τοιαύτην κεφαλὴν τῆς γῆς κατασχούσης, οὐκ Αἴαντα, ὃς πέρι μὲν εἶδος, ἀλλ᾽ ὃς τῷ κάλλει τῆς ψυχῆς πολὺ τοὺς ἡμιθέους ἐνίκα καὶ ὃς Πέρσας μὲν κλάοντας ἐκάθισεν, ἡμᾶς δὲ εἰς ὕψος ἦρεν; 2. οὐκ οἶσθ᾽ ὅτι τὸ μὲν ὑβρίζειν ἄλλων ἐστίν, ἡμῖν δὲ ἀνάγκη νύττεσθαι ξίφεσί τε καὶ ἔγχεσιν ἀμφιγύοισιν; φέρωμεν οὖν ὅ τι ἂν ὁ θεὸς διδῷ, καὶ τοὺς βάλλοντας αὐτῷ τούτῳ λυπῶμεν τῷ πεπαιδεῦσθαι φέρειν· καὶ γὰρ εἰ μὲν ἦν μείζω τὰ δεύτερα τοῦ πρώτου κακοῦ, τάχα ἂν ἦν συγγνώμη θορυβουμένοις· νῦν δ᾽ ὅ τι ἂν συμβαίνῃ δεινόν, οὐχ ὅσον γε ἐκεῖνο. ποταμοὺς δὲ περᾶν μετὰ πελάγη κοῦφον. 3. Κλέαρχον μὲν οὖν ἐβουλόμην μηδὲν ἠγροικίσθαι περὶ τὴν σὴν οἰκίαν· ἐπεὶ δὲ λυπεῖν εἵλετο μᾶλλον ἢ ἐπαινεῖσθαι, τοῦ γε αὐτὸν γενέσθαι βελτίω ποιήσομαι πρόνοιαν. δέξεται γὰρ ἐπιστολὴν μεμφομένην. 4. Λητοΐου δὲ τοῦ

[a] Plat. *Soph.* 248e.
[b] Homer *Od.* 11.549f.
[c] Plat. *Ion* 535e; cf. *Or.* 15.75.

## 134. To Nicocles

1. What! Good heavens, did you expect me[a] to spend the rest of my life in the peace of flowery meads after earth has claimed such a personage—not an Ajax who excelled in physical beauty,[b] but one who far outstripped the heroes in beauty of soul, who set the Persians lamenting[c] and raised us up on high? 2. Do you not know that arrogance is for others, and we must needs cower before swords and double-pointed spears?[d] Let us then endure whatever the god sends and grieve our assailants simply by being trained to endure. Indeed if the results were worse than the first evil, there might perhaps be pardon for panic. As it is, whatever disaster afflicts us cannot compare with that. After crossing the oceans, it is not much to cross rivers. 3. Anyway, I did not like Clearchus behaving rudely towards your family, but since he has chosen to annoy rather than to win praise, I shall make his correction my concern, and he will receive a letter of reproof.[e] 4. In mentioning Letoius[f] son of

[d] Homer *Il.* 10.147.

[e] *Ep.* 1266. Nicocles had been teacher of Clearchus and his brother, but Clearchus, now Vicar of Asia, had moved against him for his conduct in the reign of Julian. Nicocles was cleared in 365.

[f] *BLZG* 198 (ii). He is the nephew of the *principalis* Letoius (i) and himself to be a *principalis* in the 380s. He was now a pupil of Libanius, perhaps not a model one (Petit, *Étudiants* 148).

Κυνηγίου μεμνημένος <τὸ>[1] σαυτοῦ ποιεῖς καὶ πρὸς ἐπιμέλειαν ἑτέρους παρακαλῶν ἄξια τῆς ξενίας ποιεῖς. ἡμεῖς δὲ Κυνήγιον μὲν ἀνδρείως ἀποθανόντα λόγῳ πρότερον τετιμήκαμεν, πρὸς δὲ λόγων κτῆσιν τὸν ἐκείνου τὰ μὲν πείθοντες, τὰ δὲ ἀναγκάζοντες ἄγομεν.

[1] <τὸ> F., conj. Re.

## 135. Εὐαγρίῳ

1. Μέγα τοῦτο σημεῖον τοῦ ὡς ἄριστά σε ἄρξειν τὸ ζητεῖν παρ᾽ ἡμῶν κανόνας, δι᾽ ὧν ἂν ὡς ἄριστα ἄρξαις· ἐγὼ δὲ ἓν μὲν ἐκεῖνο λέγω σαφὲς καὶ βραχύ, ὅτι σε ὅμοιον χρὴ σαυτῷ γενέσθαι καὶ τὴν ἐπὶ τῶν ἐλαττόνων γνώμην ἐν τοῖς μείζοσι τηρῆσαι. 2. εἰ δὲ δεῖ καὶ διελόντας εἰπεῖν, ἕπου τοῖς νόμοις, τίμα τοὺς ἀγαθούς, μίσει πονηρίαν, μείζους ποίει τὰς πόλεις, ἡδὺ τὸ πονεῖν ἡγοῦ, κέρδος νόμιζε τὴν δόξαν. ἂν ταῦτα φυλάττῃς— φυλάξεις δέ, καὶ γὰρ πρότερον — σαυτόν τε καὶ πατρίδα καὶ γονεῖς καὶ τὸν ἀδελφὸν κοσμήσεις.

Cynegius, you behave in customary fashion, and in urging others to interest themselves in him, you behave in a manner worthy of the ties of hospitality. I have previously honoured with an oration Cynegius for his courageous death; his son I now direct to the acquisition of eloquence by persuasion and compulsion.

## 135. To Euagrius[a]

1. The fact that you ask me for rules whereby you may be an excellent governor, is itself an indication that you will be an excellent governor. I make this one brief and explicit point, that you must be consistent with yourself, and maintain in more important matters the same attitude you hold on minor things. 2. But if I must go into details, then follow the laws, honour the good, hate wickedness, improve the cities, regard work as a pleasure, and think of your good reputation as pure gain. If you keep to this—and you will, as you have done before—you will be a credit to yourself, your birthplace, your parents, and your brother.[b]

[a] *BLZG* 128 (iv), *PLRE* 285 (6). As an ex-pupil and family friend, he had had Libanius' support in his advancement to office (*Letter* 112).

[b] Euagrius was Antiochene, son of Pompeianus and brother of Libanius' old friend Olympius. He does not seem to have had much success with the application of these "rules," for he was dismissed from office, flogged and fined, though later cleared.

## 136. Σαλουτίῳ

1. Ὅταν συνέλθωσιν ἀγαθὴ γνώμη καὶ τύχη καὶ ὁ αὐτὸς ἄνθρωπος χρηστός τε ᾖ καὶ δυνατός, κοινόν τι τοῦτο πᾶσιν ἀνθρώποις καθίσταται. νῦν τοίνυν ἥ τε σύνοδος ἐκείνη λαμπρότατα φαίνεται τό τε τρίτον εὖ ποιοῦν ἠκολούθηκεν. εὐθυμοῦνται μὲν αἱ πόλεις, ἀνθοῦσι δὲ οἱ οἶκοι, καὶ ἄρχουσι μὲν ἐθνῶν οἱ ἀρχῆς ἐπιστήμονες, ἰδιωτεύουσι δὲ οὓς κάλλιον. 2. ἐγὼ δὲ τῇ μὲν ἄλλῃ τῶν παρόντων ἀπολαύω, φιλοῦμαι γὰρ καὶ οὐκ ἂν ἀρνηθείην, γράμματα δὲ παρὰ τοῦ φιλοῦντος οὐ λαμβάνων ἀδικοῦμαι. καὶ εἰ μὲν οὐκ ἦν πω ταύτην τὴν τιμὴν τετιμημένος, ἴσως ἂν οὐδὲ ἐζήτουν· νῦν δ' Εὐφράτης μοι γλυκύτερος Βοσπόρου. ἐντεῦθεν μὲν γὰρ ἐπέστελλες καὶ ταῦτα τὸ σῶμα ἔχων ἐν χερσὶν ἰατρῶν· ἐκεῖνον δὲ ἰδὼν τὸν πόρον, οὐκ ἂν μὲν φαίην ὡς ἐπελάθου μου, τοῦ δὲ γράμμασιν εὐφραίνειν οὐκ οἶδ' ὅπως ἀπέστης. 3. ἀλλά, πρὸς θεῶν, οἵ σε ἡμῖν ἐκ τῶν ἐσχάτων κινδύνων σεσώκασιν, ἀνανέωσαι τὴν τιμὴν καὶ δὸς ἐκεῖνα τὰ πρότερα. βουλοίμην δ' ἂν τὸν αὐτὸν ἄνδρα μοι

---

[a] Salutius was not in good health (Amm. Marc. 25.5.3).

## 136. To Salutius

1. Whenever good counsel and fortune combine, and the same person is both virtuous and influential, it is a blessing to be shared by mankind as a whole. Now that combination is most gloriously revealed, and the third factor has fortunately resulted. The cities are in good heart, individual families flourish, and expert administrators are governors of provinces, while those people who deserve to do so remain out of office. 2. In general, I enjoy the present situation, for I am befriended and would not deny it, but I am wronged by not receiving a letter from my friend. Had I never yet received such a token of esteem, I would not perhaps be looking for one. As it is, the Euphrates is more pleasing to me than the Bosporus, for you used to write to me from there, even while your person was in the hands of doctors.[a] But as soon as you saw that strait[b]—I would not assert that you forgot me, but somehow or another you ceased giving me the pleasure of your letters. 3. But, in the name of the gods who have saved you for us from direct perils, renew your favour and grant me what you did before. My wish would be that the same person should scrutinize my letter while endowed with the fitting honour of another

[b] Still praetorian prefect he is with the court at Constantinople, a city which Libanius refuses always to name, as much from distaste as from rhetorical convention.

δοκιμάσαι τὴν ἐπιστολὴν κεκοσμημένον οἷς εἰκός, ἀρχῇ δευτέρᾳ. δεινὸν γὰρ τὸν πρὸ τῶν ἄλλων τότε νῦν οὐδὲν ἐργαζόμενον ἔργα ἑτέρων ὁρᾶν.

---

[c] The plea to Salutius to resume writing indicates the precariousness of his position at this time when Julian's

## 137. Εὐδαίμονι

1. Καὶ σοὶ τῷ πρεσβευτῇ χάρις καὶ τῷ τὸν ὕπνον ὑμῖν[1] ἐπιδόντι καὶ τῷ φήναντι τὴν γυναῖκα τὴν μεγάλην τε καὶ καλήν, καὶ σοὶ πάλιν χάρις, ὅτι ταύτην οἴει τὴν Ὑγίειαν εἶναι. 2. ἀλλ' ὅπως ταύτην γε τὴν ἄνθρωπον ἢ μᾶλλον τὴν θεὸν μὴ ἀνῆτε, πρὶν ἂν ἐμοὶ συγγένηται καὶ περιχυθῇ καὶ διὰ παντὸς ἐλθοῦσα μέλους φυγῇ ζημιώσῃ τὴν ἀναιδῆ ποδάγραν. 3. ἐλπίζω δέ τι πλέον· οὐδὲ γὰρ τὸ νῦν μικρόν, ὃ καὶ αὐτὸ τοῦ θεοῦ τίθεμαι, παρ' οὗ τὴν νύμφην λαμβάνεις. ἤδη γὰρ ὁ ποὺς δύο μοίρας ἀπείληφε τῆς δυνάμεως ἥν ποτε εἶχεν.

[1] ὑμῖν F., conj. Re. ἡμῖν Wolf (V).

---

[a] *BLZG* 131 (ii), *PLRE* 289 (2). A teacher in Antioch, travelling to Cilicia to visit the temple of Asclepius at Aegae on Libanius' behalf to get him some cure for his gout. There, by incubation, he had a vision which he inter-

office: for it is a shame that you, at that time more actively engaged than anyone else, should now be inactive and look upon the activities of others.[c]

friends were under suspicion of magic aimed at Valentinian's health (Zos. 4.1), and both emperors were to show themselves bitterly hostile to them (Zos. 4.2.2 ff).

## 137. To Eudaemon[a]

1. I am grateful both to you, my envoy, and to him who brought sleep upon you and revealed to you that tall and lovely lady, and I am again grateful to you for believing her to be Good Health. 2. But take care that you do not let her go, be she human or, more likely, divine, before she joins me and embraces me, and penetrating every limb condemns to exile my accursed gout.[b] 3. But I hope for more: what I already have received is not a little thing—I attribute it to the god, from whom you have got this bride. Already my foot has recovered two thirds of the strength it once had. The hands are

preted as Hygieia. Libanius reports some improvement in consequence.

[b] This attack of gout struck at the celebration of the Olympia in August, and confined him to bed for its duration (*Or.* 1.139). This would in any case have prevented him from delivering the Olympic oration, even if he had not already refused the task (*Ep.* 1243). The gout continued with brief intermissions until 371 (*Or.* 1.141–3). Letters which deal with it are *Epp.* 1239, 1274, 1300–1, 1483, 1518.

αἱ μὲν χεῖρες τοῖν Ἠπειρώταιν, τὸ δὲ δῶρον Ἀσκληπιοῦ. 4. πιστεύειν οὖν χρὴ καὶ περὶ τοῦ λειπομένου. τοῦτο δὲ εἰ γένοιτο, δραμούμεθα παρὰ τὸν φιλόδωρον θεὸν βεβαιωσόμενοί τε τὸ δοθὲν καὶ σοὶ δᾷδα ἅψοντες ἐν τοῖς γάμοις· πρὶν δὲ κομίσασθαι τὸ πᾶν, οὐκ ἀσφαλές, οἶμαι, μείζω τῆς δυνάμεως τολμᾶν.

## 138. Ἀκακίῳ

1. Ἥσθησαν καὶ ἐγέλασαν ἅπαντες οἱ τῆς κωμῳδίας ἀκούσαντες· ἤκουσαν δὲ πλὴν ὀλίγων πάντες, καὶ οὐδεὶς ἦν, ὃς οὐκ ἂν ἐβουλήθη ποδάγρᾳ κατειλημμένος οὕτως αὐτὴν δύνασθαι κωμῳδεῖν. 2. ἐγὼ δὲ οὐχ, ὡς οἴει, τὸν νόμον ὑπερπεπήδηκα τὸν τῶν ἄρτι δεξαμένων τὴν βασιλίδα ταύτην, ἀλλὰ καὶ σκληρότητα ὁδοῦ καὶ ὄστρακα καὶ θέατρον καὶ θηρίων θέαν καὶ πάντα μᾶλλον ᾐτιώμην τοῦ κεῖσθαι ἐπὶ κλίνης ἢ ὅπερ ἦν. συνεξηπάτηντο δέ μοι καὶ ἰατρῶν ἐν οἷς ἡ

[a] Acacius (iii), Libanius' literary friend in Cilicia, a composer of epic (*Letter* 58), and one with more than a passing interest in matters medical, had already composed an oration in honour of Asclepius in 362 in thanksgiving for recovery from illness (*Ep.* 695). Now in 364, he composes a comedy inspired by Libanius' attack of gout, and has sent

those of the two Epirotes,[c] the gift that of Asclepius. 4. So I must be confident for the rest. If this comes to pass, I will hasten to the generous god both to confirm the gift and to light the torch for you at your marriage. But before a complete recovery is made, it is unsafe, I believe, to venture beyond one's strength.

[c] His doctors; cf. *Or.* 1.140; *Letter* 138.2.

## 138. To Acacius[a]

1. Everyone who listened to your comedy was delighted and applauded, and those who listened to it were practically everyone: there was not one who would not have wished, on being afflicted with gout, to be able to make a comedy of it in this way. 2. As for myself, I have not, as you think, overstepped the rules of those who have recently welcomed this mistress; I grumbled at the rough road, the pavement,[b] the theatre, and the spectacle of the beasts as the cause of my lying abed, anything rather than the real reason.[c] And those doctors of consummate skill were as deceived as I.

him a copy. From the information here given by Libanius, Seeck (p. 44) identified this work with the ps.-Lucianic *Ocypus*. This identification is plausible but falls short of certainty, especially in view of the standardised treatment of such themes in the Second Sophistic.

[b] Cf. P. Oxy. xxxi.2532, line 3. For the use of *testa* ( = ὄστρακα) in pavement construction cf. Cato *R.R.* 18.7.

[c] Cf. *Ocypus* 7 ff, 54 ff, 85 f.

ἰατρικὴ πᾶσα. 3. καρπωσάμενος δὲ τὴν ἀπάτην μῆνα ὅλον καὶ μέλλων εἴσεσθαι ὅ τι ἐστί, πάλιν διεκωλύθην ὑπὸ τῶν οὐκ ἀγνοούντων, φαίην ἄν, ἀλλ' οὐκ ἐθελόντων ἀνιᾶν. πυκναῖς δὲ αὐτῆς ταῖς εἰσβολαῖς χρωμένης καὶ δενδροτομούσης καὶ δῃούσης μᾶλλον ἢ οἱ Λάκωνες τὴν Ἀττικὴν ἐνέδωκα καὶ ἀπέδωκα τῷ πάθει τοὔνομα δεινῆς ἀναισχυντίας ἡγούμενος ἐξελεγχόμενον ἀρνεῖσθαι. σὺ δ' ἀκούων μηνὶ τετάρτῳ τὰ ὄντα οἴει παρημελῆσθαι τὸν νόμον. ὁ δὲ λαβὼν τὴν αὑτοῦ μοῖραν οὐκ ἔμελλεν ἀεὶ βιάσεσθαι τὴν ἀλήθειαν. 4. φθέγξῃ δὲ καὶ σὺ ταὐτά μοι μικρὸν ὕστερον, μᾶλλον δέ, πρὸς μὲν τὸν[1] θεὸν εἴρηταί σοι παραπλήσια, καὶ κέκληται σύμμαχος ἐπὶ ποδάγραν· ἀγροὶ δὲ καὶ ἵπποι καὶ πονηρὸς οἰκέτης οὐχ ὑποδεξάμενος φερόμενον νῦν μὲν ᾄδεται πρὸς ἡμᾶς, προϊὸν δὲ τὸ ἔτος πάσας αἰτίας ἐξαλείψει πλὴν μιᾶς. 5. ἡμεῖς δὲ γενόμενοι χορός, ἐσμὲν δὲ πλείους ἢ καθ' ὅσους ὁ κωμικός, ὑπὸ σοὶ κορυφαίῳ τιμήσομεν ᾠδαῖς τὴν ἐρῶσαν τῶν ποδῶν.

[1] τὸν Wolf (Ms.) τὴν F.

3. And after enjoying the fruits of this deception for a whole month, and just as I was about to discover what it was, I was once again forestalled by them not through their ignorance, I dare say, but through their refusal to worry me. So it made frequent incursions, harried and devastated more than ever the Spartans did in Attica,[d] and I gave in and gave the illness its proper name,[e] for I thought it dreadfully obstinate to be found out denying the obvious. You hear the facts three months afterwards, and think that I have broken the rules. But anyone who has got what is destined for him is not likely always to do violence to truth.[f] 4. You too will say the same as I very soon, or rather, you have addressed the god in similar terms, and have summoned him as an ally against gout.[g] Now we hear the repeated refrain of your estates, horses, the rascal of a servant who refuses to support you as you are driven along, but as the year goes on it will erase every excuse bar one. 5. And we will form a chorus, more in number than that of comedy,[h] and under you as its leader we will honour with song her who has such a passion for feet.

[d] Thuc. 1.108, 3.26.

[e] Cf. *Ocypus* 12 ff.

[f] Cf. *Ocypus* 117.

[g] Asclepius. For Acacius' declamation in his honour cf. *Ep.* 695 (of 362).

[h] That is, more than two dozen.

## 139. Ἀντωνίνῳ[1]

1. Ἔδει τὸν ἐπιστείλαντά σοι περὶ τοῦ σκύτους καὶ τῶν πληγῶν καὶ τὴν αἰτίαν προσθεῖναι τῶν πληγῶν· οὕτω γὰρ οὐκ ἂν ὥσπερ νῦν ἐλυπήθης. φαίνῃ γάρ μοι λίαν ἀλγεῖν, οὐχ ὅτι πληγὰς ἔλαβεν ὁ σὸς υἱός, ἀλλ' ὅτι μὴ μεγάλα ἁμαρτὼν οὐκ ἄν ποτε ἐδόκει πληγῆναι. 2. ἐγὼ δὲ ὡς ἔχω περὶ τούτων, ἄκουσον· ἢν μέν τις τῶν νέων ἀδικῇ τι τοιοῦτον, ὃ μηδὲ εἰπεῖν καλόν, ἐκβάλλω καὶ οὐκ ἐῶ τὸν χορὸν ἀναπίμπλασθαι τῆς νόσου· κατὰ δὲ τῶν ὑπτίων εἰς λόγους αἱ πληγαί. τῶν μὲν γὰρ τὰ ἕλκη φοβοῦμαι καὶ ἀπελαύνω, τοὺς δὲ ἀφυπνίζω τῷ σκύτει. 3. τοῦτ' ἔλαβον καὶ τὸν σὸν υἱὸν ἀδικοῦντα. τὸ γάρ τοι βιβλίον ἀφεὶς ἐπεδείκνυτο τάχος ποδοῖν καὶ δίκην ἔδωκεν ἐν τοῖς ποσίν, ἵν' ἑτέρου δρόμου φροντίζῃ τοῦ τῆς γλώττης. 4. μὴ τοίνυν δευτέραν προστίθει δίκην τὴν σὴν ὀργὴν μηδ' ἡγοῦ τὸν παῖδα κακόν, βλέποντά τε πρὸς τὸν ἀδελφὸν ἤδη καὶ ἐρῶντα τῶν σῶν καὶ ἴσως δυνησόμενον ἴσα.

[1] Ἀντωνίνῳ F. (V) Ἀκακίῳ Wolf (S W Vind).

---

[a] *BLZG* 77 (i): an Armenian who had received reports of corporal punishment inflicted on his son, who was in his

## 139. To Antoninus[a]

1. Your correspondent who informed you about the strap and the beating ought to have told you the reason for the beating, too. In that case you would not have been so aggrieved as you now are: for it seems to me that you have taken offence not so much because your son has had a beating, but because you thought he never would have done except for some grave misconduct. 2. But just listen to my attitude towards this matter: if one of my students conducts himself so badly that it cannot decently be mentioned, I expel him and refuse to allow my class to be infested by such contagion. Beatings however are employed against those who are idle in their studies. In the case of the first, I am afraid of the damage they cause, and so expel them; these last I waken up with the strap. 3. This was the error of which I found even your son guilty: he put his book down and showed a clean pair of heels, and he was punished and brought to heel, so that he might concentrate upon a different kind of chase in future—a linguistic one. 4. So do not punish him a second time by being angry with him, and do not think him to be vicious. He now regards his brother, is devoted to yourself, and perhaps will be just as able.

first term as Libanius' pupil. On corporal punishment see Festugière, *Antioche* 111 ff. As Libanius gets older, he becomes more reluctant to resort to the strap (e.g. *Or.* 2.20).

## 140. Σελεύκῳ

1. Ἀνεπνεύσαμεν ἀκούσαντες ὅτι τὸν ἆθλον ἐκεῖνον τὸν καλὸν καὶ δίκαιον διήνυσας. ἡμῶν δὲ τὰ μὲν ἔργα οὐκ ἂν ἴσως ἐπαινεθείη, μικρὰ γάρ, τὴν γνώμην δὲ οἶμαι καὶ παρὰ τοῖς θεοῖς εὐδοκιμεῖν· καὶ γὰρ ἐστενάξαμεν καὶ ἐδακρύσαμεν καὶ παρήλθομεν σοῦ τὴν λύπην. καὶ νῦν ὥσπερ ὑμεῖς χαίρομεν, ὅτι πᾶν τὸ πέλαγος ἐπλεύσθη. 2. χαίρω δὲ καὶ δι' ἐκεῖνο, ὅτι παλαιόν τι τῆς ὑμετέρας οἰκίας νόμιμον σώζετε[1] καὶ δῶρα δύνασθε πέμπειν καὶ μετὰ τὸν σκηπτόν. 3. νῦν μὲν οὖν ἴσως οὐ πολλῶν παρόντων, ταχέως δὲ καὶ πολλῶν παρόντων πέμψετε. τοιαῦτα γὰρ τὰ τῆς Τύχης· ἔδωκεν, εἶτα ἀφείλετο. πάλιν ὧν ἀφείλετο δέδωκε πλείω. τέρψιν γάρ, οἶμαι, τινὰ ταύτην τέρπεται κινοῦσα τὰ τῶν ἀνθρώπων καὶ οὐκ ἐῶσα τοὺς αὐτοὺς ἐπὶ τῶν αὐτῶν μένειν. 4. οὐδ' ἂν εἴποις ὅτι πλείους καθεῖλεν ἢ ἦρεν. ἀναμιμνήσκου δὲ πάντα τἄλλα ἀφεὶς Ὀδυσσέως τοῦ γυμνοῦ, ὡς φύλλων δεηθεὶς εἰς τὸ κρύπτειν ἃ κρύπτειν ἔδει, μετὰ πολλῶν χρημάτων οἴκαδε ἦλθε. 5. σοὶ δὲ

[1] σώζετε F., conj. Re. σώζεται Wolf (V)

## 140. To Seleucus

1. I sighed with relief upon hearing that you had completed that noble, just task. My own achievements may not be particularly praiseworthy, for they are trifles, but my intentions, I feel, are commendable even among the gods, for I lamented and wept, and outdid you in grief.[a] And now I rejoice, as you do, that we have sailed the ocean through. 2. I rejoice for this reason too, that you maintain the long established custom of your house and can send me gifts, even after that bitter blow.[b] 3. Well, perhaps now you send them with not many lookers-on, but soon there will be many. Such is Fortune's way:[c] she gives, and then takes away, and then again gives more than she has taken. She gets some such delight, I feel, by upsetting the condition of men and refusing to allow people to stay as they are. 4. Nor could you say that she has cast down more people than she raised up. Discounting all else, think of Odysseus, when he was naked, needing leaves to cover what needed to be covered, and yet going home with many possessions.[d] 5. Some god

[a] The death of Julian. Libanius has completed the Monody.

[b] The New Year presents date the letter to early 365. Seleucus has just been fined for his activity under Julian.

[c] Cf. *Ep.* 1266.7. Misson, *Recherches sur le paganisme de Libanius* 50 ff.

[d] Homer *Od.* 6.127 (cf. *Letter* 142.2); 8.389 ff.

δώσει μὲν θεῶν τις χρυσὸν ἀντὶ χρυσοῦ, δέδωκε δέ, ὃ πολλῷ παντὸς χρυσίου βέλτιον, πάλαι μὲν γυναῖκα, νῦν δὲ θυγατέρα χρυσῆς ἀτεχνῶς γενεᾶς· ἣν οὖσαν ὁπόσων λέγεις ἐτῶν εἰδέναι ὁπόσα ἔφης θαυμαστὸν οὐδέν. ἡ γὰρ τοῖν γονέοιν φύσις καὶ τοῦτο πιστὸν ποιεῖ. ὅπου γὰρ τοιοῦτος μὲν γεωργός, τοιαύτη δὲ ἄρουρα, πολλῆς, οἶμαι, τῆς ἀνάγκης μέγα τι φῦναι καὶ διαφέρον τῶν ἄλλων. ἄγε οὖν ἡμῖν τὸ μουσόληπτον παιδίον καὶ ὁράτω πόλιν ἐν ᾗπερ ἐσπάρη. 6. τὸν Εὐστάθιον δὲ μηδεὶς ἐπειγέτω μηδὲ διαφθειρέτω τοῖς δευτέροις τὴν χάριν μηδὲ τοιούτους ἡμᾶς ἀποφαινέτω χρήστας, οἵους φεύγειν παραινεῖ Φωκυλίδης.

---

[e] He had married Alexandra in Antioch in 360; his daughter, Olympias, was born in 361.

## 141. Θεμιστίῳ

1. Οὐκ ἔλαθές με ῥῆμα μέγα περὶ ἐμοῦ φθεγξάμενος ἐν ἀγορᾷ τε καὶ ὄχλῳ. μεμήνυκε δ' αὐτὸ Βιθυνὸς ἀνήρ, ὃς ἐρᾷ τῆς μεγάλης ποτὲ πόλεως

---

[a] Bouchery p. 256, F/Kr. no. 59. One of a batch of letters delivered by Celsus (§6; cf. *Epp.* 1474, 1476) to friends and officials in Constantinople, January 365. The occasion for writing was the receipt of a friend's letter

will give you gold for gold, but he has already given you something far better than all the gold in the world—in times past, a wife, and now a daughter[e] of a generation of pure gold. It is no surprise that she, at her age, has all the accomplishments you say she has, for the natural gifts of her parents lend credence even to this. With such the sower and such the soil, something far and away surpassing all else is bound to be produced. Well, then! let this gifted child see the city in which she was begotten. 6. As for Eustathius,[f] let no pressure be put upon him, nor yet let the favour be spoiled by its consequences, nor let him show us to be such creditors as Phocylides tells us to avoid.[g]

[f] Seeck's identification with Eustathius (iv, *PLRE* 3), the wronged husband of *Letter* 77, seems most unlikely. He is mentioned in *Ep.* 1471.

[g] Ps.-Phocyl. 83: μηδέποτε χρήστης πικρὸς γένῃ ἀνδρὶ πένητι (Never be an angry creditor to a pauper).

## 141. To Themistius[a]

1. The important statement about me which you made in the city square before a large audience has not escaped my notice. My informant was a Bithynian, a man passionately devoted to the city which,

reporting complimentary remarks made by Themistius in Constantinople about the excellence and purity of Libanius' rhetorical style, as compared with the current fashion. Libanius, flattered, replies in kind.

καὶ κειμένης. ἔγραφε γὰρ βουλόμενός με χάριν σοι τοῦ ῥήματος εἰδέναι. 2. ἐγὼ δὲ οὐκ ἔχω, καὶ μὴ ὅτι τῶν πτερνῶν ἃς ἔφης οὐχ ὁρᾶν τοὺς ἄλλους δὴ τὰς ἐμάς, ἀλλ' οὐδ' ἄν, εἰ τὰς βλαύτας ἔλεγες, ᾔδειν ἄν σοι χάριν. ἃ γὰρ σὺ σαυτὸν ἐπαινεῖς, διὰ τί ἄν σοι τούτων χάριν εἰδείην ἐγώ; ἐμοὶ γὰρ καὶ σοὶ λόγοι οἱ πολιτικοὶ μορφῆς μιᾶς καὶ τῶν αὐτῶν τοκέων καὶ ἀδελφοὶ καὶ προσέτι δίδυμοι. 3. ἀνάγκη οὖν πᾶσα ψεγομένων μὲν τῶν ἐμῶν καὶ τοὺς σοὺς ἀκούειν κακῶς, ἐπαινουμένων δὲ κοινὸν ἀμφοῖν καὶ τὸν ἔπαινον εἶναι. σὺ τοίνυν εἰπεῖν μέν τι περὶ τῶν σαυτοῦ λόγων ἐθελήσας, φυγὼν δὲ τὸ φορτικὸν δι' ἐμοῦ ταὐτὸ ποιεῖς. 4. ἀλλ', ὦ μακάριε, ἔασον τὴν ἀγέλην τῶν χηνῶν καὶ σὲ καὶ αὑτοὺς ἀγνοεῖν, καὶ νομιζόντων σὲ μὲν χῆνα, κύκνους δὲ αὑτούς. εἰδόσι γὰρ δὴ ταῦτα ἐν Ἀργείοις ἀγορεύουσι καὶ οὐ μεταθήσουσι τὴν δόξαν

---

[b] Nicomedeia, destroyed in the earthquake of 358.

[c] Other orators could not "get within a mile of" Libanius as regards style. Libanius models himself upon the purely classic Attic school, so much so that he is labelled Demosthenes ὁ μικρός by the Byzantine commentators. The prevailing fashion was for the Asianic style—the flowery stuff of Himerius or Gregory Nazianzen (cf. Norden, *Antike*

once great, is now laid low.[b] He wrote and wanted me to be grateful to you for what you had said. 2. But I cannot be: nor would I be grateful to you for the mention not just of the clean pair of heels you say I show to most people but even of the shoes I wear in doing so.[c] Why should I be grateful to you for your own self-praise? Your public orations and mine are of a kind and of the same parentage. They are brothers, twins in fact.[d] 3. So it is bound to be the case that, if mine are criticized, yours too are ill-spoken of, while if mine are praised, then the praise too belongs to us both alike. So when you want to talk about your own oratory, to avoid vulgar ostentation, you achieve this same result by means of me. 4. My dear good man, leave that flock of geese to stay in ignorance both of you and of themselves: let them think you to be the goose and themselves the swans.[e] They make their remarks "among the Argives who know these things,"[f] and

*Kunstprosa* 2:463–4). The reference to shoes and heels is a private joke between the two.

[d] Libanius insists on the close kinship between his own and Themistius' oratory in *Ep.* 376.5.

[e] Swans for the ancients are melodius birds, so much so that Horace dubs Pindar *Dircaeum cycnum* (*Od.* 4.2.25), but their singing was proverbially reserved for their dying song (e.g. by Themistius himself, *Or.* 18.223d).

[f] Homer *Il.* 10.250.

οὔτε τὴν αὑτῶν οὔτε τὴν ἡμετέραν. 5. δοκοῦσι δέ μοι τὰ μὲν ἡττᾶσθαι, τὰ δὲ κρατεῖν καὶ οὐ πάντα ἡττᾶσθαι. ἢ οὐχ ἑώρακας αὐτοὺς πίνοντας μὲν ὑπὲρ τὸν Κρατῖνον, ἐσθίοντας δὲ ὑπὲρ τὸν Ἡρακλέα, μαγείρων δὲ πλήθει τρυφῶντας, πολλῶν δὲ θύρας οἰκιῶν εἰδότας, ὥστε κἀκείνοις εἶναι τὸ μηδὲ ἐγγὺς αὐτῶν ἡμᾶς εἶναι κατὰ τὰς πτέρνας; 6. ἐκείνους μὲν οὖν ἔα τέρπεσθαι τοῖς αὑτῶν, ὡς ἂν φαῖεν, ἀγαθοῖς· σὺ δὲ ἔχων τὸν σαυτοῦ μαθητὴν Κέλσον ποίει βελτίω. ποιήσαις δ' ἄν, εἰ μηδὲν ἀγνοήσειε τῶν ἐν τῷ μακρῷ σοι τούτῳ δημιουργηθέντων χρόνῳ.

---

[g] Aristoph. *Peace* 700 ff.

[h] For example, Eurip. *Alc.* 747 ff. Proverbially Ἡρακλῆς ξενίζεται.

[i] Libanius' customary prejudice against high-living in Constantinople (*Or.* 1.75). The passage is very close to *Or.*

## 142. Σελεύκῳ

1. Ἐδάκρυσα ἐπὶ τοῖς γράμμασι καὶ πρὸς τοὺς θεοὺς ἔφην· 'τί ταῦτα, ὦ θεοί;' δοὺς δὲ καὶ τῶν ἄλλων οἷς πιστεύω μάλιστα τὴν ἐπιστολὴν κἀκεί-

---

[a] Seleucus' disgrace is now complete (Spring 365): he is banished to Pontus (§ 5) and forbidden to enter cities there.

they will not change either their own opinion or ours. 5. It seems to me that in some respects they come off worst, in others they are all right and do not have the worst of it at all. Have you not seen them out-drinking Cratinus,[g] and out-eating Heracles,[h] revelling in the number of their cooks, and acquainted with the doors of many households, so that they too can say that we are nowhere near enough to them to catch a sight of their heels?[i] 6. So leave them to enjoy their so-called blessings. You have with you Celsus, your pupil: improve him. This you would do if he were left in ignorance of none of the works you have composed over this long period of time.

30.8, where the excesses of the monks are thus described. Thus it appears that we have not simply a straightforward opposition of Attic and Asianic rhetoric, but also the covert criticism that these geese in Constantinople behave and sound like the contemporary fathers of the church, with Asianism a characteristic of their current preaching.

## 142. To Seleucus[a]

1. I burst into tears at your letter and to the gods I exclaimed, "Ye gods, what does this mean?" I gave your letter to those of the rest whom I particularly trust and saw that they too were affected in the

The punishment of Julian's one-time priests and supporters continues apace, and Libanius allows only a trusted few to read Seleucus' letter.

νους ταὐτὸν εἶδον παθόντας πρὸς τὴν ἐπιστολήν. ἐλογίζετο γὰρ ἕκαστος, ὧν ἄξιος ὢν τυχεῖν ἐν οἷς ἠνάγκασαι διάγειν. 2. ἐγὼ δὲ οἷς κἀκείνους καὶ ἐμαυτὸν παρεμυθησάμην ἐρῶ· καὶ γάρ σοὶ τοῦτο ἀρκέσειν οἶμαι. εἰσῆλθέ με Ὀδυσσεὺς ἐκεῖνος, ὃς ἐπειδὴ τὴν Τροίαν κατήνεγκεν, ἐκομίζετο διὰ τῆς θαλάσσης, ὡς οἶσθα, ἡμεῖς δὲ οὔτε κλάδων ἐπὶ τὰ αἰδοῖα δεόμεθα μηδ᾽ αὖ δεηθείημεν οὔθ᾽ ὑπὸ τῶν οἰκετῶν τυπτόμεθα καθαρός τέ σοι πάσης παροινίας ὁ οἶκος. 3. εἰ δ᾽ εἴργῃ πόλεων καὶ τῶν ἐν ἐκείναις λουτρῶν, ἐνθυμοῦ, πόσοι παρὸν ἐν πόλει διατρίβειν ἐν ἀγροῖς αἱροῦνται τὰς ἡδονὰς ἡδίους τῶν ἐκεῖ θορύβων κρίνοντες. εἰ δὲ ἦσθα Ἀχιλλεὺς καὶ ἐχρῆν σε ἐν Πηλίῳ συνεῖναι τῷ Κενταύρῳ, τί ἂν ἔδρας; ἀποδρὰς ἂν εἰς τὰς πόλεις ᾤχου συμφορὰν τὸ ὄρος ἡγούμενος; 4. μή, πρὸς Διός, ὦ Σέλευκε, μὴ κόπτε σαυτὸν μηδ᾽ ἀμνημόνει τῶν στρατηγῶν ἐκείνων, οἳ ἄρτι τὰ τρόπαια στήσαντες, ὁ μὲν ἦν ἐν δεσμοῖς, οἱ δὲ ἔφευγον. οὐδὲ γὰρ ὅπως πονοῖμεν, ἐκεῖνα ἐμανθάνομεν, ἀλλ᾽ ὅπως ἐν τοῖς δεινοῖς ἐκεῖθεν κουφιζοίμεθα. 5. σὺ δ᾽ ἔχων καιρὸν εἰς ἐπίδειξιν ἀνδρείας ὀδύρῃ καὶ τοὺς Πέρσας οὐ δείσας τὰ δένδρα ἡγῇ δεινὸν καὶ τὸν

same way by it, for each of them reflected on the conditions in which you have been forced to live as compared with those you deserve. 2. I will tell you in what terms I consoled both them and myself, and I think this will satisfy you. The thought of Odysseus of old came to me, who after the fall of Troy was carried over the sea, as you know; we however had no need of branches to cover our nakedness[b]—and never will, I hope—nor are we beaten by our slaves.[c] Your household is free of excess of all kinds. 3. If you are barred from cities and the baths in them, think how many they are who can live in a city and yet choose to live in the country, regarding their pleasures as sweeter than the commotions of town. If you were Achilles and had to live with the Centaur on Pelion,[d] what would you have done? Run away and made off for the cities, thinking the mountain to be your bane? 4. No, Seleucus! in Heaven's name, do not torture yourself. Do not forget those famous generals who after their recent victories finished up, one in chains, the others in exile.[e] Nor did we learn of such things to distress ourselves but to obtain relief therefrom in our distress. 5. You have the opportunity to display your courage, and yet lament. You were not afraid of the Persians, yet you dread the

[b] Homer *Od.* 6.128. The citation is repeated from *Letter* 140.

[c] Homer *Od.* 17.233 f. [d] Cheiron.

[e] Miltiades, Themistocles, Pausanias: stock topics for declamation.

μὲν ἥλιον τὸν περὶ τὸν Τίγρητα ἤνεγκας, σκιὰν δὲ ἔχων ἐκ φύλλων ἐν Πόντῳ τῶν ἐν ἄστεσιν ἀγορῶν ἐπιθυμεῖς καὶ φῂς εἶναι μόνος· ὃ ἥκιστ' ἂν ἀνδρὶ φιλολόγῳ συμβαίη. πῶς γὰρ ἄν σε καταλίποι Πλάτων καὶ Δημοσθένης καὶ ὁ χορὸς ἐκεῖνος, οὓς ἀνάγκη μένειν, ὅπουπερ ἂν ἐθέλῃς; 6. τούτοις τε οὖν διαλέγου καὶ τὸν πόλεμον ὃν ὑπέσχου σύγγραφε, καί σου τὰ παρόντα οὐχ ἅψεται βλέποντος εἰς ἆθλον οὕτω μέγαν. τοῦτο καὶ Θουκυδίδῃ τὴν φυγὴν ἐποίησεν ἐλαφράν, καὶ διῆλθον ἄν σοι τὸ πᾶν, εἰ μὴ ἠπίστω καλῶς. 7. πάνυ γε ἡγοῦ τῇ γραφῇ χαριεῖσθαι πᾶσιν ἀνθρώποις. εἶδες μὲν γὰρ ἔργα μετὰ πολλῶν, μόνῳ δὲ σοὶ τῶν ἑωρακότων ἀξία τῶν ἔργων ἡ φωνή.

forests. You bore the heat of the sun by the Tigris,[f] and yet, though you have the leafy shade of Pontus, you hanker after city squares and say that you are all alone. That is the last thing that could happen to a man of culture. How would Plato, Demosthenes and the rest of that company, who are bound to stay with you wherever you like—how would they desert you? 6. So commune with them, and write the history of the war as you promised to do, and your present circumstances will not affect you as you fix your gaze on so great a prize. This is what made exile a light thing for Thucydides,[g] too, and I would have given you the whole story, were it not that you know it well enough. 7. You may be quite sure that by writing it you will oblige all mankind. You, and many more, saw the events; you alone of the eye-witnesses have an eloquence equal to the events.[h]

[f] As a member of Julian's expedition.

[g] Thuc. 5.26.

[h] Cf. Suidas s.v. Seleucus; a grammaticus Seleucus of Emesa wrote, among other things, Παρθικὰ δύο. Seeck identifies this with the history which Libanius here requests, despite the difference of profession and place of origin. *PLRE* correctly states that nothing more is known of this work.

## 143. Θεοδώρῳ

1. Ἔχω τὸν Ἀριστείδην, πρᾶγμα πάλαι ποθούμενον, καὶ σοὶ χάριν ἔχω μικροῦ τοσαύτην, ὅσηνπερ ἄν, εἰ αὐτὸν ἡμῖν ἀναστήσας τὸν ἄνδρα ἐπεπόμφεις. 2. καὶ παρακάθημαί γε τῇ γραφῇ τῶν ἐκείνου τι βιβλίων ἀναγινώσκων ἐρωτῶν αὐτόν, εἰ αὐτὸς ταῦτα. εἶτ' αὐτὸς ἀποκρίνομαι ἐμαυτῷ· 'ναί, ταῦτά γε ἐκεῖνος.' καὶ γὰρ ἔπρεπε τοιούτων λόγων τοιαύτην μορφὴν εἶναι μητέρα· οὕτω πάντα θεοειδῆ καὶ καλὰ καὶ κρείττω τῶν πολλῶν. 3. ἀλλ' ὅ μοι συνέβη περὶ τὸ πρᾶγμα τοῦτο παθεῖν, διηγήσομαί σοι. τὴν αὐτὴν ταύτην ᾐτήκειν χάριν Ἰταλικιανὸν ἐκεῖνον, ὁ δ' εὐθὺς ἔπεμψεν. ἐγὼ δὲ ἠπίστουν τοῦτον ἐκεῖνον εἶναι· τῆς τε γὰρ νόσου τῆς πολλῆς ἀπᾴδειν τὸ πρόσωπον τήν τε κόμην ἄλλον τινὰ μηνύειν. οὐ γὰρ εἶχον εὑρεῖν, ἐξ ὅτου τοσαύτην ἔθρεψεν ἄν. 4. ἡγούμην οὖν Ἀσκληπιὸν ἡμῖν ἥκειν ἀντὶ τοῦ

[a] F/Kr. no. 11, *BLZG* 308 (iii), *PLRE* 897 (11). Theodorus at this time was governor of a province in the diocese of Asia. Since he has apparently easy access to relics of Aelius Aristeides, who lived at Adrianutherae in Bithynia, it is likely that he was governor of Bithynia.

## 143. To Theodorus[a]

1. I have the portrait of Aristeides,[b] something I have long desired, and I am almost as grateful to you as if you had resurrected the man himself and sent him to me. 2. And I sit by his portrait, read some book of his and ask him whether he was the one who wrote that. Then I answer my question myself. "Yes, he did that." Indeed, it was only proper that such a handsome figure should produce such eloquence. 3. But I will tell you my experience on this subject. I had made this very same request of Italicianus,[c] and he sent me a copy straight away. But I could not believe that this was Aristeides, for the face seemed to be out of keeping with his serious illness[d] and the hair indicated that it was someone else, for I could not see how he should have had such a growth of it. 4. So I began

[b] Aelius Aristeides, a leading member of the Second Sophistic, was Libanius' greatest source of inspiration in matter, style, and deportment. He was his model in the *Monodies* and in *Oration* 64; and Libanius' account of his meeting with Julian echoes that of Aristeides with Marcus Aurelius (*Or.* 1.120). Moreover, one element in his valetudinarianism is imitation of Aristeides; cf. *Or.* 1.9, R. A. Pack, "Two Sophists and Two Emperors," *CP* 42 (1948) 17 ff.

[c] *BLZG* 187, *PLRE* 466.

[d] Aristeides recounts the cures for various illnesses transmitted to him by Asclepius at various points in the *Hieroi Logoi* (Aristeides ed. Keil, 2:413 f, 426 f).

ῥήτορος καὶ οἷος ἦν ἐν Δάφνῃ. τοῦτον ἐν Ὀλυμπίου τιθέναι πλησίον τῆς μεγάλης εἰκόνος[1] ἣ τὸν Ἀπόλλω μετὰ τῆς κιθάρας μέσον Ἀσκληπιοῦ καὶ τῆς Ὑγιείας δείκνυσιν — ἀνάθημα τοῦτ' ἦν Ὀλυμπίου τοῦ πατρὸς Ὀλυμπίου διὰ χρόνον πάλιν οἴκαδε εἰσελθόν, ἥρπαστο γὰρ ὑπ' ἀνδρῶν φοβερῶν — ταῦθ' ἡμῶν βεβουλευμένων ἧκε τὰ δεύτερα πείθοντα περὶ τῶν προτέρων, ταὐτὸ γὰρ ἀμφοτέραις εἶδος, καὶ πρὸς ἀλλήλους ἐλέγομεν ὡς τὸν μὲν Ἰταλικιανὸν εἰκὸς ἦν τι καὶ παραμελῆσαι, Θεόδωρος δὲ πάντως ἂν τὸν ὄντα ἐξεῦρεν. 5. οὕτως ἡμῖν ἀνθ' ἑνὸς δύο πέπομφας. πέμψεις δέ, οἶμαι, καὶ τὴν τρίτην· ἐπιθυμῶ γὰρ δεινῶς χεῖράς τε καὶ πόδας ἰδεῖν, ἃ φῂς ἔχειν τὴν τρίτην. ἀλλά σου δέομαι καὶ τὸν τόπον[2] μηνύσαι τῆς εἰκόνος καὶ παρὰ τῶν γερόντων πυθέσθαι, τίς ὁ νοῦς τῶν τριχῶν· ἴσως γάρ τις σώζεται περὶ τῆς κόμης λόγος.

[1] εἰκόνος F., conj. Re. εἰκὸς Wolf (Ms.)
[2] τόπον F., conj. Re. τύπον Wolf (Ms.)

---

[e] The temple in the city itself, *Or.* 15.79, 30.51.

[f] Apollo is father of Asclepius, who is in turn father of

to form the opinion that instead of a picture of the orator I had received one of Asclepius, similar to the way he is represented in Daphne. So I decided to place it in the temple of Zeus Olympius,[e] near the great painting showing Apollo with his lyre in between Asclepius and Hygieia[f]—which was a dedication of Olympius, father of Olympius,[g] lately restored to its place after being removed by people who intimidate us—after such deliberations on my part, your second portrait arrived which convinced me of the authenticity of the first, for the features were the same in both cases. We began to say to one another that Italicianus could conceivably be mistaken, but Theodorus would certainly have discovered the real one. 5. So you have sent us two instead of one, and, I am sure, you will send the third also. I am awfully eager to see the hands and feet, which you say appear on the third. But please give me some notion of the location of the picture and ask the old men what is the idea of the hair. Some story is perhaps preserved about it.[h]

Hygieia. These are the three healing deities of the Greeks.

[g] *BLZG* 222 (i), *PLRE* 644 (4).

[h] Aristeides' home seems to have been preserved as part shrine, part museum; he was the one person of note produced by the town.

## 144. Ἀμφιλοχίῳ ἐπισκόπῳ

1. Ὁμολογῶ καὶ λελυπῆσθαι καὶ λιάν, ὡς ἐπυθόμην ἐφ' ἕτερά σε ἥκειν, καὶ σεσιγηκέναι καί μοι τοῦτο ᾧ[1] μάλιστα τοὺς ἐχθροὺς ἐνίκων, ἀπολωλέναι. ὁπότε γὰρ σοῦ μνησθείην καὶ τῶν σῶν ἀγώνων, ἔφυγον οἱ θρασεῖς. 2. ἕως μὲν οὖν ἤκουον ἐν ἀγρῷ σε καθῆσθαι καὶ τὸ ῥεῦμα ἑστάναι τὸ πολὺ ἐκεῖνο καὶ καλόν, τὰ τῶν ἐζημιῶσθαι πεπεισμένων ἐποίουν· ἐπεὶ δὲ πάλιν ἐπυθόμην ἁρπαγήν τε γενέσθαι καλὴν καὶ εἶναί σε ἐπὶ τῶν θρόνων καὶ δεδόσθαι τινὰ ἀφορμὴν πρὸς τὸ χρῆσθαι τοῖς λόγοις, ἥσθην καὶ τούς τε ἡρπακότας ἐπαινῶ καὶ πάλιν τὴν σὴν ἡγοῦμαι καρποῦσθαι ψυχήν. 3. ἀκούω γὰρ ὡς κινεῖς μὲν τὸν ὄχλον, πολὺ δὲ τὸ θαῦμα, λαμπραὶ δὲ αἱ βοαί, καὶ οὐκ ἀπιστῶ. τίς γὰρ ἂν εἴης νῦν, ὃς καὶ ἡνίκα ἐφοίτας, πηδᾶν ἐποίεις τοὺς γέροντας; 4. Ἀντίοχος δὲ καὶ ὁ τούτου κηδεστὴς ὁ ῥήτωρ σφᾶς τε

[1] ᾧ F. ὡς Laurent. iv. 14. om. Wolf (other Mss.)

---

[a] F/Kr. no. 74, *BLZG* 59 (iii), *PLRE* 58 (4). Foerster dated this letter to 377, but it clearly follows closely upon Amphilochius' elevation to the bishopric of Iconium, which occurred in 373. A more correct dating is therefore to 374.

## 144. To Bishop Amphilochius[a]

1. I confess to have been exceedingly distressed upon learning that you had adopted a different way of life, and to have kept quiet and so lost me the particular means whereby I used to get the better of my foes; for whenever I made any mention of you and your achievements, the rascals took to flight. 2. So while ever I heard that you were settled on your estate and that fine and copious flow of oratory was stilled, my attitude was one of conviction that I had been robbed. But again now that I have heard of their justified seizure of you and of your occupation of your chair,[b] and the renewed opportunity you have of employing your eloquence, I am delighted, I commend them for their seizing of you, and I feel that once more your genius bears fruit. 3. I am told how you move the people, of the great admiration inspired, and of the applause, and I do not disbelieve it. What would you be like now, when even as a student you made old men leap to their feet in excited applause?[c] 4. Antiochus and his son-in-law, the rhetor, count themselves and their

[b] Amphilochius, Libanius' pupil in 361 (*Epp.* 634, 670), was later advocate before retiring to his father's estate at Ozizala. After three years of silence there, he was "seized" by the Christians to become bishop of Iconium.

[c] Typically Libanius' love of rhetoric overcomes his distaste for Christianity when it comes to matters of personal relationships. Compare his attitude to John Chrysostom (Sozomen *H.E.* 8.2.2).

καὶ τὴν πόλιν μακαρίζουσι τοῦ κτήματος μείζω τε ἤ τινα[2] τῶν ἄλλων ἡγοῦνται διὰ τὸ σοῦ τε καὶ τῆς σῆς σοφίας ἀπολαύειν, οἱ δὲ[3] παῖδες μὲν Ἀντιόχου, τῆς δὲ τοῦ ῥήτορος γυναικὸς ἀδελφοὶ πλείοσι νῦν χρῶνται τοῖς περὶ τοὺς λόγους πόνοις ἐννοοῦντες, οἷος αὐτοῖς ἐν τῇ πατρίδι κάθηται λογιστής.

[2] ἤ τινα F., conj. Re. ἢ τὴν Wolf (Mss.).
[3] οἱ δὲ F. οἵ τε Wolf (Mss.).

## 145. Ἑορτίῳ

1. Οὐκ οἶσθα, ὦ φίλε Ἑόρτιε, τῶν προσβαλόντων μοι νοσημάτων οὔτε τὸ πλῆθος οὔτε τὸ μέγεθος οὔτ᾽ ἐφ᾽ ὅσον προῆλθε τοῦ χρόνου. οὐ γὰρ ἄν ποτε ὑπερβὰς τὸ συναλγεῖν ἐμέμφου. νῦν δὲ ἡ ἄγνοια πανταχοῦ τοῖς ἀνθρώποις βλαβερὸν καὶ δὴ καὶ σὲ κατηγορεῖν ἐπῆρεν ἀντὶ τοῦ παραμυθεῖσθαι. ἐγὼ δέ σοι οὐκ ἐγκαλῶ τὸ τὰς δυσκολίας ἡμῶν ἀγνοεῖν. 2. καίτοι φαίη τις ἂν τῶν ὥσπερ σὺ ῥᾳδίως ἐπιτιμώντων, ὡς ἀγνοεῖς μὲν τῷ μὴ πυνθάνεσθαι, οὐ πυνθάνῃ δὲ τῷ μισεῖν, καὶ οὕτως ἂν

[a] *BLZG* 171. This letter was written in or soon after 381 when Libanius, then in his 67th year, found himself a target for the criticism that he was tiresome and over-

city lucky in their acquisition, and they think that, because they enjoy yourself and your learning, they have something more than most men. The sons of Antiochus, brothers of the rhetor's wife,[d] now apply even more effort to eloquence as they reflect upon the quality of the critic[e] who is settled in their home town.

[d] Antiochus and his family remain unknown.
[e] Demosth. *Ol.* 1.10.

## 145. To Heortius[a]

1. My dear Heortius, you have no idea how many and how serious are the ills that afflict me, nor how long I have endured them. Otherwise you would not have so neglected sympathy as to reprove me now. As it is, ignorance is universally harmful to mankind,[b] and indeed it has induced you to offer accusation instead of consolation. I make no complaint against you for your ignorance of my discomfiture. 2. Yet it may be said by those who express such easy disapproval as you do, that your ignorance is due to failure to inquire, and your failure to inquire to dislike, and so by adducing a

bearing, and rebutted it with the tirade of *Oration* 2. (Martin—in Libanios, *Discours* 2:11–13—denies the connection between this letter and *Or.* 2, preferring to date the letter to 353/4, but the argument is not persuasive.)
[b] Cf. Plat. *Phileb.* 49c-d, Lucian *de Cal. non Tem. Cred.* 1.

ὑπεροψίαν προφέρων αὐτὸς ἐνέχοιο μείζοσιν. ἐγὼ δὲ τοῦτο οὐ ποιήσω φιλίαν ἰσχυρὰν ὑβρίζειν οὐκ ἀξιῶν συκοφαντίᾳ. ἀλλ᾿ ὅταν τι γένηται τοιοῦτον, ζητήσας αἰτίαν τοῖς πράγμασιν ἐπιεικεστέραν οὕτω πρὸς ἐμαυτὸν ὑπὲρ ἐκείνων ἀπολογοῦμαι. 3. σὺ δὲ οὐκ ἐν καιρῷ ῥητορεύεις ἄλλους εἶναι λέγων τοὺς αἰτιωμένους, οὓς αὐτὸς ἀνέπλασας διὰ τῆς ἐπιστολῆς. ἐπεὶ τί παθὼν οὐκ ἐπεστόμιζες, ἀλλ᾿ ἐπείθου; ὑπεροψίας δὲ μνησθείς, εἰ μὴ δώσεις δίκην, Ἡρακλεῖ χάριν ἔχειν ἀλεξικάκῳ. ἐγὼ δὲ ἤδη πόλιν ὅλην τοῦτο φθεγξαμένην τετιμώρημαι λόγῳ.

## 146. Τατιανῷ

1. Τῶν πρώτων σου γραμμάτων εὐθὺς ἡμῖν ἐν ἀρχῇ τῆς ἀρχῆς ἡκόντων, εἶτα ἑτέρων οὐχ ἡκόντων θαυμάζειν ἐπῄει τοῖς φίλοις καὶ ζητεῖν, ὅτῳ ποτὲ τοῦθ᾿ οὕτως ἔσχεν. 2. ἐγὼ δὲ αὐτοὺς οὐκ

[a] After breaking off abruptly in the middle of 365, the corpus of Libanius' letters resumes equally abruptly in the middle of 388. It is not entirely coincidental that these are the years of the outbreak of the revolt of Procopius and of the suppression of that of Maximus. From the intervening period there remains a scatter of a dozen and a half letters of varying dates, of which the two preceding are samples.

charge of arrogance you yourself would be liable to more serious charges. But I shall not behave like this, for I have no intention of violating a firm friendship by humbug. Whenever anything of this sort occurs I look round for some more reasonable cause in the facts and so make excuses to myself on their account. 3. You do not employ your rhetoric reasonably when you say that it is other people who level the charges, which you yourself have invented in your letter. Otherwise, why was it that you did not silence them, but believed them? For your mention of my arrogance, be thankful to Heracles, averter of evil, that you escape scot-free.[c] Before now I have delivered an oration to punish a whole city for saying that.[d]

[c] Cf. Lucian *Alex.* 4.
[d] *Or.* 2.

## 146. To Tatianus[a]

1. Your first letter reached me right at the start of your term of office and then was followed by no more. This occasioned surprise among my friends and inquiries as to why this came to pass. 2. I

For Tatianus, *BLZG* 285 (i), *PLRE* 876 (5). Praetorian prefect in succession to Cynegius who had died in office in March 388, he was certainly in office by mid-June (*Cod. Th.* 16.4.2). The present letter, with its punning start on ἀρχή, indicative of the close familiarity between the two, can hardly be earlier than that, considering the interval between Tatianus' two letters.

εἴων ἀπορεῖν οὐδὲ σὴν τοῦτο νομίζειν μεταβολήν, οὐ γὰρ σὸς οὗτος ὁ τρόπος, ἀλλ' ἐπὶ τὴν αἰτίαν ἣν ἔσχον ὡς πονηρὸς εἰς τοὺς κρατοῦντας γεγονώς, ἦγον τῆς σιωπῆς τὴν αἰτίαν κωλύειν λέγων τὸν νόμον τὰς τῶν τηλικούτων πρὸς τοὺς τοιούτους ἐπιστολάς, 'τῆς μέμψεως δὲ ἐξελεγχθείσης' ἔφην 'ὄψεσθε[1] τὰ γράμματα.' 3. ταῦτα εἶπον, ταῦτα προσεδόκησα, ταῦτα ἐξέβη τῆς αὐτῆς ἡμέρας σὴν ἐνεγκούσης ἐπιστολὴν καί τινων ἄλλων, ἐν αἷς ἦν μανθάνειν ὡς ἀφείθημεν ἐλεύθεροι. 4. καὶ οὐκ ἠγνοοῦμεν τὸν συνηγωνισμένον τοῖς πράγμασι προσθέντα γε αὐτὸν τοῖς ἀπ' ἐκείνων. καὶ γάρ, εἰ μὴ λέγεις, ἀλλὰ βεβοήθηκας. καὶ πρέποι ἂν σοὶ μὲν τοῦτο μὴ λέγειν, ἐμοὶ δὲ λέγειν. ὁ γὰρ εὖ παθὼν οὐκ ὢν κακὸς τοῦτο ποιήσει. 5. ἐγὼ δέ σε καὶ ἀπόντα φιλεῖν εἶχον ἐν τῷ σῷ παιδὶ καὶ προσάγων τῷ Πρόκλου στόματι τοὐμὸν ἀμφοτέ-

[1] ὄψεσθε F. (conj. Re.) ὄψεσθαι Wolf (Mss.)

---

[b] In the uneasy days following the Riot of the Statues early in 387, and while the revolt of Maximus was at a critical point in the West, Libanius had to face three separate charges of disaffection: (1) Thrasydaeus accused him of being a supporter of Maximus (*Or.* 32.27). This is the one dismissed in the present letter. (2) The scheme concocted

would not let them remain in their puzzlement, or think that this marked a change of feeling on your part, for that is not your way. The grounds for your silence I attributed to the grounds of complaint preferred against me—of my alleged disloyalty towards our rulers. I told them that normal practice forbade people in your position to write to those in mine. "When this accusation is proved baseless," said I, "you will see his letters." 3. That is what I said, that is what I anticipated, and that is what came to pass on the very day which brought a letter from you and from certain others. These gave me to understand that I was acquitted, a free man.[b] 4. I was not unaware that the one who had assisted me in my career lent his services in dealing with its accidents.[c] Indeed you have certainly helped, even if you do not admit it. The mention of this might not be proper for you, but it is for me, for the beneficiary who is not an ingrate will do so. 5. Even in your absence I have been able to show my affection for you in your son; as I apply my lips to those of

by the *Comes Orientis,* who egged on an old drunkard to accuse him in similar terms. This was laughed out of court (*Or.* 1.262–5). The formulation of this charge is noted in *Epp.* 853, 855. (3) Eustathius, *consularis* in 388–9, puts up the ruined decurion Romulus to accuse him of divination against the emperor (*Or.* 54.40). The formulation of this charge is mentioned in *Ep.* 844.

[c] Tatianus had been *consularis* and *Comes* in the early 370s, which is presumably the period of assistance here mentioned.

ρους ἡγούμην φιλεῖν καὶ τῇ γε ἐμαυτοῦ συνέχαιρον οὕτως ὑμᾶς ἀμειβομένῃ νικώσῃ πάντα τὰ πρὸς ἄρχοντας αὐτῇ πεπραγμένα καὶ μάλα εἰκότως· καὶ γὰρ ὑμεῖς τοῖς ὑμετέροις αὐτῶν τὰ τῶν ἄλλων εἰς ταύτην.

---

[d] Proclus (Proculus)—*BLZG* 248 (iii), *PLRE* 746 (6)—*Comes Orientis* in 383–4 and now prefect of the City at

## 147. Μάγνῳ

1. Ἔξεστί σοι καὶ ἀπόντι θεραπεῦσαι μεθ' ἡμῶν τὸν Ὀλύμπιον Δία τὸν Ὀλυμπίοις παρ' ἡμῶν ἐν Δάφνῃ τιμώμενον. ἥκουσι μὲν γὰρ οἱ διαλεξόμενοι τοῖς παρ' ὑμῖν ἀθληταῖς καὶ πείσοντες, ὡς νόμος· δέονται δὲ τοῦ πρὸς ἅπαντα βοηθήσοντος αὐτοῖς ὅσα τε ἀρχόντων δεῖται καὶ ὅσα τῶν ἄλλων. 2. σοὶ δ' οὐ πολλῶν ἂν δέοι πρὸς οὐδένα ῥημάτων σωφρονούσης τε τῆς Αἰγύπτου καὶ ποιούσης ἅ σοι δόξειεν ὁρώσης κἀκείνους ὑφ' οἷς Αἴγυπτος ἐν κέρδει ποιουμένους, εἴ σοί τι χαρίσαιντο. οὐδὲν οὖν ἀδικῶ τοὺς μὲν ἄλλους ὑπερβάς, πέμψας δὲ αὐτοὺς οἷ χρῆν. 3. ἀγωνι-

---

[a] *BLZG* 200 (iv), *PLRE* 534 (7): a famous iatrosophist at Alexandria; cf. Eunap. *V.S.* 497–8.

Proclus,[d] I think to kiss you both, and am delighted with my native city for repaying you so and excelling all that she has ever done for her governors—and rightly so, for you have both by your actions excelled anything that anyone else has done for her.

Constantinople. There is little more distasteful about Libanius' attitude to officialdom than his gross flattery of the man in his letters and his vilification of him in private orations.

## 147. To Magnus[a]

1. Even though absent you can join us in worshipping Olympian Zeus who is honoured at the Olympia here in Daphne.[b] People are coming to negotiate with your athletes and induce them to come, as is customary. They need someone to help them in all matters requiring the intervention of governors and others. 2. You would not need to tell a long story to anyone, since Egypt shows sound sense and does as you decide when she sees even those under whose jurisdiction she is placed counting it to their advantage if they oblige you. So I do them no harm at all if I neglect the rest and send them to where they ought to go. 3. If competitors

[b] The Olympia of 388. This letter was written some months before, at the latest in early summer. Libanius uses his influence to make the festival a success, as he had done in 364. His motives were, of course, religious; the attitude of most spectators far from it, as he had shown in his Oration on the Plethron (*Or.* 10).

ζομένων οὖν τῶν παρ᾿ ὑμῶν ἡκόντων καὶ θαυμαζομένων ἐπαινέσεται μὲν ὁ Ζεὺς τοὺς δαπανωμένους ἀντιδαπανώμενος,[1] εὑρήσει δέ τι καὶ σὸν ἐν τοῖς δρωμένοις καὶ διδοὺς ἀγαθόν τι Λητοΐῳ τῷ δείξαντι τὸν υἱὸν ἀθλοθέτην δώσει καὶ τῷ σοφῷ Μάγνῳ τῷ τοῖς ἐν ταῖς παλαίστραις εὐδοκιμοῦσι παραινέσαντι δεῦρο πλεῖν. 4. ἔχω δὲ κἀγὼ νέον τρέχειν τε καὶ λέγειν ἀγαθὸν καὶ στεφάνου τε ὁμοῦ καὶ τρίβωνος ἄξιον.

[1] ἀντιδαπανώμενος F. -δαπανῶντας Wolf (Va Vo) -τος V. ἀντιδαπανῶν Seeck.

## 148. Εὐσεβίῳ

1. Ἔτι πρέσβεις Ἔμεσα πέμπει καὶ στεφάνους βασιλεῦσιν εἰδυῖα μὲν τὴν ἑαυτῆς πενίαν, αἰσχυνομένη δὲ ὅμως τοῦ τῶν πόλεων ἐκπεσεῖν ἀριθμοῦ καίτοι τῶν πραγμάτων αὐτὴν ἐκβεβληκότων

[a] *BLZG* 145 (xxvii), *PLRE* 305 ff (26), F/Kr. no. 34. For this embassy from Emesa which Libanius supports cf. Liebeschuetz, *Antioch* 268. Its task was to congratulate the emperor on his successes against Maximus and, equally important, to complain about the decline in curial

come from you and are admired, Zeus will commend them by giving them due recompense for their outlay, and he will find in the events something of your own too, and by granting some blessing to Letoius[c] for appointing his son to present the games, he will also grant it to the wise Magnus who has persuaded those who have won fame in the training schools to sail here. 4. I too have a youngster good at running his course and in eloquence,[d] and who deserves both the victor's crown and the scholar's gown.

[c] *BLZG* 198 (ii). Ex-pupil of Libanius in 364, nephew of the *principalis* of the 360s.

[d] Cimon (*BLZG* Arabius (ii), *PLRE* 92). Now advocate at the court of the *consularis* Eustathius, and not very successful. Libanius had originally wanted him to be a rhetor (*Letter* 169). For earlier problems caused by his illegitimacy cf. *Letter* 121, note.

## 148. To Eusebius[a]

1. Emesa still sends envoys and crowns to the emperors. Though she knows her own poverty well enough, she is still ashamed to drop out of the list of cities, even if circumstances have forced her out of it

numbers which endangered its city status. This was a recurrent theme of Libanius throughout the decade; in *Or.* 27.42 (dated to 385) Emesa is described as τὴν οὐκέτι πόλιν. Malalas (13:645) reports that Theodosius later promoted Emesa to be metropolis of the newly constituted province of Phoenicia Libanensis.

πάλαι. 2. ὁ γὰρ ὀφθαλμὸς τῆς Φοινίκης καὶ τὸ τῶν θεῶν οἰκητήριον καὶ τὸ τῶν λόγων ἐργαστήριον καὶ ἡ πηγὴ τῶν ἀγαθῶν[1] εὐθυμιῶν, καὶ οὐκ ἂν ἐξαριθμήσαι τις τὸ πλῆθος τῶν ἀγαθῶν, αὕτη τοίνυν ἡ πολλή τε καὶ καλὴ τὰ πολλὰ μὲν ἀπολώλεκεν, ὁρᾶται δὲ ἐν οἰκίαις ὀλίγαις ταὐτὸ ταῖς ἄλλαις πεισομέναις, εἰ μὴ βοηθήσαις τι. 3. οἷον γὰρ δή τι τὸ κείνων; ὁ μὲν ἀγχόμενος ἀπέδοτο, ἡ τιμὴ δὲ οὐ τοῦ πεπρακότος, ὁ δὲ πριάμενος καθελὼν λαβὼν ὅσα ἤθελεν ἄγων ἄλλοσε ἐχρῆτο. πάνυ δή τι μικρὸν τὸ λειπόμενον, παλαιᾶς μὲν εὐδαιμονίας μεμνημένοι, τὰ νῦν δὲ δακρύοντες. καὶ ξένος δὲ ὅστις ἐκεῖσε ἔλθοι, κατὰ τάχος ἀπέρχεται πειρώμενος μὴ πάντα ὁρᾶν ὡς πανταχόθεν οὐσῶν εἰς ὀδυρμὸν ἀφορμῶν. 4. τὴν οὖν οὐκέτ᾽ οὖσαν, τὴν γὰρ ἀντὶ τοιαύτης τοιαύτην δεῖ νομίζειν οὐκ εἶναι, πάλιν ἡμῖν ὁ θεῖος Ἀρκάδιος ποιείτω πόλιν. πρέποι γὰρ ἂν αὐτῷ τοιαῦτα διδόναι τῇ γῇ καὶ ποιεῖν τοὺς βουλομένους αὐτὸν ἐπαινεῖν εὐπορωτέρους. 5. ὧν δὲ σὺ κύριος ὡς οὐδενὸς οἱ πρέσβεις ἀτυχήσουσιν, εὖ οἶδα. τῷ τε γὰρ εὖ

[1] After ἀγαθῶν <καὶ> F., conj. Re.

[b] Cf. *Or.* 2.35.

[c] Cf. ὀφθαλμὸς Σικελίας Pind. *Ol.* 2.10. So Catullus on

long ago.[b] 2. She was the cynosure[c] of Phoenicia, the dwelling place of the gods, the manufactory of eloquence, the source of blessed tranquillity,[d] and none could count the number of her blessings. But now this once-populous and beautiful city has lost the greater part, and is to be seen in the few houses that remain, which will suffer the same fate as the rest unless you provide some assistance. 3. And what a grievous fate theirs is! The owner burdened by debt, sells up but the money he gets for the sale is not his, while the purchaser demolishes and seizes whatever he likes and takes it off and uses it elsewhere. There are precious few left, and these remember their former prosperity and bewail their present lot. Any stranger who goes there leaves quickly, for he tries not to see everything since there is cause for lamentation on every side. 4. This lifeless place—for a place that has sunk so low from its former high estate cannot be considered living—let the divine Arcadius[e] once more make into a city. It would be fitting for him to bless the world so, and to give greater scope to those who want to praise him. 5. I am well aware that the envoys will not be unsuccessful in anything which lies in your

Sirmio, 31.1 f. Phasganius was Ἀσίας ὀφθαλμόν (*Or*. 1.117).

[d] Cf. Amm. Marc. 14.8.9.

[e] Arcadius is Augustus (Honorius not yet so), and is now emperor in residence in Constantinople. Theodosius is still in the west, clearing up the remnants of the revolt of Maximus, who was killed 28 Aug. 388.

ποιεῖν χαίρεις καὶ τὸν ἐπεσταλκότα ἐμὲ παρεῖναί τε νομιεῖς καὶ κοινωνεῖν τοῖς πρέσβεσι τῆς σπουδῆς.

## 149. Πρόκλῳ

1. Ἤδη τῶν πρέσβεων ᾑρημένων ἤρετό τίς τινα ξένος πολίτην, ὁπόσοι τινὲς εἶεν. ὁ δὲ ἔφησε· 'τρεῖς.' ἐγὼ δὲ τοὺς τρεῖς ἀκούσας, καὶ γὰρ ἔτυχον παρών, οὐ τρεῖς ἔφην πρεσβεύειν, ἀλλὰ τέτταρας. 2. 'πῶς,' ἤρετο, 'τέτταρες;' 'ὅτι πολὺ πρὸ τῶν τριῶν' ἔφην 'ᾑρέθη Πρόκλος ὑπ' αὐτῶν τῶν ἐν τῇ πόλει παρ' αὐτοῦ πεποιημένων ὁδῶν τε καὶ στοῶν καὶ λουτρῶν καὶ ἀγορῶν. φιλεῖν μὲν γὰρ ἀνάγκην ἔχει τόν γε αὑτοῦ πόνον, τὸ δὲ ἐρᾶν δεινὸν πεῖσαι μηδὲν ὀκνεῖν ὑπὲρ τῆς ἐρωμένης.' 3. καλὸν δὲ τὸ τὸν αὐτὸν βούλεσθαί τε ἡμᾶς εὖ ποιεῖν καὶ δύνασθαι. δύναται δὲ δυνάμεως δυοῖν εἴδεσιν, ἔχει γὰρ δὴ καὶ τὸ τοῦ πατρὸς σθένος· οἷν ἀμφοῖν ὑπὲρ ἡμῶν χρήσεται πρὸς τὴν

---

[a] *BLZG* 248 (iii), *PLRE* 746 (6), F/Kr. no. 36.

Proclus, *Comes Orientis* four years before, when his building projects in Antioch were begun, was a target of private abuse in the *Orations*, despite such public protes-

power. You delight in doing good and you will think of me, the writer of this letter, as present with you and sharing in the efforts of the envoys.

## 149. To Proclus[a]

1. When the envoys had already been picked, a visitor here asked one of our citizens how many they were. He replied, "Three." I happened to be present and, upon hearing this "Three," I remarked that there were not three in the embassy, but four. 2. "How do you mean? Four?" he asked; to which I replied, "Long before these three Proclus was picked, by reason of his building constructions in the city, streets, colonnades, baths, and squares.[b] A man must needs love his own handiwork anyway, and love is potent to persuade him to shrink from nothing for the sake of the beloved." 3. It is a good thing that the same person should have both the wish and the power to be our benefactor. His power is twofold, for he also possesses his father's might, and he will employ both this and his own on

tations of goodwill as here. This letter is a companion to *Ep.* 851, and is addressed to him as prefect of the city in support of the embassy of three (for which see Petit, *Vie Municipale* 418 f, Liebeschuetz, *Antioch* 268–271). This embassy accompanied that from Emesa (*Letter* 148) with the same objectives.

[b] On Proclus' buildings in Antioch cf. *Or.* 10; also Liebeschuetz, "Finances of Antioch," *Byzantinische Zeitschrift* 52 (1959): 354 note.

ἀρχαίαν ῥώμην τὴν βουλὴν ἀπανάγων, ὡς μὴ μόνον ἐν τῇ στοᾷ τῇ παρὰ σοῦ φαίνεσθαι τοῦ δήμου τὴν εὐθυμίαν ἑσπέρας ἑκάστης ᾄσμασιν, ἀλλὰ καὶ τῆς βουλῆς δι' ὧν ἂν βουλῇ πρέπῃ.

## 150. Ῥιχομήρει

1. Τῆς ἡμέρας ἐκείνης, ἐν ᾗ σοι τὸ πρῶτον συνεγενόμην, καὶ τῶν λόγων τῶν οὐ πολλῶν μέν, καλῶν δὲ μέμνημαι καὶ μεμνήσομαι καὶ ζῶν κἂν τελευτήσω. μέμνημαι δὲ καὶ τῶν ἡνίκα ἐλειτούργεις τιμῶν δι' ἀμφοῖν λαμπρότερος ὑπὸ σοῦ γεγενημένος. 2. τί οὖν ἀντὶ τούτων σοὶ παρ' ἡμῶν; πρῶτον μὲν εὐχαὶ τὴν ἀπὸ τοῦ γήρως ἰσχὺν ἔχουσαι· δεύτερον δὲ ἡ ἐπὶ ταῖς σαῖς εὐπραξίαις ἡδονή. σὺ μὲν γὰρ ἐργαζόμενος ἔχαιρες καὶ κρύπτων τὰ πεδία τοῖς ἀπὸ τῶν ἐναντίων νεκροῖς, ἡμεῖς δὲ παρ' ἀγγέλων ἀκούοντες τὰς νίκας. 3. ἔχαιρον δὲ οὐ μόνος, ἀλλὰ μεθ' ὅλης

[a] *BLZG* 251, *PLRE* 765. This letter, like the two following to other military men, was delivered by the same three-man embassy which had passed through Constantinople on its way to the headquarters of Theodosius in the West.

[b] For the meeting of Richomer and Libanius in winter

our account, in restoring our council to its pristine power, so that there is to be seen not only in the colonnade that you erected the rejoicing of the common folk in their songs every evening,[c] but also that of the city council, in the conduct that becomes a council.

[c] On the night life of Antioch, which was encouraged by its unique public lighting system, see *Or.* 11.267.

## 150. To Richomer[a]

1. I remember that day when I first met you, and the brief but elevating conversation we enjoyed, and I shall remember it all my life and after. And I remember also the honours in your time of service here, when I came to enjoy more prestige from you on both counts.[b] 2. Well, then, what have you had from me in return? First, prayers—the potent prayers of old age:[c] secondly, delight at your successes. Your pleasure is in action, and in covering the ground with the corpses of the foe, mine in hearing of the news of your victories.[d] 3. I was not alone in my pleasure, but had the whole city for

383–4 see *Or.* 1.219. Richomer's visit and, on his return to Constantinople, his invitation to attend his inauguration as consul of 384, is accompanied by the imperial grant of the honorary prefecture; cf. Petit, "Sur la date su *Pro Templis,*" *Byzantion* 21 (1951): 293.

[c] Libanius was now 74.

[d] He was serving in Italy under Theodosius, putting down what was left of Maximus' revolt.

τῆς πόλεως· ᾗ τούτων εἰκότως ἂν ἀποδοίης χάριν, ἀποδοίης δ' ἂν διὰ τῶν παρ' αὐτῆς ἀπεσταλμένων πρέσβεων, ἀνδρῶν μιμουμένων πατέρων τε καὶ πάππων ἔθη τε καὶ πολιτείαν· οὓς μοι δοκεῖς ἀποπέμψειν ἡμῖν ἔχοντας λέγειν πρὸς τὴν πόλιν ὡς παρὰ τὴν σὴν εὔνοιάν τε καὶ βοήθειαν ἐξ οὐρίων ἔπλευσαν.

## 151. Προμότῳ

1. Ἀλλ' εἰ καὶ ὁ παρελθὼν ἠδίκηται παρ' ἐμοῦ χρόνος οὐκ ἐπεσταλκότος σοι καὶ ταῦτα ὄντι ἐν τῷ τῶν φίλων ἀριθμῷ, γιγνέσθω τὰ προσήκοντα περί γε τὸν μετ' ἐκεῖνον, εἴτε μέλλοις ἀντεπιστέλλειν εἴτε μή. μέγιστον μὲν γὰρ ἐκεῖνο, μικρὸν δὲ οὐδὲ τοῦτο. 2. καὶ γὰρ αὐτὸ τὸ γράφειν ἡδίω ποιεῖ τὸν γράφοντα, ἄλλως τε κἂν πρὸς τοιοῦτον ἐπιστέλλῃ, μισοῦντα μὲν τυραννίδα καὶ ὕβριν, φιλοῦντα δὲ βασιλείαν καὶ νόμους, ἐμβαίνοντα δὲ ἡδέως εἰς κινδύνους ἅπαντας, ὅπως ἥδε ἐκείνην

[a] *BLZG* 250, *PLRE* 750. The letter is companion to the preceding, conveyed by the same three-man embassy to Theodosius (§ 4).

company. You may with reason feel grateful to her for this, and express your gratitude through the envoys she has sent, men whose personal character and political standpoint emulate those of their fathers and grandfathers.[e] You will return them to us, I believe, and they will be able to tell the city that their course was set fair in consequence of your good will and support.

[e] Libanius' devotion to family tradition in the municipalities recurs throughout his works, his tone being that of the decurion *manqué*; cf. *Or.* 1.3 ff, 57 ff, 2.10 f.

## 151. To Promotus[a]

1. Even if time that is past has not received its due from me—since I have not written to you, although I am counted among your friends—let me do my duty with regard to the period hereafter, whether you intend to reply or not.[b] Of these alternatives the first is much the best, but the second is not without its points. 2. Indeed, the very act of writing cheers the writer, especially when writing to such as yourself with your hatred of tyrannical arrogance, your love for lawful monarchy, and your readiness to undertake all hazards to ensure that it

[b] The tone here is more reserved than in the letters to the other generals. The two were perhaps not personally acquainted; Promotus, as far as is known, had never been in Antioch.

ἐκκόψειε. 3. καί μοι δός, ὦ γενναῖε, χάριν, τὴν αὐτὴν δὲ[1] καὶ τῷ βασιλεῖ δώσεις. ποίησον δή με τῶν παρόντων τὸν ἀπόντα μὴ ἧττον εἰδέναι τὸν πόλεμον ἢ τῇ σαυτοῦ χειρὶ χρησάμενος ἤ τινος ἑτέρου τῶν τὰ τοιαῦτα ὑπηρετούντων. ἡ φωνὴ δὲ ἔστω σὴ τοῦ μηδὲν τῶν πεπραγμένων ἀγνοοῦντος μήτε μεῖζον μήτε ἔλαττον. 4. ἔχεις δὲ τοὺς ἐμοὶ τοῦτο κομιοῦντας τρεῖς ἄνδρας, οὓς ἄλλα τε κοσμεῖ καὶ τὸ τὰ σὰ θαυμάζειν. ἐχέτωσαν οὖν μετὰ τῶν ἄλλων λέγειν ὡς καὶ τοῦτο ἡμῖν φέρουσι δῶρον στρατηγοῦ ῥήτορι πεπομφότος.

1 'Num δὲ <ἦν>' F.

## 152. Ἐλεβίκῳ[1]

1. Ὅσης ἡμᾶς εὐφροσύνης ἀπεστέρησας ἡμᾶς μὲν ἀφείς, τὸ δὲ σὺν ἄλλοις εἶναι μεῖζον ἡγησόμε-

1 Ἐλεβίχῳ in Mss. of the Letters. Ἐλλεβίχῳ in Orations. Hellebichus in Cod. Th.

---

a *BLZG* 167 (Hellebichus, cf. *Cod. Th.* 9.39.1), *PLRE* 277 (Ellebichus, as in the Orations and elsewhere).

b He had been resident in Antioch as *magister militum* since 385 when he formed this friendship with Libanius and requested a panegyric from him (*Ep.* 2, *Or.* 1.232; 22.2). During the Riots of the Statues early in 387, he had been absent in Constantinople, but he was appointed to the commission of enquiry along with Caesarius, *magister*

will cast out the usurper.[c] 3. And grant me a favour, noble sir, and you will grant the same to the emperor too. Ensure that I, though absent, may know no less about the war than those on the spot, either by your own hand or by that of another who performs such services. And let your voice be that of one unaware of no detail of action, whether great or small.[d] 4. You have three men to bring me this account whose greatest recommendation is their admiration of your achievements. So let them be able to report, along with everything else, that they are bringing this gift, sent by a general to an orator.

[c] Maximus.

[d] Libanius seeks to consolidate this newly formed friendship by requesting information on which to exercise his oratory. Promotus was to be consul in the following year.

## 152. To Elebichus[a]

1. Ah! what happiness did you take from us when you left and thought it more important to be with others:[b] for how good it was to tell each other

*officiorum,* and was left to continue the task when Caesarius returned to court to report. He was generally commended for his clemency and tact, and received, probably in 388 close to the time of this letter, the mini-panegyric *Oration* 22. By now he had been recalled to take part in the final campaign against Maximus, here referred to; cf. *Or.* 22.41.

νος. οἷον γὰρ δὴ ἦν ἑσπέρας μὲν πρὸς ἀλλήλους εἰπεῖν ὅτι δεῖ φανείσης ἡμέρας ὡς σὲ δραμεῖν, προσθεῖναι δὲ τὸ ἔργον καὶ φανείσης δραμεῖν ἰδεῖν τέ σε καὶ λαλοῦντος ἀκοῦσαι καὶ εἰπεῖν τι καὶ αὐτοὺς ἡδίους[2] γενομένους ἀπελθεῖν. 2. οὐ μὴν πάντα γε ἐγκαλοῦμεν τῇ Τύχῃ. καὶ γὰρ εἰ τὴν σὴν συνουσίαν ἀφῃρέθημεν, οἷς γε ἀκούομεν εὐφραινόμεθα. ἀκούομεν δὲ εὔνοιαν εἶναί σοι τὴν βασιλέως καὶ ἐπιστολὰς ἐκείνῳ τε γράψαι καὶ σοὶ λαβεῖν πρεπούσας λαμπροτέρας παρεχούσας ἐλπίδας. 3. τῇ χαρᾷ δὲ ἡμεῖς ταύτῃ τὴν ὑπὲρ ἡμῶν σου λύπην ἀμειβόμεθα μεμνημένοι τῶν δακρύων ἐκείνων, ἃ μεθ' ἡμῶν ὑπὲρ ἡμῶν ἀφῆκας. τὴν οὖν δοῦσαν ἃ δέδωκε θεὸν ἱκετεύομεν ὃ μήπω δέδωκε δοῦναι καὶ τὴν ἡδίω παντὸς ὕπνου παρασχεῖν ἀγρυπνίαν. 4. ἐκείνου μὲν οὖν τῷ τῶν θεῶν ὑπάτῳ μελήσει· σοὶ δὲ νῦν μελησάτω τῶν πρέσβεων παίδων ὄντων ἐμῶν· οἱ γὰρ περὶ αὐτούς μοι πόνοι ταύτην ποιοῦσι τὴν προσηγορίαν. 5. καὶ μάλιστα μὲν ἐγγύθεν ἀμῦναι ὑπὸ

[2] τε after ἡδίους Wolf (Mss.): del. F.

[c] For such evening conversations cf. *Ep.* 2, and deputations during the enquiry into the Riots, *Or.* 22.41.

of an evening that we must hurry to see you at break of day, to translate it into action, and at daybreak to hurry to see you, listen to your conversation, enter into it ourselves and leave, cheered at heart.[c] 2. Yet we do not rail at Fortune entirely, for even though deprived of your presence we are overjoyed at what we hear. We hear of the good will of the emperor that you enjoy and of letters proper for him to write and you to receive which augur well for a more brilliant career. 3. By this joy we repay you for your grief on our account, remembering the tears you shed with us and for us.[d] We entreat the goddess[e] who has given you what she has given to give you what she has not yet given you and to provide you with wakefulness more pleasing than any sleep. 4. So that will be the concern of the consul of the gods; but now let your concern be for our envoys, children of mine,[f] for my labours upon them give them this title. 5. If possible, aid

[d] Cf. *Or.* 22.20, 22.

[e] Fortune (§ 2). The use of this term and that of τῷ τῶν θεῶν ὑπάτῳ (§ 4) show him to be a pagan, like Richomer. His name indicates barbarian origin, and it is notable that Libanius' relations with the two are warmly intimate despite his normal prejudice against barbarians. With Christian generals of barbarian extraction, like Victor, he is more cool and formal.

[f] On Libanius' regard for his pupils as his children cf. Petit, *Étudiants* 33 f.

τῷ θειοτάτῳ βασιλεῖ καθήμενος· εἰ δ' ἔτι τοῦτο μέλλει, γράμματά γέ[3] ἐστιν ἔχοντα καὶ αὐτὰ τὸ δύνασθαι.

[3] γέ F., conj. Re.  τέ Wolf (Mss.).

## 153. Ἐντρεχίῳ

1. Ἐγὼ δέ σε ἐβουλόμην ἀμφότερα ὁμοῦ δύνασθαι, οἴκοι τε εἶναι καὶ παρ' ἡμῖν, καὶ μεθ' ἡμῶν μὲν ἐπιμελεῖσθαι λόγων, Νίκαιαν δὲ κοσμεῖν καὶ συνέχειν Ἀρισταινέτῳ τὴν οἰκίαν. 2. Νικαίας δέ μοι καὶ μεμνῆσθαι καὶ μέλειν καὶ τιμᾶν τῶν δικαίων ἂν εἴη, ἥδε γάρ ἐστιν ἡ τῷ κόλπῳ με δεξαμένη καθάπερ τὸν Διόνυσον ἡ Θέτις τῶν Βακχῶν αὐτῷ τυπτομένων. 3. φιλῶν δὲ Νίκαιαν καὶ τὸν Ἀρισταινέτου τάφον πῶς οὐκ ἂν καὶ τὸν ἀντ' ἐκείνου τοῖς ἐκείνου γενόμενον φιλοίην; ἔνι δὲ καὶ φιλοῦντα μὴ ἐπιστέλλειν ὥσπερ αὖ καὶ μὴ φιλεῖν ἐπιστέλλοντα, ἐπεὶ καὶ αὐτὸς ἡμᾶς καὶ ὃν οὐκ ἐπέστελλες ἐφίλεις χρόνον.

---

[a] Libanius resumes correspondence with an old friend from Julian's day and before (*BLZG* 126, *PLRE* 278).

[b] Aristaenetus, who died in the earthquake at Nicomedeia in 358, was native of Nicaea, and Entrechius, a kinsman and perhaps son-in-law (so Seeck), acted as guardian for his family.

them from close at hand as you sit at the feet of our most divine emperor: but if this is still in the future, there are letters which themselves can produce this result.

## 153. To Entrechius[a]

1. I wanted you to be able to do two things at once, to stay at home and to be with us, with us to interest yourself in eloquence, and yet to be a leading light in Nicaea and maintain the household of Aristaenetus.[b] 2. It would be only right for me to recall Nicaea, to show concern and respect for her, for she it is who took me to her bosom as Thetis did Dionysus when his Bacchae were flogged.[c] 3. In my affection for Nicaea and the last resting place of Aristaenetus, I cannot but feel affection too for the man who has taken his place for his descendants. It is possible for someone not to write, for all his affection, as again it is for him not to feel affection, for all his letters, and this you personally have proved by your affection for me even during the time you did

[c] After his explusion from Constantinople, Libanius sought refuge and employment in Nicaea (*Or.* 1.48), whose patron deity was Dionysus; hence the Homeric reference (*Il.* 6.136). From there, in 345, he was invited, by decree of the council confirmed by the governor of Bithynia, to move to the provincial capital Nicomedeia, from which he had originally been banned.

4. ἔπειθε δέ σε φιλεῖν τὸ ζητοῦντα μὲν λόγους ἥκειν Ἀθήναζε, φανῆναι δὲ οὓς ἐζήτεις ἔχοντα. τὰ δ' ἐφεξῆς ἅπαντα τῶν λόγων τούτων, ἀρχαί τε ἐπ' ἀρχαῖς, αἱ δεύτεραι παριοῦσαι τῷ μέτρῳ τὰς προτέρας, ἔρως τε βασιλέως Πέρσας ἐληλακότος καὶ μετ' ἐκεῖνον ὑπάρχου φιλανθρώπῳ βασιλεῖ τιμίου, ὃς μετὰ σοῦ τὸ πλέον τῆς οἰκουμένης ἐπελθὼν ἅπαντά σοι πιστεύων παραδοὺς τὴν Παλαιστίνην ἄγειν λαμπρότητος ἀφορμὰς παρέδωκεν. 5. ἀλλ' εἰς ταῦτα μὲν ἐπιθυμίᾳ τῶν σῶν ἐπαίνων ἤχθην· λαβὼν δέ σου τὴν ἐπιστολὴν καὶ τὸ μῆκος κατιδὼν ᾤμην αὐτὴν ἐρεῖν τί μοι καὶ περὶ τῶν υἱέων, ἐν ὅτῳ τέ εἰσι καὶ τίνες αἱ ἐλπίδες. εἰκὸς δὲ εἶναι χρηστὰς σοῦ τοὺς σεαυτοῦ παιδεύοντος. 6. εὑρὼν δὲ αὐτοὺς οὐδαμοῦ μάλα ἠχθέσθην οὐχ ὡς οὐκ ὄντων ἐν τοῖς πρέπουσι πόνοις, πῶς γὰρ ἂν οἵ γε ἐκ σοῦ; ἀλλ' ὅτι μοι ἔδοξας[1] οἴεσθαί με μηδένα αὐτῶν ἔχειν λόγον καὶ ταῦτα τοῦ κινοῦντος ὄντος οὕτω μεγάλου.

[1] ἔδοξας F., conj. Re. ἔδειξας Wolf (Mss.).

---

[d] These credentials for office are approved of both by Julian and Libanius, *Or.* 18.158.

[e] Only two governorships are known, Palestine in

not write. 4. Your affection was inspired by your journey to Athens in search of eloquence and your obvious possession of the eloquence you sought.[d] Everything thereafter was a consequence of this eloquence, one official post after another, each succeeding one excelling the previous ones in importance,[e] the love of our emperor who routed the Persians, and after him that of a prefect whom our generous emperor held dear.[f] He it was who traversed the greater part of the civilized world with you, trusted you implicitly, and in offering you the governorship of Palestine offered you the opportunities for fame. 5. I have been diverted to this topic by my desire to sing your praises. When I got your letter and saw its length, I thought that it would tell me something about your sons too, of their situation and prospects. They are likely to be of the best, since you are the teacher of your own children. 6. But when I found no mention of them at all, I was sadly put out, not at the idea that they are not engaged upon fitting labours,[g] for that would be impossible for sons of yours, but that I felt that you had a notion that I was not interested in them, for all that the stimulus for this is so great.

361–2 and Pisidia in 362–4. It appears that others followed in the period after 365 when Libanius' letters are interrupted.

[f] Julian and his praetorian prefect Salutius Secundus.

[g] πόνοι are, for Libanius, the labours in oratory *par excellence.*

## 154. Εὐσεβίῳ

1. Ἀκούων σου τὴν προθυμίαν ἣν ἀντέταξας οὖσαν δικαίαν τῇ τῶν παρ' ἡμῶν πρέσβεων ἀδικίᾳ λύειν πειρωμένῃ τὰ τῆς βουλῆς δόγματα χαίρων τὰ τῶν χαιρόντων ἐποίουν· νῦν δ' ἀκούσας τἀκείνων νενικηκέναι καὶ σοὶ μάτην ἅπαντα πεπονῆσθαι λυπούμενος τὰ τῶν λυπουμένων ποιῶ· ῥίψας τὰ βιβλία δακρύω τὸν ὑπ'[1] ἐμοὶ ποιμαίνοντα τοὺς νέους οὐκ ἔχων. 2. ἀλλ' ὁ μὲν χειμὼν ἐν ἀρχῇ, δεινὸς δὲ οὗτος οὕτως ὡς μηδὲ τοῖς ἐν ταῖς κλίναις εἶναι διάγειν ἄνευ κακῶν. Εὐσέβιος δὲ ὁ σοφιστὴς μισθωσάμενος ὄνους ἔρχεται θαρρεῖν οὐκ ἔχων ὡς οὐκ ἀπολεῖται. τῇ μητρὶ δὲ αὐτοῦ παραμυθίαν μὲν ἄλλην οὐχ ὁρῶ, τὴν ἀπὸ σοῦ δὲ ἐλπίδα. 3. πάλιν τοίνυν ἅπτου τῆς βοηθείας αὐτὸν ἔχων δεικνύντα σοι, πηλίκοις δικαίοις τετειχισμένος ὡς οὐδ' ὁτιοῦν ἔχων ἰσχυρὸν ἐλαύνεται.

[1] ὑπ' F. ἐπ' Wolf (Mss.).

## 154. To Eusebius[a]

1. When I heard of the eagerness which you so justly arrayed against the injustice of our envoys when they tried to have the council's decrees rescinded, I rejoiced and was glad.[b] But now that I hear that they have prevailed and that all your labour has been in vain, I grieve and am filled with vexation. I cast my books aside and weep at not having with me him who acted under me as shepherd to my flock.[c] 2. But the winter is just beginning,[d] and this is so harsh that not even in bed can we remain without harm. The sophist Eusebius has hired mules and is coming with no confidence that he will not be undone. For his mother I see no consolation other than her hopes of you. 3. So once again apply yourself to his defence, while you have him to demonstrate to you that, although protected by such justifiable claims, he is being harried as though he has not a single line of defence.

[a] *Magister Officiorum,* as in *Letter* 148.

[b] *Letters* 154–159 reflect Libanius' determination in support of a protégé. For the matter at issue here see Additional Note in Appendix.

[c] Eusebius xxii, *BLZG* 143, *PLRE* (24) 305.

[d] The winter is that of 388/9.

## 155. Θεοδώρῳ

1. Ἔδει μὲν ἡμᾶς ἐν ἡδονῇ νῦν εἶναι τῶν ἀδίκως Εὐσεβίου τοῦ σοφιστοῦ λαμβανομένων κεκρατημένων, ὃ κοινὸν ἂν ἦν κέρδος ἐκείνων τε καὶ ἡμῶν, ἡμῶν μὲν οὐκ ἀδικουμένων, ἐκείνων δὲ οὐκ ἀδικούντων, ὃ δὴ καὶ αὐτὸ τοῖς εὖ φρονοῦσι κέρδος· ἐπεὶ δὲ τῇ λίαν φιλονεικίᾳ τοσοῦτον ὅσον βεβούληνται καὶ δεδύνηνται καὶ διατετμήμεθα πρότερον, ὥσπερ βόες ὑπὸ ζυγῷ τὰ περὶ τὴν γῆν, αὐτοὶ τὰ περὶ τοὺς λόγους πονοῦντες, δίκαιος ἂν εἴης Ἀθηνᾶ τῷ Ὀδυσσεῖ γενέσθαι κἂν τῷ μετ' Εὐσεβίου τοῦ σοφιστοῦ στῆναι παντὶ τῷ τῶν σοφιστῶν ἔθνει λῦσαι τὸν φόβον. 2. καὶ γὰρ οὐδὲ δικαίων ἁνὴρ ἀπορεῖ πολλὰ μὲν ἔχων ἀναγνῶναι τῆς βουλῆς γράμματα, πολλὰ δὲ τοῦ φιλανθρωποτάτου βασιλέως. 3. οἱ δ' οὔτε τὰ αὐτῶν αἰδούμενοι οὔτε τἀκείνου φοβούμενοι μεταφέρειν ἐφ' ἃ βούλονται πειρῶνται τὸν τῶν ἔργων μὲν ἐκείνων ἀφειμένον, ταῖς δὲ τῶν Μουσῶν ᾠδαῖς δεδεμένον·[1] ὃ οὔποτε Θεόδωρος ὁ καλὸς ἀνέξεται πρὸς τὸ τιμᾶν τοὺς λόγους ἀνάγκην ἔχων τὸ διὰ λόγους ἐνταῦθα οὗπέρ ἐστιν ἥκειν.

[1] δεδεμένον F., conj. Re. δεδομένον Wolf (Mss.).

## 155. To Theodorus[a]

1. We ought now to be delighted at having overcome the unjust assailants of the sophist Eusebius, for that would have been a boon both to them and to us. We would not suffer injury and they would inflict none, and that indeed is a boon to men of good sense. But since by their excessive contentiousness they have been able to do exactly as they liked and we in the past have been cut off by our labours in rhetoric, like oxen under the yoke labouring on the land, you would be right to act as Athena to Odysseus[b] and, in taking the side of Eusebius the sophist, to free the whole sophistic profession from fear. 2. Indeed the man has no lack of just grounds either, for he can adduce many decrees of the city council and many of our most generous emperor. 3. But those people have no regard for their own decrees or fear of the emperor's, and they are trying to transfer him to a position of their own liking, though he enjoys immunity from those duties, and is attached to the songs of the Muses. The noble Theodorus will never endure this, since he is forced to honour eloquence by the fact that he has reached his present position because of his eloquence.

[a] *BLZG* 310 (ix), *PLRE* 899 (17).

[b] Cf. *Epp.* 835, 855. Homer *Il.* 10.277 ff; *Od.* 1.48 ff, 5.5 ff, 13.187 ff.

## 156. Πρόκλῳ

1. Ὁ πολλοὺς μὲν λόγους καὶ ποιήσας καὶ διδάξας, ἐφ᾿ ἅπασι δὲ αὐτοῖς ἐνεγκάμενος κρότον, οὐχ ἥκιστα δὲ ἐπὶ τοῖς εἰς σὲ συγκειμένοις ἐκβάλλεται μὲν τοῦ αὐτοῦ βίου καὶ τῆς ἀτελείας, ἣν ἔχει παρὰ τοῦ βίου, βουλεύειν δὲ ἀντὶ τοῦ παιδεύειν ἀναγκάζεται παρά τε τὰ τῇ βουλῇ δόξαντα καὶ τὰ τῷ θειοτάτῳ βασιλεῖ, ὧν ἀμφοτέρων ἐστὶ γράμματα, κἂν ὁ πατήρ σου κελεύῃ δεῖξαι, δείξει. 2. φυλάττων τοίνυν σαυτῷ μὲν κἀκείνῳ τὴν δόξαν, ἣν ὡς ἐρῶντες λόγων ἔχετε, φυλάττων δὲ καὶ ἐμοὶ τὸν συνεργόν, οὗ τῇ βοηθείᾳ κρύπτεταί μου τὸ γῆρας, ἀγανάκτησον καὶ μὴ περιίδῃς πρᾶγμα οὕτως ἀσεβὲς ἀρχὴν ἐν ταῖς ὑμετέραις ἀρχαῖς λαμβάνον.

## 157. Ἀβουργίῳ

1. Οὐκ ἔλαθές με τηρῶν ἀκριβῶς τὴν πάλαι γενομένην φιλίαν οὐδ᾿ ὅτι χαίρεις ὁρῶν χαίροντα τοῖς ἡμετέροις πόνοις τὸν μέγαν Τατιανόν· ταυτὶ γὰρ οἱ μὲν ἥκοντες ἡμᾶς ἐδίδαξαν, οἱ δὲ ἐν

## 156. To Proclus

1. The man[a] who has both composed and given instruction in many orations, and won applause in them all, not least in those dedicated to you, is being expelled from his own way of life and the immunity he enjoys because of it, and is being compelled to take the position of decurion instead of teacher, contrary to the decrees both of the council and our divine emperor. He has letters from both, and if your father[b] bids him produce them, produce them he will. 2. So in protecting both for yourself and for him the reputation you have of being lovers of eloquence, and in protecting for me also my colleague, by whose aid my old age is disguised, rise up in wrath and do not ignore so impious an act that has its beginning at a time when you both hold office.[c]

[a] Eusebius xxii.

[b] Tatianus, praetorian prefect.

[c] Proclus was prefect of the city of Constantinople at this time.

## 157. To Aburgius[a]

1. It has not escaped my notice that you scrupulously maintain our long-standing friendship and that you rejoice to see the great Tatianus rejoice at my labours, for this is the information that comes to

[a] *BLZG* 36, *PLRE* 5.

ἐπιστολαῖς. 2. οὔκουν ἡγησάμην ἐνοχλήσειν, εἰ χάριν αἰτοίην ὑπὲρ ἧς πρὸς μὲν αὐτὸν οὐκ εἶχέ μοι μνησθῆναι καλῶς, ἐπὶ σὲ δὲ ὑπὸ τοῦ πρέποντος ἐπεμπόμην. ἔστι δὲ ἃ δεῖ γενέσθαι παρὰ σοῦ τοῖς θεοῖς τοῖς λογίοις. 3. Εὐσέβιος, οὑμὸς ὁμιλητής, δεομένης αὐτοῦ τῆς βουλῆς ἐν τοῖς ψηφίσμασι μιμήσασθαι τὸν πρόγονον καὶ ὁμώνυμον καὶ ποιεῖν ῥήτορας πείθεται καὶ καταστὰς εἰς τοὺς τοιούτους πόνους καὶ πολλοῦ γε ὧν ἄξιος τιμᾶται πάλιν ψηφίσμασιν αἰτοῦσιν αὐτῷ τιμὰς παρὰ τοῦ βασιλέως. καὶ ἦν ὁ μὲν οἷς ἔλαβε λαμπρός, ἡ δὲ οἷς ἐπήγγειλεν, ὁ δὲ οἷς ἔδωκεν. 4. ἑλόμενοι δὲ αὖ τὸν σοφιστὴν πρεσβευτὴν οὐχ ὡς βουλευτήν, ἀλλ' ὡς οὐχ ἀπολοῦντα τοῦτο ἐν ᾧπερ ἦν, καὶ τοῖς παρ' αὐτοῦ λόγοις τῆς πρεσβείας ὠφελημένης καὶ ταῦτ' ἀπαγγέλλοντες αὐτοὶ μετὰ ταῦτ' Εὔριποι γενόμενοι τὴν ἐναντίαν ἦλθον καὶ δεῖν ἔφασαν τὸν σοφιστὴν ποιεῖν ὧν ἀφεῖται παρὰ τῶν νόμων. 5. δεινὸν οὖν, εἴτε μηδεὶς ἀτελὴς ἔσται σοφιστής, ἀλλ' οἱ λόγοι τοιαῦτα πείσονται, εἴτε μόνος οὐκ ἔσται, ἀλλ' οἷος Ἀργείων, ὥς πού φησιν Ὅμηρος, ἀγέραστος ἔσται, καὶ ταῦτα ὧν

[b] An Aristeidean concept employed by Libanius in his later years to supplement or supplant that of Fortune

me by new arrivals or by letters. 2. So I felt that I would not be a nuisance if I beg a favour for which, though I could not decently mention it to him, I could with perfect propriety betake myself to you. There must be some deference paid by yourself to the gods of eloquence.[b] 3. Eusebius, a pupil of mine, being requested by the city council in its decrees to follow in the footsteps of his forebear and namesake and to produce orators, consented so to do. He undertook such labours and being highly respected, he was again honoured by decrees which sought honours for him from the emperor. He was ennobled by the honours received, the council by its petition, and the emperor by his grant. 4. Then they chose the sophist as their ambassador, not as being a councillor but without prejudice to his existing status, and the embassy was assisted by his eloquence, as they themselves acknowledged, but then they did an about-turn and took the opposite direction.[c] They asserted that the sophist should illegally perform the duties from which he was excused. 5. So it is a shocking thing that no sophist shall be immune and the profession of rhetoric put up with such treatment, or else that he alone shall not be, but instead, as Homer somewhere says, shall be "alone of the Argives without a

which had been all-important in the first part of the Autobiography; cf. *Or.* 1.234 ff, 238, 274. *Epp.* 1051, 1085, 1089. Misson, *Recherches sur le paganisme de Libanios* 50 ff.

[c] See the narrative in *Or.* 32.

οὐδενὸς ὕστερος, ἵνα μηδὲν εἴπω πλέον. 6. καὶ μὴν καὶ περὶ τῶν τιμῶν τῶν ἀνῃρημένων ἔστιν αὐτῷ δεικνύειν ὡς τούτῳ μόνῳ μενοῦσι, καὶ τὰ γράμματα ἐγγύς. δὸς οὖν σαυτὸν σύμμαχον μέλλων δώσειν τῇ τοῦ δικαίου μερίδι.

## 158. Μαρδονίῳ

1. Οὐ μόνον ἐπὶ τὴν χρηστότητά σου καταφεύγομεν, δι' ἣν πολλοῖς οὐδὲν εἰδὼς αὐτῶν ἄλλ'[1] ἢ ὅτι ἄνθρωποι, βεβοήθηκας, ἀλλ' ὅτι καὶ φίλους ἡμᾶς πάντοτε ἐνόμισας καὶ οὕτω καλεῖς. 2. ἡμεῖς τοίνυν, οὓς οὕτω καλεῖς, κινδυνεύομεν· Εὐσέβιος μὲν ὁ σοφιστὴς ὑπὲρ τοῦ σχήματος, ἐν ᾧ ζῇ, τοιαῦτα γὰρ οἱ παρ' ἡμῶν πρέσβεις ἐνεανιεύσαντο, ἐγὼ δὲ ὑπὲρ τοσαύτης ῥοπῆς, ἣν εἶχον ἐκ τοῦ τὴν γλῶτταν ἔχειν τὴν Εὐσεβίου τὴν ἀπὸ τῆς Ἀττικῆς, ἧς εἰς τὴν τῶν νέων ἐπιμέλειαν ἀπέλαυον. 3. ἀλλ', ὦ πολλοῖς μὲν ἤδη βεβοηθηκώς, πολλοῖς δὲ βοηθήσων, οὐδέποτε δὲ παυσόμενος, καὶ νῦν δεῖξον τοῖς ἀνθρώποις σεαυτόν.

[1] ἄλλ' F. ἀλλ' Wolf (Mss.).

prize,"[d] especially when he is second to none, to put it at the least. 6. And yet, upon the matter of the honours of which he has been deprived, he can show that they will remain his and his alone, and he has the documents to hand. So enlist yourself as his ally and take the side of justice.

[d] Homer *Il.* 1.118 f; cf. *Ep.* 818.3.

## 158. To Mardonius[a]

1. I have recourse not just to your generosity, whereby you have assisted many people though you knew nothing of them save their existence, but to the fact that you have always regarded me as your friend and call me so. 2. Well, we whom you call so are in jeopardy—Eusebius the sophist with regard to the professional status in which he lives, for our envoys have had the sauce to impugn that, and I with regard to the great support I obtain from Eusebius' acquisition of pure Attic eloquence, of which I have availed myself for the supervision of my students. 3. But my dear sir, who have already helped many in the past and will never cease to do so in the future, even now show your mettle to these fellows.

[a] *BLZG* 203 (ii), *PLRE* 558 (2).

## 159. Τατιανῷ

1. Εἴ με ἐθέλεις καὶ φθέγγεσθαι καὶ χορὸν ἔχειν καὶ λόγους ποιεῖν καὶ μὴ φίλους μὲν ἡμῖν συνάχθεσθαι, ἐχθροὺς δὲ ἐπιχαίρειν, στῆναι δέ μοι τὰς συνουσίας καὶ μὴ χωρεῖν ᾗ πρόσθεν, τήρησον ἡμῖν ἐν τῷ παιδεύειν νέους Εὐσέβιον. 2. ὃς ἐμοῦ πολλάκις σιγῇ καθημένου ῥέων αὐτὸς καὶ λέγων τοὺς φοιτῶντας παρ' ἡμᾶς βελτίους ἀπέπεμψεν, ἀλλὰ καὶ τοῦ νοσήματος ἐπιόντος οὐκ ἐνόσουν τοῖς διδασκάλου χρῄζουσιν, ἦν γὰρ οὗτος διδάσκαλος. βλάβη δέ, ὅση τοῖς τοιούτοις γίγνοιτ' ἂν ἀπὸ γήρως, οὐκ ἐγίγνετο. ὅλως γὰρ νεανίσκος ἀνεῖχε πρεσβύτην. 3. μὴ οὖν με ταύτης τῆς ἐπικουρίας ἐκβάλῃς ἢ ταχέως ἄφωνον ἀκούσῃ με κείμενον. ταυτὶ δὲ οὐ κατὰ τὴν Θέτιν αἰτῶ τὴν προεισενεγκοῦσαν τῷ Διὶ τὸ μὴ δεθῆναι. σοὶ μὲν γὰρ οὐδὲν παρ' ἡμῶν οὔτε μεῖζον οὔτε ἔλαττον, σὺ δὲ εἰς ἡμᾶς πολλὰ διὰ παντὸς ἐπιδείκνυσαι τοῦ χρόνου. καί σοι τοῦ καὶ νῦν ἡμᾶς εὖ ποιεῖν ἀνάγκη τὸ πολλάκις πρότερον εὖ πεποιηκέναι.

## 159. To Tatianus

1. If you want me to speak, to retain my school and to compose my orations, and if you do not want my friends to condole with me while my enemies rejoice, or my classes to be halted and not to progress as in times past, then please retain Eusebius in the profession of teaching. 2. Often, while I have sat by in silence, he personally by the flow of his eloquence has sent my pupils away much improved; moreover, when I suffered any bouts of illness, I did not suffer through their lack of a teacher, for he was there to teach them. Any harm which might have ensued for such as them from my old age did not ensue, for there was a youngster providing full support to an old man. 3. Do not then deprive me of this support, or you will soon hear of me as prostrate and dumb. This request I make not in the fashion of Thetis after previously helping Zeus escape from his bonds.[a] You have received from me nothing either great or small, though all the time you give me so much evidence of your goodwill. So, to compel you to act as my benefactor now, you have your many benefactions in the past.

[a] Homer *Il.* 1.396 f.

## 160. Τῷ πατριάρχῃ

1. Τῶν εἰρημένων τούτων ἐν τοῖς γράμμασι τὰ μὲν ᾔδειν πάλαι, τὰ δὲ νῦν μεμάθηκα. καὶ πλείων ἡ λύπη μοι τῇ προσθήκῃ τῶν γραμμάτων γέγονε. τίς δ' οὐκ ἂν ἀχθεσθείη τοιούτου γένους χρόνον οὕτω πολὺν κάμνοντος; 2. ὑπὲρ δὲ τῶν ἀδικούντων ὑμᾶς διελέχθη μὲν ἡμῖν οὐδεὶς ἐν ἐπιστολαῖς· εἰ δὲ καὶ πολλοὶ τοῦτ' ἐπεποιήκεσαν, οὐδὲν ἂν ἔπραττον οὐδ' ἂν ἐμαυτὸν ὑμᾶς ἀδικῶν ᾐδίκουν. 3. ὃν δ' οἴει τῆς ἡμετέρας ἄρξειν καὶ εἶναί που πλησίον ἡμῖν, λόγος ὑμᾶς ὥσπερ ἡμᾶς οὐκ ἀληθὴς ἐξηπάτηκεν. ἀλλ' ἡμεῖς μὲν ἀπατώ-

[a] *BLZG* 162, *PLRE* 385. M. Stern, *Greek and Latin Authors on Jews and Judaism,* 2:580–599.

Seeck and *PLRE* identify him as the Jewish patriarch Gamaliel vi, Stern (582) as Gamaliel v. His son was a pupil of Libanius (*Ep.* 1098, although Stern is doubtful), and he himself was familiar with Greek literature (*Epp.* 1085.3, 1105.1). He is thus notable for his acceptance of Hellenic culture. His temporal power was very great, as was his influence upon imperial policy (*Ep.* 974). The governor Hilarius was disgraced at his persuasion (*Ep.* 1105), and Hesychius executed (Jerome *Ep.* 57; *PL* xxii.570). Gamaliel vi was, for a time, honorary prefect (*Cod. Th.* xvi.8.22), and under him the status of the patriarchate in Tiberias was little different, in practice,

## 160. To the Patriarch[a]

1. Of this information in your letter, some I knew long ago, the rest I have only now discovered. And my grief has been increased by the postscript to your letter. No one could fail to be upset at the troubles that have afflicted such a nation for so long.[b] 2. No one in correspondence has approached me on behalf of your oppressors, but however many might have done so, I would never have abetted them or injured myself by injuring you. 3. As for him whom you take to be the future governor of our city and to be somewhere in our vicinity, a false story has misled you, as it did us.[c]

from that of a client ruler. Cf. M. Goodman, *State and Society in Roman Galilee* (Oxford Centre for post-Graduate Hebrew Studies 1983) 114–8.

[b] The Roman administration tried to adhere to the policy of maintaining Judaism as a *religio licita,* but the activities of monks and the fulminations of bishops and priests, most recently by John Chrysostom, led to unofficial acts of repression. The latest outrage against the Jews had been the razing of the synagogue at Callinicum in this same year, which Seeck (p. 453) suggested is the trouble here mentioned.

[c] This appears to refer to the attempted return of the disgraced governor Lucianus and the rebuff offered by his claque of supporters to his successor Eustathius in summer 388; cf. *Or.* 56.9 ff, Seeck, "Libanius gegen Lucianus," 91 ff.

μενοι πεπαύμεθα, δεῖ δὲ καὶ ὑμᾶς νῦν, εἰ καὶ μὴ πρότερον.

## 161. Πρόκλῳ

1. Ἡμεῖς δὲ οὐ πεπόνθαμεν τὸ τῆς παροιμίας, ἥ φησιν ἔρωτα ὕβρει λύεσθαι, ἀλλ' ἐλαυνόμενοι καὶ παιόμενοι καὶ τί κακὸν οὐκ ἀκούσαντες ὅμως ἐσμὲν ἐρασταὶ καὶ τῶν αὐτῶν ἐπιθυμοῦμεν κἂν δέχηταί τις, ἐρχόμεθα μεθ' ἡδονῆς οὐδὲν εἰρῆσθαι τῶν εἰρημένων νομίζοντες. 2. τοῦ δὲ ἄνδρα ἀγαθὸν εἶναι τὸν Θαλάσσιον καὶ τῆς βουλῆς ἐκείνης εἰκότως ἂν μετασχεῖν πολλοὶ μὲν οἱ μάρτυρες, ὁ δ' ἀντάξιος πάνυ πολλῶν Πρόκλος. οὗ τοῖς ἔργοις οὐδὲ εἷς λόγος ἴσος. ὃς ἡνίκ' ἦρχεν ἡμῶν, τοῖς τὸν ἄνδρα συκοφαντοῦσιν εἶπεν ὅτι δεῖ πεπαῦσθαι τοῦτο ποιοῦντας ὡς αὐτοῦ γε οὐκ ἀπατησομένου. 3. τοῦ δὴ τότε ταῦτα εἰπόντος εἴη ἂν καὶ πρὸς τοὺς νῦν διαβάλλοντας τοῖς αὐτοῖς χρήσασθαι ῥήμασι καὶ μεταδοῦναι πεῖσαι τοῦ συνεδρίου τῷ μήτε μικρὸν μήτε μεῖζον ἐν μηδενὶ μηδὲν εἰς ταύτην ἡμαρτηκότι τὴν ἡμέραν.

---

[a] There is a gap in Libanius' correspondence after *Letter*

However, we have stopped being misled: so too must you be now, even if never before.

## 161. To Proclus[a]

1. We have not been affected in the way that the proverb has it, which says that love is dissolved by injury;[b] though badgered and beaten and called every name under the sun, we are still in love and desirous of the same things as before. If anyone welcomes us, we go with pleasure and think that none of these words has been said. 2. There are plenty of witnesses to say that Thalassius[c] is a good man and well worthy of becoming a member of the Senate there, but Proclus is equal to very many. No words can describe adequately what he has done. When he was our governor,[d] he told those who traduced the man that they must stop doing so, for he was not going to be hoodwinked. 3. For one who said that then it would be proper to use the same expressions against his present traducers and to induce them to allow him membership of the Senate, since he has never been guilty of any fault, great or small, in any single matter up to this day.

160; on the events leading to *Letters* 161–164 see Appendix.

[b] Cf. *Ep.* 801.1.

[c] *BLZG* 291 (iv), *PLRE* 888 (4).

[d] As *Comes Orientis* in 383–4. A comparison with the invective against Proclus in *Or.* 42.38–44 makes this dignified sounding appeal appear the more distasteful.

## 162. Ὀπτάτῳ

1. Ὅταν ἀριθμήσω τὰς βοηθείας, αἷς αἰτοῦντος ἐμοῦ πολλοὺς πολλῶν ἐρρύσω κακῶν, εἶτ' εἰς τὰς λοιδορίας ἀποβλέψω τὰς καθ' ἡμῶν, καὶ γὰρ αὐτὸς ἦν ἐν αἷς ὁ Θαλάσσιος, ὃν πεποίημαι φίλον, οὐ τῆς αὐτῆς ἄμφω ψυχῆς εὑρίσκω. καὶ κάθημαι δὴ πολλάκις κατὰ χθονὸς ὄμματα πήξας, εἰ ὃν ἔδει μάχεσθαι τοῖς τι καθ' ἡμῶν λέγουσιν, οὗτος αὐτός τε ἔλεγε καὶ ἄλλους ἐβούλετο. καὶ γὰρ εἴ τι καὶ ἐγκαλεῖν εἶχες, ἀλλ' οὐ τοσαύτην ἔδει τὴν τιμωρίαν λαβεῖν. 2. γενέσθω τοίνυν, ὦ γενναῖε, τὰ δεύτερα βελτίω καὶ τούτοις ἐκεῖνα ἐξαλειφέσθω. καὶ γενοῦ Στησίχορος ἡμῖν παλινῳδίαν ᾄδων. ἢν γὰρ σὺ τοῦτο ποιήσῃς, οὐδεὶς ὅστις οὐκ ἀκολουθήσει. καὶ γὰρ τὰ ἄλλα καλῶς ποιοῦντες πείθονταί σοι. δείξας οὖν ἡμῖν τὸν ὀργιζόμενον δεῖξον καὶ τὸν διηλλαγμένον.

---

[a] *BLZG* 226 (ii), *PLRE* 649 (1). This flattering letter, with its classical references, should be compared with the

## 162. To Optatus[a]

1. When I count the times you have at my instance assisted and protected many people from many troubles, and then look at the abuse you have levelled against me, for I too am involved in the abuse suffered by Thalassius, whom I have made my friend, I cannot think that both these attitudes belong to the same person. And here I sit, with eyes often fixed on the ground,[b] wondering why the man who ought to take issue with those who make allegations against me was the very one to make such allegations and to want others to do the same. Indeed even if you had accusation to make against me, you should not have exacted a punishment like this. 2. So, noble sir, let second thoughts prevail,[c] and let your first thoughts be erased by them. Be a Stesichorus and sing us your recantation.[d] If you do so, everyone will follow your lead. In fact, in all else they quite rightly defer to you. So, now that you have shown us yourself in your anger, show us also yourself reconciled.

venomous picture of the intriguing and illiterate villain of *Or.* 42.11–32. He had been foremost in getting Thalassius blackballed.

[b] Homer *Il.* 3.217.

[c] The proverbial δευτέρων ἀμεινόνων, Plat. *Legg.* 4.723d, Eurip. *Hippol.* 436. *Paroem. Gr.* 1.62.

[d] Cf. Plat. *Phaedr.* 243a, *Paroem. Gr.* 2.210.

## 163. Ἐλεβίκῳ

1. Δεινὸν μὲν ἡμῖν καὶ τὸ τοιαῦτα ἐν μέσῃ τηλικαύτῃ βουλῇ περὶ ἡμῶν εἰρῆσθαι· καὶ γὰρ εἰ τοὐμὸν ὄνομα ὑπερεπήδων οἱ τὸν ἐμὸν λέγοντες κακῶς φίλον, ἀλλὰ κατ᾽ ἀμφοῖν ὄντοιν γε φίλοιν ἀφίετο τὰ βέλη. 2. λύπη μὲν οὖν κἀντεῦθεν· λυπηρότερον δὲ ἐκεῖνο τὸ σοῦ παρόντος τε καὶ συγκαθημένου καὶ δυναμένου τοσοῦτον ὅσον ἄξιον μηδένα ὑπὲρ ἡμῶν γενέσθαι λόγον. οὐ γὰρ ἐπείσθην τοῖς ἀπαγγέλλουσιν ὅτι καὶ καθ᾽ ἡμῶν παρὰ σοῦ· σύ τε γὰρ χρηστὸς καὶ φίλος ἡμῖν τε οὐδεμίαν τοιαύτην παρὼν ἐνεωράκεις κακίαν. 3. οὐ συνεπέθου μὲν οὖν, οὐκ ἐβόησας δέ, τῇ σιγῇ δὲ ἠδίκεις. εἰ γάρ, ὡς ἐπίστασαι καλῶς, ἐμέ τε καὶ Θαλάσσιον ἐβόησας,[1] ἀπείχοντ᾽ ἂν ἡμῶν οἱ νῦν βάλλοντες· νῦν δὲ οὐδὲν ἦν τὸ κωλύον. 4. ἐπεσταλκότων τοίνυν τινῶν ὡς οἱ τέως πολεμοῦντες κατέθεντο τὰ ὅπλα καὶ οὐκ ἐπαινοῦσι μὲν τὰ πεπραγμένα, βούλοιντο δ᾽ ἂν ὧν εἶργον μεταδοῦναι καὶ τὸν δεξόμενον φανῆναι, τὰ αὐτά

[1] ἐβόησας F., conj. Re. ἐβοήθησας Wolf (Mss.).

---

[a] In this address to a military man Libanius makes effective use of military terms. His general attitude

## 163. To Elebichus[a]

1. It is a dreadful thing for me to have such remarks made about me in open session of so august a Senate. Indeed, even if my friend's traducers skipped over mentioning me by name, they yet made both of us their targets, since we are friends. 2. I am grieved in consequence, but more grievous still is the fact that while you were present and at the session, with all the influence you so deservedly possess, no single word was spoken on our behalf. I disbelieved the reports that you actually spoke against us, for you are a good friend and had never seen any such defect in me when you were here.[b] 3. Well, you did not join in the attack; but you raised no protest, and so you injured us by your silence. For, as you well know, if you had provided vocal support for Thalassius and me, our present attackers would now be steering clear of us. As it is, there is nothing to stop them. 4. However, I learn from correspondents that some of our enemies at that time have now grounded arms, and do not approve of the action taken, and would like him to participate in the privileges from which they barred him, and to be clearly seen to be a recipient of them.

towards Elebichus, though one of disappointment at Thalassius' rejection, is more balanced and consistent than that of his letters to Proclus and Optatus, who are signalled as the most vocal opponents in *Or.* 42.

[b] Cf. Plat. *Gorg.* 477b.

τε πάλιν αἰτοῦμεν κἂν τύχωμεν, οὐδὲν ἀηδὲς πεπονθέναι φήσομεν.

## 164. Εὐσεβίῳ

1. Οἶσθά που Θαλάσσιον, ἐν ᾧ μοι τὰ μέγιστα· τί γὰρ ἴσον παρ' ἐμοὶ τῇ περὶ τοὺς λόγους διατριβῇ; τούτῳ βίος μέν, εἴ τις ὀρθῶς ἐξετάζοι τὰ πράγματα, ἄμεμπτος, φθόνος δὲ παρ' ἐνίων δι' αὐτὸ τοῦτο καὶ τὸ μὴ δύνασθαι ταὐτὰ νοσεῖν ἑαυτοῖς. 2. τὸ δὴ πιστεύεσθαι παρὰ τοῖς ἄρχουσιν ἐκ τοῦ κολακεύειν οἱ τοιοῦτοι λαβόντες ἄλλους τε σεσυκοφαντήκασιν ἐν δείπνοις καὶ δὴ τοῦτον ὄντα ἀγαθόν, οἱ δ' ἑλκυσθέντες ἠπείλησαν. 3. γίγνεται δή τις ἐνταῦθα σύμβουλος Θαλασσίῳ γενέσθαι τοῦ σεμνοῦ συνεδρίου· τὸν γὰρ ἀπειλήσοντα ῥᾳδίως οὐκ ἔσεσθαι. καλῶς εἰπεῖν ταῦτα εἰπὼν ἔδοξέ μοι, καὶ ἐπιτρέπω. 4. τοῦ πράγματος δὲ εἰσηγμένου τῶν τις ἐν τῇ βουλῇ δυνατῶν ἠδικημένος μὲν οὐδὲν ὑφ' ἡμῶν, οἰόμενος δὲ δι' ἀπάτης, πολλοὶ δὲ οἱ τοῦτο ποιοῦντες, ἠναντιοῦτο λέγων οἷα εἰκὸς τὸν οἰόμενον αὑτῷ δίκην ὀφεί-

So I repeat my request and, if successful, I shall deny having experienced any unpleasantness.

## 164. To Eusebius

1. You know Thalassius, I am sure. In him I repose the greatest confidence, for what in my eyes can possibly equal an engagement in rhetoric? His life, if the facts are carefully examined, has been irreproachable, but envy has arisen among some people for this very reason and the fact that he is incapable of experiencing the same ailments as they.[a] 2. Such fellows as these have gained the ear of the governors by their flatteries, and at their dinner parties have retailed scandalous gossip against other people, him in particular, for all his virtues, and the others have been dragooned into making threats against him. 3. Thus Thalassius was advised by someone here to become a member of the august Senate, since he would not be the target for unwarranted threats. This argument seemed a cogent one to me, and I agreed to it.[b] 4. When the matter was brought up, an influential member of the Senate, who had suffered no injustice at our hands but had been deceived into thinking that he had—and there are plenty of people to deceive him so—opposed it with arguments to be expected of one who feels that he has the right to punish us, and by

[a] Cf. *Or.* 42.7–9.
[b] *Ibid.* 3–6.

λεσθαι παρ᾽ ἡμῶν. καὶ ἐκράτει δὴ βοῶν. 5. τούτοις δ᾽ ἡμῶν ἀχθομένων καὶ μηκέτ᾽ ἐνοχλεῖν ἐγνωκότων ἦλθον ἐκεῖθεν ἐπιστολαὶ παύουσαί τε τὴν λύπην καὶ φάσκουσαι μεθ᾽ ἡμῶν ἔσεσθαι ταῦτα ζητούντων τοὺς τότε ἐν ἐχθρῶν μοίρᾳ. 6. φίλοις μὲν οὖν τοῖς ἐπεσταλκόσιν οὖσιν οὐκ ἦν ἀπιστεῖν· πανταχοῦ δὲ τὸ σὸν μεγάλη πρὸς τὸ κατορθοῦσθαί τι ῥοπή.

## 165. Πρόκλῳ

1. Σὺ μὲν ἡμῖν ἐγκαλεῖς τὸ παύσασθαι γράφοντας, ἡμεῖς δὲ σοὶ τὸ μηδὲ ἐπεσταλκέναι πρὸς ἡμᾶς, ἀφ᾽ οὗ ταύτης ἥψω τῆς ἀρχῆς τῆς μεγάλης, ὥστε με μᾶλλον εἰδέναι Φοινίκῃ χάριν ἢ Θρᾴκῃ. 2. θαυμαστὸν δὲ καὶ τοῖς ἑταίροις ἐφαίνετο τὸ μηδεμίαν ἡμῖν ἐλθεῖν ἐκεῖθεν ἐπιστολήν, καὶ προσιόντες ἠρώτων, ὅτῳ τοῦτο γέγονεν. ἐγὼ δὲ ἠρυθρίων μέν, ἐπειρώμην δὲ ὅμως λέγειν τι, λέγειν δὲ οὐδὲν ἐδόκουν, ἀλλ᾽ ἀεὶ τὸ λεγόμενον

[a] Proclus has evidently made an effort to reduce the ill-feeling between Libanius and himself engendered by the affair of Thalassius. This reply from Libanius draws a veil over their public differences; however, in private and probably unpublished orations like *Or.* 42, he continues to fulminate against Proclus.

his outcries, he gained the day.[c] 5. We felt aggrieved at this and had made up our minds not to make any more unwelcome solicitations, but then there came letters from there which put an end to our annoyance, asserting that persons previously on the side of our enemies[d] were now on our side in our request. 6. So, since it was our friends who sent us this news, we could not disregard it. In every case, your support is of great assistance in putting matters right.

[c] This is probably Optatus (*ibid.* 6, though in the oration deception is as nothing compared with the man's natural viciousness).

[d] Cf. Dem. *c. Aristocr.* 61.

## 165. To Proclus

1. You reproach me for ceasing to write to you. I reproach you for not having sent me a single line since the day you entered upon this great office, with the result that I am more grateful to Phoenicia than to Thrace.[a] 2. It appeared remarkable to my friends too that no letter reached me from you, and they began to come along and ask me the reason for this. For all my blushes, I still tried to give them some sensible explanation, but I was held to be talking nonsense and my remarks always appeared

Proclus had been *consularis* in Phoenicia and *Comes* in Antioch before holding his present post as prefect of the city in Constantinople.

ἀσθενὲς εἶναι ἐφαίνετο. 3. μόλις δὲ ἐνεθυμήθην καὶ εὗρόν τι καὶ εἶπον ὅτι, 'ὦ φίλοι, τούτου τοῦ πράγματος αἴτιον οἱ λόγοι πολλοί τε καὶ παρὰ πολλῶν τῷ καλῷ Πρόκλῳ καὶ ποιούμενοι καὶ δεικνύμενοι καὶ ῥώμην ἔχοντες ὅσην εἰκὸς παῖδας ἀκμαζόντων τῶν πατέρων, ἡμεῖς δὲ ἐν γήρᾳ τε πολλῷ καὶ τῷ μόλις κινεῖσθαι.' 4. ταῦτα λέγων οὐ κακῶς ἐδόκουν λέγειν. εἶθ' ἡκόντων τουτωνὶ τῶν νῦν γραμμάτων ἕτερον ἀνέφυ ζήτημα τὸ 'τί ταύτην ἐποίησε τὴν ἐπιστολήν;' οὐ γὰρ δὴ θεῶν τις τὸ γῆρας ἀποξύσας ἔθηκέ με νέον ἡβώοντα. πάλιν τοίνυν ἐνταῦθα πάντα κινῶν ἀεί τι νομίζων εὑρήσειν εὗρον οὐδέν. εἶθ' ὑπ' αὐτῆς τῆς ἀπορίας εἶδον ὅτι χρὴ παρὰ σοῦ μεταπέμπεσθαι τὴν λύσιν.

## 166. Πρίσκῳ

1. Ὅσῳ μέτρῳ τὴν πόλιν ἡμῶν ἥκων εἰς αὐτὴν

---

[a] *BLZG* 246 (i), *PLRE* 730 (5). Eunap. *V.S.* 478, 481–2. F/Kr. no. 69. Written to Priscus, the Neoplatonist companion of Julian, for whom he always entertained affection and respect, and using another philosopher, Hilarius, as emissary, this letter allows Libanius to exercise his Platonic learning for the benefit of an appreciative reader, and

lame. 3. At length, after much pondering, I thought of something. "My friends," I told them, "the reason for this is to be found in the many orations from many people composed and delivered for the noble Proclus. They have the force expected of the offspring of men in their prime.[b] I however am at an advanced age, when inspiration is hard come by."[c] 4. Such comments seemed plausible, but then your present letter arrived and produced another inquiry: what had produced this letter? Clearly it was not that a god had stripped the old age off me and left me a youth in my prime.[d] So once again, I explored every avenue and, though always thinking to find some answer, I found none. Then from my very puzzlement I saw that I must send to you for the answer to the riddle.

[b] Cf. Plat. *Resp.* 5.459b. For λόγοι as ἔκγονοι cf. *Letter* 181.
[c] Libanius is now 76.
[d] Cf. Homer *Il.* 9.446.

## 166. To Priscus[a]

1. The improvement the good Hilarius[b] effected

occasions the expression of longing for the dead Julian. Fatouros and Krischer (p. 453) identify the hints of Platonic diction in the letter.

[b] *BLZG* 178 (v), 179 (viii); *PLRE* 435 (7), (9). F/Kr. are surely right in identifying the Hilarius of Eunap. *V.S.* 482 with this Hilarius (Seeck and *PLRE* to the contrary).

ὁ χρηστὸς Ἱλάριος[1] ἀπέφηνεν ἀμείνω, τοσούτῳ χείρω δραμὼν εἰς τὴν Ἑλλάδα βελτίω μὲν τῆς ἡμετέρας οὖσαν, μᾶλλον δέ, τοῖς ἅπασι νικῶσαν. 2. τοῖς δ᾽ οὖν ἀφαιρεθεῖσιν ἃ μάλιστα ἔχειν ἤθελον οὐδὲν ἀφαιρεῖ τοῦτο τῆς λύπης καὶ μάλιστα τοῖς ἄγαν γεγηρακόσιν ἡμῖν· ἐπεὶ τῷ γε ἐν νεότητι ἢ γήρᾳ μέν, οὐ μὴν ἐν τοσούτῳ, τά γε ἀπὸ τῶν ἐλπίδων ὑπάρχει πλοῦν τε αὐτὸν ὅμοιον τῷ προτέρῳ ποιήσεσθαι καὶ αὖθις ἐνταῦθα ἔσεσθαι καὶ τοῖς δεξιωτέροις συνέσεσθαι δεχόμενόν τε τοὺς ὡς αὐτὸν ἰόντας καὶ τὴν ἴσην ἀποδιδόντα καὶ τὰ μὲν λέγοντα, τὰ δὲ ἀκούοντα, καὶ τὰ μὲν ἐπαινοῦντα, τὰ δὲ ἐπαινούμενον. 3. ἀλλ᾽ ἐκεῖνα μὲν ἐκείνων· τὸ δ᾽ ἡμέτερον, ἓξ μὲν καὶ ἑβδομήκοντα ἔτη γέγονα, τὸ λειπόμενον δὲ οὐ πολύ. καὶ ὁ μὲν ἥξει κομίζων καλὴν διήγησιν, καλὴ γὰρ δήπουθεν ἡ περὶ τῆς Ἑλλάδος, ἑτέρους δὲ εὐφραίνων ἐμὲ ζητήσει. 4. τούτων μὲν οὖν ἡμῖν ὕστερον ἀπολαύσειεν ἡ πόλις· Ἱλάριον[2] δὲ μακάριον ἐπέρχεταί μοι καλεῖν ὀψόμενον τὰ κάλλιστα τῶν ὑπὸ τὸν ἥλιον, τάς τε ἐν τῇ Πελοποννήσῳ πόλεις

[1] Ἱλάριος F. (conj. Sievers 133 and 185; Seeck 179 viii): cf. infra §§ 4, 6, Ep. 950. 3 F.; om. V Va Vo Σαλούστιος Wolf (W Vind.)

in our city by his arrival is directly proportionate to the deterioration created by his departure for Greece—a Greece superior to my home town, in fact surpassing it in every particular. 2. When deprived of what one most wanted to have, one's grief is not thereby decreased, particularly for me at my advanced age. When one is young or old, though not so old as I, one may hope that one's course will be like the previous one[c] and that one will once more be back here to associate with persons of superior intelligence, welcoming those who approach and giving them their due, speaking, listening, giving and receiving praise. 3. That is what they can look forward to. But I have now reached the age of seventy-six and have not much time left.[d] He will come back with a fine tale to tell—and obviously it will be a fine tale since it is about Greece—and while delighting others he will look in vain for me. 4. This, I trust, is what our city will enjoy hereafter. It occurs to me to call Hilarius blessed, for he will see the finest sights under the sun,[e] the many great cities in the Peloponnese, Phocis, and Boeotia and

[c] A variation on the proverbial δευτερος πλοῦς.

[d] Firmly dates the letter to 390. Priscus is even older, since he was over 90 when he died in 395–6.

[e] Cf. *Ep.* 668.2, *Letter* 81.8; Aeschin. *de Fals. Leg.* 41.

---

[2] Ἱλάριον F. (V Va Vo) Σαλούστιον W Vind. Σαλλούστιον Wolf.

τὰς πολλὰς καὶ μεγάλας Φωκέας τε καὶ Βοιωτοὺς καὶ τὴν ἐνεγκοῦσαν αὐτὸν καὶ τὸν ἀστέρα δὴ τῆς Ἑλλάδος, τὴν Ἀθηναίων πόλιν, καὶ ἕτερον ἀστέρα, Πρίσκον τὸν καλῶς μὲν εἰδότα τὸν Πλάτωνα, καλῶς δὲ τὸν ἐκείνου μαθητήν, ἀποπέμποντα δὲ τοὺς ὁμιλοῦντας αὐτῷ φρονιμωτέρους, ὃ καὶ αὐτὸς οἶδα πολλάκις κερδάνας. 5. ταὐτὸ δ' ἂν εἶπε περὶ αὐτοῦ κἀκεῖνος, ᾧ φιλοσοφίας ὁ θεὸς τὴν ψυχὴν ἐμπλήσας ἔδωκε Ῥωμαίων μὲν ἄρχειν, βαρβάρους δὲ ἐλαύνειν, ἐπεὶ καὶ τὴν τελευτὴν αὐτὴν ἐν τῷ Πέρσας ἐλαύνειν ἐδέξατο μέγα ποιούμενος, εἰ Πρίσκῳ δοκοίη τὰ προσήκοντα ποιεῖν. 6. ποίει τοίνυν καὶ τὸν Ἱλάριον[3] βελτίω καὶ δίδου πρὸς ἡμᾶς αὐτὸν τοῦτ' ἐπιστέλλειν· δίκαιός τε γὰρ ἀνὴρ καὶ οὐκ ἀποκρύψεται.

[3] Ἱλάριον F. (V Va Vo) Σαλούστιον W Vind. Σαλλούστιον Wolf.

---

[f] Eurip. *Hippol.* 1122.
[g] Aristotle.

## 167. Θαλασσίῳ

1. Λέγε Καλλιοπίῳ μὴ κακῶς τὸ ἔαρ λέγειν ὡς ἄγον τῇ Ῥώμῃ τῶν ἡμετέρων νέων διὰ θαλάττης

the city that bore him, the cynosure of Greece,[f] the city of Athens, and that other cynosure, Priscus, with his deep knowledge of Plato and of his disciple,[g] who sends out his associates with a fuller wisdom, as I myself know since it has often stood me in good stead. 5. The same tale would have been told of him by our great emperor whose soul the god filled with philosophy[h] and who was granted the empire of Rome, and victory over the barbarians, for even when he received his death wound in the hour of victory over Persia, his great concern was that his conduct should be seen to be approved by Priscus.[i] 6. So make some improvement in Hilarius too and allow him to write and tell me of it, for he is a fair-minded man and will not conceal it.

[h] Julian. For Priscus and other friends at Julian's deathbed, cf. Amm. Marc. 25.2.23.

[i] A specific instance of Julian's respect for Priscus' moderating influence is to be found in *Or.* 1.123, where it worked to Libanius' advantage.

## 167. To Thalassius[a]

1. Tell Calliopius[b] not to blame the spring for carrying some of our students by sea to Rome. I am

[a] *BLZG* 291 (iv), *PLRE* 888 (4). Thalassius was now, in 390, in Constantinople, possibly in connection with his unsuccessful application for membership of the Senate.

[b] *BLZG* 102 (v), *PLRE* 175 (3). Onetime assistant to Libanius in Antioch, now *magister epistularum* to the emperors (cf. *Ep.* 18).

τινάς. οὐ γὰρ ἐγὼ τοῦθ' ὅ[1] φησι ποιῶ τὸ κακὸν οὐδ' ὑβρίζω μὲν τὴν Ἑλλάδα φωνήν, κοσμῶ δὲ τὴν Ἰταλῶν, οὐδ' ἂν εἴποι πατὴρ οὐδεὶς τοιοῦτον αὑτῷ τί με συμβεβουλευκέναι. 2. ἀλλ' ἔστι ταῦτα ἀνοίας ἐλπιζούσης ἃ μάλιστα βούλεται. νοῦς δὲ εἴ σφισιν ἐνῆν, ἐδέχοντ' ἂν τὴν ἀπὸ τῶν πραγμάτων παραίνεσιν. ἡ δ' ἐστὶν ἐξετάζειν τοὺς ἀποδοθέντας πολλαῖς πόλεσιν παρ' ἐκείνης τοὺς οὐ πολλῷ τῶν βοσκημάτων διαφέροντας.

[1] τοῦθ' ὅ F. τοῦτο Wolf (Mss.).

## 168. Σαπώρῃ

1. Αἱ τοῦ θειοτάτου βασιλέως πρὸς σὲ καταλλαγαὶ σοὶ μὲν ἀποδεδώκασι τὴν οὐσίαν, ἅπαντας δὲ ἀνθρώπους εὔφραναν οὐχ ἧττον ἢ τὸν ἀπειληφότα τὴν οὐσίαν. ἀμοιβαὶ δὲ αὗταί σοι τῆς χρηστότητος, ᾗ χρώμενος ἐν τηλικαύτῃ δυνάμει

---

[a] *BLZG* 269, *PLRE* 803. By 381 Sapores was friendly enough towards Libanius to visit him in the company of other commanders (*Or.* 2.9). Since then he had been disgraced and his property confiscated, and only lately had he been restored to favour. Of Persian origin, he was probably a pagan, like other commanders, which would recommend him to Libanius and to the praetorian prefect Tatianus, though not to his predecessor Cynegius.

not responsible for this trouble he mentions: I don't insult the Greek language and exalt Latin, nor could any parent say that I have ever given him such advice.[c] 2. It results from stupidity, where the wish is father to the thought. If they had any sense at all, they would be advised by the facts—that is, they would examine those who have been returned from there to their several cities not much different from sheep.

[c] The beginning of the sailing season brought the annual exodus of ambitious youngsters to Italy to study Latin and law, with an eye to their advancement in the administration. Libanius often and bitterly inveighs against this practice, which reduced the prestige of the traditional Greek education in rhetoric; cf. *Or.* 1.214, 40.5, 48.28 f (the flight to Rome, with parental consent); *Or.* 1.234, 2.43 f, 62.21 ff (the competition of Latin, law, and even shorthand): Liebeschuetz 243 ff, Petit, *Vie Municipale* 358 ff.

## 168. To Sapores[a]

1. The reconciliation of our most divine emperor to yourself has restored you your possessions and has afforded all mankind no less happiness than it did you on recovering them. This is the reward for your goodness, which you employed in a position of such influence; and you were often called by the

πατὴρ ἐκλήθης πολλάκις δείξας ὡς ἔστι καὶ στρατιωτῶν ἡγούμενον μὴ χαλεπὸν εἶναι. 2. ταυτὶ δὲ τὰ παρὰ τοῦ βασιλέως πέπρακται μὲν νῦν, ἑωρᾶτο δέ μοι πάλαι, καὶ πρὸς τοὺς ἑταίρους προὔλεγον ὡς ἃ γέγονε γενήσεται. μάντιν δὲ ἐποίει με τοῦ βασιλέως ὁ τρόπος ὁ βραδὺς μὲν εἰς δίκην, ταχὺς δὲ εἰς χάριν καὶ μέμψεις φιλανθρωπίᾳ λύων καὶ λύπας ἰώμενος. 3. ὃ δὲ ἐγκαλεῖς, τὸ μηδὲ λόγον ὑπὲρ τῶν τοιούτων ἐλθεῖν αὐτῷ παρ' ἡμῶν ἤ, εἰ μὴ λόγον, ἐπιστολήν, μεῖζον ἦν ἢ κατὰ τὰ δοθέντα μοι παρ' αὐτοῦ, καὶ τὸ δόξαι θρασὺς εἶναι δεδιὼς ἐκωλυόμην ἢ τοῦτο ποιεῖν ἢ 'κεῖνο. τουτὶ δὲ κἀπὶ τῶν ἐμαυτοῦ πραγμάτων ἐφυλαξάμην· πρὸς ἃ καὶ αὐτὰ κατηγοροῦντά μου ταὐτὸν ἂν ἀπεκρινάμην. 4. καὶ μὴν τό γε σοὶ πέμψαι παραμυθίαν ἐν γράμμασιν εἶχεν ἂν τὸν ἐπιτιμῶντα· καὶ πλέον δ' ἂν οἱ κακοήθεις ἐποίουν. ὑφ' ὧν ἐγὼ πολλὰ πολλαχοῦ παθὼν οἶδα ὅσον ἐστὶ κακὸν ἄνθρωπος κακοήθης καὶ ὡς ἀπὸ συλλαβῆς ὅ γε τοιοῦτος ῥᾳδίως ἀνάψειεν ἂν πυράν. 5. ἀμφοτέρων οὖν κηδόμενος, καὶ σοῦ

---

[b] Despite his commendations of individual generals, Libanius retains a deep mistrust for the average military man in relations with civilians; cf. *Or.* 46.13 f, 47.3 ff.

name of father, since you proved it possible even for a military commander not to be harsh.[b] 2. This action of our emperor has only lately occurred, but I had foreseen it long ago, and I used to tell my friends in advance that what has happened would happen. I gained this second sight from the behaviour of our emperor, slow to punish but quick to oblige. By his generosity he does away with reproaches and heals our pain. 3. Your accusation, that he received from me no word on such matters, or, in default of that, no letter, is disproportionate to his favours to me: I was afraid to be thought impertinent, and so was prevented from doing either one or the other. I took care not to do so even in matters affecting myself, and I would have given the same reply if you made this accusation against me in that case too. 4. In fact, even to have sent you a letter of consolation would involve reproof; and the malicious would go further. I have on many occasions suffered much at their hands and I know what a penance a malicious fellow can be, and how such a person can easily create havoc from the utterance of a mere syllable.[c] 5. So in my concern for both you and

[c] Publicity caused by the revelation of letters received could well cause trouble for the writer, e.g. *Or.* 1.43, 175, 178. The prudent suppression of the correspondence from 365 to 388 surely stems from this consideration. In any case, from 387 Libanius had had to face three charges of treason so that writing to a disgraced commander could be dangerous for them both.

καὶ ἐμοῦ, κάλλιον ἡγησάμην τὴν σιγὴν ὑπούσης τινὸς καὶ τοιαύτης ἐλπίδος σεαυτῷ διαλέξεσθαι καὶ τῆς λύπης ἀφαιρήσειν τοῖς παρὰ τῆς σῆς φρονήσεως φαρμάκοις, δι' ἣν τὰς ἐν τοῖς ὅπλοις νίκας ἀναιρούμενος προσετίθεις ἕτερον ἀγαθὸν οὐκ ἔλαττον, τὴν πρὸς τὸ σεσωσμένον πρᾳότητα. 6. οἶμαι μὲν οὖν σοι ταῦτα ἀρκέσειν·[1] εἰ δ' ἡδέως ἂν καὶ μακροτέρων ἀκούσαις, πρὸς ἥκοντά σε τοῦτο ἔσται.

[1] ἀρκέσειν F., conj. Re. (D) ἀρέσκειν Wolf (other Mss.).

## 169. Τατιανῷ

1. Ὑπὲρ ὧν νυνὶ γράφω, πάλαι μὲν ἴσως ἐχρῆν, ὄκνος δέ τις διεκώλυε· τοῦ πράγματος δὲ κατεπείγοντος οὐκέτ' ἔξεστιν, εἰ καὶ λίαν ἐθέλοιμι, μὴ λέγειν. καὶ γὰρ ἂν καὶ χαλεπήναις ὕστερον ἀκούσας, ὅτι μὴ πρότερον ἤκουσας. 2. τί οὖν αἰτῶ καὶ τὶ βούλομαι λαβεῖν παρ' ἀνδρὸς ἡδομένου τῷ καλὰς διδόναι χάριτας; παῖς ἐκ γυναικὸς ἀγαθῆς ἐγένετό μοι καὶ τοιαύτης ὡς τὸν ἐκείνης τρόπον μικρὸν ποιῆσαί με νομίσαι πλούτους μεγάλους πατέρων θυγατέρας ἐχόντων.

myself, I thought silence was best, while ever some such hope subsisted that you would think things over to yourself and relieve your dejection by the cures provided by your own good sense. That is how you used to win your victories in arms and to them add another benefit no less important, your gentleness towards what you have preserved. 6. These remarks, I believe, will satisfy you, but if you would like to hear them at even greater length, this will be done upon your arrival here.

## 169. To Tatianus[a]

1. I ought perhaps to have written to you long ago upon the subject of my present letter, but some hesitation held me back. But since the matter presses, I can no longer keep silent, however much I might wish it, for you might even be angry if later on you heard what you had not heard previously. 2. What then is my request, and what is it that I want to get from a man who enjoys granting well-deserved favours? I have a son born of a good woman, and such a one that her character makes me think little of the great wealth of fathers with

[a] *Letters* 169–170 are prologue to the last tragedy in Libanius' life. On this see note in Appendix.

3. γενόμενον δὲ τὸν παῖδα ῥήτορα γενέσθαι βουλόμενος, ἐπειδὴ τὸ δύνασθαι λέγειν εἶχεν, εἰς τοὺς συνδίκους ἐνέγραψα, καὶ χρυσὸν μὲν οὐ συνέλεξε πολύν, ἡ γλῶττα δὲ αὐτῷ πολλοὺς ἐπαίνους ἠνέγκατο καὶ τῶν πρὸς αὐτὸν μεμαχημένων αὐτὸ τοῦτο ποιούντων. 4. γνοὺς δ' ἅπαν τὸ πρᾶγμα τοῦτο ὁ παρὰ τοῦ Διὸς αὐτοῦ τὴν βασιλείαν λαβὼν βοηθεῖ βοήθειαν ἡμῖν πρέπουσαν τῇ αὑτοῦ φύσει. καὶ κρείττων τῶν κωλυόντων γενόμενος ἔδωκεν εἰς αὐτὸν διαβῆναι τὰ ὄντα μοι τὰ μικρά, καὶ διέβη. 5. ἀντὶ μὲν οὖν ταύτης τῆς τιμῆς ἀεὶ τῆς βελτίονος τύχης ἀπολαύοι βασιλεύς· τῶν φίλων δὲ ἡμῖν τῶν μὲν αὐτὸν ἐπὶ τὴν βουλὴν ἀγόντων, τῶν δὲ ἐν ᾧπερ ἦν τηρούντων, καὶ

---

[b] F/Kr. no. 13. Libanius had been affianced to his cousin, Phasganius' daughter, but she died on the eve of his return to Antioch (*Or.* 1.95). Inside the next year he had formed a union with the freedwoman who was the mother of Cimon and his partner for the rest of her life. Now she had just died (*Or.* 1.278). Eunapius' comment that she was of inferior status is confirmed here and in *Letters* 188.5, 189.1.

[c] Syndics = advocates. Cimon was attached to the court of the *consularis* in the time of Icarius in 384, and remained there until 388–9, when Eustathius scoffed at

marriageable daughters.[b] 3. After my son was born I wanted him to become an orator since he had the gift of eloquence, and I enrolled him among the advocates and, though he did not make much money,[c] his oratory won him much praise even from those who had been on the opposite side. 4. Upon realizing all the facts of this matter, our emperor who has gained his empire from Zeus himself helped me with assistance consonant with his own generosity.[d] After overcoming the opposition, he allowed my paltry possessions to pass to my son, and this has been done.[e] 5. So in return for this token of esteem may our emperor ever enjoy success. But as some of our friends wanted to introduce my son into the town council,[f] while others were for him staying as he was, and these last seemed better

his lackadaisical attitude (*Or.* 28.9, 54.12). On the advantages of the profession of advocacy cf. *Or.* 48.7; Wolf, *Schülwesen* 76 f.

[d] Libanius can, in addressing a pagan official, make covert play with the name of the emperor Theodosius by referring to the "gift of Zeus." The emperor and any Christian official might have found this offensive, and even with a pagan this must be disguised as a literary conceit.

[e] In 388. It may well have suited the supporter of a programme of curial recruitment, as Tatianus was, to oblige his friend Libanius by this donation, since Cimon would immediately become liable to claims for curial service.

[f] An ironical play on "friends," since they include opponents like Thrasydaeus and those whom Libanius constantly describes as his enemies.

δοκούντων ἄμεινον φρονεῖν τῶν δευτέρων εἴχετο μὲν τοῦ λέγειν, δείσας δὲ τά τε πλοῖα καὶ τὸν σῖτον καὶ τὴν θάλατταν τάς τε ἐν τῷ βουλεύειν πληγάς, ὃ μηδ᾽ ὑπὲρ λόγων ἐπεπόνθει πώποτε, μίαν εὑρίσκει καταφυγὴν ζώνην τε καὶ τὸ ἄρξαι. 6. καὶ δακρύων ἅμα δεῖταί μου θαρρῆσαι πέμψαι πρὸς σὲ τὴν τοῦτο ποιήσουσαν ἐπιστολήν· πάντως δὲ αὐτὸν ἀγαπήσειν ἅπαν τὸ διδόμενον, ἅπαν γὰρ ἕξειν τὴν αὐτὴν ἀσφάλειαν, ὥσπερ αὖ καὶ χρόνον ἅπαντα, κἂν μὴν οὗτος ᾖ. ταυτὶ γὰρ ἔστιν ὁρᾶν ἐν πολλοῖς παραδείγμασι. 7. λῦσον δὴ τὸν φόβον, ὦ γενναῖε, καὶ τῷ νέῳ καὶ τῷ γέροντι. καὶ γὰρ εἰ τεθνεῶτος ἤδη μου ταῦτα συμβήσεται τὰ δεινά, λόγος ἀνδρῶν σοφῶν εἶναι καὶ ὑπὸ γῆς τό τε χαίρειν καὶ τὸ λυπεῖσθαι.

---

[g] On the burdens imposed on decurions, including the sitegia, see my Introduction to *Orations* 48 and 49. The

## 170. Ἀβουργίῳ

1. Καὶ διὰ ταύτης τῆς ἐπιστολῆς ἃ διὰ τῆς προτέρας αἰτοῦμεν. ᾐτοῦμεν δὲ δι᾽ ἐκείνης εὔ-

---

[a] Aburgius is now the senior ex-prefect still resident in Constantinople, the rest having died, like Cynegius, or

advised, he kept on with his oratory. But he is afraid of shipping, grain cargoes, the sea, and of the floggings involved by curial serice—a thing he had never experienced even in learning rhetoric,[g] and finds one sole recourse, to enter the imperial service and to hold an official post.[h] 6. Tearfully he begs me to pluck up courage to send you a letter to secure this. In any case, he says, he will welcome absolutely anything that is offered, for anything will involve the same security, and the same applies to the period too, even if it is only for a month: that can be seen in many examples. 7. Then, noble sir, relieve both the young man and the old of their fear. For even if these horrors happen to him after my death, it is a saying of wise men that pleasure and pain can be experienced even in the underworld.[i]

school system throughout antiquity was notorious for the flogging of pupils.

[h] ζώνη, the baldric, is the mark of the official in imperial service.

[i] A Platonic theme, e.g. *Phaed.* 68a, *Axioch.* 371c ff.

## 170. To Aburgius[a]

1. In this letter too I make the request I made in my previous one.[b] In that I requested your goodwill

returned to their homes in the West, like Neoterius. As such, he wielded considerable influence, not least with the present holder of the office.

[b] *Letter* 157.

νοιάν τε τὴν παρὰ σοῦ καὶ βοήθειαν καὶ τὸ δοῦναί τέ σε τὰ γράμματα παρεῖναί τε τοῖς ἀναγιγνωσκομένοις καὶ ποιεῖν ἰσχυρὰ τοῖς παρὰ σοῦ ῥήμασι. μέγα δ' ἂν ἐν τοῖς τοιούτοις ἐνέγκαι τι καὶ νεῦμα. 2. ἐνθυμοῦ δὲ ὅτι σοι φεύγειν οὐκ ἔνι τήνδε τὴν βοήθειαν διὰ τὴν ἀπὸ τῆς προτέρας ἀνάγκην. ὁ γὰρ ἐμῷ παιδὶ βεβοηθηκὼς Εὐσεβίῳ πῶς οὐκ ἂν καὶ Ἀρραβίῳ παιδί γε ὄντι καὶ αὐτῷ καὶ μᾶλλόν γε ἢ 'κείνῳ; τὸ μὲν γὰρ τῶν λόγων καὶ παρὰ τῷδε, τὸ δὲ καὶ δι' αἵματος οὐ παρ' ἐκείνῳ.

## 171. Ἱεροφάντῃ

1. Πολλὰ ἀγαθὰ γένοιτο καὶ τῷ γεγραφότι καὶ τῷ κεκομικότι τὰ γράμματα. πάνυ γὰρ ἐλπίζω τὸν μετὰ ταῦτα χρόνον ἀμείνω τοῦ πρὸ αὐτοῦ ἔσεσθει τῆς σῆς φωνῆς τε καὶ χειρὸς τὸν χειμῶνα λυούσης. 2. χειμῶνα δὲ λέγω νῦν τὴν ἐκ πολλῶν συνειλεγμένην λύπην. τά τε γὰρ κατὰ τῶν ἀγαλμάτων τετολμημένα πληγὴ μεγάλη τό τε καταπεπατῆσθαι μὲν τῶν ἡμετέρων λόγων τὴν

[a] *BLZG* 178. Obviously pagan, and perhaps a title rather than a proper name. Seeck's suggestion that he was brother of Siburius (*Ep.* 963) is wrong.

and assistance, and that you should provide a letter, attend its reading and confirm it with your own comments. In such matters even a nod can have great effect. 2. Reflect that because of the obligation imposed by your earlier assistance you cannot escape assisting me in the present instance. For after your help to my child Eusebius,[c] you are bound to help Arrhabius,[d] since he too is my child, and more so than Eusebius, for he is connected by eloquence also, whereas there is no blood connection with Eusebius.

[c] On παῖς as the relationship of pupil to teacher cf. *Or.* 62.27, *Epp.* 137, 1266. Also Petit, *Étudiants* 33.

[d] The forename of Cimon. The names appear without distinction, but Cimon is the one more commonly used after the grant of inheritance and *de facto* legitimization.

## 171. To Hierophantes[a]

1. May many blessings light upon the writer and the bearer of your letter. I very much hope that the time hereafter will be better than the past, with your voice and hand to quell the storm. 2. And by the storm I mean the grief which has now arisen from a combination of causes. It is a great blow that outrages have been committed against the statues[b]

[b] Refers not to the anti-pagan legislation of the emperors but to the violence that accompanied it. The chief offenders were the monks, whose excesses (cf. *Or.* 30) were to culminate in the destruction of the Serapeum at Alexandria in June 391.

βασιλείαν, μεθεστάναι δὲ ἑτέρωσε τὸ κράτος πληγὴ καὶ αὐτὸ δευτέρα τις νοσήματά τε ἄλλο ἐν ἄλλῳ μέρει τοῦ σώματος οἰκοῦντά μοι χαλεπὰς μὲν ἐργάζεται τὰς νύκτας, ἀηδεστέρας δὲ τὰς ἡμέρας πολλοί τε τῶν εὖ παθόντων ὑφ' ἡμῶν οὐ βούλονται τῶν εὖ παθόντων εἶναι. 3. καὶ τοῦτο δ' ἂν δάκοι καρδίαν· φίλοι τε ἡμῖν ἀδελφῶν τεθνᾶσι κρείττονες τῶν τ' ἀρχόντων οὐκ ὀλίγοις τεθνηκέναι δοκοῦμεν, ὃ βοηθείας ἀποστερεῖ τοὺς δεομένους βοηθείας. ἀλλ' οὐδὲ ἡμῖν αὐτοῖς ὑπάρχει βοηθεῖν τὰς μείζους βοηθείας, ἃς οἶσθα. 4. ταῦτ' οὖν καὶ πρὸς τούτοις ἕτερα λήξειν ἡγοῦμαι τῆς σῆς ἐλθούσης ἡμῖν ἐπιστολῆς. καὶ κατὰ τοῦτο οὖν εἰκότως ἂν πολλάκις ἡμῖν γράφοις, ὅπως ἧτται πολλαὶ γίγνοιντο τῶν χειρόνων. εἰ δὲ προσθείης τοῖς γραμμασι καὶ τὸ διαλέγεσθαί τι τοῖς θεοῖς ὑπὲρ ἡμῶν, λαμπροτέραν ἔσῃ πεποιημένος τὴν ἐπικουρίαν.

---

[c] A recurrent theme of his later years, e.g. *Or.* 1.154, 213, 234; *Or.* 2.43. One reason for the decline in Greek studies, implicit in his protests against the growth of Latin and law, is that Greek was not admissible for use in law until 439 (*Nov. Theod.* 16). Cf. *Letter* 167.

and that the preeminence of our Greek eloquence has been trampled underfoot, and it is another blow too that this preeminence has gone elsewhere:[c] the different ailments that reside in different parts of my body make my nights miserable and my days joyless,[d] and many of those to whom I have done a good turn refuse to acknowledge it. 3. And this would strike one to the heart.[e] Friends who were more to me than brothers are dead,[f] and by quite a number of our governors it is thought that I too am dead,[g] and that deprives those who need help of the help they need. I cannot even get help for myself upon the major matter you are aware of. 4. Such things and others besides I believe will cease now that your letter has arrived. So then, you might write to me often with good reason, so that many reverses may be inflicted on my inferiors. If, in addition to your letter, you were also to commune with the gods on my behalf, you will have rendered me assistance even more noteworthy.

[d] He had had a nervous breakdown in 382–3 (*Or.* 1.202 ff). In 386 he had a recurrence of gout, neuralgia, and associated migraine (*Or.* 1.243 ff, *Or.* 36.15), which continued until 389 (*Or.* 1.268, 280), when his sight also began to fail (*Or.* 1.281).

[e] Aristoph. *Ach.* 1; cf. *Ep.* 257.

[f] In particular, Olympius.

[g] Cf. *Or.* 1.254. Although the target there is the Christian *Comes,* Deinias, Libanius has earned the enmity of a string of pagan *consulares* besides, most recently Eustathius.

## 172. Ῥιχομήρει

1. Ἐξετάζων ἐγὼ τὰ παρὰ τῶν θεῶν εἰς ἐμὲ χρηστὰ τοῦτο μέγιστον εὑρίσκω, τὴν σὴν φιλίαν, καὶ τιμῶ τὴν ἡμέραν ἐκείνην, ᾗ τοῦτ᾽ ἐδέξατο, ὅτε πρῶτον ἰδόντες ἀλλήλους συνήσθημέν τε ἀλλήλοις καὶ ἐποιοῦμεν οἷα ἂν οἱ πολύν τε χρόνον ὡμιληκότες καὶ διὰ μακρᾶς συνηθείας ἥκοντες. καὶ ἐπειδὴ ἦν ἀνάγκη μένειν μὲν ἐμοί, πορεύεσθαι δὲ σοί, μετὰ δακρύων ταῦτα ἐπράττετο. 2. σοὶ μὲν οὖν ἡ φήμη μικρὰ περὶ ἡμῶν ἐκόμιζεν, ὡς λέγομέν τε καὶ γράφομεν νέων τε ἐν μέσῳ καθήμεθα μανθάνειν τι τῶν ἡμετέρων ἢ πειθομένων ἢ ἀναγκαζομένων· τὰ σὰ δὲ λαμπρά τε καὶ σεμνὰ καὶ μεγάλα, στρατηγίαι τε καὶ μάχαι καὶ νῖκαι καὶ τὸ μὴ εἶναι τύραννον μηδὲ δοῦλον τὸν ἐλεύθερον θεόντων ἐφ᾽ ἅπαν τῶν καλῶν βασιλέως τε καὶ σοῦ καὶ τὰ μὲν σοφίᾳ, τὰ δὲ χερσὶν αἱρούντων. 3. ταυτὶ μὲν οὖν λόγων τῶν μὲν τετύχηκε, τῶν δὲ τυγχάνει, τῶν δὲ τεύξεται. καὶ μισθὸς τοῖς

---

[a] F/Kr. no. 71. Cf. *Letter* 150 and notes.

[b] The friendship began on Richomer's arrival as *magister militum* in Antioch in 383. On leaving to assume the consularship of 384, he invited Libanius to attend his inau-

## 172. To Richomer[a]

1. As I count one by one the blessings I have from the gods, my greatest blessing I find to be your friendship. I revere that day which brought it about, when first we saw each other, and had pleasure in each other's company and behaved as though we had known each other a long time and had long enjoyed such intimacy. And when I was forced to stay and you to go, this was done tearfully.[b] 2. Well, rumour used to bring you some items of news about me, that I deliver and compose my orations, that I sit surrounded by pupils who are either persuaded or forced to learn something of my art. But yours is a career of fame, renown, and greatness, of military commands, battles, victories, the suppression of tyranny, and the rescue of free men from slavery, as our emperor and your self hasten to all deeds of high endeavour, and by wisdom or by main force win the day.[c] 3. Such conduct has received its meed of praise, and does and will do more; and the reward for your successes

guration. Libanius refused this honour, but received instead an honorific letter from the emperor (*Or.* 1.219), offering him the honorary prefecture (cf. Petit, "Sur la date du *pro templis*," 293 f).

[c] The campaigns in Italy and the final defeat of Maximus in 388. Richomer is still there in attendance on Theodosius.

κατωρθωκόσιν οὗτος ὥσπερ τοῖς μετ' Ἀγαμέμνονος ἃ τοῖς ἔργοις προσέθηκεν Ὅμηρος. 4. αἰτοῦμεν δὲ παρὰ τῶν θεῶν τε καὶ ὑμῶν ἐλθεῖν τε ὑμᾶς ὡς ἡμᾶς καὶ τὴν ἐπιθυμίαν ἡμῖν ἐμπλῆσαι καὶ καλλίω ποιῆσαι τὴν Δάφνην τῷ τοῦ βασιλέως κάλλει. 5. καὶ γὰρ εἰ μὴ Ῥώμη γε ἡμεῖς, μήθ' ἡ μήτηρ μήθ' ἡ παῖς, ἀλλ' οὐκ ἀναξία γε τῆς τοιαύτης δωρεᾶς χαίρουσα πόλις ἐν ταῖς τοῦ κρατοῦντος εὐπραξίαις καὶ τῷ μήπω τεθεάσθαι τὸν θεοειδῆ λυπουμένη.

## 173. Τατιανῷ

1. Τὰ περὶ τῆς εἰς σὲ τιμῆς γράμματα ταυτησὶ τῆς δικαίας ἥξονθ' ἡμῖν, ἥξει γάρ, ἔφθη τῆς τιμῆς ὁ λόγος, ὃς δι' ὁπόσης[1] εἰσέρχοιτο πόλεως, ἑορτὴν ποιῶν καθ' ἑκάστην ἔρχεται. τὰς γὰρ οὔσας τε διὰ σὲ καὶ σωζομένας καὶ ηὐξημένας ἔδει δήπου καὶ πηδᾶν καὶ ᾄδειν καὶ χορεύειν καὶ οἷς ἂν ἦν ἀμείβεσθαι τὰς πολλάς τε καὶ μεγάλας καὶ λαμ-

[1] δι' ὁπόσης F. διὰ πάσης Wolf (Mss.).

---

[a] Tatianus had just been designated consul for 391. Libanius seems to add a covert reproach that he has not been informed of it personally, a reproach more openly

is this, just as Homer bestowed it on the deeds of those who went with Agamemnon. 4. We pray the gods and yourself that you visit us, fulfil our desires and glorify Daphne with the glory of the emperor.[d] 5. For even if we are not Rome, neither the mother city nor her daughter,[e] still our city is not unworthy of such a benefaction, for she rejoices in our emperor's success and grieves that she has not yet beheld his divine person.

[d] Libanius constantly pleaded that the emperor should visit Antioch; cf. *Or.* 20.45, 22.18. On his view of the emperor's concern for Daphne cf. *Or.* 1.262, 20.44.

[e] Rome and Constantinople. Theodosius had visited Rome for three months in the summer of 389, with Richomer in his train.

## 173. To Tatianus

1. The letter informing us of this well-deserved honour conferred upon you, when it comes—as come it will—has been anticipated by the report of it.[a] However great each city may be that it reaches, it proceeds through it and brings universal joy: for the cities which owe to you their existence, their preservation, and increase must surely jump, sing, and dance for joy, and make what repayment they can for the great and notable acts of benefaction

expressed in the companion letter to Proclus (*Ep.* 991). That the correspondence between them was too one-sided for his peace of mind is shown in *Ep.* 987.6.

πρὰς εὐεργεσίας, ἀνθ᾽ ὧν οἱ τὰς πόλεις ἔχοντες θεοὶ ταυτὶ τὰ νῦν διὰ τοῦ θειοτάτου βασιλέως ἔδοσαν. 2. ἡμεῖς δὲ οἱ περὶ τὰς Μούσας καὶ μᾶλλον ἑορτάζομεν μετά τε τῶν ἄλλων εὖ παθόντες ἀνθρώπων καὶ πλέον ἐκείνων τι λαβόντες εὐρυτέρας τῆς παιδεύσεως ὑπὸ σοῦ γεγενημένης ποιήσεως συναφθείσης τῇ παρ᾽ Ὁμήρου δι᾽ αὐτῶν τῶν Ὁμήρου. 3. οὗτος δὲ ὁ πόνος ἠγαπᾶτο μὲν καὶ πρότερον καὶ ἦν ἐν χερσὶ διδασκάλων τε καὶ μαθητῶν τυγχάνων ὧνπερ Ἰλιὰς καὶ ἣν ἐπ᾽ ἐκείνῃ πεποίηκεν Ὅμηρος· ἀκριβωθεὶς δὲ τῇ τρίτῃ χειρὶ καὶ τοῦ κάλλους γενομένου μείζονος μειζόνως ἤστραψεν ὁ πόνος, καὶ ἐφ᾽ ὅτιπερ ἂν τῆς ἀγέλης ἔλθῃς, εὑρήσεις Τατιανόν. ᾧ καὶ αὐτὸς γεγένημαι βελτίων χρησάμενος μὲν καὶ τοῖς πρώτοις, μᾶλλόν γε μὴν ἐνδιατρίβων τοῖς δευτέροις κινῶν τοῖς σοῖς ἐμαυτὸν εἰς τὰ ἐμαυτοῦ. 4. ἐκεῖνα δὲ ἃ δεῖν ᾠήθης αὖθις εἶναι παρὰ σοί, θαυμαστὸν ὡς οὐκ ἔστι παρὰ σοὶ δεδομένα κομίζειν ᾧ καλῶς εἶχε δοῦναι· δέδοται γὰρ τῷ πάντα

[b] For Tatianus' consistent efforts to promote the rehabilitation of the curiae cf. Petit, *Vie Municipale* 386 ff. Both he and Proclus seem ready to distance themselves from Libanius, whose practice at this time, in his efforts to

received, and it is in return for this that gods, who hold cities in their keeping, have made this present gift through our most divine emperor.[b] 2. We who are connected with the Muses are even more joyful, for we are favoured along with the rest of mankind and have gained even more than they, since you have broadened the scope of our educational training with a poem connected with the Homeric theme with actual Homeric material. 3. This work was well-received even before this, and was handled by both teachers and pupils, in the same way as the *Iliad* and Homer's later composition.[c] It was revised a third time and as its beauty increased, the work flashed with increased lustre, and to whatever part of the class you go, there you will find Tatianus.[d] I too have been improved by it, after utilizing its first edition, and particularly by concentrating on the second, using your composition as inspiration for my own. 4. Yet it is odd that what you thought should be with you again is not with you, since it was entrusted to the conveyance of the most proper

gain immunity for Eusebius, Thalassius, and Cimon, does not match his precepts—that the curia must be supported and its decline stopped.

[c] The *Odyssey*.

[d] This epic poem on a Homeric theme apparently combines Homeric material with verses of his own composition. That it should undergo three revised editions and be accepted as a regular school text is testimonial to the literary ability of Tatianus no less than to his position.

ἀρίστῳ Πρόκλῳ. καὶ τοῦτο ἴσασι Πάγραι, οὗ φέρων εἰς χεῖρας Ὀλύμπιος ἔθηκεν αὐτῷ τὴν διφθέραν. 5. ἃ καὶ πρὸς τὸν χρηστὸν διῆλθον Παλλάδιον, ὃς ἔχων ἃ βούλοιτο πράττειν, ἃ τοῖς νόμοις ἀρέσκει μόνα πράττων διετέλεσεν.

---

[e] The copy of the second edition was evidently entrusted to Proclus on his return from his tenure as *Comes* in 384.

[f] Pagrae (Malalas 202) or Phlegrae (*Or.* 5.41) was the first post station on the main road north from Antioch (*Or.*

## 174. Κύρῳ

1. Οὐκ αἰσχύνομαι τῶν βουλευόντων ἁπάντων κηδόμενος καὶ πάντας ἐμαυτοῦ πολίτας ἡγούμενος καὶ χαίρων τε ἐν ταῖς ἐκείνων τιμαῖς καὶ στένων ὑβριζομένων. εὑρίσκω δὲ τοῦτο καὶ τοῖς τιμῶσιν ἀγαθόν· εὑρίσκω γὰρ τοὺς τοιούτους ἄρχοντας εὐδοκιμοῦντας. 2. εἶναι δὲ σὲ τούτων μᾶλλον ἢ 'κείνων βουλόμενος τὸν ἀδελφὸν τὸν Ἀπολλωνίδου πληγὰς ἀκούων λαβεῖν ἐπλήγην

---

[a] *BLZG* 113 (iii), *PLRE* 238 (1). His province is unknown.

[b] An Apollonides is addressed by Libanius in 393 (*Ep.* 1095), when he supports his old pupil Leontius (*BLZG* vi, *PLRE* 14) as suitor for his daughter. Since Leontius had

emissary—entrusted as it was to the most excellent Proclus.[e] To that Pagrae[f] bears witness, for it was there that Olympius took the envelope and delivered it to him personally. 5. This information I also gave to the good Palladius,[g] who, although able to act as he likes, has continued to act only in conformity to the law.

1.93). Olympius, Libanius' friend now dead, had done his duty of ceremonially escorting the outgoing governor, as well as rendering this service for Libanius.

[g] *BLZG* 230 (xvii), *PLRE* 660 (13), outgoing official returning to Constantinople, who is now acting as Libanius' messenger.

## 174. To Cyrus[a]

1. I am not ashamed of any concern for all city councillors, in regarding them all as my fellow citizens, in rejoicing at the honours done them and grieving at the insults they suffer, and I find this to be a blessing to those who honour them, for I find such governors enjoying high repute. 2. I want you to be one of them rather than of the other sort and, when I heard that the brother of Apollonides[b]

been *consularis* of Phoenice in 392, the presumption is that Apollonides was likely to be a *principalis* in his community, and that his brother was a fairly important decurion. If Libanius protests against corporal punishment inflicted on decurions as such, he is likely to have protested even more sharply in this case.

τὴν ψυχὴν εὐνοίᾳ τε τῇ ἐκείνου καὶ σῇ. πῶς γὰρ οὐ δεινὸν Κύρον τὸν ἐν παιδείᾳ γεγενημένον δοκεῖν βλάβην γεγονέναι ταῖς βουλαῖς παραινοῦντα ταῖς πληγαῖς ἄλλοσέ ποι βλέπειν καὶ ζητεῖν καταφυγὴν τὸ βουλεύειν φυγόντας; 3. εἰ μὲν οὖν ἦν λῦσαι τὰ πεπραγμένα, τοῦθ' ἡμᾶς ἔδει ποιεῖν· ἐπεὶ δὲ τοῦτο οὐκ ἔστιν, ἡμερώτερος ὁ λοιπὸς γιγνέσθω χρόνος καὶ παρέχωμεν ἀφορμὰς τῇ φήμῃ βελτίονας.

---

[c] The reign of Theodosius once more saw a decline in official behaviour towards the curiae. In 380 all decurions were immune from torture and floggings (*Cod. Th.* 12.1.80). By 392 only the *principales* were excused these punishments, the lower grade decurions being increasingly

## 175. Ἀνατολίῳ

1. Ἦλθόν τινες παρ' ὑμῶν ὡς ἡμᾶς. ὧν ἦν ἡμῖν ἀκούειν, ὅπως μὲν ἐπλήγης τὴν ψυχὴν ὑβριζομένων ἡμῶν, οἷα δὲ ἐφθέγξω, οἷα δὲ ἐβόησας, οἷα δὲ ἐποίησας. 2. τὸ μὲν οὖν τὴν οἰκίαν ὑμῶν μηδένα πόνον φεύγειν, ᾧ γένοιτ' ἂν τὰ ἡμέτερα βελτίω, θαυμαστὸν οὐδέν· καλὸν δέ σε παύσασθαί

had taken a lashing my heart was lashed, out of my regard for both him and you. It is bound to be a shock that Cyrus, that educated gentleman, should be thought to have become a bane to the city councils, when by his floggings he advises them to look elsewhere and to seek refuge in flight from curial duties.[c] 3. So, if it were possible to undo what has been done, it would be our duty to do so: but since this is impossible, let the remainder of your term be more gentle and let us provide better claims for fame.

victimized (*ibid.* 12.1.126). This, Libanius constantly repeats, is one of the chief reasons for their flight. Both Proclus and Tatianus were notably heavy-handed (*Or.* 46.8), and Cyrus, like Eustathius in Antioch, seems to have followed the official lead in his manhandling of decurions.

## 175. To Anatolius[a]

1. People have reached us from you. From them I was able to hear how sore at heart you were at the insults heaped upon me, of your comments, your protests, and your actions. 2. Well, it is no surprise that your family avoids no task conducive to my betterment, but it is right that you should

[a] *BLZG* 69 (vi), *PLRE* 61 (9), son of Libanius' old friend Anatolius (ii),(4) of Cilicia, brother of Apolinarius and Gemellus, who were to help Cimon after his injury on his way home. An influential senator at this time.

τε καὶ παῦσαι τὴν σπουδὴν ταύτην καὶ σιωπῆσαι καὶ ἐᾶσαι νικᾶν τοὺς τῆς νίκης ταύτης ἐπιθυμοῦντας. οὓς εὐξαίμην ἂν ἐγὼ πολλὰ τοιαῦτα καὶ νικᾶν καὶ φιλοτιμεῖσθαι ταῖς νίκαις. 3. σὺ δ' ἡμῖν τὸν ἡμέτερον ἀπόπεμψον πείσας μηδὲν τῶν τοιούτων νομίζειν ἀφόρητον. καὶ μήτε ἀρχῆς ἐπιθυμείτω μήτε ἄλλου τινὸς ὧν οὐ θέμις, ἀλλ' ἀγρῶν καὶ δένδρων καὶ μελιττῶν τὸ αὐτῶν ἐργαζομένων. εἰ μὲν γὰρ προσεῖχεν οἷς ἔλεγον, οὐδ' ἂν ὕβριστο· παριδὼν δὲ ἐκεῖνα παρὰ σοῦ πεισθήτω μὴ πλείω χρόνον ἀποστερεῖν ἑαυτὸν τῶν ἑαυτοῦ.

---

[b] See Appendix, Note on *Letters* 169–170. The date is now 391. Cimon's nomination to the governorship of Cyprus has been cancelled following heated protests in the Senate. In the debate in the Senate Libanius himself, no less than Cimon, came in for criticism and abuse (*Epp.* 1000.3, 1002.4).

## 176. Ἡρακλείῳ

1. Οὐ τοσοῦτον οἶδα ἔχων, σὺ δέ μοι καὶ τοσοῦτον δίδως πρᾶγμα ποιῶν ἐρῶντος, ὃ ποιεῖν ἤρξω πάλαι. τοιοῦτος δὲ ὁ δαίμων οὗτος ὁ τὸ τόξον

cease and put a stop to this enthusiasm of yours: stay silent and let those who hanker after a victory of this kind have it. My prayer would be for them to win many such victories and pride themselves upon them! 3. Send me my boy home: make him believe that there is nothing intolerable in any of this. Do not let him desire office or any other forbidden fruit, but fields and trees and bees that mind their own business; for if he had paid attention to what I told him, he would have been spared such insult. But though he ignored that, let him take your advice not to deprive himself of his own any longer.[b]

Whereas his commendation of Cimon's appointment had been sent to two of his friends of prefectural standing, Libanius now implores three family or personal friends of less standing, but perhaps of more reliability, to get the lad out of Constantinople, where he seems to have been ready to stay for another attempt in a case that Libanius now recognized as hopeless.

## 176. To Heracleius[a]

1. I did not know I had so much, but you offer just me so much, behaving like a lover, as you began to do long ago. Such is the nature of this god to

[a] *BLZG* 172 (iv), *PLRE* 419 (7). At present *praeses Armeniae,* he had been advocate in Antioch in the 380s (*Or.* 28.9, 13; 54.13, 76), and therefore a colleague of Cimon.

ἔχων καὶ τὸ πῦρ, καὶ τὸν οὐ καλὸν πολλάκις καλὸν ἀναγκάζει νομίζειν καὶ θαυμάζειν τε καὶ ἕπεσθαι καὶ ἐπαινεῖν καὶ τοῖς οὐκ ἐπαινοῦσιν ἐγκαλεῖν οὐκ ἐπαινοῦσι. 2. τοιοῦτον δή τί μοι δοκεῖς πεπονθέναι καὶ αὐτός· εἶναι λόγους ἐν ἡμῖν οἵους οὐ παρ' ἄλλῳ νομίζεις. εἶτα τοὺς ἄλλους οὐ πείθων ἀγανακτεῖς εἰκότως οὐ πειθομένων. ἐγὼ δὲ χαίρω μὲν ὑπὸ σοῦ φιλούμενος, δέομαι δέ σου τῆς ἐν τοῖς ἐπαίνοις ὑπερβολῆς ἀφελεῖν, ὅπως μὴ τοὺς αἰτιωμένους ἔχοιμεν μηδὲ τοὺς καταγελῶντας. 3. τοῦτο μὲν οὖν μοι χαριῇ· χαριῇ δὲ καὶ αὐτὸν Νεμέσιον ποιήσας πρὸς ἡμᾶς δίκαιον. ἥκει δὲ ταυτί σοι γράμματα ποιοῦντά σοι τὸν λόγον εὐσχήμονα. 4. τὰ δ' ἐν τῇ Μεγάλῃ πόλει περὶ τὸν οὐκ ἀξιώσαντα δέξασθαι τὴν ἡμετέραν παραίνεσιν, ὕβρισται μὲν ὁ ἐμός, ὕβρισμαι δὲ ἐγὼ τῶν καταβοώντων ἐχόντων οὓς ἔτερπον. 5. ἀλλ' ἐμοὶ μὲν οὐ πάνυ δεινὰ ταῦτα πολλὰ τοιαῦτα ἐνηνοχότι· τὸν δ' ἀκούω τῇ διὰ ταῦτα λύπῃ νοσεῖν καί τινα καὶ φόβον ἔχειν ταύτην τὴν νόσον. 6. πέμπε δὴ πρὸς αὐτὸν

[b] Eros; cf. Moschus 1.18–23, *ibid.* fr. iv (*Bucolici Graeci*, ed. A. S. F. Gow, Oxford 1952, pp. 139, 152).

[c] *PLRE* 622 (1), an Armenian, pupil of Libanius in the

whom belong the bow and the torch;[b] he often forces us to think of the ugly as beautiful, to admire it, to pursue and commend it, and to reprove those who do not commend for not doing so. 2. You too seem to me to have been affected by some such passion: you think that there is in me an eloquence without peer. Then when you fail to convince the rest, you are annoyed, though they have good grounds for not being convinced. I am glad to be the object of your affections, but I beg you to put off exaggeration in your commendations, that I may not have people to accuse me or yet to make a mock of me. 3. Do me this favour, then, and favour me also by allowing Nemesius[c] too to do his duty towards me. This letter comes to you giving you a decent pretext. 4. As for what happened in the capital to my son after he refused to accept my advice,[d] he has been insulted and so have I, since our detractors had an audience they could delight. 5. As far as I am concerned, I am not particularly worried by this, since I have put up with plenty of this sort of thing, but I am told that he is sick with grief because of it, and that this sickness even gives some cause for anxiety. 6. Send him a letter, then, and let this advise him at

350s and now a decurion, Nemesius wished to visit Antioch, but required the governor's permission to leave (cf. *Ep. 1019; Petit, Étudiants* 50, 160).

[d] Libanius now comes to his main point, the plea to get Cimon away from Constantinople. This backs up *Epp.* 1000–1.

ἐπιστολήν, ἡ δὲ συμβουλευέτω γνωρίσαι ποτὲ τὴν πατρίδα καὶ μὴ τὴν τιμῶσαν ἀτιμάζειν. 7. ἀλλὰ σύ γε[1] αὐτὴν ποιήσεις καὶ ἄνδρας ἔχειν [καὶ] πλείους[2] τοὺς μὲν πείθων μὴ φεύγειν, τοὺς δὲ κατιέναι. εἰ δὲ δὴ καὶ τὸ τῶν ἀέρων εἰς ἄρχοντα ἤρχετο, καὶ τούτους ἂν ἐποίεις ἡμερωτέρους.

[1] In Mss. the letter ends with ἀτιμάζειν, ἀλλὰ σύ γε marking the beginning of another letter. Corrected by Wolf.

[2] [καὶ] πλείους F.  καὶ πόλεις Wolf (Mss.).

## 177. Συμμάχῳ

1. Χρηστῆς νυκτὸς ἀπολαύσας διὰ τοιούτων ὀνειράτων γενομένης ἡμέρας συγγενόμενος τοῖς φίλοις ἔλεγόν τε τἀν τῇ νυκτὶ πρὸς αὐτοὺς καὶ ἅμα προὔλεγον ἔσεσθαί τι καλὸν εἰς ἔργον τὸ φανθὲν ἄγον. 2. τῆς τοίνυν ἡμέρας προελθούσης εἰς ὥραν τρίτην ὄντων τε ἡμῶν ἐν μέσοις τοῖς πόνοις Κοδράτος ὁ βέλτιστος, ὁ μακάριος — πῶς

[a] *BLZG* 284 (i), *PLRE* 865 (4), F/Kr. no 63. Cf. *Q. Aurelii Symmachi quae supersunt,* ed. Seeck, 1883 (repr. 1961).

For Symmachus, the chief supporter of paganism in

long last to recognize his own city and not to dishonour her who honours him. 7. You at least will ensure that she has even more men, by inducing people either not to flee from her or else to return to her. Indeed if the weather too were in a governor's control, you would make even that more gentle.[e]

[e] If Heracleius at a distance can provide this one example of curial recruitment (by persuading Cimon to return), he will be doing what governors on the spot had found impossible. Reference to the weather suggests a date in late winter of 391.

## 177. To Symmachus[a]

1. I enjoyed a good night, such were my dreams. When it was day I met my friends, told them of my dreams of the night and also foretold that something good would happen since the vision would bring it to fruition.[b] 2. So the day proceeded to the third hour and I was in the midst of my task when Quadratus, that excellent, that blessed fellow—for

Rome and consul in 391, to write to Libanius as a mark of friendship was a most prestigious event, marking rapprochement between the most famous pagan publicists of East and West. The letter does not survive. The earliest date of its writing is likely to be autumn 391.

[b] As a devoted pagan, Libanius throughout his life was a firm believer in oneiromancy (*Or.* 1.67, 143, 245), though he well recognized the risks (239).

γὰρ οὐ μακάριος ὁ σοὶ συνδιατρίψας; — εἰσελθὼν ὡς ἐμὲ τίθησιν εἰς χεῖρά μοι τὴν ἐπιστολὴν τοῦτ᾽ αὐτὸ λέγων, ὅτι σή. 3. καὶ παραχρῆμα πᾶν τὸ λυποῦν ἔφευγε, — πολλὰ δὲ ταῦτα ἦν πολὺν ἤδη χρόνον ἐγκείμενά τε καὶ ὀδυνῶντα — καί μέ τις εἶχεν ἡδονὴ μείζων τῆς ἐν τοῖς φιλοχρημάτοις γιγνομένης, ὅταν ἔλθῃ ποθὲν αὐτοῖς χρήματα. 4. καὶ ταυτὶ μὲν πρὸ τῆς ἀναγνώσεως· ἤδη δὲ ἑρμηνέως τυχούσης δεινὸν ἡγησάμην, εἰ μὴ τὴν πόλιν ἐμπλήσαιμι τοῦ δώρου τῆς Τύχης, καὶ παραδοὺς τρισὶ τῶν φίλων τὴν ἐπιστολὴν ἐκέλευον πᾶσαν ἐπιόντας τὴν πόλιν τοῖς ἡδέως ἔχουσι πρὸς ἡμᾶς δεικνύειν καὶ τοῖς οὐχ οὕτω, τοῖς μέν, ὅπως χαίροιεν, τοῖς δ᾽, ἵνα ἀποπνίγοιντο. 5. οἵδε μὲν οὖν ἐσίγων τὴν τῶν ἀνιωμένων σιγήν, οἱ δ᾽ ἦσαν ἐν ἑορτῇ σοῦ ταύτην αὐτοῖς ποιοῦντος τὴν ἑορτὴν εὐδαιμόνιζόν τε καὶ ἐμὲ καὶ σέ, τοῦ τετιμῆσθαι μὲν ἐμέ, σὲ δὲ τοῦ τετιμηκέναι· κεχαρίσθαι γὰρ ἐν τούτῳ σε τοῖς λογίοις θεοῖς ἐγείραντα τοὺς νέους ἐπὶ τοὺς λόγους, ἐν ᾧ καὶ τὴν ἄρχουσαν εὖ πεποίηκας πόλιν τοὺς ἀρχομένους

[c] The time of day is 9–10 a.m. Quadratus is otherwise unknown.

he must surely be blessed since his time is spent in association with you—came in and placed the letter into my hand, saying quite simply that it was from you.[c] 3. And straightaway all my troubles fled—and these were many that have long assailed me, causing me pain.[d] A joy possessed me greater than that of misers when they happen to get money. 4. And that was before the reading of it! When a translator had been got for it,[e] I thought it a shame not to fill the whole city with the gift of Fortune, and so I handed the letter over to three of my friends and told them to go through the whole city and to show it both to those well disposed towards me and to those who were not, in the first case for their pleasure, in the second, that they should choke with chagrin.[f] 5. So these last maintained a resentful silence, and the others were in holiday mood, this holiday of theirs being your doing, and they counted me blessed for the honour received and you for that bestowed, for you had obliged the gods of eloquence by rousing the students towards eloquence at the very time when you conferred kindnesses even upon the ruling city by exhorting your subjects to proper

[d] In particular, the disasters that had afflicted Cimon.

[e] Like his uncle Phasganius, Libanius had no Latin. Letters from such as Symmachus and Postumianus had to be translated (cf. *Letter* 181).

[f] Cf. *Ep.* 1059.5. As he grew older Libanius increasingly recognized his unpopularity in Antioch, which had come as such a shock to him in *Oration* 2.

ἐφ' ἃ δεῖ παρακαλῶν. 6. ἐν μὲν οὖν τοῖς γράμμασιν, ὅπερ αὐτὸς ἔφης, ἔφθης· ἐγὼ δὲ νενίκηκα τῷ φιλῆσαι πρότερος. ἀπὸ γὰρ ἐκείνου δὴ φιλῶ τοῦ χρόνου, ὃς πατέρα τὸν σὸν δεῦρο ἡμῖν ἤγαγε τῶν θεῶν οἷς ἡμῶν μέλει τοῦτο ἡμῖν διδόντων, ὅπως ἡμῖν ᾖ καὶ θεᾶσθαι τὸν ἄριστον Σύμμαχον. 7. ὃς τέταρτος μὲν ἧκε, μόνος δὲ εἰς αὑτὸν ἐπέστρεφε τὴν πόλιν ἀγαθῶν ἀμείνων δεικνύμενος ἔν τε τοῖς ἄλλοις καὶ ἐν ἐξετάσει λόγων, ᾧ με καὶ τρέχειν ὡς αὐτὸν καθ' ἡμέραν ἔπεισε. καὶ ἦμεν ἐν τῷ τι περὶ τῶν παλαιῶν ἀεὶ λέγειν, ὧν ὁ τόκος παιδεία τοῖς ἄλλοις. 8. ὁρῶν δέ με οὐ πάνυ τῶν ἀποβλήτων ἁνὴρ πολλὰ περὶ τῆς σῆς φύσεως διεξιὼν ᾔτει παρὰ τῶν θεῶν γενέσθαι τι τοιοῦτον, ὅ σε ποιήσει τῶν ἐμῶν πόνων μεταλαβεῖν. καὶ προσετίθην ἐγὼ τὴν αὐτὴν εὐχήν, καὶ τούτοις οὕτω διετέθην ὥσθ' ἣν ἔσχον ἂν περὶ σοῦ γνώμην πεπραγμένων, ταύτην ἔσχον στάντων ἐν εὐχῇ τῶν πραγμάτων. τοιγαροῦν ἥσθην τε πλέοντος ἐξ

[g] Symmachus was renowned for his oratory. The fragments appear in Seeck's edition. Now consul, Symmachus had been prefect of the city of Rome in 384–5; cf. Symm. *Relationes* (Letters Bk. x).

[h] His father was L. Aurelius Avianius Symmachus

matters.[g] 6. In your letter, as you yourself remark, you have anticipated me; but I have had the better of you in being the first with my affection: it dates from the time which brought your father to us here, when the gods, under whose care we are, granted us that we should even see the excellent Symmachus.[h] 7. He came as one of four, but alone he attracted the city to himself since he showed himself better than the good, particularly in his appreciation of eloquence, and in so doing he induced me to hasten to him every day. And we were continually engaged in discussion of the classical authors, whose products form the basis of education. 8. When he saw that I was not one to be dismissed out of hand, he told me much of your ability and prayed that by grace of the gods there would occur some such eventuality as would make you participate in my exertions.[i] And I made the same prayer too, and was so affected by this that, even while its fulfilment remained a matter for prayer, my attitude towards you was as it would have been, had it been fulfilled. At any rate, I rejoiced when

Phosphorius, *PLRE* 863 (3), prefect of Rome in 364–5. Libanius evidently refers to the embassy of 361 sent to Constantius, which met Julian at Naissus on the way home; cf. Amm. Marc. 21.12.24; Seeck, *Regesten der Kaiser und Päpste für die Jahre 311 bis 476 n. Chr.* (Stuttgart 1919) p. 208 for his stay in Antioch.

[i] In 361, the young Symmachus was still studying rhetoric, aged no more than 20.

οὐρίων κἂν τῇ ταραχῇ τῆς θαλάττης ἔδεισα καὶ πάλιν λείας γενομένης ἐχάρην. 9. προκαλούμενος οὖν με φίλον εἶναι τὸν ὄντα προκαλῇ καὶ κελεύων ἀντεπιστέλλειν, ὃ καὶ μὴ κελεύοντος ἂν ἐπράττετο. ἴσην δὲ ἀπαιτων ἐπιστολὴν οὐ δυνατὰ ζητεῖς. καὶ γὰρ ἂν ἴση μὲν ᾖ τῷ μέτρῳ, μὴ χείρων δὲ τὸ εἶδος, αὐτῷ γε τῷ γράφοντι γίγνεται φαυλοτέρα. δεῖ γάρ με πρότερον καὶ αὐτὸν γενέσθαι Σύμμαχον, εἰ μέλλει τῶν σῶν τἀμὰ μὴ λελείψεσθαι.

---

[j] Symmachus had composed and delivered a panegyric on the usurper Maximus. After his fall, Symmachus was disgraced and prosecuted for treason. He sought refuge in

## 178. Τατιανῷ

1. Ἔχω τὴν τιμὴν λαβὼν ἔν τε τῇ φιάλῃ καὶ τῷ διθύρῳ γραμματείῳ, τὸ μὲν ἐλέφαντος, ἡ δέ ἐστιν ἀργύρου. καὶ τοῖς μὲν ἄλλοις, οἳ τὴν σὴν οὐκ ἐπίστανται φύσιν, θαυμαστὸν τοῦτο ἐδόκει καὶ οὐκ ἐλπιζόμενον ἥκειν, ἐμοὶ δὲ ἐλπίδα τε ἐπλήρωσε καὶ μαντείαν· εἶπον γὰρ ἥξειν τὰ ἥκοντα πρὶν

your course was set fair, was afraid when you were tempest-tossed, and glad when it was all plain sailing once again.[j] 9. So in inviting me to be your friend, you invite one who is a friend already, and in bidding me write to you in reply, you bid me do what I would have done even without your bidding. But when you demand a letter equal to your own, you are seeking the impossible. It may be its equal in length and no worse in style, but it becomes inferior simply because of its composer. I must myself first become a Symmachus, if my letters are not to fall short of yours.

a Christian church, and was pardoned, the charges being dropped. He then wrote an apology and a panegyric on Theodosius, who thereupon restored him to favour (Socr. *H.E.* 5.14; cf. Symm. *Ep.* 2.13, 31; 8.69).

## 178. To Tatianus

1. I have received your compliment consisting of the silver goblet and ivory writing tablets.[a] Other people, who do not know your nature, regarded its coming as remarkable and unexpected, but it fulfilled my expectation and auguries, for I said that what has come would come, before ever it arrived.

[a] Tatianus had sent Libanius a belated peace offering, acknowledging the congratulations sent upon his entry to the consulship of 391. It came as a great relief to Libanius after the recent snubs he had endured. For γραμματεῖον δίθυρον cf. *Or.* 51.11; Pollux *Onom.* 4.18.

ἥκειν. 2. ὧν ἐλθόντων τε καὶ φανέντων καὶ δοθέντων δρόμος τῶν ἐπιτηδείων παρ' ἡμᾶς χαιρόντων τε καὶ συγχαιρόντων. ἐγὼ δὲ τῆς μὲν τιμῆς ἐζηλούμην, τῷ δὲ ὡς τιμήσομαι προειπεῖν ἐθαυμαζόμην. 3. τιμὴ δέ μοι καὶ τὸ διὰ τοιούτου κεκομίσθαι τὴν τιμήν, ᾧ κόσμος μὲν ὁ πατήρ, κόσμος δὲ αὐτὸς αὑτῷ τῇ τε ἀρετῇ καὶ τῷ τρόπῳ καὶ τῷ κάλλει τῶν λόγων· ὧν εἰς κάλλος ἀπήλαυσε καὶ τὰ σὰ τυχόντα φωνῆς πρεπούσης. 4. πεποίηται δέ τί σοι καὶ παρὰ τοὐμοῦ γήρως, οἷον εἰκὸς παρὰ γήρως γενέσθαι, ῥώμην μὲν οὐ παραδεικνύον, ἔρωτα δέ. τίς δ' οὐκ ἂν ἐρασθείη τοιαῦτα μὲν εὑρίσκοντος ὑπάρχου, τοῖς δὲ εὑρισκομένοις προστιθέντος τὰ τέλη; δι' ὧν πάλιν γίγνομαι μάντις καί φημι σὲ μὲν αὖθις ἴσα πέμψειν ἐφ' ἴσοις, ἐμαυτὸν δὲ καὶ λήψεσθαι καὶ γράφειν.

[b] Priscianus, *BLZG* 245 (ii), *PLRE* 728 (4); cf. *Epp.* 1022, *Letter* 179. He had evidently delivered a panegyric to Tatianus on the occasion of his consulship.

## 179. Ἀνατολίῳ

1. Πρὸς εἰδότας μέν, ὅμως δὲ ἀπήγγειλεν ὁ καλὸς Πρισκιανός, οἷος μὲν ἔξω γένοιο τοῦ βουλευ-

2. When they arrived, were displayed and handed to me, my acquaintances rushed to visit me, with gratification and congratulation; I became an object of envy for the compliment done me, and of surprise for having foretold that I would be complimented. 3. I am also complimented that your compliment has been received through the agency of such an emissary,[b] whose prestige lies in his parentage and his personal gifts of virtue, conduct, and his glorious eloquence, which your own achievements, after obtaining a voice that befits them, have enjoyed to glorious purpose. 4. A piece has been composed for you by me even in my old age, of a kind to be expected from old age, showing evidence not of power but of affection.[c] Who could not but feel affection for a prefect who plans such measures, and brings his plans to completion? In consequence, I resume the role of seer, and foretell that you will again send the like on like occasions, and that I will both receive it and write in acknowledgement.[d]

[c] For this oration see Foerster, 11:634. Libanius was now 77.

[d] He was to be disappointed in his forecast, for in the next year the fall of Tatianus was engineered with brutal efficiency by Rufinus.

## 179. To Anatolius

1. The noble Priscianus informed me, though I already knew it, of your attitude towards my son both outside and inside the Senate House, and of

τηρίου περὶ τὸν ἡμέτερον, οἷος δὲ ἐν αὐτῷ, καὶ οἷος μὲν μελλούσης ῥηθήσεσθαι τῆς δίκης, οἷος δὲ λεγομένης, οἷος δὲ ἐκβάσης, ὡς ἐξέβη. 2. πάντων οὖν σοι τούτων ἔχομέν τε χάριν καὶ ἐπαινοῦμεν, ἅ μοι δοκεῖ καὶ παρ' αὐτῶν ἐπαινεῖσθαι τῶν θεῶν, ὥσπερ αὖ καὶ τὰ τῶν ἀδελφῶν σου περὶ τὸν αὐτόν. ἃ εἰ μὴ τότε ἔκαμόν τε ἐκεῖνοι καὶ εἰσήνεγκαν φροντίδας καὶ ἰατροὺς καὶ ἀγρυπνίαν καὶ δαπάνην, ᾤχετ' ἂν οὗτος ἢ ἄνευ ποδὸς ἔζη. 3. τούτων δὴ τῶν τε λόγων[1] καὶ ἔργων ἴσθι κεισομένην ἐν ἐμοὶ μνήμην ἀθάνατον. χάρις δὲ καὶ Πρισκιανῷ τῆς τε λύπης ἣν ὑπὲρ ἡμῶν ἐλυπήθη καὶ τῆς ἡδονῆς μεθ' ἧς τὰ ὑμέτερα διηγεῖτο. οὐ γὰρ δὴ διηγεῖτο μόνον, ἀλλὰ καὶ μετὰ τοῦ χαίρειν ἡμῶν μὲν εὖ παθόντων ὑφ' ὑμῶν, ὑμῶν δὲ εὐδοκιμούντων. 4. ἀλλὰ κἀκεῖνο μέντοι πρόσθες· πεῖθε τὴν μεγάλην βουλὴν ὡς οὔτ' ἐμὸν ἐκεῖνο τόλμημα οὔτε τοῦ πεπορευμένου, τῶν δ' ἀναπτερωσάντων οὐ μίσει μὲν τοιαῦτα διαλεχθέντων, ἰδεῖν δὲ καλῶς τὸ πρᾶγμα οὐ δυνηθέντων. μήτ' οὖν ἐμέ τις ὡς ἀγνοήσαντα τὰ ἡμέτερα μεμφέσθω κἀκείνῳ τις ἐχέτω συγγνώμην.

[1] καὶ before λόγων Wolf (Mss.), om. F.

your attitude both before and while the case was pleaded, and after it was settled in the way it was. 2. So I am grateful to you for all this and praise the actions which, I am sure, are praised by the gods themselves, as too was your brothers' kindness towards him.[a] Had they not undertaken those exertions then, supplying him with care and medical attention, and spending watchful nights and money on him, he would be dead, or alive without his leg. 3. Of these words and actions, then, you may be sure that there will remain with me a memory imperishable.[b] I am grateful to Priscianus too for the grief he evinced on my account and for the pleasure he took in speaking of you. He gave no bald recital, but spoke with pleasure, since I was the recipient of your kindness and you won acclaim for it. 4. But grant me this one thing more. Persuade the august Senate that it was no misconduct either of mine or of my son who had made the journey, but of those who egged him on, making the remarks they did not through hatred, but through inability to view the situation properly. Do not, then, let anyone reprove me for being unaware of my station, and let my son be pardoned.

[a] Apolinarius and Gemellus of Tarsus, who saw to Cimon's welfare after his accident; cf. *Or.* 1.279. At the time of writing Cimon had still not arrived home. It is clear from *Ep.* 1026.5 that he died shortly after reaching Antioch (*pace* Martin, Libanios, *Autobiographie* 279).

[b] A reminiscence of Aeschin. *in Ctes.* 182.

## 180. Ῥιχομήρει

1. Πολλὰ πολλάκις ἡμᾶς εἰς ἑορτῶν ἄγει μνήμην. ἐν οὖν τῇ μνήμῃ τῶν ἑορτῶν καὶ τῶν ἡμερῶν ἐκείνων μνημονεύομεν, παρ' ὧν ἡμῖν ἐδόθη τὸ σοὶ συνδιατρίψαι, καὶ τιμῶμεν τὰς ἡμέρας ἐκείνας τῷ τῶν ἑορτῶν ὀνόματι τὰ δίκαια ποιοῦντες. 2. σὺ γὰρ δὴ καὶ ἥκων ἡμῖν καὶ συνὼν ἡμέρας μέλιτος ἡδίους ἡμῖν ἐποίεις τὰς ὁμιλίας, ὥσθ' οἱ μὲν ἀπῄεσαν μεστοὶ χαρᾶς, οἱ δ' εἰσῄεσαν ἐπ' ἴσοις, καὶ πᾶν μὲν λυπηρὸν ἐπεφεύγει, παρεῖχες δὲ εὐφροσύνης ἀφορμάς. ὁ δὲ πλέον τῶν ἄλλων ἔχων ἦν ἐγὼ ζητούμενός τε ἀεὶ καὶ καλούμενος καὶ πρὸς τῷ τοίχῳ λόγων ἀκούων ὧν οὐκ ἄλλοι. 3. τὸ οὖν ἐκ τούτων καὶ ἐμοὶ καὶ τῇ πόλει φίλτρον ἐγγενόμενον πέπηγέ τε καὶ μένει καὶ οὐδενὶ κινηθήσεται. καὶ εὖ τε πράττοντι συγχαίρομεν †καὶ τά τε†[1] δυσκολώτερα τοῦ

[1] καὶ τά τε Mss. Edd. Reiske suggested corruption. Num εἴτε καὶ τὰ?

---

[a] After the death of Cimon in 391 Libanius suffered another breakdown. His physical ailments got worse, and his eyesight began to fail, so that his letters were interrupted for some time (cf. *Ep.* 1026.6). In due course he

## 180. To Richomer

1. Plenty of things often lead me to the recollection of holidays:[a] so in the recollection of holidays, I also call to mind those days when it was granted me to spend my time with you, and I honour those days with the name of holidays, and quite rightly too![b] 2. In fact when you came and joined us, you turned our association into days sweeter than honey for us, so that some used to go away filled with joy, while others entered with a like end in view, and every trouble had vanished, while you provided the means for happiness. And the one who enjoyed that more than the rest was I, for I was ever the object of your inquiry and invitation, and against the wall[c] I would hear words which no others heard. 3. The resulting affection engendered in the city and myself has stayed firm and endures, and will never be moved. We rejoice with you in your success, and in the event of something more irksome than is

resumed his teaching and his declamations, but now at home (*Or.* 1.280). The present letter is written after this break and, with its recollections of holidays past, may be dated to the early months of 392 after the New Year festival.

[b] For the same sentiments addressed to Richomer cf. *Ep.* 1007.

[c] Cf. *Ep.* 892.1; Plat. *Gorg.* 485d.

προσήκοντος τετύχηκεν εὐχαί τε ἡμῖν πρὸς τοὺς θεοὺς πανταχοῦ σε τύχης ἀπολαύειν τῆς βελτίονος δεῦρό τε αὖθις ἐλθεῖν σὺν τῷ θείῳ βασιλεῖ καὶ πάλιν ἐπιβῆναι τῆς φίλης τῷ Ἀπόλλωνι Δάφνης, ἣν ἐτίμησας δρόμῳ τε τῷ εἰς αὐτὴν καὶ τῷ διὰ πάσης τοὺς ὀφθαλμοὺς ἐνεγκεῖν, καὶ ταῦτα ἐν μιᾶς ἡμέρας μέρει· τῶν γάρ, οἶμαι, πραγμάτων ἐφ᾽ ἑαυτὰ καλούντων οὐκ ἐνῆν πλέον τι τῇ Δάφνῃ χαρίσασθαι. 4. τουτὶ μὲν οὖν δοῦναι τῶν θεῶν, ὧν ἱερὰ πολλὰ μὲν ἡμῖν ἐν τῇ πόλει, πολλὰ δὲ περὶ αὐτήν· τἀμὰ δέ, καὶ ὧν ἐστερήμεθα καὶ ἐν οἷς κείμεθα, γράμμασι μὲν οὐκ ἔδοξέ μοι διὰ μῆκος παραδοῦναι, τῇ φωνῇ δὲ ἀφεῖναι τοῦ χρηστοῦ Παλλαδίου. ᾧ μισθὸν εἴ σε φαίην ὀφείλειν, οὐκ ἂν αἰτιάσαιο· μέτριον γὰρ οὕτω δή τι καὶ ἐπιεικῆ παρέσχεν αὑτὸν πρὸς πάντας ἀνθρώπους, καὶ οὐδεὶς ὑπ᾽ οὐδενὸς ἠδίκηται διὰ τὸ Παλλάδιον δύνασθαι, ὥστε σοι πᾶσαι μὲν ἀπὸ εὐφημίαι στόματος, ἔγκλημα δὲ οὐδὲ ἓν οὐδαμόθεν.

proper,[d] our prayers to the gods are that everywhere you may enjoy better fortune, and come here once more with our divine emperor, and again set foot in Daphne, the beloved of Apollo. You honoured it by a flying visit and casting your eyes on the whole of it, all in part of a single day, for obviously, since affairs of state demanded your attention, you could not favour Daphne any further.[e] 4. This then is for the gods to grant, whose many temples we have in and around our city.[f] As for my own affairs, my loss and my present plight, I have decided not to dwell upon them at length by letter, but to entrust them to the voice of the good Palladius,[g] If I were to say that you owe him reward, you would not hold that against me, for he has behaved so sensibly and decently towards everyone, and nobody has been victimized by anyone because of Palladius' influence, and in consequence from every lip comes acclamation of every kind for you, and not a single reproach from any quarter.

[d] The text here is uncertain.

[e] The plea repeats that of *Letter* 172.

[f] For the temples remaining in Antioch in 384 see *Or.* 30.51.

[g] The death of Cimon in particular, as shown in *Ep.* 1026. Palladius (cf. *Letter* 173) seems to be returning to court after holding office as *Comes Orientis*; *BLZG* 230 (xvii), *PLRE* 660 (13). He stood very close to Richomer, and on this occasion is deputed by Libanius to supplement the letter with full verbal information.

## 181. Ποστουμιανῷ

1. Οἱ πάντα ὁρῶντες θεοὶ καὶ τοῖς πεπληγμένοις τῶν ἀνθρώπων εἰωθότες βοηθεῖν ἰδόντες με καταβεβλημένον καὶ κείμενον ὑπὸ τῆς νῦν συμφορᾶς τό τε πλῆθος τῶν εἰς παραμυθίαν εἰρημένων λόγων οὐδὲν δυνηθὲν φάρμακόν τι τοῦτο ἰσχυρὸν τὴν σὴν ἐξεῦρον ἐπιστολήν. 2. ἧς ἦν μέν τι κέρδος καὶ προτεινομένης ἔτι Ἱλαρίου τοῦ καλοῦ τοῦτο ποιοῦντος, πλέον δ' ἑρμηνευομένης, πόνος δὲ ἄρα τὸ πρᾶγμα γεγένηται τοῖς ἄγουσιν εἰς τὴν ἡμετέραν φωνὴν τὴν ὑμετέραν, καὶ ὁ νικήσας <τῷ>[1] τὸ προσιὸν ἑλεῖν[2] ἐστεφανοῦτο. 3. ἐγὼ δὲ ῥᾴων ἐδεικνύμην τῇ τιμῇ καί μέ τις τῶν συνήθων εἶδε μειδιάσαντα, καὶ τὸ νέφος οὐκέτ' ἦν ἴσον οὔτ' ἐπὶ τῆς ψυχῆς οὔτ' ἐπὶ τοῦ προσώπου. καὶ θαυμαστὸν οὐδὲν τιμὴν τοσαύτην ἤκουσαν δι' ἐπιστολῆς τοῦ πρώτου Ῥωμαίων — ὁ δὲ τοῦτ' εἰπὼν εἶπε· πάντων ἀνθρώπων — ἰσχύσαι λύπης ἀφελεῖν τι καὶ καταμίξαι τι γαλήνης. 4. δοκεῖς δέ μοι δίκαιος εἶναι πειρώμενος κατὰ τὸν Αἰγινήτην

[1] <τῷ> F.
[2] ἑλεῖν F. ἐλθεῖν Wolf (Mss.).

## 181. To Postumianus[a]

1. The all-seeing gods whose habit it is to assist the afflicted among mortals have seen me cast down and prostrate under my present misfortune and all expression of consolation to be of no avail, and they have devised your letter to be the potent charm that it is.[b] 2. Even its delivery was of good effect, while the noble Hilarius[c] was performing that act, and its translation even more. The translators were put to it to render your Latin into Greek, and the best at comprehending each succeeding passage[d] was crowned as victor. 3. I showed more cheerfulness at your compliment, and some of my friends saw me smiling, and the cloud lay not so heavily either upon my heart or on my brow.[e] It is no cause for surprise that such a compliment addressed by letter from the foremost of the Romans—and that means the foremost of all mankind—should have the power to relieve my pain somewhat and to infuse some calm into it. 4. But it seems to me that, though you attempt to be just, as Aeacus of

[a] A member of one of the noblest of Roman families. *BLZG* 243 (iii), *PLRE* 718 (3). F/Kr. no. 67. Date: 392.

[b] The terminology throughout the letter is thoroughly pagan.

[c] *BLZG* 179 (vii), *PLRE* 435 (8), *consularis* of Palestine. Since he handed over the letter to Libanius, it must have come by the imperial post.

[d] Cf. *Decl.* 3.27 (Foerster V:218.3).

[e] Cf. Anaxandr. Comic. fr. 58 (ii.160 K).

Αἰακὸν ἓν οὐ δίκαιον ποιεῖν φεύγων ἐν οἷς ἐπιστέλλεις τὴν Ἑλλήνων γλῶτταν. ἣν σὺ προσέθηκας τῇ παρὰ τοῦ γένους πολλῇ μὲν ἐπιθυμίᾳ, πολλοῖς δὲ ἱδρῶσι, τοῖς μὲν ἐν ἡλίῳ, τοῖς δὲ πρὸς λύχνον, δι' ὧν ἐνέπλησας τὴν ψυχὴν Ὁμήρου τε καὶ Ἡσιόδου καὶ τῶν ἄλλων ποιητῶν Δημοσθένους τε καὶ Λυσίου καὶ τῶν ἄλλων ῥητόρων. 5. εἴποι δ' ἂν Ἡρόδοτός τε καὶ Θουκυδίδης καὶ πᾶς ἐκείνων ὁ χορὸς εἶναι χώραν καὶ αὐτοῖς ἐν τῇ σῇ διανοίᾳ καὶ τούτου μάρτυρας εἶναι τοὺς πεποιημένους σοι λόγους τοὺς πολλούς τε καὶ καλούς. 6. καὶ ταῦτα οὐ νῦν μὲν ἔγνωσται, πρότερον δὲ ἠγνοεῖτο, ἀλλὰ καὶ πρὸ τῶν ἐπιδείξεων ἐπιστεύετο[3] καὶ ἐν αὐταῖς καὶ μετ' ἐκείνας λόγος οὐκ ὀλίγος περὶ τῶν σῶν ἐκγόνων,[4] λόγων. τουτὶ δὲ κοινὸν ἁπάσης οἰκίας, ᾗ θεοὶ πρόγονοι, τὸ δ' ἄγαν τῆς ὑμετέρας γενεᾶς. 7. κτησάμενος δὴ καὶ

[3] πρὸ τῶν ἐπιδείξων ἐπιστεύετο F., conj. Re. πρῶτον ἐπιστεύετο V, corrected. πρὸ followed by lacuna Vo. πρῶτον ἐπιστεύοντο Wolf.

[4] ἐκγόνων suggested F. ἐγγόνων edd. (Mss.), but cf. Plat. Symp. 209d.

---

[f] Judge of the dead, along with Minos and Rhadamanthys (Plat. *Gorg.* 523e). F/Kr. (p. 447) create unnecessary problems by linking ἓν οὐ δίκαιον ποιεῖν with πειρώμενος. The

Aegina was,[f] in one respect you act unjustly, in that you avoid the use of Greek in your letter.[g] You supplemented your native tongue with knowledge of it by dint of much eagerness and much industry, both by day and by lamplight, and in consequence you have filled your soul with Homer, Hesiod, and the rest of the poets, and Demosthenes, Lysias, and the rest of the orators. 5. Herodotus, Thucydides, and all their company could claim that there is room for them too in your intellect, and as witness of this they could cite the many fine orations you have composed. 6. And this is not something that was unknown in the past and recognized but lately, but before, during, and after your declamations there was no little expression of confidence in those offspring of yours,[h] the expressions of your eloquence. This is a characteristic of every family which has gods in its ancestry, but particularly of your own lineage.[i] 7. So, having gained such a knowledge

reference to Aeacus seems to indicate that Postumianus' letter was indeed a consolatory epistle on Cimon's death.

[g] For Libanius Greek is the sole medium for a proper education. On the importance of the authors listed in §§ 4–5 for the traditional education system see Festugière, *Antioche* 216, 509; Norman, "The Library of Libanius," 158 ff.

[h] Plat. *Symp.* 209d.

[i] This revival of the concept of the divine origin of noble families is in the mouth of Libanius indicative of cultural preeminence only.

ταῦτα ἐπ' ἐκείνοις ὡς δύνασθαι πείθειν, εἰ λέγοις σαυτὸν Ἀθηναῖον, χρῶ πρὸς ἡμᾶς παροῦσιν ἀγαθοῖς καὶ τὰς ἐσομένας ἐπιστολάς — δῆλον[5] γὰρ ὡς ἀρξάμενος οὐ παύσῃ — μὴ πέμψῃς πάλιν εἰς ἑρμηνέων στόματα. 8. τοῦδε μὲν οὖν σὺ κύριος, παρὰ δὲ τῶν θεῶν αἰτῶ δοῦναί μοι τὴν σὴν ἰδεῖν κεφαλὴν ἐν ἀρχομένου τάξει, καθάπερ πάλαι τὸν σὸν θεῖον ἔγνων, ᾧ παῖδα τρέφεις ὁμώνυμον ἐν τῇ πόλει τῆς θεοῦ τῆς δι' ἀγῶνος αὐτὴν λαβούσης. 9. τοῦτό τε οὖν ἐστί μοι πρὸς ὑμᾶς δικαίωμα καί τι καὶ ἕτερον, ὃ δεῖ σε μαθεῖν· ἐν ᾧ γὰρ ἔτει γῆν καὶ θάλατταν ἐπεῖχε τῷ τοῦ ὑπάτου καὶ ὀνόματι καὶ σχήματι πάππος ὁ ὑμέτερος, τότε τῆς μητρὸς ἐκδραμὼν ἐφάνην ἡλίῳ.

[5] δῆλον F. (V) δῆξον Vo. δεῖξον Wolf.

---

[j] Seeck (*BLZG* 243 ii) identified this uncle with Postumianus, praetorian prefect in 383, by reason of the name but the fact that the son of the addressee is the homonymous member of the family tells against this. *PLRE* 719 more cautiously leaves everything an open question, and both the uncle and the son appear in the *Anonymi.* Certainly, in matters of religion at least, there is a wide gap between the Christian praetorian prefect and

of Greek, as well as of Latin, that you would carry conviction if you were to describe yourself as an Athenian, employ your present gifts upon us, and your future letters—for obviously, having once begun, you will not stop—do not again send to the lips of interpreters. 8. This, then, is something in your own power; but from the gods I pray that it be granted me to see your person in the position of governor, as long ago I saw your uncle, whose name is borne by the son you are bringing up in the city of the goddess who obtained it by trial of strength.[j] 9. This then is the basis of my claim upon you, but there is something else too, of which you should be aware. In the very year when your grandfather held sea and land with the title and position of consul I came forth from my mother's womb and saw the light of day.[k]

the Neoplatonist Postumianus. The mythical struggle between Athena and Poseidon for the lordship of Attica was most graphically represented in antiquity by the sculptures on the western pediment of the Parthenon and other works of art (Pausan. i.24.3,5) which Libanius had himself seen (*Ep.* 962), and which he could reasonably expect this student to see during his time in Athens.

[k] From other references for his age given by Libanius, he was born in 314 (*Or.* 1.139; 143). The senior consul for that year was C. Ceionius Rufius Volusianus, the grandfather here mentioned. See stemmata of the Caecinae Sabini and of the Ceionii Rufii (*PLRE* 1136, 1138).

## 182. Φιρμίνῳ

1. Οὐδ᾽ εἰ πᾶσάν μοι τὴν οὐσίαν ἐδεδώκεις τὴν σαυτοῦ καὶ πρὸς αὐτῇ τάς τε τῶν συγγενῶν ἁπάσας καὶ[1] τῶν φίλων, οὐκ ἂν ἦσθα μείζω τῶν νῦν δεδομένων δεδωκώς. 2. τί γάρ μοι τοῦ παρόντος ἢ μεῖζον ἢ ἴσον; Φιρμῖνος ῥίψας τὸν στρατιώτην ἐνέδυ τὸν σοφιστήν. καὶ θρόνος ὁ τούτῳ πρέπων καὶ βάθρα καὶ βίβλοι καὶ νέοι παιδευόμενοι καὶ λόγοι ποιούμενοί τε καὶ δεικνύμενοι δονοῦντες θέατρον μουσικόν· τοιοῦτον γὰρ οἱ Καππαδόκαι. 3. καὶ βραδέως μὲν ταῦτα, οἶσθα γάρ, ἐφ᾽ ἅ σε παρεκάλουν, κέρδος δὲ ὅμως καὶ νῦν, ὦ φίλε Ἀλκιβιάδη, ταῦτά σοί τε καὶ ἐμοί. ὥστε καὶ τοῦ πρώτου ταῦτ᾽ ἀγγείλαντος ὡς ἡμᾶς ἐφίλησα μὲν τὴν κεφαλήν, ἐφίλησα δὲ τὼ ὀφθαλμὼ καθίσας τε ἐγγὺς ἐμαυτοῦ πολλὰ μὲν ἠρόμην περὶ σοῦ, πολλὰ δὲ ἤκουσα, πάντα καλά, εὐεργέτην τε ἡγησάμην ἐμαυτοῦ μετὰ σὲ τὸν δόντα τὰ τοιαῦτα μηνύειν. 4. πάλιν τοίνυν

[1] <τὰς> F., conj. Re., after καὶ

---

[a] *BLZG* 156 (ii), *PLRE* 339 (3); Petit, *Étudiants* 125–7; F/Kr. no. 73.

[b] In 372 Basil wrote *Ep.* 116, encouraging Firminus to escape from army service, which was not to his liking. It

## 182. To Firminus[a]

1. Even had you given me all your possessions, and all those of your relations and friends besides, you would not have given me more than you have done now. 2. What could surpass or equal your present gift? Firminus has cast off the soldier and donned the sophist's guise. And now there is a professor's chair that befits him, benches, books, students under instruction, the composing and declaiming of orations which excite a cultured gathering, which is what the Cappadocians are.[b] 3. And though this career, to which I invited you, has come late in time, as you know, yet even now, my dear Alcibiades,[c] it is pure gain for you and myself. So when the first messenger came with this news, I kissed his head and his eyes, and set him down beside me, and made many inquiries about you, and heard much in reply, all of it good, and regarded him as my benefactor next only to you who allowed him to give me such information. 4. Once again

has therefore taken him twenty years to achieve this. He has now retired at the end of over 30 years of service. Basil implies that the reason for Firminus' resort to a military career was the need to avoid curial service, which may be the cause of this long delay. His present appointment to a municipal chair as sophist, probably in Caesarea in Cappadocia, at last secured him immunity from curial impressment.

[c] So Socrates addressed his pupil, Plat. *Alc.* i.109d, 133b; *Symp.* 218d.

ἥσθην λαβών σου τὴν ἐπιστολὴν καὶ πάλιν ἥσθην λαβών σου ταύτην τὴν δευτέραν, — δύο γάρ ἐστον, κἂν πάνυ πολλὰς αὐτὰς ἐν τοῖς γράμμασι λέγῃς. 5. ἥσθην δὲ καὶ τοῖς εἰρημένοις περὶ σοῦ παρὰ τοῦ καλοῦ Κυνηγίου τοῦ τὸν ὁμώνυμόν τε καὶ πάππον κεκοσμηκότος, ὃν ἐγὼ συμφοιτητῶν μάλιστ᾽ ἠγάπηκα, καὶ τὸν ἀδελφὸν μὲν γάρ, ἀλλὰ μετ᾽ ἀμύμονα. 6. πῶς ἂν οὖν οὕτω διατεθεὶς ὑπὸ τῆς μεταβολῆς τοῦ τηλικαῦτα κεχαρισμένου κατεφρόνουν; κείσθω γὰρ τὸ ῥῆμα τὸ σὸν ὡς μηδὲ ἐπιστέλλειν. σὲ δ᾽ ἐχρῆν ἄλλην τινά που ζητεῖν αἰτίαν, μᾶλλον δέ, οὐδὲ ζητεῖν τὴν οὕτω δήλην ἔδει. τίς γὰρ οὐκ ἔγνω τὴν Κίμωνος τελευτήν; ὃν καὶ αὐτὸς ᾔδεις καὶ οὗ λέγοντος ἀκήκοας καὶ ὃν πολλάκις ἐπῄνεσας. 7. τοῦτον τοίνυν κείμενον πενθῶν ἐκαθήμην ἀνάγκαις ταῖς παρὰ τῶν φίλων σιτίων ἁπτόμενος λεγόντων μὴ δεῖν ἐπισπᾶσθαι θάνατον μηδὲ προσαπόλλυσθαι,[2] καὶ ἐπιστολὰς τὰς μὲν δεῦρ᾽ ἰούσας οὐκ ἄνευ δακρύων ἐδεχόμην, πέμπειν δὲ οὐ μάλα οἷός τε ἦν. 8. ᾤμην δὲ Φιρμῖνον τὸν δίκαιον μαθητήν, εἰ καὶ μὴ μακρά, μικρά γε ἐν τοῖς αὑτοῦ πολίταις ἐρεῖν περὶ μικρῶν τῶν

[2] προσαπόλλυσθαι Wolf (Mss.) προαπόλλυσθαι F., conj. Re.

then I was pleased at receiving your letter and was again pleased at receiving this second one—for two there are, however many you may say they are in your letter.[d] 5. I was also pleased at the news of you given by the noble Cynegius, who is such a credit to his namesake and grandfather[e] to whom I as a fellow student was especially devoted—and to his brother too, but second to that blameless man.[f] 6. So how could I, who have been so moved by your change of career, ever despise—to use your own words—one who has given me this pleasure, so as not to write to you. You should have looked for some other reason, or rather, there was no need for you to look for a reason so obvious. Everyone has heard of the death of Cimon; you knew him personally, you heard him speak, you often praised him. 7. Now he is dead and I have sat in mourning for him, touching food under duress from my friends, who tell me that I must not embrace death and die as well. Letters arriving here I received not without tears, and I have been quite incapable of sending any. 8. I thought that Firminus, my upright pupil, would among his own fellow citizens give, if

[d] Basil also remarks (*Ep.* 116) that Firminus was not the best of correspondents.

[e] Cf. Plat. *Resp.* 1.330b. Cynegius the elder was probably a fellow student with Libanius in Athens; the younger, the bearer of the letter to Libanius, a student of Firminus.

[f] Homer *Il.* 2.674, 17.280.

τοῦ Κίμωνος καὶ ποιήσειν ὃ τῶν ἡμῖν ὡμιληκότων τινὲς ἔπραξαν. 9. ὅρα οὖν εἰ μηδέν σοι τῶν πρὸς ἡμᾶς ὠλιγώρηται, κἂν εὕρῃς, τόθ᾽ ἕτερον ἄδικον καλεῖν.

[g] Priscio was one of such ex-pupils who delivered a funeral address over Cimon; cf. *Ep.* 1037. Firminus had evi-

## 183. Χρύσῃ

1. Ἠβουλόμην μὲν ἔχειν ὑπὲρ ἀμεινόνων γράφειν, σιγῆσαι δὲ οὐκ ἔστιν οὐδὲ θάτερα διὰ τὸ πάντα ἐθέλειν σε τὰ ἡμέτερα εἰδέναι. ἴσθι τοίνυν πένθει πένθος προστεθὲν καὶ λύπῃ λύπην καὶ δάκρυα δάκρυσιν. 2. ἔτι γὰρ ἡμῶν ζητούντων τε Κίμωνα καὶ ποιούντων ἃ τοὺς ζητοῦντας εἰκὸς δαίμων τις ἐξάιφνης ὥσπερ πνεῦμα ἐμπεσὼν τὴν Ἀρχελάου[1] μὲν θυγατέρα, Σευήρου δὲ γυναῖκα ἀπήνεγκεν οὕτως ὀξέως ὡς φθῆναι τὴν τελευτὴν

[1] Ἀρχελάου F., conj. Seeck. ἀρχαίαν μου Wolf (Mss.).

[a] *BLZG* 107 (ii). Chryses in 392 is the subject of a grateful and enthusiastic letter of commendation (*Ep.* 1042). An Egyptian, friend of Cimon and Libanius (less certainly a pupil), he had travelled the cities of the East in 391 displaying his eloquence. In Constantinople he had reconciled Proclus with Cimon, and on his return he had

not in detail, at least in brief outline, an account of the brief career of Cimon, and would do as some of my former pupils have done.[g] 9. So see whether you have not failed in your duty towards me, and if you find that you have not, then accuse someone else of injustice.

dently been in Antioch at some time before Cimon's death—probably in the 380s, to judge by the praise for his eloquence.

## 183. To Chryses[a]

1. I would like to be able to write on more cheerful matters, but I cannot leave their exact opposite unmentioned because of my desire that you should know all my circumstances. So you must know that sorrow has been piled upon sorrow, grief upon grief, tears upon tears. 2. While I still felt the loss of Cimon and was behaving as was to be expected in this state, an evil spirit suddenly descended like a whirlwind upon the daughter of Archelaus, Severus' wife,[b] and carried her off so quickly that she was dead before the arrival of the doctors they had sum-

mourned Cimon's death along with Libanius. He was not a sophist, despite his rhetorical ability; from § 7 below he appears to be a physician. He had returned to Egypt in 392.

[b] *BLZG* 84 (iv). In 390 Libanius could hope for Archelaus, perhaps resident in Constantinople, to gain some office (*BLZG* 456; *Ep.* 954). Severus, *BLZG* 277 (xv), cannot be identified more precisely.

τοὺς κεκλημένους ἰατρούς. 3. ἡμεῖς δὲ οὐ γείτονες μόνον τῶν εἰρημένων ἀνδρῶν, ἀλλὰ καὶ φίλοι πλείω παθόντες ὑπ' αὐτῶν ἀγαθὰ καὶ πάλαι καὶ νῦν ἢ ποιήσαντες αὐτοὺς ὠφελεῖν μὲν οὖν οὐ πάνυ δυνάμεθα, συμπενθεῖν δὲ ἐπιστάμεθα. 4. καὶ δὴ καὶ νῦν ἄνδρα χρηστὸν ὁρῶντες ἐρριμμένον ἐνθυμούμενον ὡς δεῖται μὲν αὐτῷ τὰ τέκνα μητρός, ἡ δὲ οἴχεται, τοῖς αὐτοῖς οἷσπερ ἐκεῖνος ἐχόμεθα τά τε παρόντα ἐλεοῦντες τοῦ τε Κίμωνος ἐπεισιόντος καὶ τῆς οὐχ ὁρωμένης ἐκφορᾶς ὁρωμένης. 5. ἔδει δή σε τῇδέ τε εἶναι καὶ δύο φίλους ὀρθοῦν, Σευῆρόν τε καὶ ἐμέ. τὸν δὲ πατέρα τῆς ἀπελθούσης ἐν τηλικαύτῃ πόλει πείθομαι πολλοὺς ἔσεσθαι τοὺς ἀναστήσοντας, εἰ καὶ τὸ μέγεθος τῆς πληγῆς δεινὸν κατασχεῖν ἐπὶ τοῦ πτώματος θυγατρὸς ἀπελθούσης, οἵαν οὐκ ἄλλος ἔθρεψε πατήρ. 6. ἀλλ', ὦ φίλτατε Χρύση καὶ πολλὰ δὴ πονήσας ὑπὲρ ἡμῶν, ἃ μὲν ἀκοῦσαι χρὴ παρ' ἡμῶν τὸν ἐζημιωμένον, ἀκήκοε κἂν ἔλθῃ ποτὲ ὁ πατήρ, ἀκούσεται· σὺ δ' ἐπιστολαῖς ἀμφοτέρους ποίει ῥᾴονας. ἔστι δέ σοι δύναμις λόγων τοῖς μὲν ἁμιλλωμένη τῶν σοφιστῶν, τοὺς δὲ καὶ νικῶσα.[2]

moned. 3. I am not just a neighbour of the men I have mentioned, but a friend too, and I have received more kindness from them, both now and in the past, than I have conferred; and so, though quite unable to help them, I am capable of joining them in their grief. 4. Indeed when I now see a good man cast down and reflecting how his children miss their dead mother, I am in the same situation as he and pity him in his present plight, as the thought of Cimon presents itself to me and I visualize that funeral procession that I cannot see. 5. You ought to be here to raise up two friends, Severus and myself. I am sure that in such a great city the father of the dead woman will have many to raise him up, even though the terrible blow of the loss of a daughter, the like of whom no other man has had, is enough to keep him down. 6. The bereaved husband has heard what he should hear from me, and her father will hear it too, when he comes.[c] But, my dearest Chryses who have so often toiled on my behalf, by your letters relieve us both. You have oratorical powers rivalling or surpassing

[c] He had evidently composed a funeral address.

[2] *καὶ νικῶσα* F. *νικῶσα*, in lacuna, V. *καὶ παρενεγκοῦσα* Wolf (Vo. in lacuna).

7. παῦσον δὲ καὶ ἐμοὶ τὴν μαινομένην ἀγρυπνίαν· μὴ γὰρ δὴ οἵου τι τὸν χρόνον δεδυνῆσθαι, ἀλλ' ὁ μὲν ἐνιαυτός τε καὶ μήν, ἐγὼ δὲ ἐν ἐκείνοις οἷσπερ ἄρτι παραδοὺς τὸν Κίμωνα τῇ σορῷ.

## 184. Ἀρισταινέτῳ

1. Ἡγούμενος βούλεσθαί σε μηδὲν τῶν ἡμετέρων ἀγνοεῖν, εἰ καὶ μηδὲν ἔχοιμι γράψαι καλόν, ἅ γε ἔνεστι γράφειν οὐ σιωπήσομαι. 2. ἐπλήγην τῇ τελευτῇ τοῦ παιδός, ἣν ἐποίησεν ἡ τινων παρ' ὑμῖν φιλονεικία. τὰ δ' ἀπὸ τῆς πληγῆς ἐκείνης δάκρυα τὰ πολλά, τούτοις γὰρ αὐτὸν ἐξῆν τιμᾶν, εἰ καὶ μὴ τοῖς μείζοσι, τοῦ τῶν ὀφθαλμῶν ἔργου παρείλετο τὸ πλέον, καὶ νῦν ἔχομεν ὀφθαλμοὺς ἐλεουμένους. 3. ἄλλος μὲν οὖν ἂν ἐμνήσθη καὶ διαθήκης πενίαν ἐνεγκούσης καὶ κύματος ἑτέρου μείζω ταύτην πεποιηκότος· ἐμοὶ δὲ ταυτὶ μὲν ἐν οὐ πολλῷ λόγῳ καὶ χρημάτων ἀπολλυμένων οὐκ ἔστιν ὅτε μοι ταραχὴ τὴν ψυχὴν κατέλαβεν· ἀλλ' ὅ με κατέδυσεν ὥσπερ τι πλοῖον, οἶσθά που

[a] *BLZG* 87 (ii), *PLRE* 104 (2). Kinsman and ex-pupil of Libanius, in 392 he succeeded Proclus as prefect of the City of Constantinople.

those of professors. 7. And put a stop to my raging insomnia too. Do not think that time has had any effect: a year and a month have gone by, and my plight is still as it was just after I had consigned Cimon to the tomb.

## 184. To Aristaenetus[a]

1. I believe that you wish to be unaware of none of my circumstances, and so even if I have nothing good to write about, I shall not be silent on what I can. 2. I have been smitten by the death of my son, which was caused by the rancour of certain persons among you there.[b] Too many tears I have shed in consequence of that blow—for I could honour him with them, even though with nothing further—these have deprived me of my eyesight for the most part, and my eyes are now in a pitiable state.[c] 3. Another might have made mention also of the inheritance that brought me poverty[d] and of another buffeting that has made this poverty the greater, but I am not much concerned with this, and the loss of money has never caused me any perturbation. But what has sunk me without trace, as it were, is

[b] Libanius avoids mention of Aristaenetus' predecessor Proclus, who had consistently opposed Cimon's advancement (so also *Letter* 188). Proclus' bloody removal by the new praetorian prefect Rufinus had perhaps been too scandalous for him to mention it.

[c] Cf. *Or.* 1.281.

[d] The inheritance of Olympius; cf. *Or.* 1.275 ff, *Or.* 63.

Καλλιόπιον καὶ τὸν ἐκείνου τρόπον καὶ τοὺς ἐκείνου λόγους καὶ ὅσην περιέφερεν[1] ἐν ἑαυτῷ παιδείαν. 4. οὗτος τοίνυν θρηνῶν ἔτι μετ᾽ ἐμοῦ τὸν ἐμὸν οἴχεται καὶ τέθαπται παῖς ὢν δήπου καὶ αὐτὸς ἐμός, σπέρματι μὲν οὔ, πόνοις δὲ ἐμοῖς τεθραμμένος. 5. τεθνεῶτος δὲ πέπτωκε μὲν τὰ τῇδε διδασκαλεῖα, ἐμοὶ δὲ πένθος τοῦθ᾽ ἕτερον οὐκ ἔλαττον. παραμυθία δέ, καὶ γὰρ ταῦτ᾽ ἔδει σε μαθεῖν, παρὰ μόνης τῆς Θεοφίλου ψυχῆς τούτῳ πλέον τοῦ χρόνου νέμοντος ἢ τοῖς ἄλλοις ἅπασιν. 6. ἔστι δὲ ἐπιστήμων τῶν τοιούτων φαρμάκων καὶ ῥέουσιν ἀπ᾽ αὐτοῦ νῦν μὲν κρουνοὶ φιλοσοφίας, νῦν δὲ ῥητορικῆς· ἐν αὐτῷ γὰρ ἄμφω, καὶ γάρ ἐστι πολὺς μὲν ἐν ἐκείνῳ, πολὺς δὲ ἐν τούτῳ. καὶ δὴ καὶ τοῦ γάμου χάριν μὲν αὐτὸς οἶδεν ἡμῖν, πλείω δὲ ἡμεῖς αὐτῷ πείθοντι πολλοὺς ἐπιμελεῖσθαί τε σφῶν αὐτῶν καὶ βιβλία μᾶλλον ἢ χρυσίον διώκειν. 7. οὗτος παρ᾽ ἐμὲ βαδίζει καθ᾽ ἡμέραν, οὗτος μάχεται τῷ πάθει, οὗτός μοι τηρεῖ τὸν νοῦν χαλεποῖς ἐλαυνόμενον πνεύμασιν, οὗτός μοι βοηθεῖ ταύτην τὴν βοήθειαν νῦν μὲν πείθων ἔχεσθαι τῶν λόγων, νῦν δὲ ἀναγκάζων καὶ οὐκ

[1] ὅσην περιέφερεν F. ὅσηνπερ ἔφερεν Wolf (Mss.).

this. You know Calliopius, I am sure, and the character, eloquence and learning that he possessed. 4. Well, while still in mourning with me for the death of my son, he is dead and buried, himself also assuredly a child of mine, not by blood but reared by my labours.[e] 5. At his death the schools here have collapsed, and this is cause of grief no less than the first. My consolation—for you must know that too—comes from the character of Theophilus[f] alone, who spends more of his time on this than on all other things put together. 6. He is well versed in healing arts of this sort, and there flow from him springs now of philosophy, now of rhetoric, for both reside in him and he is much occupied in the one and in the other. Moreover, he is grateful to me for sponsoring his marriage, but I am more grateful to him for persuading many to care for their own well-being and to follow books rather than gold. 7. He comes to me each day, he combats my affliction, he keeps me sane when I am driven by the winds of misfortune, and he gives me this assistance, now persuading me to apply myself to oratory, now com-

[e] *BLZG* 102 (iv), *PLRE* 175 (4), his assistant in his later years. Like Eusebius (*Letter* 170) he is παῖς by virtue not of blood, but of eloquence. For the damage caused to the school by his death cf. *Letter* 188.6.

[f] *BLZG* 312 (v). He is commended in very similar terms in *Letter* 189.

ἐῶν τὴν τάξιν λιπεῖν. 8. ἀνθ' ὧν ἕξει μὲν καὶ τὴν τῶν λογίων θεῶν εὔνοιαν, ἐχέτω δὲ καὶ τὴν σήν, μᾶλλον δέ, πάλαι μὲν τοῦτο ἔχει καὶ φιλεῖται φιλῶν, δεῖ δέ τι προστεθῆναι παρὰ σοῦ διὰ τἀκείνου πρὸς ἐμέ. τὰ μὲν γὰρ παρ' ἐμοῦ καὶ τοὐμοῦ γήρως καὶ τῶν ἐμῶν πολιῶν εὐχαί, σοὶ δὲ ἡ Τύχη καλῶς ποιοῦσα καὶ πλέον τι δέδωκεν. 9. εἰ μὲν οὖν τῇδε ὢν ἐτύγχανες, καὶ αὐτὸς ἄν με παρεμυθοῦ λέγων τι καθ' ἡμέραν· νῦν δὲ κτῆμα γεγονὼς τῆς μεγίστης πόλεως ἐπαίνει δι' ἐπιστολῶν τὸν παραμυθούμενον, ἀμείνω γὰρ αὐτὸν εἰς ταῦτα ποιήσεις· καὶ τἄλλα δὲ ἢν ἐπαινῇς, ἀληθῆ τε ἐρεῖς καὶ τὰ δίκαια ποιήσεις ἄνδρα ἀμειβόμενος ἐν τοῖς σοῖς ἐπαίνοις ὡς ἥδιστα διατρίβοντα.

---

[g] τηρεῖν τὴν τάξιν appears as Libanius' watchword with regard to all sections of society (e.g. *Or.* 48.31 ff). As regards his own profession it is not merely metaphorical; λόγοι are inseparable from πόνοι, as in the Autobiography (*Or.* 1.1), and the service of letters is as much a *militia* as any other.

[h] For λόγιοι θεοί in his later life, cf. *Or.* 1.234 f, 238, 274; *Epp.* 907, 1085, 1089. Fortune, which in the Autobiography appears as his guardian angel, is less prominent

pelling me and forbidding me to quit my post.[g] 8. In return for this he will have the goodwill of the gods of eloquence and let him have yours too—or, I should say, he has had it for a long time now and is both your admirer and admired, but there should be some extra contribution from you because of his kindness towards me. From me, in my old age and with my grey hairs, he gets merely prayers, but Fortune has justly given you something more than this.[h] 9. So, were you here, you too would console me in person with daily conversation. As it is, you have been acquired by the capital;[i] so write and commend him for so consoling me, for you will make him better at it. And besides, if you do praise him, you will be speaking the truth and doing him justice by paying him his due, for he dwells on your praises with the utmost pleasure.

in the later sections. Here the *λόγιοι θεοί* are the mark of Libanius himself, Fortune that of Aristaenetus. Although the family of Aristaenetus was Christian, Libanius makes easy use of the terms of pagan religion and rhetoric, knowing that he will be indulged because of the ties of kin and culture.

[i] The settlement in Constantinople seems to have been of fairly long standing. This resume of the events of the past three years does not denote any frequent correspondence or recent intimate association between them. In fact, the attainment of the prefecture may well have been Libanius' stimulus to resume the correspondence.

## 185. Πρισκίωνι

1. Οὐ ταῦτα ἤλπιζον ἔσεσθαι τὰ νῦν γεγενημένα, πολὺ δὲ βελτίω τούτων καὶ πολλήν μοι φέροντα τὴν εὐθυμίαν, ὅτι Πρισκίων ἐκεῖνος ὁ πολλὰς μὲν ἀνῃρημένος ἐν δικαστηρίοις νίκας, πολλὰς δὲ ἐν θεάτροις τοῖς δεχομένοις λόγους, ἐμπλήσας δὲ τῶν αὑτοῦ πόνων τὴν γῆν καὶ βασιλέα καταστήσας ἡδίω τοῖς γεγραμμένοις περὶ αὑτοῦ. τοῦτον τοίνυν τὸν Πρισκίωνα ᾤμην εἰς Ἱλάριον τὸν γενναῖον ἀδελφοῦ βελτίω γενήσεσθαι καὶ λόγοις λεγομένοις καὶ ἔργοις πραττομένοις καὶ συγγράμμασι ποιουμένοις καὶ δόξῃ τῇ μὲν αὐξομένῃ, τῇ δὲ φυτευομένῃ, μάχαις τε καὶ πολέμοις τοῖς πρὸς τοὺς οὐ ταὐτὰ[1] βουλομένους. 2. ἐνεποίουν δέ μοι ταυτασὶ τὰς ἐλπίδας παραινέσεις τε ἃς πρὸς ὑμᾶς ἐπεποιήμην ὑποσχέσεις τε ὑμέτεραι καὶ τὸ παιδείας ἄμφω μετεσχηκέναι ἀπὸ[2] τῶν αὐτῶν καὶ διατριβῶν καὶ ἀνθέων καὶ τὸ κόσμον ἔσεσθαι σοὶ μὲν ἐκεῖνον θαυμαζόμενον, σὲ δὲ ἐκείνῳ. τὰ δ' ὑμέτερα εἰπεῖν παραλείπω, οἷά

[1] ταὐτὰ F., conj. Re. ταῦτα Wolf (Mss.).
[2] ἀπὸ F., conj. Re. αὐτοῖς Mss. αὐτῆς Wolf.

## 185. To Priscio

1. I did not expect that what has now happened would ever be like this. I looked for something much better than this and productive of much good cheer for me, for Priscio is he who has won many victories in the courts and in the rhetorical lecture rooms; he filled the earth with his labours and has pleased the emperor by his writings about him.[a] Well, I thought that this Priscio would be better than a brother towards the noble Hilarius,[b] with the delivery of orations, the performance of actions, the writing of compositions, the increase and the generation of his renown, and by battling and campaigning against those who do not entertain this same desire. 2. This expectation had been engendered in me by the advice which I had given you and by your promises to me, and by the fact that you had both partaken of learning from the same sources,[c] the same discourses and flowery meads, and that the admiration he won would be a glory for you, and yours for him. The abilities which were characteris-

[a] Priscio (*BLZG* 245, *PLRE* 729) had begun his career as advocate in Antioch before becoming a sophist in Palestine. Earlier in this year he had delivered a panegyric on the emperor.

[b] *BLZG* 178 (vii), *PLRE* 435 (8); governor of Palestine, where Priscio was practising.

[c] Both were pupils of Libanius.

γε ἦν. ταῦτα μὲν προσεδόκων, ἀκούω δὲ ἕτερα, μῖσος καὶ ὑποψίας καὶ ῥήματα σεσιγῆσθαι δίκαια, ἃ λέγειν μὲν ἔστι μοι, ῥηθήσεται δὲ οὐδέποτε. 3. βουλομένου δέ μου πότερον αἰτιᾶσθαι μᾶλλον ἄξιον μαθεῖν ἔλεγεν ὁ ἀπαγγέλλων τὸν σοφιστήν· τοῦ γὰρ ἄρχοντος χάριτας μὲν καλὰς δόντος, τὰς δ' οὐ τοιαύτας οὐ δυνηθέντος τῷ μὴ καὶ ταύτας λαβεῖν χαλεπήναντα τὸν σοφιστὴν ῥήματα ἀφεῖναι γλώτταις ἁπαλαῖς[3] ἐναντία. καὶ οἶδα μὲν τούτοις τὸν ἐμαυτοῦ παῖδα λυπῶν, πατρὸς δὲ οἶμαι καὶ τοῦτο, παῖδα λυπεῖν εἰς ἐπανόρθωσιν. 4. τὰ πεπραγμένα μὲν οὖν οὐκ ἔνι μὴ πεπρᾶχθαι, ἔξεστι δέ σοι γενέσθαι βελτίονι καὶ δοῦναι τοῖς παρ' ὑμῶν δεῦρο ἀφικνουμένοις λέγειν ὡς ἔστιν ὁ δεινὸς παιδεύειν[4] Πρισκίων εἰς τὸν δεινὸν ἄρχειν Ἱλάριον τοιοῦτος οἷόσπερ εἰς ἀμφοτέρους ἐγώ.

[3] ἁπαλαῖς F. ἁπάσαις Wolf (Mss.).

[4] παιδεύειν F., conj. Re. παίδευσιν Wolf (Mss., with ἄρχειν superscribed.)

## 186. Μοδεράτῳ

1. Εὐδαίμων ὁ γενναῖος ὁ τὰ τῶν ἀρχαίων ποιητῶν εἰδώς τε καὶ μιμούμενος ἔφη πρός με παρὰ σῶν μεμαθηκέναι γραμμάτων ὡς πάνυ ἂν

tic of you both, I forbear to mention. This then was my expectation, but what I hear is the opposite of it—hatred, suspicion, words better left unsaid and which I could repeat, but never will. 3. When I wanted to find out which of you was more to blame, my informant told me that it was the sophist; for when the governor offered reasonable favours and was unable to offer any that were not, the sophist took umbrage at not getting them and gave vent to comments quite at variance with the soft answer. I know that in saying this I am causing discomfiture to a son of mine, but I also believe it is a father's duty to cause his son discomfiture for his correction. 4. What is done cannot be undone, but you can improve and allow those who arrive here from you to say that Priscio, the gifted teacher, treats Hilarius, the gifted governor, as I treat them both.

## 186. To Moderatus[a]

1. The noble Eudaemon,[b] who both knows and imitates the classical poets, has told me that he has learned by letter from you that you would be very

[a] *BLZG* 213, *PLRE* 605. Despite his earlier prejudice against the military, Libanius in his later years is eager to seek out friendship with eminent soldiers. In this case, he begins correspondence following a hint received at second hand. Moderatus replied, and Libanius acknowledges his letter (*Ep.* 1059).

[b] *BLZG* 131 (i), *PLRE* 289 (3). He had been friendly with Libanius for over 35 years.

ἡσθείης ἡμετέροις γράμμασιν. 2. ἐγὼ δὲ τῷ μὲν οὐκ ἀπιστήσας, σοὶ δὲ ἔχων τῆς ἐπιθυμίας χάριν καὶ τῇ γε δῶρόν μοι τοιοῦτον προξενησάσῃ Τύχῃ πέπομφα τήνδε τὴν ἐπιστολὴν οὐ πολλῶν μὲν ἐσομένην ἀρχήν — πῶς γὰρ ἂν ἐν οὐ πολλῷ τῷ μετὰ ταῦτα χρόνῳ; — δεῖξαι δὲ δυναμένην ὡς, εἰ νέος ἦν, πλῆθος ἂν ἐπιστολῶν ἦλθέ σοι καλῶς μὲν οὕτως ἡγουμένῳ στρατιωτῶν, καλῶς δὲ οὕτω κηδομένῳ πόλεων ὡς ἔχεσθαί τε τοῦ λόγου αὐτὰς καὶ δεδιέναι μή τις αὐτὸν ἑτέρα πόλις λάβῃ. 3. ἐμοὶ μὲν οὖν φιλοτιμία τὸ τοιοῦτον κτήσασθαι φίλον, σοὶ δὲ εἰ τὸ ἐμέ, σκόπει, τάχα γὰρ ἂν ἔλθοι ποθὲν αἰτία· πρὸς ἣν μάχου[1] πολλὰ δὴ νενικηκὼς ἐν μάχαις. 4. τοῦ δὲ πάντ᾽ ἔχοντός μοι Θαλασσίου τῆς οἰκίας φροντίσας ἴσθι φροντίσας <τῆς>[2] ἐμῆς καὶ τὴν φροντίδα τεῖνον ἐφ᾽ ἅπαντα τὰ ὄντα αὐτῷ καλέσας τε τοὺς αὐτοῦ καὶ ποιήσας φανερὸν ὡς, εἴ τι ῥᾳθυμηθείη, κἂν μικρόν, οὐ περιόψει.

[1] μάχου F. μάχῃ Wolf (Mss.)
[2] <τῆς> F., conj. Re.

pleased with a letter from me. 2. I do not disbelieve him, and I am grateful to you for your desire and to the Fortune that has sponsored such a gift to me, and so I have sent this letter to be the start of no long correspondence—for how could that be possible in the no long time left to me—but enough to prove that if I were a young man a mass of correspondence would reach you, since you command your troops so well and care so well for the cities that they are attached to the regiment billeted there and are afraid that some other city may get it.[c] 3. I am proud to have gained such a friend, but consider whether you should have me for a friend, for some complaint may perhaps arise about it. But oppose it, after the many victories you have won in combat. 4. You must know that in your concern for the family of Thalassius[d] who means everything to me, you show concern for mine: extend your concern to all that is his, summon his servants and demonstrate that you will not put up with any shortcomings, however slight.

[c] This is praise indeed—or flattery. Most cities were only too eager to get rid of their resident garrisons.

[d] Libanius' assistant, the Thalassius of *Or.* 42. He owned property in Samosata (*Or.* 42.37). Moderatus thus seems to have been in charge of the Euphrates frontier.

## 187. Βρασίδᾳ

1. Οὐδὲν θαυμαστὸν ἄτιμον ὄντα σιωπᾶν· ἡμεῖς δὲ παρ' ὑμῖν ἀπ' ἐκείνης ἄτιμοι τῆς ἡμέρας, ἐν ᾗ μειζόνων ἴσως ἢ χρῆν ἐρασθέντες ἠλαυνόμεθα. 2. ἤλαυνε δὲ ἡμᾶς δαίμων κακός, δι' ὃν οὐ κακὸς ἄνθρωπος, οὐ γὰρ ἦν κακός, κακῶς μὲν ἐξῆλθεν ἐνθένδε, κακῶς δὲ ἐπέζευσε, κακῶς δὲ διέπλευσε, κακῶς δὲ τοῖς μὲν αὑτὸν ἔδωκε, τοῖς δὲ οὐκ ἔδωκε. τοῦ αὐτοῦ δαίμονος καὶ τὸ ζεῦγος καὶ τὸ ἀναβῆναι καὶ τὸ πτῶμα καὶ τὸ περὶ τὸν πόδα καὶ ὁ μὴ προσδοκηθεὶς μέν, ἐπελθὼν δὲ θάνατος. 3. σπουδὴν δὲ τὴν ὑμετέραν οὐκ ἀγνοῶν οὐδὲ ἔργα καὶ λόγους καὶ μάχας οἶδα μὲν ὑμῖν ὧν ἐβουλήθητε χάριν, τὸ δὲ μὴ δεδυνῆσθαι οὐκ αἰτιῶμαι, ἀλλ' ἐν εὐεργέταις μὲν ὁ χρηστὸς Ἀνατόλιος, ἐν εὐεργέταις δὲ ὁ καλὸς Βρασίδας, τῶν δ' ἠναντιωμένων τούτοις οὐδένα μεμφόμεθα· φιλούντων γὰρ ἂν αὐτοὺς ἴσως ἔργον ἐποίουν.

---

[a] *BLZG* 97 (ii), *PLRE* 164. F/Kr. no. 14. This letter appears to resume correspondence after a gap of nearly four years: certainly it is the first since Cimon's failure to secure advancement two years before. The tone of resigna-

## 187. To Brasidas[a]

1. It is not surprising for one in disgrace to stay silent.[b] I have been in disgrace with you people since the day when I was repulsed in my yearning for something which perhaps was beyond the reach of my aspirations. 2. I was repulsed by an evil spirit, and because of it a man who was certainly not evil, with evil omen left here, travelled overland, and crossed the straits with evil omen, and with evil omen offered himself to one group and refused himself to another.[c] It was the same spirit that was responsible for his conveyance and his mounting of it, for his fall, for the accident to his foot and the unexpected death that befell him. 3. I am not unaware of your support, of your actions, your words, and the opposition you encountered, and I am grateful to you for your intentions and do not complain of their lack of success. Among my benefactors I count the good Anatolius[d] and the noble Brasidas, but I have no reproach for anyone who opposed them, for what they did was done perhaps out of self-interest.[e]

tion here—his loss is not due to the wickedness of men but to fate, in the shape of an evil spirit—is very different from the outburst which concludes the Autobiography.

[b] ἀτίμια carried with it the inability to make a public defence in law.

[c] The Senate and the curia.

[d] See *Letter* 179.

[e] Cf. *Letter* 188.5.

4. καὶ ταῦτα δ' ἐγὼ προλέγων τὸν ταλαίπωρον οὐκ ἔπειθον ἐξηπατημένον ὡς οὐδὲν αἰτήσει τοιοῦτον, ὃ μὴ ῥᾳδίως αὐτῷ παρ' ὑμῶν ἔσται δι' ἐμέ. 5. ἔχετ' οὖν τῷ μὲν οἰχομένῳ συγγνώμην ὧν ἤλπισεν, ἐμοὶ δὲ τοῦ σιγῆσαι. πρὸς γὰρ αὖ τοῖς ἄλλοις βραδύτερος ὅ τε νοῦς μοι γέγονε καὶ ἡ γλῶττα καὶ ἡ χεὶρ ὑπὸ τῆς κατεσθιούσης με λύπης.

## 188. Μαρκελλίνῳ

1. Καὶ σὲ ζηλῶ τοῦ Ῥώμην ἔχειν κἀκείνην τοῦ σέ· σὺ μὲν γὰρ ἔχεις ᾧ τῶν ἐν γῇ παραπλήσιον οὐδέν, ἡ δὲ τὸν τῶν ἑαυτῆς πολιτῶν, οἷς πρόγονοι δαίμονες, οὐκ ὕστερον. 2. ἦν μὲν οὖν δή σοι μέγα καὶ τὸ μετὰ σιγῆς ἐν τῇ τοιαύτῃ διάγειν καὶ τὸ λόγους ὑπ' ἄλλων λεγομένους δέχεσθαι — πολ-

[a] Ammianus Marcellinus, the historian; cf. *PLRE* 547 (15); F/Kr. no. 62; E. A. Thompson, *The Historical Work of Ammianus Marcellinus.*

This letter is of prime importance for our knowledge of Ammianus' life and work. (i) It is the one piece of evidence that he was an Antiochene; (ii) and that in 392 he was resident in Rome and was giving readings from the books of the *Histories* which were already finished (but that the work as a whole was not yet complete); (iii) and that, although he was not a frequent correspondent, he was familiar enough with Libanius to receive from him this

4. I foretold it to my poor son, but he took no notice because of his delusion that any request of his would easily be obtained of you on my account. 5. So now that he is dead, pardon him for his presumption and me for my silence. For besides all else, my mental faculties, my tongue, and my hand have lost their cunning through the grief which consumes me.

## 188. To Marcellinus[a]

1. I envy you for possessing Rome and her for her possession of you. You possess something without peer in the world, she someone not inferior to her own citizens whose ancestors were divine.[b] 2. It was certainly a great thing for you both to live in such a city in silence and to listen to the eloquence

unsolicited letter and for the sophist to expect him to be aware of matters concerning Cimon, Calliopius, and himself.

However, G. W. Bowersock, in *Journal of Roman Studies* 80 (1990): 247–248, gives a brief summary of an alternative identification of this Marcellinus: that he is a young associate of the doctor Magnus (7) of Nisibis and has no connection with the historian.

[b] ἔχειν with the accusative of places is Homeric, and especially used of the gods (e.g. *Il.* 5.890). Here the mention of the gods does not merely glance at the divine origins of Rome, but heightens the compliment to Ammianus. That the claim of divine origin was taken seriously by the noblest Romans of the time, if only as a social cachet, is shown by the claims of the family of Postumianus (*Letter* 181).

λοὺς δὲ ἡ Ῥώμη τρέφει ῥήτορας πατράσιν ἀκολουθοῦντας — νῦν δ', ὡς ἔστιν ἀκούειν τῶν ἐκεῖθεν ἀφικνουμένων, αὐτὸς ἡμῖν ἐν ἐπιδείξεσι ταῖς μὲν γέγονας, ταῖς δὲ ἔσῃ τῆς συγγραφῆς εἰς πολλὰ τετμημένης καὶ τοῦ φανέντος ἐπαινεθέντος μέρος ἕτερον εἰσκαλοῦντος. 3. ἀκούω δὲ τὴν Ῥώμην αὐτὴν στεφανοῦν σοι τὸν πόνον καὶ κεῖσθαι ψῆφον αὐτῇ τῶν μέν σε κεκρατηκέναι, τῶν δὲ οὐχ ἡττῆσθαι. ταυτὶ δὲ οὐ τὸν συγγραφέα κοσμεῖ μόνον, ἀλλὰ καὶ ἡμᾶς, ὧν ἐστιν ὁ συγγραφεύς. 4. μὴ δὴ παύσῃ τοιαῦτα συντιθεὶς καὶ κομίζων οἴκοθεν[1] εἰς συλλόγους μηδὲ κάμῃς θαυμαζόμενος, ἀλλ' αὐτός τε γίγνου λαμπρότερος καὶ ἡμῖν τοῦτο δίδου. τοιοῦτον γὰρ πολίτης εὐδοκιμῶν· κοσμεῖ τοῖς αὐτοῦ τὴν πόλιν τὴν ἑαυτοῦ. 5. σὺ μὲν οὖν ἐν ὁμοίοις εἴης· ἡμῖν δ' ἐν πένθει κειμένοις εἰ μή τις θεῶν ἀμύνειεν, οὐκ ἔσθ' ὅπως οἴσομεν. ὃς γὰρ δὴ μόνος ἦν ἡμῖν οὐ κακὸς ἐκ μητρὸς ἀγαθῆς, εἰ καὶ μὴ[2] ἐλευθέρας, οἴχεται καὶ τέθαπται λύπῃ τελευτήσας, ἡ δ' ἔργον ἦν ὕβρεως. οἵτινες δὲ οἱ

[1] οἴκοθεν F. ἐκεῖθεν Wolf (Mss.)

[2] εἰ καὶ μὴ F. εἰ μὴ καὶ Valesius (V Vo) ἀλλὰ καὶ Wolf (Vind D)

produced by others—and Rome produces many orators who follow in their fathers' footsteps[c]—but now, as I am told by new arrivals from there, you either have taken or will take part in recitations, since your history is divided into numerous sections where each published portion wins approval and invites another.[d] 3. I am told that Rome itself crowns your work and that her verdict is that you are superior to or not inferior to other authors. This is an honour not merely for the historian but also for us to whom the historian belongs. 4. Don't stop composing such works, and taking them out to the literary clubs, and do not weary of exciting admiration, but win greater glory for yourself and give us this also. For that is what a citizen's renown means: he adorns his native place with his own handiwork. 5. So I trust that you will remain in like situation. As for myself, I lie prostrate with grief, and I shall find it unendurable without a god's protection. My only son, no bad lad, and child of a mother who was a good woman, even though not free, is dead and buried, dying of grief in conse-

[c] For instance, Symmachus.

[d] The recitation of excerpts was a traditional method of publication in antiquity (cf. the story of Thucydides listening to Herodotus reciting from his works at Olympia). In this case, Libanius' statement that portions of the history were still to be published lends more precision to *PLRE*'s cautious conclusion that Books 26 to 31 were published together after 390.

προπηλακίσαντες, παρ᾽ ἑτέρων μάνθανε, ἡμεῖς δὲ αὐτοὺς καὶ παθόντες αἰδούμεθα. 6. ζέοντος δὲ ἔτι τοῦ κακοῦ Καλλιόπιος ἐκ μέσων ἡρπάσθη βιβλίων καὶ πόνων, καὶ γίγνεται ἕλκος ἐφ᾽ ἕλκει καὶ χείρω τὰ τῶν νέων. καὶ τοῦτ᾽ ἂν ἀκούσαις καὶ τῶν τἀκείνου νειμαμένων. ἐμοὶ δὲ καὶ τὰ πρὸ αὐτοῦ[3] καὶ αὐτὸς καὶ τὰ μετ᾽ αὐτὸν οἰμωγῶν τε ἀφορμαὶ καὶ δακρύων, ὧν ἐπὶ τὰ γραφόμενα ῥεῖ τὰ πλείω.

[3] αὐτοῦ F., conj. Re. τοῦ Wolf (Mss.)

---

[e] This is the most explicit statement that Libanius gives of the original servile status of Cimon's mother. He hints at it in *Or.* 1.278 and in *Letters* 169.2 and 189.

## 189. Ἀρισταινέτῳ

1. Καλῶς σοι τεθρήνηται τἀμὰ κακά, ἥ τε τοῦ παιδὸς τελευτὴ τοῦ διὰ τὴν μητέρα δεινὰ παθόντος ἥ τε Καλλιοπίου τοῦ τοῖς τῶν παλαιῶν λόγοις λυσιτελοῦντος ἥ τε τῶν ὀφθαλμῶν ἀσθένεια καὶ τὸ ἀπολωλὸς αὐτοῖς τὸ πολὺ καὶ τὸ οὔπω τὸ μικρόν, ὥστε πάλιν ἔρρει δάκρυα κατὰ τῶν γεγραμμένων. 2. καὶ θαυμαστὸν οὐδὲν τοιούτων ἠξιῶσθαι παρὰ

quence of the insult he suffered. The identity of those who abused him so you must learn from others, for even in my distress I hold them in respect.[e] 6. And while the evil still raged, Calliopius was snatched away from the midst of his books and labours, and one wound occurred after another, and my students' education has suffered.[f] This you could hear also from those who have inherited his property. For me the events before his death, his death itself, and the events thereafter have been a source of lamentation and tears, most of which flood onto my writings.

[f] *BLZG* 102 (iv), *PLRE* 175 (4); Petit, *Étudiants* 87. Cf. *Letter* 184.4, which shows F/Kr. to have erred in their identification here. It would appear that this death occurred in term time, and that the letter thus belongs to the latter part of 392.

## 189. To Aristaenetus

1. You have duly lamented my troubles,[a] the death of my son who suffered terribly on his mother's account and that of Calliopius who did yeoman service to the study of classical literature, my weakened eyesight, and the loss of a great part of it, with little remaining, and in consequence tears once again rained down upon my writings.[b] 2. And it

[a] Aristaenetus, acknowledging *Letter* 184, has replied with a letter of consolation upon his afflictions there listed.

[b] Cf. *Letter* 188.5–6.

σοὶ τὰς ἐμὰς συμφορὰς συγγενείας τε βουλομένης καὶ τοῦ τῆς φιλίας νόμου καὶ τοῦ περὶ τοὺς λόγους, ὧν τὰς ἀρχὰς ὅθεν οἶσθα λαβὼν ἐπὶ τοσοῦτον προὔβης ὡς οὕτως εἶναι καλὸς ἐν ἐπιστολαῖς. 3. ὅθεν δέ μοι τὸ κλαῦσαι γέγονεν, ἐκεῖθεν καὶ ἡ παραμυθία. τὸ γὰρ Ἀρισταίνετον τοιαῦτα περὶ τοιούτων εἰπεῖν δεδυνῆσθαι καὶ εἶναι ῥήτορα πολλοῦ τινος ἄξιον ἀνίστη μέ πως ἀπὸ τοῦ πτώματος καὶ ἦν τῇ ψυχῇ φάρμακον. 4. σὺ μὲν οὖν τὸν Θεόφιλον ἡγῇ μακάριον <ἐμοὶ>[1] ὁμιλοῦντα. ἔστι δὲ τοῦτο ἐμόν, ὅτι βιβλίων τε καὶ παιδείας ἀνδρὶ γέμοντι σύνειμι καθ᾽ ἑκάστην ἡμέραν τὰ μὲν αὐτὸς ὡς αὐτὸν ἰών, τὰ δ᾽ ἐκείνου βαδίζοντος ὡς ἐμέ. 5. ἐν δὴ τοῖς λόγοις τοῖς ἐν ταῖς συνουσίαις ἐπαινοῦμέν τε τοὺς τοσοῦτόν σε πεποιηκότας θεοὺς καὶ ἅμα παρ᾽ αὐτῶν αἰτοῦμεν εἶναι τοὺς αὐτοὺς περὶ σὲ τά τε ἄλλα ἀνδρῶν ἄριστον ὄντα καὶ χαίρειν ἐν ταῖς τῶν συνήθων εὐπραξίαις εἰδότα καὶ οὐ χαίρειν γε μόνον, ἀλλὰ καὶ συμπράττειν, ὅπως ἐν λαμπροτέροις εἶεν. οὗ πεῖραν καὶ ὁ γενναῖος Θεόφιλος τὴν μὲν ἔλαβε, τὴν δὲ λήψεται.

[1] <ἐμοὶ> F., conj. Re.

is no surprise that my misfortunes have had such a reception from you following the dictates of our kinship, and the conventions of friendship and of rhetoric, wherein you received your initiation from the source you know[c] and have made such progress as to achieve such competence in epistolary style. 3. But the source of my laments has become the source of my consolation. For Aristaenetus to have been able to speak so well on such subjects and to be an orator of mark revived me somewhat from my slough of despond and was solace to my soul. 4. Now, you count Theophilus lucky for his association with me, but the luck is mine, in that I am every single day in the company of a man brimful of books and learning, either going to see him myself or having him come to see me.[d] 5. During our conversation in such meetings we praise the gods who have made you so great, and also beg them to maintain this same attitude towards you,[e] since you are the best of men and, in particular, capable of rejoicing in your friends' successes, and not only of rejoicing but also contributing to the enhancement of their prestige. And the noble Theophilus has had and will have experience of this.

[c] Libanius himself.

[d] Cf. *Letter* 184.6.

[e] For this pagan terminology in addressing a kinsman who was Christian, cf. *Letter* 184.8.

## 190. Φιρμίνῳ

1. Ἠρχόμην μὲν τοῖς τῶν οἰκετῶν ποσὶν εἰς τὸ βουλευτήριον, προσελθὼν δέ τις ἐρχομένῳ καὶ δοὺς ἐπιστολὴν εἶπεν· 'ἥδε σοι παρὰ Φιρμίνου,' καὶ ἥσθην. ἔκειτο δὲ ἄρα γράμματα ἐν γράμμασι, καὶ οὕτως ἑτέραν εἶχον ἀφορμὴν εἰς ἡδονὴν δύο τῆς μιᾶς γενομένων. ἔμελλε δέ, οἶμι, νικήσειν τὰς δύο τὸ τρίτον, ἡ διφθέρα· ἧς εὐθὺς μὲν ἠβουλόμην ἀπολαύειν, ὁ χορὸς δὲ οὐκ ἐπέτρεπεν. 2. ἦν οὖν ἐν χερσὶν ἡμῶν τὰ εἰωθότα σκοπουμένοις ἅμα, τίς ἂν ὑποκριτὴς πρέπων γένοιτο τοῖς δράμασι, καὶ ὁ μὲν εὕρητο καὶ ἐφαίνετο νέος ἀπὸ τῶν ἐμῶν ἀρδευόμενος πόνων πάντων, ὡς ἤκουσαν, τὸν αὐτὸν ἑλομένων· ὁ δὲ τὰ γράμματα κομίσας ἐφειστήκει βαρὺς ἀξιῶν πρὸ τῆς ἀναγνώσεως γενέσθαι σοὶ τὴν ἐπιστολήν. διαφεύγειν δὲ οὐκ ἔχων ἐπείσθην, μᾶλλον δέ, ἠναγκάσθην κινῆσαι τὴν τάξιν καὶ πρότερα ποιῆσαι τὰ δεύτερα. 3. καὶ νῦν μέν σοι ταῦτα, ἥξει δέ, ἢν ὁ θεὸς ἐθέλῃ, καὶ τὰ μετὰ τὴν θοίνην, τὰ μὲν σοὶ διαλεξόμενα,

---

[a] Although still suffering from gout, Libanius has resumed his lectures in the school by the *Bouleuterion*.

## 190. To Firminus

1. I was setting out to the City Hall carried by my servants[a] when someone came up to me on my way and gave me a letter, saying "This is for you from Firminus," and I was glad. But it turned out that there was a composition enclosed in your letter, and so I had another reason for being pleased, since the two became one. And there was a third item which was likely to surpass the other two—your envelope.[b] I wanted to enjoy that immediately, but my class would not let me. 2. The usual texts were in my hands and I was considering who was the proper actor for the plays: he was discovered, and turned out to be a young fellow who was being nurtured by my labours, for everybody chose him as soon as they heard him.[c] Your messenger stood by insistent that you should have your answer before the reading took place. I could not evade it and was persuaded, or rather compelled, to reverse my usual order and put first things last.[d] 3. For the present then, I send you this much: but there will come, god willing, the aftermath of the feast, to be imparted to

[b] The letter is written on papyrus but the cover is parchment.

[c] An insight into his treatment of classical texts in his lectures: in the case of plays one of his pupils both reads and acts the passage.

[d] Echoing the proverbial δευτέρων ἀμεινόνων (e.g. Plat. *Legg*. 4.723d), he amends his usual watchword τηρεῖν τὴν τάξιν.

τὰ δὲ τῇ φιλολόγῳ πόλει, ἥν μηδεὶς καιρὸς τοῦτο ἀφέλοιτο τὸ καλόν.

## 191. Θεοφίλῳ

1. Ἐγὼ μὲν ἐγέλασα, σὺ δὲ ὀργῆς ἔσῃ μεστὸς ἀκούσας τὸ πεπραγμένον. ἦν ἐν σπουδῇ καὶ εὐχῇ καὶ σοὶ καὶ τοῖς τὰ σὰ μιμουμένοις εἰς ἐμὲ φανῆναί τέ με ἐν τῷ διδασκαλείῳ καὶ τὴν οἴκοι κλίνην ἀφέντα χρήσασθαι τῇ ἐν τῷ διδασκαλείῳ· ἐγὼ δὲ ἕτερα μὲν ᾔτουν παρὰ τῶν θεῶν τῶν περικλυζόντων τοῦτο πειθόντων κακῶν, ἔπραττον δὲ ὅπερ ἦν βουλομένοις ὑμῖν. 2. καὶ αἱ μὲν ἐλπίδες ὑμῶν δρόμον ἐκ τῆς ἀγορᾶς εἰς τὸ βουλευτήριον τῶν λαμπρῶν διδασκάλων ἔσεσθαι πηδώντων, κροτούντων, χαιρόντων, εὐθυμουμένων, τοῖς θεοῖς εἰδότων χάριν, ἕτερος δ' ἂν ἐμνήσθη καὶ λύχνων·

---

[a] *BLZG* 312 (v), F/Kr. no. 15. Theophilus had recently been in Antioch, where he consoled Libanius upon the deaths of Cimon and Calliopius (*Letters* 184, 189). Indeed Seeck (p. 464) suggests that he is still there and that Libanius, now bedridden, communicates with him by letter, but this seems extreme. He had been able to visit Theophilus and had also made his way to his schoolroom, carried in a litter (cf. *Letter* 190). In 392 he was still working as usual in his schoolroom (*Ep.* 1046). In *Or.* 1.280,

you and to your cultured city,[e] and I trust that no eventuality may rob her of this glory.

[e] Cf. Plat. *Legg.* 1.641e. The city is Caesarea in Cappadocia. Libanius promises a dissertation in response to Firminus' composition.

## 191. To Theophilus[a]

1. Though I found it a joke, you will be filled with anger at hearing what has happened. You and those who behave like you towards me prayed insistently that I should make my appearance in the schoolroom, and leave my couch at home to use that at school. My prayer from the gods was something different, for the troubles that overwhelm me induced this attitude, but still I acted as you wished. 2. What you expected was a rush from the marketplace to the City Hall on the part of our foremost teachers, with excitement, applause, rejoicing, good will, and thanksgiving to the gods—and if some people had their say, with lanterns too.[b] But I knew

referring to 391, he notes that he was able to fulfil the routine professional duties of teaching, but his compositions were delivered indoors (cf. *ibid.* 281, *Letter* 193.7). Now in 393 he gives notice that he intends to deliver a public declamation, but this is snubbed. His infrequent appearances in public and the recent interruptions of his teaching course had left him without support.

[b] Compare the resounding success of his first declamation in Antioch forty years before (*Or.* 1.87 ff), where his audience were queuing to get into the City Hall before daylight.

ἐγὼ δὲ ᾔδειν μὲν αὐτοὺς καὶ ὧν ἐπιθυμοῦσι καὶ ἃ φρονοῦντες ἔρχοιντο παρ᾽ ἐμέ, καὶ διὰ τοῦτο ἔμελλον, ὅπως μηδεὶς αὐτῶν λυπήσεται. 3. προὔλεγον μέντοι τὴν ἐσομένην λύπην καὶ ὡς πένθος τοῦτο ἐκείνοις. ἀλλ᾽ ὅμως σοῦ καὶ βοῶντος καὶ κελεύοντος ἠναγκαζόμην καὶ ἐφερόμην. τῶν δὲ οὐδεὶς οὐδαμοῦ, μᾶλλον δέ, ἐξ οὕτω πολλῶν δύο, παρ᾽ ὧν οἶμαι λήψεσθαι δίκας τοὺς οὐχ ἥκοντας. 4. ἐμοὶ μὲν οὖν, ὅπερ ἔφην, ταυτὶ γέλως μαντείας τε τυχόντι καὶ ὡς οὐκ ὄντα με ζητήσουσιν εἰδότι· σοῦ δὲ δέομαι μὴ κινῆσαι νῦν τὴν ὀργήν, ἣ πολλάκις ἐπὶ τοὺς ἀδικοῦντας ὥσπερ τι τῶν ἄνωθεν ἠνέχθη βελῶν. ὄψει γὰρ δὴ καὶ ἡσυχάζων ἐπ᾽ ἀλλήλους ἰόντας τοὺς νῦν τούτους ἀλλήλους ἐπ᾽ ἐμὲ παρακαλοῦντας.

## 192. Οὐρανιανῷ

1. Ἐγὼ τοὺς μὲν ἐροῦντάς τι δυσχερὲς περὶ τῶν σῶν υἱέων ἡγησάμην ἔσεσθαι πολλοὺς[1] ὁρῶν

[1] πολλοὺς F. πολλὰς Wolf (Mss.)

[a] *BLZG* 315. Uranianus has delivered a wigging to his sons after receiving news of some misconduct of theirs. Throughout his teaching career Libanius had generally supported his pupils against ill-judged criticisms from

them, their desires, and their feelings when they attend me, and so I dallied so that none of them should be annoyed.[c] 3. You see, I foretold the annoyance there would be and how grievous this would be for them, but still at your protests and bidding I was carried along under duress. And not one of them turned up at all, or more precisely, out of all that number a couple did so, and I think the absentees will punish them for it. 4. So, as I told you, I found this a joke, for my prophecy came true and I know that they will want me dead.[d] But please do not now stir up your anger which has often visited wrongdoers like a bolt from the blue. Indeed, without stirring a finger, you will see those fellows who now incite each other to attack me attacking each other.

[c] For the reactions of his enemies at his silence cf. *Or.* 1.280.

[d] His letters at this time increasingly speak of the imminence of death, e.g. *Letter* 186.2, *Epp.* 1068.2, 1088.

## 192. To Uranianus[a]

1. I thought that your sons would have plenty of detractors, seeing that unjustified abuse is levelled

their parents. In some cases earlier in his career the misinformation had come from a sycophant (e.g. *Epp.* 660, 1395), in others from βασκανία (*Ep.* 1403). In any case these parents had unwittingly been misled by calumny (cf. Festugière, *Antioche* 111 ff). Now, however, Uranianus is roundly taken to task for being willingly misled; the father has shown moral failure.

παρὰ πολλῶν κακῶν κατ᾽ ἀγαθῶν ἀνδρῶν γινομένας ἀδίκους λοιδορίας· οὐ μὴν σέ γε ἐνόμιζον ἡδέως τε τούτων ἀκούσεσθαι τῶν λόγων καὶ ταχὺ πιστεύσειν[2] καὶ ποιήσειν τὰ τῶν ἠπατημένων ἄνδρα τοσαῦτα μὲν ἔτη γεγονότα, πολλοῖς δὲ πράγμασιν ἐν πολλῷ χρόνῳ πεπαιδευμένον, εἰδότα δὲ τούς τε ἀληθῶς ὄντας σοι φίλους καὶ τοὺς λέγοντας μέν, ῥηγνυμένους δὲ τοῖς σοῖς καλοῖς. 2. ἐπεὶ δὲ οὕτως ἡρπάσθης καὶ ἐλήφθης καὶ παρωξύνθης καὶ ἐχαρίσω διὰ τῶν πεπραγμένων τοῖς βουληθεῖσιν αὐτὰ ταῦτα πραχθῆναι, λυποῦμαι μὲν ὑπὲρ ἀμφοτέρων, καὶ σοῦ καὶ τῶν σῶν υἱέων, τῶν μὲν τοιαύτην δόντων δίκην, σοῦ δὲ τοιαύτην λαβόντος· τοσοῦτον δ᾽ ἂν εἴποιμι νῦν, ὅτι, εἰ ἦσαν κακοί, τοὺς νῦν κακῶς λέγοντας εἶχον ἂν ἐπαινοῦντας. 3. οὐδὲ γὰρ νῦν ὡς πονηροὶ μισοῦνται, ἀλλ᾽ ὄντες χρηστοὶ συκοφαντοῦνται· φαῦλοι δὲ ὄντες οὐκ ἂν τοῦτο ἔπασχον. ἦσαν γὰρ ἂν οἵουσπερ αὐτοὺς ἤθελον εἶναι τῶν <πώποτε γενομένων οἱ>[3] κάκιστοι. 4. νῦν μὲν οὖν σαυτὸν εὔφραινε τῷ θυμῷ χαριζόμενος, τοῦ χρόνου δὲ ποιοῦντος τἀληθῆ τῶν ψευδῶν δυνατώτερα πολλὰ μὲν σαυτὸν αἰτιάσῃ τὸν πεπεισμένον, πολλὰ δὲ καταράσῃ τοῖς πεπει-

against good men by plenty of rascals, yet I did not expect that you would be glad to listen to these remarks and quick to believe them and to behave in such misguided fashion—a man of your age, well-schooled in many matters over a long period of time, and able to discriminate between your true friends and the self-styled friends who burst with spleen at your goodness. 2. But now that you have been taken, hook, line, and sinker, and lost your temper and by your actions obliged those people who wanted just that to happen, I am sorry for both you and your sons, your sons for suffering such punishment and you for inflicting it. This much I would state at present, that if they were rascals, they would have their present traducers singing their praises. 3. They are now not objects of hatred for their viciousness but of calumny for their goodness. Had they been rogues, they would not have had this to put up with, for they would have been just what the biggest blackguards on earth wanted them to be. 4. So now enjoy yourself and indulge your temper, but when time causes truth to prevail over falsehood, then you will be full of self-reproach for being taken in, and of curses for those who took you in:

---

[2] *πιστεύσειν* F., conj. Re. *πιστεύειν* Wolf (Mss.)

[3] <*πώποτε γενομένων οἱ*> F., cf. Isocr. *Hel.* 38. *τε* followed by lacuna, Wolf (Mss.).

κόσι, ζητήσεις δὲ τὸν ἀπολωλότα χρόνον, τὸν δὲ εὑρήσεις οὐδαμοῦ.

## 193. <Ῥουφίνῳ>[1]

1. Ἔτι τοίνυν τὴν ἐν ἅπασιν ἡδονὴν ἀνθοῦσαν τότε νῦν ὁρῶμεν ἐν ἀκμάζουσιν, ἐν γέρουσιν, παισί, γυναιξίν, ἐλευθέροις, δούλοις, καὶ γὰρ δοῦλος ἐμιμεῖτο δεσπότην. φαίνεται δ' ἡμῖν καὶ τὰ ῥόδα τά τε ἔνθεν καὶ ἔνθεν τά τε ἄνωθεν πετόμενα καὶ τούτων τὰν τοῖς[2] γόνασιν ἱζάνοντα καὶ τοῖς ὑπὸ τῇ χλαμύδι μετ' εὐσχημοσύνης κινουμένοις δακτύλοις ἐπὶ τὰ κάτω φερόμενα. 2. λόγος δὲ εἷς μόνος ἐν τῇ τοσαύτῃ πόλει Ῥουφῖνος καὶ τὰ τούτου καὶ τί μὲν ἔπραξε, τί δ' εἶπεν ἢ πρὸς βουλὰς ἱκετευούσας[3] ἢ πρὸς τοὺς περὶ ταύτας ἐν ὁμιλίαις ἢ πρὸς τοὺς ἐπὶ τῷ παιδεύειν καθημένους. 3. εὔχονται δὲ γυναῖκες οὐ παροφθεῖσαι οὐδ' ἀμεληθεῖσαι οὐδὲ ἀπελαθεῖσαι, λόγων δὲ

[1] The superscription is missing in the Ms., where Ep. 1105 ends and is followed by a lacuna of considerable length. Wolf printed this letter as attached to the preceding one, although he noted the point of division and identified the addressee as Rufinus. F. suggests that the beginning of this letter is missing.

[2] τὰν τοῖς F., conj. Re. ταυτοῖς Wolf (ταυτοῖς Ms.)

[3] ἱκετευούσας F., conj. Re. ἱκετεύσας Wolf (Ms.)

you will seek to retrieve the misspent time that is past, and find that you simply cannot.

## 193. <To Rufinus>[a]

1. . . . That pleasure which at the time blossomed forth in everyone we still see now in men full-grown, in old men, boys, women, free men and slaves, for the slave copies his master.[b] We also remember the roses showered upon you from either side and from above, some settling on your knees and brushed off elegantly by the movement of your hands under your cloak. 2. There is only one story told in this great city—Rufinus and everything about him, what he did, what he said, whether to the councils as suppliants or to their members in private session, or to the occupants of professorial chairs. 3. Women who have suffered no neglect, no lack of considera-

[a] *BLZG* 255 (xii), *PLRE* 778 (18). F/Kr. no. 66. Rufinus, Tatianus' successor as praetorian prefect, was a Christian bigot who conducted his official feudings with high-handed viciousness (cf. Seeck, "Libanius gegen Lucianus" 95 ff).

[b] The letter as we have it begins in full flight with a flattering eulogy of Rufinus' flying visit to Antioch in the winter of 392–3, which had resulted in the fall of Lucianus and the deposition of Florentius. The fragmentary *Or.* 1.282 refers to this last. (Cf. Libanios, *Autobiographie* ed. Petit, p. 205, note 1, for the most convincing account of relations between Libanius and Rufinus.) The servility and obsequiousness of the aged Libanius towards a powerful but utterly ruthless prefect are in sad contrast to the independence he had once cherished.

τυχοῦσαι πρᾴων τε καὶ ἡμέρων, εὔχοντ᾽ οὖν αἱ γυναῖκες σώζεσθαι μέν σοι τὴν τοῦ γενναίου βασιλέως εὔνοιαν, σώζεσθαι δὲ βασιλεῖ τοὺς σοὺς ὑπὲρ αὐτοῦ πόνους ἐλθεῖν τε αὖθις ὡς ἡμᾶς τὸν τῶν πόλεων ἰατρὸν ἀναβῆναί τε πάλιν εἰς Δάφνην δευτέρων ἀκριβεστέρων, — ὡς νῦν γε ἱέραξ ἡμῖν ἦσθα τάχος τε πτεροῦ τοῦ κείνου μιμούμενος καὶ τῷ πᾶσαν ἐθέλειν εἰδέναι ἐν βραχεῖ τὸ μὴ πᾶσαν ἰδεῖν κεκωλυμένος — ταῦτ᾽ οὖν τὰ διαφυγόντα τῶν σῶν ὀφθαλμῶν τυχεῖν καὶ μὴ τῶν ὀφθέντων ἔλαττον[4] ἔχειν· εἰ δὲ καὶ μετὰ τῶν ἀρίστων βασιλέων, ὧν[5] πολὺς ἔρως τῇ πόλει — καὶ θαυμαστὸν οὐδὲν τῶν σεσωκότων ἐρᾶν τὴν σεσωσμένην, — τίς ἡμῖν ἴσος εἰς εὐτυχίας λόγον; 4. εἰ δ᾽ οὖν τι καὶ μεῖζον τὰς θείας ἐκείνας κεφαλὰς ἔτι πείθοι μένειν, αὐτὸς ἡμῖν ἥκειν μεθ᾽ ὁμοίου τοῦ δρόμου καὶ δεικνύναι με μάντιν ἀγαθόν. οἶσθα γὰρ ἃ[6] προεῖπον, ὅτι τὸν οὕτω ταχέως ἀπελθόντα

[4] ἔλαττον F. ἐλάττω Wolf (Ms.)
[5] ὧν F. οὐ Wolf (Ms.) οὗ Re.
[6] ἃ Wolf (Ms.) ὃ F.

---

[c] So called because of the killing of Lucianus and the removal of Florentius, both of whom had aroused the ire of Libanius. They had been the subjects of his harangues,

tion or rebuff, but met with kind and gentle words—the women, then, pray that the goodwill of our noble emperor may be preserved for you, and that there be preserved for the emperor your labours on his behalf, and that once more the healer of cities may visit us[c] and go up to Daphne again, more meticulously on this second occasion—for then you were like a hawk, imitating it in speed of wing,[d] and in your desire to acquaint yourself with all of it in a short time you were prevented from seeing it all—so they pray that what has escaped your glance may meet it and not be worse off than what you have seen. Should you come in company with our excellent emperors to whom the city is greatly devoted—and it is not surprising that the city they have saved should be devoted to its saviours[e]—who could rival us in any assessment of our good fortune? 4. However, should matters of greater importance still induce those sacred personages to stay behind, come yourself with like speed and show me to be a good prophet, for you know what I foretold—that I thought, when you left so quickly,

which probably provided material for Rufinus to act against them. Zosimus (5.2.1–4) put the incident after the death of Theodosius in 395 but, as Seeck showed (*op. cit.*), it almost certainly happened in this visit to Antioch early in 393 (when the roses were in bloom).

[d] A variation on the proverbial δευτέρων ἀμεινόνων. For the speed of hawks cf. Hom. *Il.* 13.86, 15.237.

[e] Saved as a result of the emperor's clemency after the riots of the Statues in 387.

καὶ ταχέως ἡμῖν ἐπανήξειν οἴομαι. 5. ὅτι δὲ ἐλθὼν τῶν αὐτῶν μεταδώσεις, οὐδὲν δεῖ πυθέσθαι τῶν μάντεων δεικνυμένων τῶν ἐσομένων τοῖς ἤδη γεγενημένοις. καὶ γὰρ ἕλξεις τῇ σαυτοῦ χειρὶ τὸν θρόνον ἐγγύς τέ μου καθίσαι ἐθελήσεις ἡσθήσῃ τε ἐγγύθεν ὁρῶν τὰς πολιὰς θήξεις τέ μοι τὸν νοῦν τοῖς σαυτοῦ νοήμασιν ἐγώ τέ σε θηράσω πάλιν κεκτημένον μὲν τὴν ἡμετέραν φωνήν, φάσκοντα δὲ οὐκ ἔχειν. 6. ὃ δὲ ᾔτησα μὲν ἐν τῇ πόλει πολλάκις, ᾔτησα δὲ κἀν τῷ ποταμῷ τῷ πολλῷ μὲν τοῦ χειμῶνος, ὀλίγῳ δὲ νῦν, τοῦτο καὶ νῦν δέομαι δοθῆναί μοι, τίνων τε ἐγένου γονέων καὶ τἀν τοῖς διδασκαλείοις ἔργα δι᾽ ὅσων πεπόρευσαι. καὶ γὰρ εἰ πολλὰ τὰ βεβοημένα καὶ διδάσκειν οὐκ ὀλίγα δύναιτ᾽ ἂν ὁ φίλος Θεόφιλος, ἀλλ᾽ οὐδεὶς οἷος σὺ περὶ τῶν σῶν γένοιτ᾽ ἂν ἡμῖν διδάσκαλος. 7. ἐμὲ δὲ θεάτρων μὲν ἀπέστησε τὸ γῆρας, τὸ δὲ

---

[f] Rufinus had flattered Libanius inordinately during his short visit—an intimacy upon which the sophist plumed himself (*Or.* 1.282). In 388 Rufinus needed an interpreter to deal with a letter from Libanius (*Ep.* 865.3). Now he can

that you would quickly return to us. 5. As for the fact that upon your coming you will confer the same benefits upon us, there is no need to make enquiries of the prophets, since the future events are revealed by those that have already occurred. You will draw up your chair with your own hand and will wish to place it near me and be pleased to see my grey hairs near at hand, and whet my intellect with your own ideas, and I will again pursue you now that you have acquired knowledge of our language, though you profess you have not.[f] 6. The request I often made in the city and at the river in winter[g] when it was in spate, I now beg you to grant me now that it is shallow—inform me of your parentage and your progression through all the activities in the schools.[h] However great the reports, and though my friend Theophilus could inform me of much of it, yet there could be none to inform me of your private affairs so well as yourself.[i] 7. My old age has withdrawn me from the lecture rooms, but it has not

converse passably with him when Libanius was seeing him off.

[g] The date of this letter is thus midsummer 393.

[h] Libanius volunteers to write a panegyric upon Rufinus (cf. *Ep.* 1111). The information he requests is indispensable for the beginning of a panegyric, as in *Orations* 18 and 59. This project was not fulfilled or has not survived.

[i] Cf. *Letter* 191.

τῆς χειρὸς ἔργον οὐ προσαφείλετο. μὴ νομίσῃς δὲ ἀδικήσειν λέγων τι περὶ σαυτοῦ καλόν· πολλοὺς γὰρ δὴ θαυμασομένους[7] ἄνδρας τούτῳ[8] ποιήσεις.

[7] θαυμασομένους F., conj. Re. θαυμαζομένους Wolf (Ms.)
[8] τούτῳ F., conj. Re. τοῦτο Wolf (Ms.)

robbed me of the work of my hand.[j] Do not think it wrong to tell something to your own credit. You will by doing so get many to admire you in the future.

[j] Cf. *Or.* 1.280, 282.

# APPENDIX. ADDITIONAL NOTES

## Chronology for *Letters* 92–95

The sequence of *Letters* 92–95 was established by Bidez and Cumont, but the chronology can be refined with more precision than either they or Seeck admit.

The *terminus post quem* is the the delivery of *Or.* 13, some days after Julian's entry into Antioch, i.e. towards the end of July 362.

The *terminus ante quem* is the burning of the Daphnean temple on 22 October. In the meantime *Or.* 14, for Aristophanes, has been composed and sent to Julian at his request. There is no mention of this disaster in the speech or the correspondence relevant to it. Yet the tenor of the speech is of Aristophanes' consistent devotion to the pagan religion in the face of Christian persecution. If this speech were later than 22 October, it would surely have been very different in tone.

Hence the sequence of events is:

(i) Julian arrives in Antioch, 18 July.

(ii) *Or.* 13 is delivered within a few days (*Letter* 88). Delivery about 25 July, but publication is delayed.

(iii) *Letter* 92. Publication of *Or.* 13 still has not

occurred (i.e. the text has not yet been sent to Julian). Libanius blames ill-health.

(iv) *Letter* 93, a cover note for *Or*. 13. Probably late in August.

(v) Julian, *Ep*. 96 Bidez-Cumont. Julian learns that Libanius is engaged on the composition of another oration (*Or*. 14) and demands a copy. September.

(vi) *Letter* 94. Libanius replies, sending the text of *Or*. 14.

(vii) Julian, *Ep*. 97. Julian acknowledges.

(viii) *Letter* 95. Libanius replies to this acknowledgement.

(ix) The burning of the Daphnean temple. 22 October. First mentioned, *Letter* 96.2 (early 363).

Items v–viii are all later than Julian's *Ep. ad Nilum* (cf. *Letter* 94.5).

## Additional Note to *Letters* 154–159

These six letters are a fair sample of Libanius' determination in support of his protégés, especially in matters where he himself has some personal interest. The matter at issue is the sophistic immunity of Eusebius the sophist (*BLZG* xxii), and by implication that of himself. Its antecedents are well documented (*Or*. 1.257 f; 32; 54.52; *Epp*. 850–2, 864–8, 870, 878–880), though interpretation of details is confused.

In the summer of 387, after the Riots of the

Statues, Ellebichus, lately commissioner and still general in charge at Antioch, suggested that the city send an embassy to purge itself completely of its misconduct, and he delegated to Libanius the arrangements concerning the choice of its members. Eusebius xxii, associate professor in his school, who already held sophistic immunity by decree of the city council backed by imperial assent, was prevailed upon to become one of the members, on the understanding that the performance of this curial duty was to be without prejudice to his immunity. Thrasydaeus, another nominee, conceived a bitter hostility towards Libanius, blaming him for not getting Ellebichus to excuse him from the task. So he tried to have Libanius' bastard son Cimon drafted into the curia, and to attack Libanius' own immunity, after alleging that he was guilty of treason as a secret supporter of the usurper Maximus (so *Or.* 32; the charge is finally disposed of in *Letter* 146). Thrasydaeus' efforts against Libanius were rebuffed; Eusebius returned from the embassy basking in the approval gained by a couple of imperial panegyrics, and with the added bonus for Libanius of the emperor's permission to transfer his property to Cimon in his own lifetime and so prevent the inevitable litigation attached to testamentary inheritance (*Or. 1.257–8, Epp.* 844, 845.4).

The current policy at court was to promote a revival of the curiae. Taking advantage of this, Antioch despatched an embassy of three, member-

ship unknown, to Constantinople to press for stronger support for the curia (*Epp.* 850–2), thence to proceed to Italy to congratulate Theodosius upon his successes there against Maximus (*Epp.* 864–8; summer 388). In such a climate of opinion Libanius himself might be safe enough, but Eusebius, his subordinate, had made himself vulnerable by performing the curial duty of ambassador. Disregarding the assurances previously given, the curials, egged on by the *consularis* Eustathius (*Or.* 54.52, *Ep.* 870), reversed their attitude towards his immunity and prepared yet another embassy consisting of two men, Cynegius, of the family of Letoius the *principalis,* and yet another Eusebius, who are both described as decurions (*Ep.* 878.1; *pace* Petit 419, who with Seeck identifies him with Eusebius xxii). They were to go officially to offer crowns to Theodosius for his final victory, but also to press for Eustathius' decision about Eusebius xxii to be ratified and his sophistic immunity rescinded (*Ep.* 870). Libanius wrote three tepid letters of introduction to minor potentates at court in favour of this Eusebius, possibly Eusebius xxviii, barely mentioning his status as ambassador (*Epp.* 878–880). Nevertheless they seemed in fair way to securing their objective, whereupon Eusebius xxii, now thoroughly alarmed, travelled privately to Constantinople in an attempt to retain his privileges. Armed with *Letters* 154–159, letters of introduction to the most influential officials and courtiers,

he sought, with Libanius' assistance, to counter the machinations of this last embassy which seemed to be on the verge of success (early winter 388–9). He was able to secure at least a temporary respite: he managed to retain his immunity, but the question was not finally settled, since he is to be found in 390 making yet another journey to court to secure final confirmation of his privileges (*Epp.* 918–921).

The nuances of approach to these various persons of influence are noteworthy, illustrating that adaptability which Eunapius attributed to Libanius. With the serving career officials, Eusebius xxvii, Proclus, and Tatianus, he could write, however much deferring to the influence they wielded, almost on terms of equality in consequence of his long service in rhetoric and his honorary status. His acquaintance with them was of long standing, and from the nature of their duties they were well aware of the facts of the case.

Eusebius xxvii indeed had already been active in the good cause (*Ep.* 902), so after due expressions of gratitude, Libanius proceeds to a pathetic description of the present situation, primarily as it affects himself and only secondarily as affecting Eusebius xxii. The emphasis reflects the difference in status between Libanius and his protégé, and of the importance which an official like Eusebius xxvii was likely to attribute to it.

To Proclus, already personally acquainted with

Eusebius and obliged to him for eloquence lavished on his behalf, the appeal is more personal. Libanius equates the quasi-filial relationship of his subordinate towards himself with that of Proclus towards his own father Tatianus, and bolsters it with the associated notions of honour and piety. With Tatianus himself stress is laid explicitly upon the cultural affinity between him and Libanius, and the appeal for Eusebius is based directly upon his services to Libanius' own continued well-being and that of his educational system. For Tatianus, who had some pretensions as a composer of epic, an appropriate Homeric reference serves to emphasize the pathos.

Mardonius, the eunuch master of the bedchamber at the court of Arcadius, after the routine mention of a rather tenuous friendship and the briefest exposition of Libanius' problems, is approached with the outright request to do what he normally does and grant this favour. Conventional politeness barely conceals Libanius' view that corruptibility is the hallmark of court eunuchs. Theodorus, however, receives very different treatment. His position of influence at court had been attained through his intellectual and educational qualifications, and he had already been active on Eusebius' account (*Ep.* 903). The appeal to him is phrased in moral terms and based on the identity of cultural interests. Philosophic undertones and a concern for education in general mark this approach, which is

supported by several appropriate classical references.

To Aburgius, a respected senior statesman and himself an ex-prefect, Libanius is much more deferential. He is out of active politics and remote from the case, and therefore receives a more circumstantial account of it, prefaced by the statement of the claims of friendship, both personal and mutual. The *ésprit de corps* and continuity of tradition among holders of the prefecture are subsumed to emphasize the consistency and proven legitimacy of Eusebius' claims. This is the one appeal where there is no direct reference to Libanius' own condition, the implication being that for such as Aburgius hard evidence is what is required. As a sweetener for this more impartial support the letter ends with the disguised compliment of a Homeric reference.

This affair is discussed in Seeck, *BLZG* 143 f, 450 f; Pack, *Studies* 121–3; Petit, *Vie Municipale* 418 f; Liebeschuetz, *Antioch* 267 ff. Of these the arguments of Liebeschuetz are the most coherent and convincing.

## The Events Preceding *Letters* 161–164

Between *Ep.* 914 and 915 there is a gap of some eighteen months in the correspondence, covering the period from early winter 388–9 to summer 390. In this time relations between Libanius and the city council of Antioch continued to deteriorate even further. The embassies of 388 and his orations upon

the curia (*Or.* 48 and 49) had won him few friends. Eusebius' success in avoiding the liturgies, followed by his own invidious position as principal heir of Olympius and thus possessor of still more land that had originally been curial, added fresh fuel to the fire (*Or.* 1.275 ff; 63). He was enmeshed in a web of testamentary litigation which he found alien to him, and a campaign of harassment against him and his protégés resulted in 390 in an attempt to enrol yet another of his assistants, Thalassius, into the curia.

Thalassius (who lacked the credentials that Eusebius had possessed) was eager to evade the doubtful honour of curial status. Now he went the whole way, deciding to apply for membership of the Senate in Constantinople by cooptation. His first step was to apply to the imperial bureau for the diploma granting the status of *clarissimus.* This was forthcoming but remained provisional upon his acceptance by the Senate itself, and this body, under the presidency of the urban prefect Proclus, constituted itself, as it was entitled to do, as a court of enquiry for the examination of Thalassius' application. If he survived this scrutiny he would then proceed to one of the praetorships, which involved the immediate outlay of the *summa honoraria,* a lump sum proportionate to his fortune, and he would thereafter be safe from curial impressment and the continued drain on his property which the liturgies involved. The plan went awry. Proclus himself and two other notables objected to him. His low origins,

his ownership of a sword factory (a sordid occupation), and the personal hostility he had manifested to at least one of them in the past, all told against him. His application was therefore blackballed.

The immediate reaction of Libanius was to try again. Around midsummer 390 he sent a string of letters to influential friends and acquaintances in Constantinople pressing for a review of Thalassius' application (*Epp.* 922–30, 932, 936–7), of which *Letters* 161–164 are a fair sample. Once again he was unsuccessful, and finally he produced his oration *Pro Thalassio* (*Or.* 42), ostensibly for the emperor's attention. This provided the fullest justification of Thalassius' merits, his position, and his course of action hitherto, and also proposed an alternative: that the emperor should appoint him directly to an official post that would give him automatic right of entry into the Senate. Proclus and his fellows were flayed with the choicest invective, which may have relieved Libanius' feelings but achieved no result, even if the emperor ever saw or heard the work. Thalassius, as revealed by the letters of 392–3, remained with Libanius in Antioch.

*Oration* 42, which provides the information outlined above, is commented upon by P. Petit, "Les senateurs de Constantinople."

## Note on *Letters* 169–170

Libanius had long been at odds with influential curials, more recently over the matter of immunity claimed by his assistants and over the problems of litigation which he encountered as heir to his friend Olympius. In consequence the councillors pressed him more closely at every opportunity. He had already succeeded in getting imperial permission for his bastard son Cimon to have undisputed right of access to his property by transferring it to him in his own lifetime (*Or.* 1.258), but in so doing he had made him more vulnerable. The councillors turned their attention towards Cimon, who was now the owner of what had once been curial land and so could be claimed for the liturgies. Beginning with Thrasydaeus (*Or.* 32.7), a sustained campaign had been set up to enrol him for curial duties. He had rejected the sophistic career mapped out for him by his father, with the possibility of obtaining immunity thereby, and had instead opted for that of advocate, immediately a more precarious course but one with prospects of advancement to the imperial service and security later on. He had been enrolled as advocate in the court of the *consularis* 384 to 389 (*Or.* 28.9, 54.7 ff), but despite the eulogies lavished upon him for his eloquence by his doting father, he had proved a failure at the bar. Membership of the Senate seemed to be the only solution for his problem as tensions increased between 388 and 390. In

view of what had happened to Thalassius, cooptation was out of the question. Direct appointment to an offical post that carried automatic membership of the Senate seemed to be his only escape from curial impressment.

Libanius was well enough aware of the current thinking at court on evasion of curial duties, but nevertheless he armed Cimon with two letters of introduction (*Letters* 169–170) and saw him depart to Constantinople. There is no attempt to approach the numerous friends and acquaintances with influence in the Senate, who had so signally failed him in the case of his assistant. Libanius concentrates solely upon the appointment to office, the prerogative of the praetorian prefect, whom he approaches direct.

Cimon succeeded in getting nomination for the post of *consularis* of Cyprus (*Or.* 1.283, *Ep.* 1012), but this raised such storms of protest in the Senate because of his mother's base origin (*Or.* 1.278, *Letters* 188.5, 189), that the appointment was immediately cancelled. Proclus again was the chief opponent. In 391, when Cimon's petition had finally failed, Libanius wrote to friends at court urging them to send him home, protesting that Cimon had gone there against his advice (*Or.* 1.279, *Epp.* 1000–1003). On the return journey Cimon broke a leg in an accident near Tarsus and, although looked after by Libanius' friends there, returned to Antioch dying.

Libanius was overwhelmed with grief, just as he had been at the death of Julian. He gave up composing his orations for a time (*Epp.* 1026, *Letter* 182), and constantly refers to his loss thereafter (*Letters* 179–181, *Epp.* 1037–9, 1042, 1045, *Letters* 182–184, 187). The final notice in the Autobiography is the curse called down on Constantinople and the false friends there who had done Cimon wrong (*Or.* 1.283–5).

# CONCORDANCES

I. This edition of the Letters compared with the editions of Foerster (F), Wolf (W), Fatouros and Krischer (F/Kr), and Bouchery (B). F, W, and F/Kr are cited by number, B by page.

| This edition | Addressee | F | W | F/Kr | B |
|---|---|---|---|---|---|
| 1 | Zenobius | 15 | 15 | | |
| 2 | Thalassius (i) | 16 | 16 | | |
| 3 | Hierocles (i) | 390 | 393 | 4 | |
| 4 | Anatolius (i) | 391 | 394 a | | |
| 5 | Hygieinus | 393 | 395 | | |
| 6 | Aristaenetus (i) | 405 | 407 | | |
| 7 | Datianus | 409 | 411 | | |
| 8 | Aristaenetus (i) | 414 | 1230 | | |
| 9 | Aristaenetus (i) | 427 | 1238 | | |
| 10 | Heortius | 428 | 1192 | | |
| 11 | Aristaenetus (i) | 430 | 1239 | | |
| 12 | Themistius (i) | 434 | 1241 | 37 | 51 |
| 13 | Datianus | 441 | 1033 | | |
| 14 | Phasganius | 454 | 1254 | | |
| 15 | Gorgonius (iv) | 469 | 1264 | | |
| 16 | Themistius (i) | 476 | 1134 | | 63 |
| 17 | Andronicus (ii) | 477 | 1270 | | |
| 18 | Strategius (i) | 497 | 1185 | | |
| 19 | Basileius | 501 | 1603 | 68 | |
| 20 | Anatolius (i) | 509 | 423 | | |
| 21 | Andronicus (ii) | 515 | 429 | | 85 |
| 22 | Anatolius (i) | 552 | 466 | | |

| This edition | Addressee | F | W | F/Kr | B |
|---|---|---|---|---|---|
| 23 | Mygdonius | 557 | 471 | | |
| 24 | Aristaenetus (i) | 571 | 487 | | |
| 25 | Aristaenetus (i) | 580 | 495 | | |
| 26 | Aristaenetus (i) | 326 | 329 | | |
| 27 | Acacius (iii) | 345 | 348 | | |
| 28 | Bassus | 359 | 362 | | |
| 29 | Aristaenetus (i) | 364 | 367 | | |
| 30 | Julian (Caesar) | 369 | 372 | 45 | |
| 31 | Paulus (ii) | 370 | 373 | | |
| 32 | Calycius | 379 | 382 | | |
| 33 | Euphemius (i) | 210 | 210 | | |
| 34 | Aristaenetus (i) | 21 | 20 | | |
| 35 | Aristaenetus (i) | 331 | 334 | | |
| 36 | Hygieinus | 25 | 24 | | |
| 37 | Demetrius (i) | 33 | 31 | | |
| 38 | Julian (Caesar) | 35 | 33 | | |
| 39 | Strategius (i) | 388 | 391 | 9 | |
| 40 | Anatolius (i) | 19 | 18 | | |
| 41 | Modestus | 49 | 47 | | |
| 42 | Themistius (i) | 241 | 244 | | 124 |
| 43 | Themistius (i) | 70 | 68 | | 137 |
| 44 | Themistius (i) | 86 | 84 | | 142 |
| 45 | Leontius (iv) | 88 | 86 | | |
| 46 | Anatolius (i) | 80 | 78 | | |
| 47 | Anatolius (i) | 81 | 79 | | |
| 48 | Iamblichus | 34 | 32 | | |
| 49 | Modestus | 37 | 35 | | |
| 50 | Modestus | 96 | 95 | | |
| 51 | Themistius (i) | 62 | 60 | | 162 |
| 52 | Themistius (i) | 66 | 64 | 56 | 169 |
| 53 | Florentius (ii) | 97 | 96 | | |
| 54 | Modestus | 101 | 100 | | |
| 55 | Themistius (i) | 112 | 112 | | 178 |

| This edition | Addressee | F | W | F/Kr | B |
|---|---|---|---|---|---|
| 56 | Spectatus | 115 | 115 | | |
| 57 | Euagrius (iii) | 126 | 126 | | |
| 58 | Acacius (iii) | 127 | 127 | | |
| 59 | Demetrius (i) | 128 | 128 | | |
| 60 | Priscianus (i) | 143 | 143 | | |
| 61 | Priscianus (i) | 149 | 149 | | |
| 62 | Andronicus (ii) | 150 | 150 | | |
| 63 | Modestus | 163 | 163 | | |
| 64 | Demetrius (i) | 283 | 286 | 25 | |
| 65 | Polychronius | 28 | 27 | | |
| 66 | Andronicus (ii) | 192 | 192 | | |
| 67 | Andronicus (ii) | 195 | 195 | | |
| 68 | Modestus | 196 | 196 | 30 | |
| 69 | Modestus | 197 | 197 | | |
| 70 | Modestus | 205 | 205 | | |
| 71 | Andronicus (ii) | 217 | 217 | 41 | |
| 72 | Crispinus | 263 | 266 | 26 | |
| 73 | Maximus (vi) | 275 | 278 | | |
| 74 | Modestus | 277 | 280 | | |
| 75 | Modestus | 308 | 311 | | |
| 76 | Palladius (vi) | 631 | 546 | 24 | |
| 77 | Anatolius (ii) | 636 | 551 | 39 | |
| 78 | Basileios | 647 | 1605 | | |
| 79 | Bassianus | 679 | 592 | | |
| 80 | Maximus (x) | 694 | 606 | 46 | |
| 81 | Celsus (i) | 696 | 608 | | |
| 82 | Julianus (ii) | 701 | 613 | | |
| 83 | Bacchius | 710 | 622 | | |
| 84 | Celsus (i) | 716 | 628 | | |
| 85 | Celsus (i) | 722 | 634 | 17 | |
| 86 | Julianus (ii) | 725 | 637 | | |
| 87 | Hyperechius (i) | 731 | 643 | 75 | |
| 88 | Celsus (i) | 736 | 648 | 47 | |

| This edition | Addressee | F | W | F/Kr | B |
|---|---|---|---|---|---|
| 89 | Julianus (vii) | 740 | 652 | | |
| 90 | Acacius (ii) | 754 | 666 | 27 | |
| 91 | Bacchius | 757 | 669 | | |
| 92 | Seleucus | 770 | 680 | | |
| 93 | Julian (Augustus) | 610 | 525 | | |
| 94 | Julian (Augustus) | 760 | 672 | | |
| 95 | Julian (Augustus) | 758 | 670 | | |
| 96 | Demetrius (i) | 785 | 695 | | |
| 97 | Antipatros | 797 | 707 | 49 | |
| 98 | Julian (Augustus) | 802 | 712 | | |
| 99 | Nicocles | 810 | 721 | | |
| 100 | Julian (Augustus) | 811 | 722 | | |
| 101 | Acacius (ii) | 815 | 726 | | |
| 102 | Themistius (i) | 818 | 729 | | 217 |
| 103 | Belaeus | 819 | 730 | 51 | |
| 104 | Alexander (iii) | 1351 | 1053 | | |
| 105 | Gaianus | 1364 | 1426 b | | |
| 106 | Rufinus (v) | 1365 | 1427 | | |
| 107 | Heliodorus (i) | 1376 | 1436 | | |
| 108 | Dulcitius (iii) | 1400 | 1217 | | |
| 109 | Aristophanes | 1402 | 1457 | | |
| 110 | Alexander (iii) | 1406 | 1460 | | |
| 111 | Entrechius | 1424 | 1059 | | |
| 112 | Salutius | 1426 | 1474 | | |
| 113 | Elpidius (ii) | 1120 | 1138 | | |
| 114 | Scylacius (ii) | 1431 | 1062 | 55 | |
| 115 | Philagrius (iv) | 1434 | 1218 | | |
| 116 | Themistius (i) | 1430 | 1061 | 60 | 223 |
| 117 | Hyperechius (i) | 1441 | 1069 | | |
| 118 | Datianus | 1446 | 1482 | | |
| 119 | Caesarius (iv) | 1459 | 1494 | | |
| 120 | Scylacius (ii) | 1220 | 1186 | 53 | |
| 121 | Andronicus (ii) | 1221 | 1329 | 78 | |

| This edition | Addressee | F | W | F/Kr | B |
|---|---|---|---|---|---|
| 122 | Nicocles | 1119 | 1137 | | |
| 123 | Demetrius (i) | 1128 | 1294 | | |
| 124 | Julianus (viii) | 1154 | 1039 | 54 | |
| 125 | Elpidius (ii) | 1180 | 1315 | 43 | |
| 126 | Datianus | 1184 | 1040 | 29 | |
| 127 | Salutius | 1185 | 1141 | | |
| 128 | Themistius (i) | 1186 | 1319 | | 243 |
| 129 | Alcimus | 1187 | 1320 | | |
| 130 | Euelpistius | 1210 | 1179 | | |
| 131 | Priscianus (i) | 1251 | 1342 | | |
| 132 | Priscianus (i) | 1253 | 1344 | | |
| 133 | Aristophanes | 1264 | 1350 | | |
| 134 | Nicocles | 1265 | 1351 | | |
| 135 | Euagrius (iv) | 1287 | 1369 | | |
| 136 | Salutius | 1298 | 1103 | | |
| 137 | Eudaemon (ii) | 1300 | 1379 | | |
| 138 | Acacius (iii) | 1301 | 1380 | | |
| 139 | Antoninus (i) | 1330 | 1119 | | |
| 140 | Seleucus | 1473 | 1073 | | |
| 141 | Themistius (i) | 1477 | 1510 a | 59 | 256 |
| 142 | Seleucus | 1508 | 1078 | | |
| 143 | Theodorus (iii) | 1534 | 1551 | 11 | |
| 144 | Amphilochius | 1543 | 1226 | 74 | |
| 145 | Heortius | 12 | — | | |
| 146 | Tatianus (i) | 840 | 760 | | |
| 147 | Magnus (iv) | 843 | 763 | | |
| 148 | Eusebius (xxvii) | 846 | 766 | 34 | |
| 149 | Proclus (iii) | 852 | 771 | 36 | |
| 150 | Richomer | 866 | 785 | | |
| 151 | Promotus | 867 | 786 | | |
| 152 | Elebichus | 868 | 787 | | |
| 153 | Entrechius | 901 | 819 | | |
| 154 | Eusebius (xxvii) | 904 | 822 | | |

| This edition | Addressee | F | W | F/Kr | B |
|---|---|---|---|---|---|
| 155 | Theodorus (ix) | 905 | 823 | | |
| 156 | Proclus (iii) | 906 | 824 | | |
| 157 | Aburgius | 907 | 825 | | |
| 158 | Mardonius (ii) | 908 | 826 | | |
| 159 | Tatianus (i) | 909 | 827 | | |
| 160 | The Patriarch | 914 | 832 | | |
| 161 | Proclus (iii) | 922 | 840 | | |
| 162 | Optatus (ii) | 923 | 841 | | |
| 163 | Elebichus | 925 | 843 | | |
| 164 | Eusebius (xxvii) | 926 | 844 | | |
| 165 | Proclus (iii) | 938 | 857 | | |
| 166 | Priscus (i) | 947 | 866 | 69 | |
| 167 | Thalassius (iv) | 951 | 870 | | |
| 168 | Sapores | 957 | 876 | | |
| 169 | Tatianus (i) | 959 | 878 | 13 | |
| 170 | Aburgius | 960 | 879 | | |
| 171 | Hierophantes (ii) | 964 | 883 | | |
| 172 | Richomer | 972 | 891 | 71 | |
| 173 | Tatianus (i) | 990 | 909 | | |
| 174 | Cyrus (iii) | 994 | 913 | | |
| 175 | Anatolius (vi) | 1001 | 920 | | |
| 176 | Heracleius (iv) | 1002 | 921 | | |
| 177 | Symmachus | 1004 | 923 | 63 | |
| 178 | Tatianus (i) | 1021 | 941 | | |
| 179 | Anatolius (vi) | 1023 | 943 | | |
| 180 | Richomer | 1024 | 944 | | |
| 181 | Postumianus (iii) | 1036 | 956 | 67 | |
| 182 | Firminus (ii) | 1048 | 968 | 73 | |
| 183 | Chryses (ii) | 1050 | 970 | | |
| 184 | Aristaenetus (ii) | 1051 | 971 | | |
| 185 | Priscio | 1053 | 973 | | |
| 186 | Moderatus | 1057 | 977 | | |
| 187 | Brasidas (ii) | 1058 | 978 | 14 | |

| This edition | Addressee | F | W | F/Kr | B |
|---|---|---|---|---|---|
| 188 | Marcellinus (vii) | 1063 | 983 | 62 | |
| 189 | Aristaenetus (ii) | 1064 | 984 | | |
| 190 | Firminus (ii) | 1066 | 986 | | |
| 191 | Theophilus (v) | 1075 | 995 | 15 | |
| 192 | Uranianus | 1093 | 1013 | | |
| 193 | Rufinus (xii) | 1106 | 1025 | 66 | |

II. Foerster's numeration of the Letters compared with that adopted here.

| Foerster | This edition | Foerster | This edition |
|---|---|---|---|
| 12 | 145 | 112 | 55 |
| 15 | 1 | 115 | 56 |
| 16 | 2 | 126 | 57 |
| 19 | 40 | 127 | 58 |
| 21 | 34 | 128 | 59 |
| 25 | 36 | 143 | 60 |
| 28 | 65 | 149 | 61 |
| 33 | 37 | 150 | 62 |
| 34 | 48 | 163 | 63 |
| 35 | 38 | 192 | 66 |
| 37 | 49 | 195 | 67 |
| 49 | 41 | 196 | 68 |
| 62 | 51 | 197 | 69 |
| 66 | 52 | 205 | 70 |
| 70 | 43 | 210 | 33 |
| 80 | 46 | 217 | 71 |
| 81 | 47 | 241 | 42 |
| 86 | 44 | 263 | 72 |
| 88 | 45 | 275 | 73 |
| 96 | 50 | 277 | 74 |
| 97 | 53 | 283 | 64 |
| 101 | 54 | 308 | 75 |

## CONCORDANCES

| Foerster | This edition | Foerster | This edition |
|---|---|---|---|
| 326 | 26 | 636 | 77 |
| 331 | 35 | 647 | 78 |
| 345 | 27 | 679 | 79 |
| 359 | 28 | 694 | 80 |
| 364 | 29 | 696 | 81 |
| 369 | 30 | 701 | 82 |
| 370 | 31 | 710 | 83 |
| 379 | 32 | 716 | 84 |
| 388 | 39 | 722 | 85 |
| 390 | 3 | 725 | 86 |
| 391 | 4 | 731 | 87 |
| 393 | 5 | 736 | 88 |
| 405 | 6 | 740 | 89 |
| 409 | 7 | 754 | 90 |
| 414 | 8 | 757 | 91 |
| 427 | 9 | 758 | 95 |
| 428 | 10 | 760 | 94 |
| 430 | 11 | 770 | 92 |
| 434 | 12 | 785 | 96 |
| 441 | 13 | 797 | 97 |
| 454 | 14 | 802 | 98 |
| 469 | 15 | 810 | 99 |
| 476 | 16 | 811 | 100 |
| 477 | 17 | 815 | 101 |
| 497 | 18 | 818 | 102 |
| 501 | 19 | 819 | 103 |
| 509 | 20 | 840 | 146 |
| 515 | 21 | 843 | 147 |
| 552 | 22 | 846 | 148 |
| 557 | 23 | 852 | 149 |
| 571 | 24 | 866 | 150 |
| 580 | 25 | 867 | 151 |
| 610 | 93 | 868 | 152 |
| 631 | 76 | 901 | 153 |

CONCORDANCES

| Foerster | This edition | Foerster | This edition |
|---|---|---|---|
| 904 | 154 | 1063 | 188 |
| 905 | 155 | 1064 | 189 |
| 906 | 156 | 1066 | 190 |
| 907 | 157 | 1075 | 191 |
| 908 | 158 | 1093 | 192 |
| 909 | 159 | 1106 | 193 |
| 914 | 160 | 1119 | 122 |
| 922 | 161 | 1120 | 113 |
| 923 | 162 | 1128 | 123 |
| 925 | 163 | 1154 | 124 |
| 926 | 164 | 1180 | 125 |
| 938 | 165 | 1184 | 126 |
| 947 | 166 | 1185 | 127 |
| 951 | 167 | 1186 | 128 |
| 957 | 168 | 1187 | 129 |
| 959 | 169 | 1210 | 130 |
| 960 | 170 | 1220 | 120 |
| 964 | 171 | 1221 | 121 |
| 972 | 172 | 1251 | 131 |
| 990 | 173 | 1253 | 132 |
| 994 | 174 | 1264 | 133 |
| 1001 | 175 | 1265 | 134 |
| 1002 | 176 | 1287 | 135 |
| 1004 | 177 | 1298 | 136 |
| 1021 | 178 | 1300 | 137 |
| 1023 | 179 | 1301 | 138 |
| 1024 | 180 | 1330 | 139 |
| 1036 | 181 | 1351 | 104 |
| 1048 | 182 | 1364 | 105 |
| 1050 | 183 | 1365 | 106 |
| 1051 | 184 | 1376 | 107 |
| 1053 | 185 | 1400 | 108 |
| 1057 | 186 | 1402 | 109 |
| 1058 | 187 | 1406 | 110 |

## CONCORDANCES

| Foerster | This edition | Foerster | This edition |
|---|---|---|---|
| 1424 | 111 | 1459 | 119 |
| 1426 | 112 | 1473 | 140 |
| 1430 | 116 | 1477 | 141 |
| 1431 | 114 | 1508 | 142 |
| 1434 | 115 | 1534 | 143 |
| 1441 | 117 | 1543 | 144 |
| 1446 | 118 | | |

# INDEX TO THE AUTOBIOGRAPHY

Reference is to section number. Parenthetic roman numerals indicate identifications as listed in *BLZG*, arabic those in *PLRE*.

# INDEX TO LETTERS

Reference is to Letter and section number. Parenthetic roman numerals indicate identifications as in *BLZG*. Addressees are indicated by asterisks.

# INDEX TO LETTERS

# THE LOEB CLASSICAL LIBRARY

## VOLUMES ALREADY PUBLISHED

### LATIN AUTHORS

Ammianus Marcellinus. J. C. Rolfe. 3 Vols.
Apuleius: The Golden Ass (Metamorphoses). W. Adlington (1566). Revised by S. Gaselee.
St. Augustine: City of God. 7 Vols. Vol. I. G. E. McCracken. Vol. II. W. M. Green. Vol. IV. P. Levine. Vol. V. E. M. Sanford and W. M. Green. Vol. VI. W. C. Greene.
St. Augustine, Confessions of. W. Watts (1631). 2 Vols.
St. Augustine: Select Letters. J. H. Baxter.
Ausonius. H. G. Evelyn White. 2 Vols.
Bede. J. E. King. 2 Vols.
Boethius: Tracts and De Consolatione Philosophiae. Rev. H. F. Stewart and E. K. Rand.
Caesar: Alexandrian, African and Spanish Wars. A. G. Way.
Caesar: Civil Wars. A. G. Peskett.
Caesar: Gallic War. H. J. Edwards.
Cato and Varro: De Re Rustica. H. B. Ash and W. D. Hooper.
Catullus. F. W. Cornish; Tibullus. J. B. Postgate; and Pervigilium Veneris. J. W. Mackail.
Celsus: De Medicina. W. G. Spencer. 3 Vols.
Cicero: Brutus and Orator. G. L. Hendrickson and H. M. Hubbell.
Cicero: De Finibus. H. Rackham.
Cicero: De Inventione, etc. H. M. Hubbell.
Cicero: De Natura Deorum and Academica. H. Rackham.
Cicero: De Officiis. Walter Miller.
Cicero: De Oratore, etc. 2 Vols. Vol. I: De Oratore, Books I and II. E. W. Sutton and H. Rackham. Vol. II: De Oratore, Book III; De Fato; Paradoxa Stoicorum; De Partitione Oratoria. H. Rackham.

Cicero: De Republica, De Legibus, Somnium Scipionis. Clinton W. Keyes.
Cicero: De Senectute, De Amicitia, De Divinatione. W. A. Falconer.
Cicero: In Catilinam, Pro Murena, Pro Sulla, Pro Flacco. Louis E. Lord.
Cicero: Letters to Atticus. E. O. Winstedt. 3 Vols.
Cicero: Letters to his Friends. W. Glynn Williams. 3 Vols.
Cicero: Philippics. W. C. A. Ker.
Cicero: Pro Archia, Post Reditum, De Domo, De Haruspicum Responsis, Pro Plancio. N. H. Watts.
Cicero: Pro Caecina, Pro Lege Manilia, Pro Cluentio, Pro Rabirio. H. Grose Hodge.
Cicero: Pro Caelio, De Provinciis Consularibus, Pro Balbo. R. Gardner.
Cicero: Pro Milone, In Pisonem, Pro Scauro, Pro Fonteio, Pro Rabirio Postumo, Pro Marcello, Pro Ligario, Pro Rege Deiotaro. N. H. Watts.
Cicero: Pro Quinctio, Pro Roscio Amerino, Pro Roscio Comoedo, Contra Rullum. J. H. Freese.
Cicero: Pro Sestio, In Vatinium. R. Gardner.
[Cicero]: Rhetorica ad Herennium. H. Caplan.
Cicero: Tusculan Disputations. J. E. King.
Cicero: Verrine Orations. L. H. G. Greenwood. 2 Vols.
Claudian. M. Platnauer. 2 Vols.
Columella: De Re Rustica, De Arboribus. H. B. Ash, E. S. Forster, E. Heffner. 3 Vols.
Curtius, Q.: History of Alexander. J. C. Rolfe. 2 Vols.
Florus. E. S. Forster; and Cornelius Nepos. J. C. Rolfe.
Frontinus: Stratagems and Aqueducts. C. E. Bennett and M. B. McElwain.
Fronto: Correspondence. C. R. Haines. 2 Vols.
Gellius. J. C. Rolfe. 3 Vols.
Horace: Odes and Epodes. C. E. Bennett.
Horace: Satires, Epistles, Ars Poetica. H. R. Fairclough.
Jerome: Select Letters. F. A. Wright.
Juvenal and Persius. G. G. Ramsay.
Livy. B. O. Foster, F. G. Moore, Evan T. Sage, A. C. Schlesinger and R. M. Geer (General Index). 14 Vols.
Lucan. J. D. Duff.

LUCRETIUS. W. H. D. Rouse.
MARTIAL. W. C. A. Ker. 2 Vols.
MINOR LATIN POETS: from PUBLILIUS SYRUS to RUTILIUS NAMATIANUS, including GRATTIUS, CALPURNIUS SICULUS, NEMESIANUS, AVIANUS, with "Aetna," "Phoenix" and other poems. J. Wight Duff and Arnold M. Duff.
OVID: THE ART OF LOVE AND OTHER POEMS. J. H. Mozley.
OVID: FASTI. Sir James G. Frazer.
OVID: HEROIDES AND AMORES. Grant Showerman.
OVID: METAMORPHOSES. F. J. Miller. 2 Vols.
OVID: TRISTIA AND EX PONTO. A. L. Wheeler.
PETRONIUS. M. Heseltine; SENECA: APOCOLOCYNTOSIS W. H. D. Rouse.
PHAEDRUS AND BABRIUS (Greek). B. E. Perry.
PLAUTUS. Paul Nixon. 5 Vols.
PLINY: LETTERS. Melmoth's translation revised by W. M. L. Hutchinson. 2 Vols.
PLINY: NATURAL HISTORY. 10 Vols. Vols. I-V and IX. H. Rackham. Vols. VI-VIII. W. H. S. Jones. Vol. X. D. E. Eichholz.
PROPERTIUS. H. E. Butler.
PRUDENTIUS. H. J. Thomson. 2 Vols.
QUINTILIAN. H. E. Butler. 4 Vols.
REMAINS OF OLD LATIN. E. H. Warmington. 4 Vols. Vol. I (Ennius and Caecilius). Vol. II (Livius, Naevius, Pacuvius, Accius). Vol. III (Lucilius, Laws of the XII Tables). Vol. IV (Archaic Inscriptions).
SALLUST. J. C. Rolfe.
SCRIPTORES HISTORIAE AUGUSTAE. D. Magie. 3 Vols.
SENECA: APOCOLOCYNTOSIS. *Cf.* PETRONIUS.
SENECA: EPISTULAE MORALES. R. M. Gummere. 3 Vols.
SENECA: MORAL ESSAYS. J. W. Basore. 3 Vols.
SENECA: TRAGEDIES. F. J. Miller. 2 Vols.
SIDONIUS: POEMS AND LETTERS. W. B. Anderson. 2 Vols.
SILIUS ITALICUS. J. D. Duff. 2 Vols.
STATIUS. J. H. Mozley. 2 Vols.
SUETONIUS. J. C. Rolfe. 2 Vols.
TACITUS: DIALOGUS. Sir Wm. Peterson; and AGRICOLA AND GERMANIA. Maurice Hutton.
TACITUS: HISTORIES AND ANNALS. C H. Moore and J. Jackson. 4 Vols.
TERENCE. John Sargeaunt. 2 Vols.

Tertullian: Apologia and De Spectaculis. T. R. Glover; Minucius Felix. G. H. Rendall.
Valerius Flaccus. J. H. Mozley.
Varro: De Lingua Latina. R. G. Kent. 2 Vols.
Velleius Paterculus and Res Gestae Divi Augusti. F. W. Shipley.
Virgil. H. R. Fairclough. 2 Vols.
Vitruvius: De Architectura. F. Granger. 2 Vols.

## GREEK AUTHORS

Achilles Tatius. S. Gaselee.
Aelian: On the Nature of Animals. A. F. Scholfield. 3 Vols.
Aeneas Tacticus, Asclepiodotus and Onasander. The Illinois Greek Club.
Aeschines. C. D. Adams.
Aeschylus. H. Weir Smyth. 2 Vols.
Alciphron, Aelian and Philostratus: Letters. A. R. Benner and F. H. Fobes.
Apollodorus. Sir James G. Frazer. 2 Vols.
Apollonius Rhodius. R. C. Seaton.
The Apostolic Fathers. Kirsopp Lake. 2 Vols.
Appian's Roman History. Horace White. 4 Vols.
Aratus. *Cf.* Callimachus.
Aristophanes. Benjamin Bickley Rogers. 3 Vols. Verse trans.
Aristotle: Art of Rhetoric. J. H. Freese.
Aristotle: Athenian Constitution, Eudemian Ethics, Virtues and Vices. H. Rackham.
Aristotle: The Categories. On Interpretation. H. P. Cooke; Prior Analytics. H. Tredennick.
Aristotle: Generation of Animals. A. L. Peck.
Aristotle: Historia Animalium. A. L. Peck. 3 Vols. Vol. I.
Aristotle: Metaphysics. H. Tredennick. 2 Vols.
Aristotle: Meteorologica. H. D. P. Lee.
Aristotle: Minor Works. W. S. Hett. "On Colours," "On Things Heard," "Physiognomics," "On Plants," "On Marvellous Things Heard," "Mechanical Problems," "On Indivisible Lines," "Situations and Names of Winds," "On Melissus, Xenophanes, and Gorgias."

## THE LOEB CLASSICAL LIBRARY

Aristotle: Nicomachean Ethics. H. Rackham.
Aristotle: Oeconomica and Magna Moralia. G. C. Armstrong. (With Metaphysics, Vol. II.)
Aristotle: On the Heavens. W. K. C. Guthrie.
Aristotle: On the Soul, Parva Naturalia, On Breath. W. S. Hett.
Aristotle: Parts of Animals. A. L. Peck; Motion and Progression of Animals. E. S. Forster.
Aristotle: Physics. Rev. P. Wicksteed and F. M. Cornford. 2 Vols.
Aristotle: Poetics; Longinus on the Sublime. W. Hamilton Fyfe; Demetrius on Style. W. Rhys Roberts.
Aristotle: Politics. H. Rackham.
Aristotle: Posterior Analytics. H. Tredennick; Topics. E. S. Forster.
Aristotle: Problems. W. S. Hett. 2 Vols.
Aristotle: Rhetorica ad Alexandrum. H. Rackham. (With Problems, Vol. II.)
Aristotle: Sophistical Refutations. Coming-to-be and Passing-away. E. S. Forster; On the Cosmos. D. J. Furley.
Arrian: History of Alexander and Indica. Rev. E. Iliffe Robson. 2 Vols.
Athenaeus: Deipnosophistae. C. B. Gulick. 7 Vols.
Babrius and Phaedrus (Latin). B. E. Perry.
St. Basil: Letters. R. J. Deferrari. 4 Vols.
Callimachus: Fragments. C. A. Trypanis.
Callimachus: Hymns and Epigrams, and Lycophron. A. W. Mair; Aratus. G. R. Mair.
Clement of Alexandria. Rev. G. W. Butterworth.
Colluthus. *Cf.* Oppian.
Daphnis and Chloe. *Cf.* Longus.
Demosthenes I: Olynthiacs, Philippics and Minor Orations: I-XVII and XX. J. H. Vince.
Demosthenes II: De Corona and De Falsa Legatione. C. A. Vince and J. H. Vince.
Demosthenes III: Meidias, Androtion, Aristocrates, Timocrates, Aristogeiton. J. H. Vince.
Demosthenes IV-VI: Private Orations and In Neaeram. A. T. Murray.
Demosthenes VII: Funeral Speech, Erotic Essay, Exordia and Letters. N. W. and N. J. DeWitt.

Dio Cassius: Roman History. E. Cary. 9 Vols.
Dio Chrysostom. 5 Vols. Vols. I and II. J. W. Cohoon. Vol III. J. W. Cohoon and H. Lamar Crosby. Vols. IV and V. H. Lamar Crosby.
Diodorus Siculus. 12 Vols. Vols. I-VI. C. H. Oldfather. Vol. VII. C. L. Sherman. Vol. VIII. C. B. Welles. Vols. IX and X. Russel M. Geer. Vol. XI. F. R. Walton.
Diogenes Laertius. R. D. Hicks. 2 Vols.
Dionysius of Halicarnassus: Roman Antiquities. Spelman's translation revised by E. Cary. 7 Vols.
Epictetus. W. A. Oldfather. 2 Vols.
Euripides. A. S. Way. 4 Vols. Verse trans.
Eusebius: Ecclesiastical History. Kirsopp Lake and J. E. L. Oulton. 2 Vols.
Galen: On the Natural Faculties. A. J. Brock.
The Greek Anthology. W. R. Paton. 5 Vols.
The Greek Bucolic Poets (Theocritus, Bion, Moschus). J. M. Edmonds.
Greek Elegy and Iambus with the Anacreontea. J. M. Edmonds. 2 Vols.
Greek Mathematical Works. Ivor Thomas. 2 Vols.
Herodes. *Cf.* Theophrastus: Characters.
Herodotus. A. D. Godley. 4 Vols.
Hesiod and the Homeric Hymns. H. G. Evelyn White.
Hippocrates and the Fragments of Heracleitus. W. H. S. Jones and E. T. Withington. 4 Vols.
Homer: Iliad. A. T. Murray. 2 Vols.
Homer: Odyssey. A. T. Murray. 2 Vols.
Isaeus. E. S. Forster.
Isocrates. George Norlin and LaRue Van Hook. 3 Vols.
St. John Damascene: Barlaam and Ioasaph. Rev. G. R. Woodward and Harold Mattingly.
Josephus. 9 Vols. Vols. I-IV. H. St. J. Thackeray. Vol. V. H. St. J. Thackeray and Ralph Marcus. Vols. VI and VII. Ralph Marcus. Vol. VIII. Ralph Marcus and Allen Wikgren. Vol. IX. L. H. Feldman.
Julian. Wilmer Cave Wright. 3 Vols.
Longus: Daphnis and Chloe. Thornley's translation revised by J. M. Edmonds; and Parthenius. S. Gaselee.
Lucian. 8 Vols. Vols. I-V. A. M. Harmon. Vol. VI. K. Kilburn. Vol. VII. M. D. Macleod.

LYCOPHRON. *Cf.* CALLIMACHUS.
LYRA GRAECA. J. M. Edmonds. 3 Vols.
LYSIAS. W. R. M. Lamb.
MANETHO. W. G. Waddell; PTOLEMY: TETRABIBLOS. F. E. Robbins.
MARCUS AURELIUS. C. R. Haines.
MENANDER. F. G. Allinson.
MINOR ATTIC ORATORS. 2 Vols. K. J. Maidment and J. O. Burtt.
NONNOS: DIONYSIACA. W. H. D. Rouse. 3 Vols.
OPPIAN, COLLUTHUS, TRYPHIODORUS. A. W. Mair.
PAPYRI. NON-LITERARY SELECTIONS. A. S. Hunt and C. C. Edgar. 2 Vols. LITERARY SELECTIONS (Poetry). D. L. Page.
PARTHENIUS. *Cf.* LONGUS.
PAUSANIAS: DESCRIPTION OF GREECE. W. H. S. Jones. 5 Vols. and Companion Vol. arranged by R. E. Wycherley.
PHILO. 10 Vols. Vols. I-V. F. H. Colson and Rev. G. H. Whitaker. Vols. VI-X. F. H. Colson. General Index. Rev. J. W. Earp.
Two Supplementary Vols. Translation only from an Armenian Text. Ralph Marcus.
PHILOSTRATUS: THE LIFE OF APOLLONIUS OF TYANA. F. C. Conybeare. 2 Vols.
PHILOSTRATUS: IMAGINES; CALLISTRATUS: DESCRIPTIONS. A. Fairbanks.
PHILOSTRATUS AND EUNAPIUS: LIVES OF THE SOPHISTS. Wilmer Cave Wright.
PINDAR. Sir J. E. Sandys.
PLATO: CHARMIDES, ALCIBIADES, HIPPARCHUS, THE LOVERS, THEAGES, MINOS AND EPINOMIS. W. R. M. Lamb.
PLATO: CRATYLUS, PARMENIDES, GREATER HIPPIAS, LESSER HIPPIAS. H. N. Fowler.
PLATO: EUTHYPHRO, APOLOGY, CRITO, PHAEDO, PHAEDRUS. H. N. Fowler.
PLATO: LACHES, PROTAGORAS, MENO, EUTHYDEMUS. W. R. M. Lamb.
PLATO: LAWS. Rev. R. G. Bury. 2 Vols.
PLATO: LYSIS, SYMPOSIUM, GORGIAS. W. R. M. Lamb.
PLATO: REPUBLIC. Paul Shorey. 2 Vols.
PLATO: STATESMAN, PHILEBUS. H. N. Fowler; ION. W. R. M. Lamb.

Plato : Theaetetus and Sophist. H. N. Fowler.
Plato : Timaeus, Critias, Clitopho, Menexenus, Epistulae. Rev. R. G. Bury.
Plotinus. A. H. Armstrong. 6 Vols. Vols. I-II.
Plutarch : Moralia. 15 Vols. Vols. I-V. F. C. Babbitt. Vol. VI. W. C. Helmbold. Vol. VII. P. H. De Lacy and B. Einarson. Vol. IX. E. L. Minar, Jr., F. H. Sandbach, W. C. Helmbold. Vol. X. H. N. Fowler. Vol. XI. L. Pearson, F. H. Sandbach. Vol. XII. H. Cherniss, W. C. Helmbold. Vol. XIV. P. H. De Lacy and B. Einarson.
Plutarch : The Parallel Lives. B. Perrin. 11 Vols.
Polybius. W. R. Paton. 6 Vols.
Procopius : History of the Wars. H. B. Dewing. 7 Vols.
Ptolemy : Tetrabiblos. *Cf.* Manetho.
Quintus Smyrnaeus. A. S. Way. Verse trans.
Sextus Empiricus. Rev. R. G. Bury. 4 Vols.
Sophocles. F. Storr. 2 Vols. Verse trans.
Strabo : Geography. Horace L. Jones. 8 Vols.
Theophrastus : Characters. J. M. Edmonds ; Herodes, etc. A. D. Knox.
Theophrastus : Enquiry into Plants. Sir Arthur Hort. 2 Vols.
Thucydides. C. F. Smith. 4 Vols.
Tryphiodorus. *Cf.* Oppian.
Xenophon : Cyropaedia. Walter Miller. 2 Vols.
Xenophon : Hellenica, Anabasis, Apology, and Symposium. C. L. Brownson and O. J. Todd. 3 Vols.
Xenophon : Memorabilia and Oeconomicus. E. C. Marchant.
Xenophon : Scripta Minora. E. C. Marchant.

*DESCRIPTIVE PROSPECTUS ON APPLICATION*

CAMBRIDGE, MASS. — HARVARD UNIV. PRESS
LONDON — WILLIAM HEINEMANN LTD